Teaching Social Studies
in
Early Education

Teaching Social Studies
in
Early Education

Wilma Robles de Melendez, Ph.D.

Nova Southeastern University

Vesna Beck, Ed.D.

Nova Southeastern University

Melba Fletcher, Ed.D.

Nova Southeastern University

Africa • Australia • Canada • Denmark • Japan • Mexico • New Zealand • Philippines
Puerto Rico • Singapore • Spain • United Kingdom • United States

NOTICE TO THE READER

Publisher does not warrant or guarantee any of the products described herein or perform any independent analysis in connection with any of the product information contained herein. Publisher does not assume, and expressly disclaims, any obligation to obtain and include information other than that provided to it by the manufacturer.

The reader is expressly warned to consider and adopt all safety precautions that might be indicated by the activities herein and to avoid all potential hazards. By following the instructions contained herein, the reader willingly assumes all risks in connection with such instructions.

The Publisher makes no representation or warranties of any kind, including but not limited to, the warranties of fitness for particular purpose or merchantability, nor are any such representations implied with respect to the material set forth herein, and the publisher takes no responsibility with respect to such material. The publisher shall not be liable for any special, consequential or exemplary damages resulting, in whole or part, from the readers' use of, or reliance upon, this material.

Delmar Staff:

Business Unit Director: Susan L. Simpfenderfer
Executive Editor: Marlene McHugh Pratt
Acquisitions Editor: Erin O'Connor Traylor
Development Editor: Melissa Riveglia
Executive Production Manager: Wendy A. Troeger

Project Editor: Amy E. Tucker
Production Editor: Elaine Scull
Technology Project Manager: Kim Schryer
Executive Marketing Manager: Donna J. Lewis
Channel Manager: Nigar Hale

Cover Design: Joseph Villanova
Cover Image: Map drawing. Digital imagery® copyright 2000 Photo Disc, Inc.

For more information, contact Delmar, 3 Columbia Circle, PO Box 15015, Albany, NY 12212-0515;
or find us on the World Wide Web at http://www.delmar.com or http://www.EarlyChildEd.delmar.com

Library of Congress Cataloging-in-Publication Data

Robles de Melendez, Wilma J.
   Teaching social studies in early education / by
Wilma J. Robles de Melendez, Vesna Beck, Melba Fletcher.
      p.   cm.
   Includes bibliographical references.
   ISBN 0-7668-0288-4
   1. Social sciences—Study and teaching (Early childhood)—United States. I. Beck,
Vesna. II. Fletcher, Melba. III. Title.

LB1139.5.S64 R62 2000
372.83—dc21   99-049327
                                                   CIP

Contents

▟ PART II: Creating an Early Childhood Social Studies Curriculum   71

Chapter 4: Planning Developmentally Appropriate Social Studies   72

Chapter 6: Learning about Where We Live: Geography and the Young Child

Chapter 9: Growing Up in a Multi-cultural Society   228

Chapter 10: Economics, the Environment, and Social Issues: Preparing Children to Make Informed Choices   249

Preface

Today there is much discussion about the pitfalls and benefits of our educational system. The issues span all education levels and include schools and institutions in both the public and private sector. As the new millennium begins, the focus of this debate has shifted to the education of young children, because they are the future of our society. In response to these issues and as a reflection of our personal interests and expertise, we have chosen to make our contribution to early childhood education in the field of social studies, an area of study with boundless educational possibilities. Our professional expertise includes Wilma de Melendez's work in early childhood education, Vesna Beck's experience in research and assessment, and Melba Fletcher's contributions to the field of early childhood special education. Throughout our long careers, all three of us have taught, lectured, and published books and articles about young children. Additionally, Wilma de Melendez and Vesna Beck are both scholars of social studies.

As an academic field, social studies includes many different areas of study, ranging from geography and environmental science to art and current events, among others. At first glance, such topics may seem too complex and sophisticated for young children, but we firmly believe that it is necessary to include them in the early childhood curriculum. A good background in social studies in the early years can provide a solid foundation on which later education in history, civic responsibility, and character development can be built.

Another reason we decided to write this book is in response to the national education agenda, which includes the Curriculum Standards for Social Studies. The standards include instructional expectations for all grade levels, including the early grades. The standards are reproduced in Appendix I at the back of this volume. Relevant excerpts have been incorporated into appropriate places in the chapters. As an additional resource for curriculum development, we have provided excerpts from specific standards for subject areas within social studies, such as history, economics, geography, the arts, and environmental science. We believe that this will help educators create meaningful social studies curricula and experiences for young children that are grounded in the national standards.

■■ Purpose and Organization of This Book

This book is primarily intended to help new and aspiring teachers of young children (ages 3 through 8) to create and teach a well-integrated social studies curriculum. We also believe that our book contains many resources and helpful ideas that even the most experienced teachers will find useful. This book has been designed to be a good resource for in-service training and professional development for all early childhood educators in social studies.

This book is literature-based: *Teaching Social Studies in Early Education* contains approximately 500 different children's book titles and resources. Our approach to the content is global and multi-cultural. Our perspective on diversity extends beyond integrating content and activities from different ethnic groups. We also include information regarding children with special needs and their inclusion in the early childhood classroom.

The book is divided in two parts. Part I consists of Chapters 1 through 3. This section outlines the theoretical concepts and foundations of social studies, as well as some basic guidelines for instructional planning, and a review of the various child development theories. Part II begins with Chapter 4, which provides extensive information about pedagogical concepts and teaching methodologies. Chapters 5 through 10 focus on specific areas within social studies, such as geography, the arts, civic responsibility, history, multi-culturalism, economics, current events, and environmental science. This section contains many resources and ideas for practical application of social studies content to the early childhood curriculum. The chapters that address special areas of social studies also contain information about the National Curriculum Standards for Social Studies and the specific standards for economics, history, the arts, geography, and environmental science.

Each chapter includes the following:

- Chapter Questions
- Key Terms and Concepts
- Classroom Portraits
- Concept Boxes
- Bringing Ideas into Practice
- Let's Talk About
- Recommended Children's Books

The *chapter questions* and lists of *key terms and concepts* serve as a preview of the material to follow. They can be used to promote discussions and to help readers assess and review their knowledge of the topics in each chapter. Key terms are defined in context and in a Glossary that appears at the back of this volume. *Classroom portraits* depict common situations that early childhood educators may encounter—both new and experienced teachers will be able to identify with them. These vignettes can be used to encourage alternative approaches to problems and challenges that may arise in the classroom. Discussions of various "what if . . ." scenarios can greatly enhance the use of these vignettes.

Concept Boxes expand important elements of each chapter. Each box provides additional, in-depth resources that enhance understanding of a different social studies concept. A series of boxes called *Bringing Ideas into Practice* demonstrate the practical application of the material in each chapter. The ideas and activities are a rich resource that early childhood educators can use in their curriculum. Many of the suggestions for "Bringing Ideas Into Practice," such as making dough that can be used to build relief maps, provide creative and inexpensive ways to design activities for young children.

The *Let's Talk About* boxes that appear several times in each chapter are opportunities to elicit readers' personal reactions, opinions, and experiences. Each box usually includes follow-up questions that are intended to promote additional discussion of the material in each chapter.

Lists of *Recommended Children's Books* can be found at the end of some chapters. These literature banks are resources that can be used in curriculum planning. Readers are also encouraged to bring these titles into the classroom.

Each chapter ends with *Activities* that involve three components: *reflections, collections,* and *Internet resources*. These components are intended to encourage teachers to pursue some key topics of the chapters further, to create additional teaching resources, and to use technology. Please note that the Internet addresses change very frequently and may become outdated—by the time this book is published, some of the URLs we have listed may no longer be valid. If this is the case, we urge you to search the Net for the information by using various descriptors provided in the original listings. A list of references also appears at the end of each chapter.

We hope that the content and presentation of the material in this book will serve the needs of aspiring and experienced teachers alike. Our goal has been to provide you with as much essential information as possible about teaching social studies to young children. However, it is up to you to make social studies come alive and to make a difference in the future generations.

Wilma Robles de Melendez, Ph.D.
Vesna Beck, Ed.D.
Melba Fletcher, Ed.D.

Acknowledgments

The book that you hold in your hands is a reality, thanks to the ideas and contributions of many people. The authors feel indebted to all of them. First, we want to express our appreciation to all the teachers who welcomed us into their classrooms and taught us many practical lessons. Our gratitude is further extended to all the children that we met and interacted with in classrooms in our country and around the world. We also want to say thank you to our students, who shared their ideas and vision about what makes social studies education appropriate for young children.

We also want to express our appreciation to all the reviewers of this book. Their suggestions contributed to the enhancement of this publication. Our thanks to:

Leanna Manna
Villa Maria College
Buffalo, NY

Jo Anne Welch, Ph.D.
Northeast Louisiana University
Monroe, LA

Kathy A. Head
Lorain County Community College
Elyria, OH

Linda S. Estes, Ed.D.
St. Charles County Community College
St. Peters, MO

Jan Smith
College of the Mainland
Texas City, TX

And certainly we want to express our thanks to Angela White, who helped us to finalize the typing of the manuscript, to Amy Tucker and Erin O'Connor-Traylor of Delmar Publishers, to Janet Domingo and Barbara Stratton, to Mario Robles and Sal Melendez, for their faith and confidence in this project, and to our families, for understanding the value of this endeavor.

Wilma, Vesna, and Melba

PART I

Helping Children Become Who They Are:
A Rationale for Teaching Social Studies

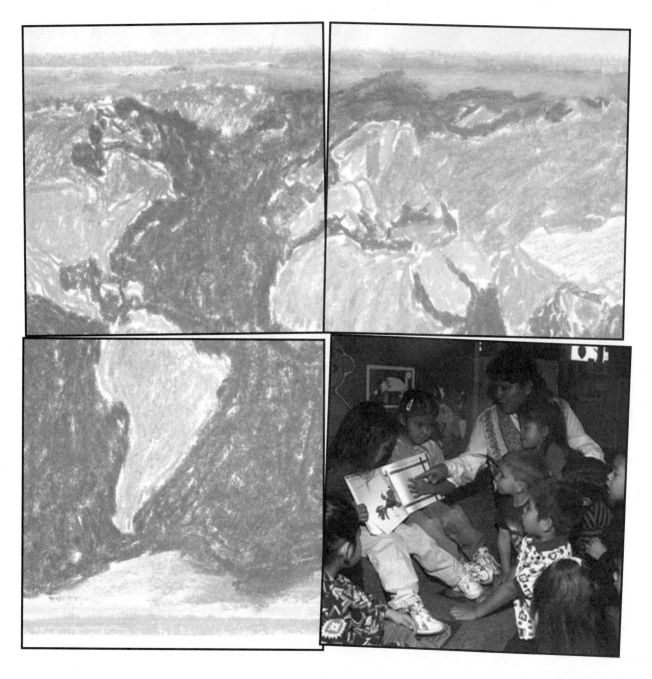

CHAPTER 1

The World Children Live In

Was it not then that I acquired all that now sustains me? And I gained so much and so quickly that during the rest of my life I did not acquire a hundredth part of it. From myself as a five-year-old to myself as I now am there is only one step. The distance between myself as an infant and myself at five years is tremendous.

—LEO TOLSTOY

Chapter Questions

After reading this chapter, you should be able to answer the following questions:

- What are the characteristics of today's society?
- How does the practice of *inclusion* affect education in early childhood?
- What is the relevance of social studies education in early childhood?
- How will a global approach to social studies prepare children for effective membership in our society?
- How can educators effectively address the individual needs of all children, including those with special needs?

Key Terms and Concepts

children with special needs
developmentally and culturally appropriate
     practices (DCAP)
developmentally appropriate practices (DAP)
family membership
global approach
inclusion
individuality

local, state, and national membership
peer group membership
social competence
social studies
socialization
triple identity (individual, national,
     and global)

Classroom Portrait: Teaching Young Children in Today's World

Marcie, a four-year-old preschooler in Chicago, was working in the housekeeping area when her teacher heard her reprimanding a doll, saying, "If you don't eat your sochi (*sic*), I will not let you fax Daddy." Puzzled, her teacher asked what she meant by faxing, to which the child replied, "Oh, that's when you write with the phone. Daddy faxes me from London at night," she added.

In Mr. Gonzalez's kindergarten classroom in Mexico City, children have just listened to a story told by a Fil-ipino teacher more than 8,000 miles away. Using video-conferencing equipment, they are now asking questions about one of the characters in the story. Their fellow classmates—in Sweden—giggle as they see the entire class from Mexico City appear on the screen.

In Mambasa, Zaire, six-year-old Lakesha works with a puzzle while her grandmother watches the evening news. On the screen, scenes from San Francisco's Chinatown flash by. "See the dragons?" says the six-year-old girl. "That's where my friend went!"

■■ The Developmental Tasks
■■ of Early Childhood Years

We all belong to that immense family we call society. The origins of the way we exist and relate to others in society lie in the early years of childhood. We know that development of our identity—*who we are* and *what we are*—actually begins between conception and age eight. It is during the first formative years, from birth to age eight, that the sense of who we are and our recognition of the perspectives of others take shape. This is the time when our social and individual selves are developed. We develop key social constructs, including membership in a family, peer group, and nationality, as well as our individual-

ity. The first eight years of life are also crucial for establishing each individual's future and ability to survive in society. During this time of life, early childhood education finds its fundamental purpose and mission: fostering the unfolding of children and making it possible for each child to develop effectively as an individual and as a social self.

Key Social Constructs Developed by Children During the Early Childhood Years

- **Individuality:** Recognition of self as a person.
- **Family membership:** Recognition of family members and awareness of belonging to a family.
- **Peer group membership:** Belonging to a group of biological and social equals.
- **Local, state, and national membership:** Identifying with the community, neighborhood, town, state, and country where the individual lives.

Development of Social Self: The Key to Being a Part of a Group

Essential to any society is the acquisition by its members of the norms and patterns governing its relationships and existence. This process starts at birth and continues throughout our lives. In classrooms everywhere, early childhood teachers witness the gradual transformation and adaptation of children to the realities and characteristic ways of their social groups. Through the process called **socialization**—acquiring knowledge about the be-

During the first eight years of childhood, children become aware of themselves and others.

Socialization starts early in life.

havior patterns considered acceptable by the group or culture—children learn the ways of the groups to which they belong. Central to the task of becoming a part of a group is achieving **social competence.** Social competence is defined as the ability to engage in successful social interactions with others and with the group to which one belongs. A socially competent individual is able to participate effectively and contribute "to the groups, communities, and larger society to which one belongs" (Katz & McLellan, 1997, p. 1). Development of a socially competent child is a central goal both of early education and of the social studies curriculum. In the classroom, through well-planned activities, children refine their knowledge about others and learn about relationships.

Children become socially competent through the following sources:

■ interactions with parents and family members
■ playing at school and in their neighborhoods with friends
■ participation in activities in the community
■ being with adults

Working with young children provides many opportunities to witness how they become competent at developing relationships. The ability to comfort a friend or to show concern for what will happen to the classroom pets during the weekends is evidence that the socialization process is already in progress. The egocentric world of children slowly broadens into a world that includes others. The process of becoming a part of a group begins as children move from simple self-recognition to recognition of others.

Developmentally Delayed Children: Exceptional Education

Any discussion of young children would be incomplete without the inclusion of the developmentally delayed child. About one out of every ten children is considered *exceptional.* This exceptionality may take the form of mental impairment, speech impediment or delay, physical disability, visual or auditory deficiency, or any combination of these and other exceptionalities. Gifted and talented children are also "exceptional."

Two federal laws, PL 94-142, enacted in 1975, and PL 99-457, enacted in 1986, collectively require that every school system in the United States provide a free, appropriate public education for every child age three to five years old, regardless of how seriously the child may be handicapped. In addition, these laws offer incentives for states to provide services for infants and toddlers as well.

Further, these federal laws require that children with developmental delays be educated with their non-handicapped peers. This practice of **inclusion**—educating **children with special needs** along with their non-disabled peers—means that educators must make accommodations for the needs of these children by individualizing their education program. However, good teachers have always made it a practice to provide for the individual needs of their students.

Some of the practices that all good teachers have consistently included are the same recommendations provided for those who work with exceptional children:

■ Divide learning materials into small steps.
■ Sequence the steps from the simplest to the most difficult.
■ Provide opportunities for lots of practice.
■ Give consistent feedback and reinforcement.

Strategies for educators to use in their work with exceptional children will be included throughout this book. These tips for accommodating individual differences will benefit all children, not just those who are labeled "exceptional." As you know, *every* child is exceptional, simply because each one is so unique and special.

Research indicates that early intervention for young children with special needs—those who are experiencing a developmental delay in cognitive, physical, language-speech, social, or self-help development—can make a positive difference. Two well-known early research efforts, the Perry Preschool Project (Berrueta-Clement, Schweinhart, Barnett, et al., 1984) and the Abecedarian Project (Ramey & Campbell, 1984), indicate that early infant stimulation can improve the intelligence quotient (IQ) and achievement test scores of children who have a physical or mental condition that puts them at risk of becoming developmentally delayed. The need for these children to become socially proficient is equal to or perhaps even greater than that of the average child. At-risk children can indeed benefit from the inclusion of social studies in the early years.

Social Studies and the Young Child

Social studies, which literally means "the study of things social," is a unified discipline with several purposes: (1) teaching cultural heritage, (2) teaching thinking and decision making, and (3) teaching social science (Welton & Mallan, 1992). Purposes 1 and 3 are content-dominant; the second purpose is process oriented. All three are intended to produce good and socially competent citizens of the global community in the twenty-first century. An appropriate and relevant social studies curriculum for young children provides a good beginning toward accomplishment of this goal. This book is intended to help you understand and assemble such a curriculum.

Helping each child discover the many gifts he or she has and guiding children in learning the ways of the society in which they live is an essential task of early childhood education. As those responsible for preparing children to meet the demands of today's and tomorrow's world, early childhood educators know the importance of carefully selecting curricular experiences. When it comes to preparing young children for civic competence and for becoming effective participants in a changing democratic society, early childhood educators recognize the role and the value of social studies. Social studies is a dynamic and exciting field of study that opens the doors for children to understand the ways of their own society and offers insights into the ways of children and people in other places. Through social studies, children see, discover, and reflect about the wide world to which they belong: the world of their families, of their neighborhoods, and of many other parts of the world.

Bringing Ideas into Practice 1–1   *Discovering Life through Social Studies*

The social studies curriculum is aimed at helping young children discover life. This is accomplished when children are given opportunities to *see, discover,* and *reflect.*

■ *See:* Create a visually challenging environment where children are exposed to a variety of books and other examples that reflect the diversity of activities and things people do. In practice, this means setting up learning centers where children can look at pictures, posters, and photographs and find a variety of objects and artifacts from different cultures.

■ *Discover:* Bring items into the classroom and offer children opportunities to try things out by touching, manipulating, or tasting appropriate objects or foods of different cultures.

■ *Reflect:* Talk about what children have experienced; discuss and openly examine ideas and perceptions derived from a variety of activities. For example, discuss stories children have read and encourage them to ponder observations made during field trips and visits. Sharing interpretations about things the children have observed or personally experienced allows them opportunities for reflection.

Becoming Aware of the World Children Live In

This book will help you create child-appropriate social studies experiences. Essential to this kind of curriculum are **developmentally and culturally appropriate practices (DCAP)** recommended by the National Association for the Education of Young Children (NAEYC) (Bredekamp & Copple, 1997). The practices, which will be examined in Chapter 2, serve to keep the curriculum responsive to the social and cultural realities of children.

Central to any appropriate curriculum is its ability to reflect what society requires from its members. We are certain that early childhood educators are already aware of what some of these future demands might be. Some of the commonly asked questions regarding the future are: "Will our lifestyles change? Will our currently held ideas and values still be valid? How will learning take place?"

Preparing Children to Face New Challenges

Early childhood educators want to equip children with all the tools—personal, social, and technological—necessary for success. Many have already begun this process.

1. The *first step* is to emphasize quality developmental practices, including development of a positive sense of self, respect toward others, and a desire to learn. Nothing will better prepare children for the future than relevant and valuable early educational experiences.

■■   Let's Talk About . . . 1–1

Preparing Ourselves for the Twenty-first Century

1. What steps do you think early childhood educators should take in order to meet the needs of the new century? Why?
2. Think about teaching strategies, child development, knowledge, skills, parental involvement, the role of the community, the impact of technology, societal demands, and related topics.

Concept Box 1–1   Preparing Children to Meet the Demands of the Future

Early childhood educators should:
- fully implement the concept of developmental appropriateness to achieve quality programs and services for all children.
- update educational practices to coincide with the realities of a diverse and global society.
- review the early childhood curriculum and develop experiences that will build skills that will enable children to interact positively with all social groups.

---

2. The *second step* focuses on aligning early childhood educational practices with the demands of a global and diverse society. As expressed in *Goals 2000* (see p. 7), children will need to have skills to live successfully in a society that will be both diverse and global. We already know what it means to live in a diverse society because our country exemplifies social and cultural diversity. We also know what it means to live in a global society. Communication technology and the latest means of transportation have literally reduced our world to a "community." Today we chat and share experiences with "neighbors" who are thousands of miles away. The classroom portraits at the beginning of this chapter remind us of many classrooms where children are communicating with each other through e-mail, fax, video, or the old-fashioned telephone in the most remote places of our shrinking world.

3. A *third step* is to provide curricular experiences that will build skills for positive interaction with all social groups. As inventions continue to bring the world closer together, children will need to possess the social and civic skills required to participate and relate with peers from all cultures and in all places. Our curricula need to be transformed in order to guarantee children will receive the appropriate experiences required to develop the skills the future will demand. The strategies presented in this book will help you transform your curriculum. This book will guide

you to create a broad variety of experiences that will allow children to develop the social and civic skills they will need for our diverse global society. Implicit in this process is the belief that social studies is an area of inquiry that encompasses all that different peoples and cultures do.

■■ Educating Children
■■ for a Different Society

As an early childhood educator, you probably share many concerns about the society and the world we live in. Every day, as early childhood educators across the country prepare and organize classroom activities, they wonder whether they are indeed teaching children what they need in order to survive in our increasingly complex society. Becoming aware of the nature and reality of our society is central to appropriate and developmentally sound teaching. It is especially relevant when you are selecting and planning curricular experiences. Particularly important is an appropriate and academically coherent early childhood social studies curriculum. But before we move forward, it is necessary to examine the unique social characteristics of our times. Getting a feel for today's world will enable you to build the effective curricular experiences children need. Remember, social studies is about people and their realities.

National Agenda for Social Studies

Expanding awareness of today's world begins when you ask yourself whether our practices and knowledge are reflective of the new social realities. Some of these include:

■ the continued impact of technology,
■ the economic and financial struggles faced by individuals and the government,
■ the wave of social violence,
■ the changing family structure,
■ the growing multi-cultural character of our country, and
■ the constant shrinking of today's world.

Early childhood educators recognize the need to revamp teaching and learning practices to respond more closely to the challenges of an increasing globally interdependent society. This need has been also evidenced at the national level with the creation of a national agenda for social studies known as *Curriculum Standards for Social Studies* (see Appendix I). Following the path of other disciplines, a task force known as the National Council for the Social Studies (NCSS), consisting of teachers, university and college educators, and school district personnel, drafted a standards document in April of 1994 (National Council for the Social Studies, 1994). The standards address ten major areas, or *strands*. These strands are organized to incorporate many different aspects of the discipline and will be presented in detail in Chapter 2.

The standards are designed to serve three purposes:

1. To serve as a framework for social studies programs designs from kindergarten through grade 12;
2. To function as a guide for curriculum decisions by providing student performance expectations in the areas of knowledge, processes, and attitudes; and,
3. To provide examples of classroom activities that will guide teachers as they design instruction to help their student meet performance expectations.
(NCSS, 1994, p. ix).

Teachers are often urged to provide children with experiences that will foster development of the social skills needed to deal in a world of diversity. Admittedly, there is a need to reassess our priorities and revise the current curricula for young children (Bredekamp & Rosegrant, 1996). We also believe that the time has come for an objective reevaluation of our programs as to what they offer to young children. Using the criterion of developmental appropriateness, we see how crucial it is to revamp our curricular practices in order to respond to the needs of these and future times. This need is further reflected in the National Education Goals, *Goals 2000*, which represent a mandate for teaching children to develop global connections and establish a priority for the community of early childhood educators.

Goals 2000 were developed in 1992 by the National Council on Education Standards and Testing in response to interest in national standards and assessment by the nation's governors, the Administration, and Congress (National Council on Education Standards and Testing, 1992). The goals still serve as guidelines for education in grades K–12 throughout the United States. There are only six goals, but they encompass the entire educational agenda for this nation:

■ *Goal 1: Readiness for School*
   By the year 2000, all children in America will start school ready to learn.
■ *Goal 2: High School Completion*
   By the year 2000, the high school graduation rate will increase to at least 90 percent.
■ *Goal 3: Student Achievement and Citizenship*
   By the year 2000, American students will leave grades four, eight, and twelve having demonstrated competency in challenging subject matter including English, mathematics, science, history, and geography. Every school in America will en-

sure that all students learn to use their minds well so they may be prepared for responsible citizenship, further learning, and productive employment in our modern economy.
■ *Goal 4: Science and Mathematics*
   By the year 2000, U.S. students will be first in the world in science and mathematics achievement.
■ *Goals 5: Adult Learning and Lifelong Learning*
   By the year 2000, every adult American will be literate and will possess the knowledge and skills necessary to compete in a global economy and exercise the rights and responsibilities of citizenship.
■ *Goal 6: Safe, Disciplined and Drug-free Schools*
   By the year 2000, every school in America will be free of drugs and violence and will offer a disciplined environment conducive to learning.

(The National Council on Education Standards and Testing, 1992)

■■ Changing Our Vision: ■■ Developing a National and a Global Sense of Citizenship

We believe that to prepare students for the new century requires an effective and responsive curriculum. A relevant social studies program plays a fundamental role in such a curriculum. By helping students to develop skills for successful and effective citizen participation, social studies offers the

Children are important citizens of the world.

■■ Let's Talk About . . . 1–2

The Children's World

How would you describe the world in which the children you teach live? According to a group of pre-K and kindergarten teachers, today's society is "a highly unpredictable society where many things don't hold true anymore." This, they said, is what makes teaching such a challenging job. In their opinion, they can no longer rely on what they taught yesterday, for today it might no longer be valid. As an early childhood teacher,

1. How do you see today's world?
2. How would you describe it?
3. What is your perception of the world today and how does it impact your teaching?

Write down your opinions. If you have not already thought about these issues, take time to begin a conversation group. Ask your colleagues the same questions posed here and find out what ideas they have.

ideal framework for children to acquire the needed skills to live in the twenty-first century society.

According to the NCSS (1994), today's social studies teaching requires a *new vision.* Because events happening in other parts of the world impact our lives every day, and because our increasing cultural diversity has transformed our social values and traditions, children need to develop an awareness and a sense of what exists beyond our national frontiers. The need to foster and develop a global view is also found in the objectives for Goal 3 of *Goals 2000,* the national agenda for educational change. The desire to develop in students a concept of citizenship that includes pride as an American and as a member of the global community is clearly identified.

■■ Global Connections: One Aim
■■ of the Social Studies Curriculum

Learning how to be an effective member of our country and of the world is a complex task that transcends many issues. What are the implications for early childhood educators? Obviously, there is a call for a new vision of teaching. This new vision includes a trifold perspective. It entails the development of a **triple identity:**

- **Individual identity:** Pride in oneself, in one's abilities and innate potential, and in the cultural background to which one belongs
- **National identity:** Recognition of one's role as a citizen of a democratic country, in this case the United States of America.

■■   Let's Talk About . . . 1–3

Triple Identity:

1. What is your opinion regarding the concept of triple identity? If you were to define your own identity, what would you say? Do you see yourself as having a triple identity? Why?
2. Is this concept applicable to young children? How would you impart it to a young child?

- **Global identity:** An awareness of being a part of the world.

Endorsed by many educators and ratified in the recent social studies standards from NCSS (1994), a curriculum based on global connections has been proposed as our way to respond to the challenges of this vision of teaching and the society of the future.

Using a Global Approach to Create a Responsive Social Studies Curriculum

Have you considered the fact that the young children we teach today will be the citizens of United States of the twenty-first century? As such, they will live with the challenges of an increasingly interdependent world society. The task of equipping children with the proper individual and social skills that will allow them to succeed in a national and global society and in a century different from ours is a major concern. There is a need to help children develop a sense of being related and affected by what happens in other parts of the world. For instance, children should recognize the fact that a rainy season in South America means a lower production of goods from that continent that will result in higher prices for people in the United States. They should also recognize that shared research work in a distant country like Korea helps improve TV communications in their hometown. The connectedness of today's world supports the need for a global approach.

A **global approach** to social studies is defined as:

> The opportunity to discover and examine the many common points people here and there share. A global approach guides children to see themselves, their culture, and their lives as interconnected and dependent upon others in any part of the world.
> Ellis (1995, p. 295)

A global approach to social studies is aimed at developing in children a sense of being part of the world. "The global village," as predicted by Marshall MacLuhan, is already a reality. We agree that more and more our lives are dependent upon events and circumstances happening in places thousands of miles away from our communities.

When asked what they would give the world, this group of kindergartners revealed their interesting perceptions of society.

Let's Talk About . . . 1–4

Do You See Yourself as Part of a Global Village?

Back in the 1960s, Marshall MacLuhan predicted that our world would shrink to the point that it would become a global village.

1. Do you agree with this notion? If you agree, what makes you believe in this concept?
2. If you disagree, state why.

According to Ellis (1995), the benefits of using a global approach are several. As you read them, see how many of them are goals reflected in today's early childhood programs. A global approach:

- offers a more systematic way to view the world.
- develops a more realistic sense of resources and of the need to preserve them.
- helps children to value and appreciate people across cultures.
- fosters a sense of tolerance.
- recognizes and develops an awareness about people's diverse ideas and ways.
- guides children to recognize that we are interdependent.

(Ellis, 1995, p. 296)

Rationale for The National Social Studies Global Connections Standard

The need for children to become able to live and work in a global society is found in today's social, political, and economic realities. As we watch the news or read the newspaper, realization of a greater interrelationship with people around the globe is highlighted. Moreover, we live in a country that mirrors the world's global diversity. In fact, in your own classroom and in classrooms around the country you can see how children reflect the diversity of world ethnicities and cultures (NCSS, 1994). As the world enters into the next millennium, visions of a global society are markedly becoming a reality. In response to the needs of this country's future citizens, who will be both American and global citizens, education must endow children with the skills and knowledge they will need. This is a goal that must permeate the entire school curriculum. A process that begins early in life, early childhood education needs to incorporate global education as one of its targets.

Recognition of the need to develop global skills and knowledge has already been established by the

FIGURE 1–1 Social Studies Curricular Strand IX: Global Connections

Performance expectations for the early grades.
Social studies classroom experiences will lead children to:

A. explore ways that language, art, music, and other cultural elements may facilitate global understanding or lead to misunderstanding;

B. give examples of conflict, cooperation, and interdependence among individuals, groups, and nations;

C. examine the effects of changing technologies on the global community;

D. explore causes, consequences, and possible solutions to persistent, contemporary, and global issues such as pollution and endangered species.

E. examine the relationships and tensions between personal wants and needs and various global concerns, such as use of imported oil, land use, and environmental protection;

F. investigate concerns, issues, standards, and conflicts related to universal human rights, such as the treatment of children, religious groups, and effects of war.

■ After reading these expectations, what is your opinion of them?

■ How many of these areas do you already include in your classroom?

■ How age-appropriate are these expectations? Why?

Source: National Council for the Social Studies. (1994). *Expectations for excellence: Curriculum standards for social studies.* Bulletin 89. Washington, DC: Author. p. 70.

social studies curriculum. As a social studies priority, the National Council for the Social Studies included *global connections* as one of its ten curricular strands. Developed to serve as guidelines for curriculum, they define expectations across the spectrum of K–12 school experiences. Recommended concepts young children should experience are outlined in Figure 1–1 above. Detailed discussion of ways to design activities with a global emphasis will be examined throughout this book. You will also find suggestions and recommendations for age-appropriate activities and materials for young children in each chapter.

■■ The Child's Ability to Learn
■■ about Others Near and Far

Is a Global Approach Appropriate for Young Children?

Concerns about the developmental appropriateness of any educational practice (see Concept Box 1–3) should always be discussed. Many professionals will question whether it is developmentally appropriate to use a global approach in early childhood education. With reason, we say that the development of a sense of global connections begins early in life. Concerned about the appropriateness of global approaches, educator Torney-Purta (cited by Ellis, 1995), conducted an exhaustive review of the literature. Through her work, she found the early childhood years to be crucial in the development of attitudes and beliefs about others. Her findings have directly supported the concept of the global approach. If children are taught early to have a broader view of the world, it is more likely that they will develop positive ideas about people and about their relationships with others.

The early childhood social studies curriculum, where the activities and lifestyles of people are explored and multiple and diverse perspectives are presented, offers diverse opportunities to form concepts about people and relationships. Well-selected content for a global social studies early childhood curriculum provides young learners with

---

Concept Box 1–2
Sample Global Themes for the Early Grades, as Derived from NCSS Curricular Strand IX

Children can learn about:
- creative and artistic representations: visual arts, music, literature (stories, poetry).
- languages.
- technology: means of communication and transportation, manufacturing, agricultural practices.
- trade: interdependence (where do goods come from; what the United States produces for the world).

- environmental conservation: saving the rain forests, saving endangered animals, recycling.
- prosocial actions: welfare of others, sharing resources, taking action to help others, human rights, how to achieve and live in peace.
- people working to help others in their communities, in our country, and in other places.

---

the knowledge society now requires to help individuals live satisfying lives.

There are, however, developmental considerations we need to address: the child's cognitive abilities and the kinds of knowledge children build during the early years. These will be discussed in the next section.

NAEYC's Definition of Developmentally Appropriate Practices (DAP)

According to the NAEYC, **developmentally appropriate practices (DAP)** is a "framework, a philosophy, or an approach to working with young children that requires that the adult pays attention to at least two important pieces of information—*what we know* about how children develop and learn and *what we learn* about the individual needs and interests of each child in the group" (Bredekamp & Rosegrant, 1992, p. 4).

Building Knowledge about the World through Piaget's Socio-Conventional and Physical Knowledge

Jean Piaget, the noted developmentalist, stated that children develop three types of knowledge: *logico-mathematical, physical knowledge,* and *socio-conventional.* Of these three, both the physical and the socio-conventional are directly dealt with through

social studies. Physical knowledge describes the concepts gained about the physical realities; for example, the geographical characteristics of a place. Socio-conventional knowledge represents the wealth of ideas established by society about the patterns of relationships and concepts held by people.

Success in life depends to a great extent on the socio-conventional knowledge individuals possess. At the heart of social studies, one finds the goal of developing a working base of socio-conventional knowledge (Seefeldt & Barbour, 1998). From birth, children initiate the lifelong process of learning the social codes and patterns of their groups. In our classrooms the process of gaining ideas about the world they live in is continued. Opportunities abound in the classroom to construct ideas about our interdependency with the world. Carefully and properly designed experiences, based on what is meaningful for young children, open doors to the conventions of a world society.

Physical Knowledge

Based on Piaget's studies (1954) about children's conception of the physical world, their understanding of objects outside their immediate world is expected to be limited. It is important to recall that Piaget pointed out that a child's ability to perceive reality evolves gradually. With experience and through the influence of the environment, children

<table>
<tr><td>

Concept Box 1–3   What is the Essence of Developmentally Appropriate Practices?

Three dimensions define the essence of developmentally appropriate early childhood practices. These dimensions of DAP need to be considered as decisions about classroom experiences and activities are made:

1. *General knowledge about child developmental principles:* Knowledge about how children grow and develop.
2. *Recognition of the characteristic individuality of children:* Knowledge of the elements that define the individual characteristics (strengths, talents) and needs of children.
3. *Knowledge about the influence and role of culture:* Knowledge about the impact of culture and of the various environments experienced by children in their development.

(Bredekamp & Copple, 1997, p. 9)

</td></tr>
</table>

However, today we are aware of findings that reveal how young children are developing an ability to manipulate concepts in a more objective fashion at an earlier period (Spencer, Blades, & Morsley, 1989; Palmer, 1994).

Demonstrating Early Social Awareness

As a general rule, Piaget's principles are still a valid frame of reference for early childhood educators. In spite of what Piaget established, researchers have found that young children, especially beginning at age four, have the ability to learn and are already using concepts depicting appropriate knowledge of events and facts in places far from their immediate world (Palmer, 1994). Researchers like Tajfel and Storm (cited by Palmer, 1994) have found that while it is true that young children's sense of space and location is oriented primarily toward what is close and familiar, today they are exposed at an earlier age and with greater frequency to people and events at distant and remote places. Two elements are responsible for this earlier awareness about other people in other locations:

come to acquire a more objective and personalized view of reality. Implications of Piagetian findings are obvious: Young children are not expected to be capable of developing an understanding of people and objects that exist outside of their own environments.

■ *Exposure to the media.* Easy access to the media, especially the popular media, literally brings the world to our door.

Classroom Portrait: **Working with Today's Young Children**

One of the developmental aspects to consider in determining the appropriateness of the global approach is the cognitive behavior of young children. During the early childhood years young children are essentially sensorimotor and preoperational thinkers (see Chapter 3). They are in the initial process of building and making sense of their world. This is the time when a young child's mind-set and concepts about others are developed. This early stage of development where initial constructs about reality are formed offers an optimal opportunity for application of the global approach to learning. Today's children show an earlier awareness of the world where they live. Factors such as exposure to the media and modern technology have contributed to the development of a sense of space at a much earlier point in children's lives. Young children today demonstrate an enhanced concept of what is found in their environment, both near and far. Although concepts may not be totally accurate, the idea of someone living far from where one is located already exists for many young children (Palmer, 1994). Early childhood educators need to consider these factors along with the individual characteristics of children, and plan the social studies curriculum accordingly.

Concept Box 1–4 Using a Global Approach: Topics that Help Young Children Build Socio-Conventional Knowledge

■ Phrases in other languages (greetings, manners, words in other languages)
■ Festivities observed by their families, their friends, and by different cultural groups in other countries
■ Eating habits and table manners, here and in other places
■ School activities here and in other countries (schedule)
■ Ways to address adults, children
 How many others can you add?

Concept Box 1–5 Using a Global Approach: Topics that Help Young Children Build Physical Knowledge

■ Characteristics of buildings, constructions in different places (shapes, height, materials used)
■ Types of animal and plant life
■ Types of soils found in different places
■ Changes based on weather
 What other topics would you add?

Personal Experiences: Ways to Learn about Reality

Personal experiential learning is basic to building knowledge about the world. This is why it is important to recognize that awareness of social reali-

■ *The sharing of ideas from parents and family members.* Adults still play an important role when it comes to imparting ideas and concepts to the young. Also, with more people traveling, greater opportunities exist for acquiring knowledge about other places, knowledge that in turn is shared with children at home.

Daily work in classrooms shows us that many children are cognizant of their social reality. While it is true that children may not fully understand what they confront, many early childhood educators realize that for some children, manipulating complex concepts is a daily reality. Today, we find young children actively engaged in discussions about the rain forests, the endangered animals in Africa, and the neighborhood's most recent violent acts. More and more we find children at a very young age immersed in the issues and problems of our society. The implications of this early awareness for the early childhood curriculum are obvious. It is evident that teaching and learning approaches in the classroom must change to accommodate this transformation. A carefully designed social studies curriculum offers opportunities to help children understand what they experience personally and through others.

▪▪ Let's Talk About . . . 1–5

Are Children Aware of People and Things in Other Settings?

To see if children show an awareness of other places, select a picture book with good illustrations or with good photographs about a topic of their interest, such as children's games, animals, toys, and so on. Engage children in conversations and show them the illustrations. See how many they are able to identify as things happening in settings nearby and far away. Use questions such as:

1. Where is this place? Do you know what they call places like this?
2. Can we find these animals/plants in our neighborhood? Why? Why not?
3. What do you think that place is like? How do you know?

Check your findings and see how many of the children's answers show they have a sense of things far from their environments. Share your findings with other colleagues.

ties is also based upon individual experiences children bring to the classroom. Their ways of processing reality are as unique and as different as their social, physical, and cultural and emotional make-up. The many times they have surprised you with their own interpretation of a story or an event in the classroom should serve as reminders of their uniqueness. As Palmer (1994, p. 2) states:

> Each child has a unique relationship with the world in which he or she is growing up: a relationship based on feelings, experiences, and interactions with people, places, objects, and events.

Personal experiences are also valuable for others. Through the sharing of their own experiences, children learn and gain awareness of each other's realities. Just consider how much is discovered when children share with their peers what they did the night before or their adventures during a family trip. This wealth of knowledge learned through others will, over time, help children develop the basis of their conventional knowledge.

A Global Approach and Development of a Sense of Equality

Acquiring awareness of diversity is another important developmental consideration that supports the appropriateness of the global approach. Fundamental to the perpetuation of our society is the ability to interact with people representing all forms of diversity. The best time to develop a sense of fairness and of tolerance and avoidance of stereotypes and prejudice is during the early years (Robles de Melendez & Ostertag, 1997). In Tajfel's opinion (cited by Palmer, 1994), young children are capable of absorbing views about others held by adults. This indicates that there is an important window of time when children begin to build attitudes toward others.

> The young child is an early, but important stage in the development of social identity—related to the in-and-out groups as specified by the surrounding culture; and the *acquisition and interpretation of fac-*

Bringing Ideas into Practice 1–2
Early Awareness of Social Realities

How many times have children surprised you with their knowledge of daily social issues? Probably many. If you are not fully aware or certain of this, simply begin by observing and talking to children. For at least a week, collect daily anecdotes. Here are some suggestions to help you collect your entries:

■ **In the classroom:** Observe children at play. Look for the roles they assume in dramatic play. Listen to what they say and look for names they use with each other. Check the language they use. Look for the comments they make and reactions they have while sharing stories.

■ **On the playground:** Observe their interactions and the language they use.

■ **With your colleagues:** Ask other classmates and teachers about occasions where they have observed children role-playing, assuming behaviors and attitudes of others, using adult-like terms or phrases, or sharing comments about current events.

---

tual information about [their] own group and other groups will be related to this frame of reference.
(Tajfel, in Palmer, 1994, p. 20, emphasis added.)

Early exposure in the classroom to people from diverse groups and to their behaviors and ways fosters positive attitudes. Through well-selected manipulatives and objects representative of all groups, visual aids (posters, pictures, photographs), and quality multi-cultural literature, children can be induced to see the world as inclusive of all people regardless of their particular differences (Derman-Sparks & The A.B.C. Task Force, 1989).

Awareness and knowledge of the characteristics and learning patterns of children in today's classrooms validate the use of the global approach to social studies. Introduction of young children to the perspectives of others is the basis of the global approach to learning. Focused on the development of

Concept Box 1–6   Developmental Considerations Supporting the Global Approach in the Early Childhood Classroom

- The early childhood years are a time for building knowledge about reality. Global relationships are a part of society's daily reality.
- Interactions with the environment are a source of knowledge. Today's children are exposed to global ideas and to diversity through the media, adults, technology.
- Perceptions and ideas about others are developed during the early years and are influenced by the environment. Exposure to appropriate classroom activities helps to form positive concepts about others.

social relationships and social settings, this new vision of teaching early childhood social studies promises to help develop the life skills members of the twenty-first century will need.

The Global Approach to Social Studies Education

Through a global and cultural approach to the social studies, children:

- build knowledge about themselves and their social relationship with people in other places.
- examine the collective experiences of people in places near and far.
- find an opportunity to see the interconnections among events and decisions made by people.
- build an appreciation for the culture of people here and around the world.
- develop a sense of appreciation for their own ways and those of others.
- develop a sense of tolerance toward the ideas, beliefs and, behaviors of others.

We are sure that you probably have many questions. These may include:

1. How will I apply the global approach to social studies?
2. How can I be sure that the curriculum I am designing will be developmentally appropriate?
3. What guidelines will I follow to select the content?
4. What strategies will be the best?
5. What materials will be best for young children?

A major goal of this book is to help you gain an understanding of the global approach. As you review each chapter, the answers to these and other questions will be found. Our journey is just beginning!

Celebrations are one of the ways people express their ideas and views about life. They are also one of the common elements shared by people across cultures (Robles de Melendez & Ostertag, 1997). In a global and cultural approach to social studies education, learning about celebrations helps children to begin their development of a sense of connection with others. Finding what makes us similar and learning about what makes us uniquely individual are the tasks of the early years and the goal of American education. In reality, no social studies curriculum is appropriately designed without consideration of cultural celebrations. These celebrations open a window to the world. Through them we can lead children to see and discover how alike we are to people in other communities and places.

The early years are a decisive time in the process of developing one's identity. Because of the crucial influence of school and of classroom experience on one's sense of identity, it is vital to offer activities aimed at helping children to validate their cultures. Acknowledgment of the children's different ways and behaviors fosters a positive sense about who they are, socioculturally speaking. Using multi-cultural and global celebrations provides opportunities for children to identify with their respective groups (Figure 1–2).

FIGURE 1–2 Using Global Celebrations: Planning Matrix

Target celebration: _____

Country/cultural group: _____

Date: _____   Age level: _____

Ideas to highlight:

Concepts:

Resources:

Activities:

Bringing Ideas into Practice 1–3   *What Do We Celebrate in August?*

The month of August is a time when many of our students are preparing to go back to school or are already starting a new school year. For many young children, this is the time when they will enter into the world of school for the first time. In those places where school opens in August, consider the feelings of some of the children as they transition into a different environment. Remember to take time to talk about those celebrations they know best: birthdays and other special family celebrations.

Around the world, August is the time when people observe many important events. These celebrations offer opportunities to learn about the following key concepts:

■ Back to school
■ Independence Day in other countries
■ Summer activities

As part of the activities to welcome children either into or back to school, remember to include opportunities for them to express their feelings and expectations. Also, take time to discuss with them what schools are like in other places. Point out details such as *types of school buildings, what children wear to school, schedules and classroom activities, what they eat at school, games they play,* and other details that might be of interest to young children.

August

Cultural Celebrations	National Celebrations	Birthdays	Other events
■ Festival of the hungry ghosts (China) (rotating) ■ International Women's Equality Day (8/26)	■ Independence Day in Bolivia (8/6); Jamaica (8/6); Indonesia (8/17); Uruguay (8/25) ■ Women's Day in Tunisia (8/13)	■ Meriwether Lewis (8/18; explorer) ■ U.S. Presidents: Herbert Hoover, Benjamin Harrison, and Bill Clinton ■ Lee De Forest (8/26; called "the father of the radio")	■ Summer vacations end ■ Back to school: Children in Caribbean countries start a new school year; children in some African and South American countries such as Kenya and Argentina are already in school ■ Moment of silence (Japan, 8/9)

Other celebrations: Remember to add other events that you know of, as well as any other events that are important to the children in your classroom.

Recommended Children's Books

Brisson, P. (1989). *Your best friend, Kate.* New York: Bradbury.

Carle, E. (1971). *Do you want to be my friend?* New York: Crowell Books.

Cole, J., & Calmerson, S. (1990). *Miss Mary Mac: And other street rhymes.* New York: Morrow.

Demi (1986). *Dragon kites and dragonflies.* New York: Harcourt, Brace Jovanovich.

Fox, M. (1997). *Whoever you are.* New York: Dial.

Kindersley, B., & Kindersley, A. (1995). *Children just like me.* New York: DK Publishing.

Martin, B., & Archambault, J. (1991). *Here are my hands.* New York: Scholastic.

Melmed, L. (1993). *The first song ever sung.* New York: Lothop. (Japan)

Spier, P. (1981). *My school.* New York: Doubleday.

Walker, B. (1993). *The most beautiful thing in the world: A folktale from China.* New York: Scholastic.

ACTIVITIES

Keeping Track of What You Learn: Your Personal Activity Log

Throughout this book, you will be guided to explore and develop an appropriate social studies curriculum. We will be discussing many ideas and concepts. In order to keep a record of what you are learning, we suggest you develop a personal activity log (PAL). To get started, you need only a notebook in which you can log your explorations. Items to include will be indicated in this section at the end of each chapter. If you are ready now, your first entries will be the following:

A. Reflections

1. In a paragraph or two, describe your expectations for an early childhood social studies curriculum.
2. As an early childhood teacher, comment on your perception of the demands society makes on education.
3. What is your opinion of the global approach? How do you define it?

B. Collections

1. In this chapter a global approach to social studies education has been proposed. Imagine you are to share this concept with parents and create a collage to demonstrate why we need a global approach.
2. One of the ideas supporting a global approach is children's early awareness of events near and far. Visit an early childhood classroom and observe children. Collect samples of children's behaviors to support this point. Samples could take the form of oral conversations, responses to a story, or pictorial representations.

C. Internet Resources*

The World Wide Web is a vast collection of resources for early childhood educators. In particular, it offers a way to keep abreast of the latest developments and materials. It is important to check Web-site addresses periodically, as they are constantly revised. Two key Web sites are:

■ **National Association for the Education of Young Children (NAEYC)**

Web site: http://www.naeyc.org

This site offers information about early childhood practices and policies.

■ **National Council for the Social Studies (NCSS)**

Web site: http://www.ncss.org

As the home page of the leading organization for social studies education, this site is a good source of professional and classroom resources.

*Please note that Internet resources are of a time-sensitive nature and URL sites and addresses may often be modified or deleted.

References

Berrueta-Clement, J. R., Schweinhart, L. J., Barnett, W. S., Epstein, A. S., & Weikart, D. P. (1984). *Changed lives: The effects of the Perry Preschool Program on youths through age 19.* (Monograph of the High/Scope Educational Research Foundation No. 89) Ypsilanti, MI: High/Scope Press.

Bredekamp, S., & Copple, C. (1997). *Developmentally appropriate practice in early childhood programs.* (rev. ed.) Washington, DC: National Association for the Education of Young Children.

Bredekamp, S., & Rosegrant, T. (1996). *Reaching potentials: Transforming early childhood curriculum and assessment,* Vol. 2. Washington, DC: National Association for the Education of Young Children.

Derman-Sparks, L., & the A.B.C. Task Force (1989). *The anti-bias curriculum: Tools for empowering young children.* Washington, DC: National Association for the Education of Young Children.

Ellis, A. (1995). *Teaching and learning elementary social studies* (5th ed.). Boston, MA: Allyn & Bacon.

Katz, L., & McLellan, D. (1997). *Fostering children's social competence: The teacher's role.* Washington, DC: National Association for the Education of Young Children.

The National Council on Education Standards and Testing. (1992). *Raising standards for American education: A report to Congress, the Secretary of Education, the National Education Goals Panel and the American People.* Washington, DC: Author.

The National Council for the Social Studies (1994). *Expectations for excellence: Curriculum standards for social studies.* Bulletin 89. Washington, DC: Author.

Palmer, J. (1994). *Geography in the early years: Teaching and learning in the first three years of school.* London, UK: Routledge.

Piaget, J. (1954). *The construction of reality in the child.* New York: Basic Books.

Ramey, C. T., & Campbell, F. A. (1984). Preventative education for high-risk children: Cognitive consequences of the Carolina Abecedarian Project. *American Journal of Mental Deficiency, 88,* 515–523.

Robles de Melendez, W., & Ostertag, V. (1997). *Teaching young children in multicultural classrooms.* Albany, NY: Delmar.

Seefelt, C., & Barbour, N. (1998). *Early childhood education: An introduction* (4th ed.). Upper Saddle River, NJ: Merrill.

Spencer, B., Blades, A., & Morsley, S. (1989). *The children in the physical environment.* Chester, U.K.: John Wiley & Sons.

Welton, D. A., & Mallan, J. T. (1992). *Strategies for teaching social studies.* Boston: Houghton Mifflin.

CHAPTER 2

Discovering the Essence of Social Studies

Social studies from kindergarten through grade three should set the tone and lay the foundation for the social studies education that follows. An important goal in these early years is to excite student interest in social studies and to capitalize on the eagerness of young children to learn.

—NATIONAL COMMISSION ON SOCIAL STUDIES IN THE SCHOOLS (1989)

Chapter Questions

After reading this chapter, you should be able to answer the following questions:

- What does the term *social studies* mean?
- Which disciplines are elements of this multi-faceted area of study?
- In what way are the needs of children met through the social studies curriculum?
- What are the characteristics of a developmentally appropriate social studies curriculum?
- What should characterize the early childhood social studies teacher?

Key Terms and Concepts

Americans with Disabilities Act
attitudes
curriculum strands
humanities

integrated curriculum
social sciences
standards
values

Classroom Portrait: Why Study Social Studies?

During a parent-teacher meeting, while looking at her child's work samples in the portfolio, Mrs. Beeman expressed her disapproval of the classroom activities. Classroom program in hand, she pointed to the place where it said, "Our classroom activities engage children in the following curricular areas: ... social studies, etc." "I'd like to know why you are taking time for social studies when my child doesn't even know how to read yet," Mrs. Beeman declared.

"Mrs. Beeman, thank you for sharing your concern. But you see, learning to read is not the only thing children need," answered Ms. Alma, the kindergarten teacher.

"Let me tell you, there are other parents who share my opinion," Mrs. Beeman added.

Ms. Alma looked at her and replied with a smile, "Reading and writing go on all the time in our classroom, particularly after five-year-olds have had a new experience. For example, see these drawings on the wall." Ms. Alma pointed to the display of illustrations. "These are a part of what we did after our last field trip. The children came back with many questions about all the statues of historical figures they saw in the park, and right away we learned their names and talked about what they did in the past!"

"Yes, I know, but don't you think that there is time later to learn about history?"

Ms. Alma understood right away what the parent meant. Like many others, Mrs. Beeman believed that social studies was only about learning dates and historical events.

■■ Social Studies:
■■ In Search of Definitions

The importance of social studies as an area of study has not always been readily understood by teachers, parents, and the public. Traditionally, and

Social studies provides opportunities to learn about ourselves and others.

particularly in the early grades, social studies has been either neglected or considered an optional subject. The vignette at the beginning of this chapter is an example of the ongoing debate about the role of social studies in early childhood classrooms everywhere. It demonstrates that full understanding of the nature and purposes of social studies has not yet been established. The implications are obvious: There is a need for educators, and particularly for early childhood teachers, to become cognizant of the relevancy of social studies and the role it should play in the curriculum.

Several early childhood social studies educators have expressed their concern about the lack of support for social studies education (Hahn, 1991). They have also indicated that this vague and loose attitude toward learning social studies in early childhood presents a risk both for young children and for our society. Although many people believe that social studies is not needed in the early childhood curriculum, particularly as our society seems to be moving into a more technologically based environment, this kind of thinking is risky, because it discourages the acquisition of the social skills individuals need to interact effectively with others and to

Bringing Ideas into Practice 2–1
Teachers' Opinions about the Importance of Social Studies

Discovering opinions about the topic of social studies helps us to analyze our own ideas as well as the ideas of others. Answer the short survey below, and then survey your colleagues or classmates. Take time to compare their responses and opinions with your own. Consider the impact these opinions have upon the development of appropriate social studies concepts and skills at the early childhood level.

Questions

1. How important to you is social studies as a component of the curriculum?

   Very Important_____ / Somewhat important_____ / Not important_____

2. In your opinion, is social studies as a subject as relevant as any of the other curricular subjects (i.e., reading, math, science)?

   YES_____   NO_____

3. Do you like teaching social studies?

   YES_____   NO_____   Not Sure_____

4. Is social studies a part of your daily planning?

   YES_____   NO_____

5. How often during the week do you include or teach social studies?

   Daily / Four days / Three days / Two days / One day / None

6. How many times did you teach social studies last week?

   Daily / Four days / Three days / Two days / One day / None

---

keep our society free and democratic in the future. In Hahn's words (1991, p. 172):

> Whatever efforts we make now to revitalize early childhood social studies will strengthen citizenship education at all levels. *Action now is a wise investment in the future* (emphasis added).

Becoming fully aware of both the nature and the purpose of the social studies helps us plan and build quality experiences that children require. It also prevents us from neglecting the context of life that children need as they continue their journey of discovery.

Defining social studies is a very challenging task, particularly because of its broad range of concepts. Just imagine trying to convey through one curriculum area the study of everything deemed "social"! There are other difficulties, as well, in defining social studies. Educator Cynthia Sunal (1990) said that the difficulty in defining social studies is partly caused by the memories we have of social studies classes we have experienced. It is impor-

tant to consider *how* those experiences have shaped the way we view the field. That's why we would like to begin this section with several questions.

As a child in school, do you remember:

- what you learned through your social studies classes?
- things you did as part of your social studies lessons?
- the activities you enjoyed the most?
- the activities you liked the least?
- some of the topics you explored? Which ones?
- which topics you liked best?
- some of the materials you used? Which ones?
- what you liked best about any of your social studies teachers? Why?

As we remember what we enjoyed and learned, some of us probably will recall what we did not like, as well. Recalling our own experiences helps us identify the relevant aspects of successful and meaningful social studies teaching.

⬛⬛ Let's Talk About . . . 2–1

What Do We Recall about Our Social Studies Classes?

Learning about the opinions of others is always a good way to discover different perspectives on a topic. Two ways to learn about the ideas of others are:

1. Ask other colleagues or friends to answer the questionnaire on p. 23.
2. Share your own answers with your colleagues and listen to their comments. See if you have any ideas in common.

Common Ideas about Social Studies

When we asked a group of early childhood teachers to share their views about social studies, we found a variety of ideas. Most of this group sees social studies as the subject area where children learn about events, people, and things people do. To some, it is the area where children just study history and geography. For a few teachers, social studies is simply the study of all things social. For still others, it is the curriculum where they explore life in different parts of the world.

Why do we find so many different ideas about social studies? The truth is, this is not an easy subject area to define. The fact that people are the focal point of social studies opens up an endless array of related areas to be explored and learned. This aspect makes social studies one of the broadest and most ambitious subject areas in the entire school curriculum. If you are among those who believe social studies deals with people and what they do, we say, "You are right!"

A Formal Definition of Social Studies

What is "social studies"? According to the National Council for the Social Studies (NCSS), **social studies** is officially defined as:

. . . the integrated study of the social sciences and humanities to promote civic competence. Within the school program, social studies provides coordinated, systematic study, drawing upon such disciplines as anthropology, archaeology, economics, geography, history, law, philosophy, political science, psychology, religion, and sociology, as well as appropriate content for the humanities, mathematics, and natural sciences. The primary purpose of the social studies is to help young people develop the ability to make informed and reasoned decisions for the public good as citizens of a culturally diverse, democratic society in an interdependent world.

(NCSS, 1994, p. vii).

Several key points are established by this definition: the *purpose* and goals of teaching social studies, the *content* to be developed, *origins* of the content, and essential *teaching strategies*. All of these points (quoted from the NCSS statement above) reaffirm the fundamental role of this curricular area in the early childhood classroom.

1. **Purpose:**
   a. "to promote civic competence."
   b. "to help young people develop the ability to make informed and reasoned decisions for the public good as citizens of a culturally diverse, democratic society in an interdependent world."
2. **Content:** "the integrated study of the social sciences and humanities."
3. **Origins of the content:** "drawing upon such disciplines as anthropology, archaeology, economics, geography, history, law, philosophy, political science, psychology, religion, and sociology, as well as appropriate content for the humanities, mathematics, and natural sciences."
4. **Essential teaching strategies:** "integrated study."

Implications of the NCSS Definition

Three key concepts that emerge from the NCSS definition of social studies have implications for early childhood educators:

1. The *first* concept is that social studies is an **integrated curriculum** comprised of a variety of disciplines. Thus, the organization of the content

---

Concept Box 2–1   Social Studies—A Fairly Recent Curriculum Area

Those among us who took social studies courses when we were in school should not assume that social studies was always a part of the school curriculum. Unlike mathematics, science, and reading, social studies as a subject area was not "born" until 1916. The term *social studies* was officially used to designate a curricular subject area by the National Education Association's Commission on Reorganization of Secondary Education in 1916. One aspect of the field has re-

mained constant throughout the years: From its inception, social studies has focused on the study of everything people do and the ways people interact in a democratic society. Today, almost a century later, the essence of the social studies is still as it was originally defined.

Source: Saxe, D. (1992). Framing a theory for social studies foundations. *Review of Educational Research, 62,* pp. 269–277.

---

should lead children to look at experiences from a variety of perspectives.

2. The *second* key concept is that knowledge about the social studies is developed through the systematic and well-integrated study of all the areas included in the **social sciences** and the **humanities** (see Figure 2–1). This means that planning needs to reflect a careful and logical selection of topics to be studied, with appropriate attention focused on the cognitive processing abilities of children. Considering that children construct knowledge in a gradual and progressive manner, activities should provide time for children to explore and process ideas at their own pace (Bredekamp & Copple, 1997).

3. The *third* concept is that the social studies curriculum has a clear and relevant social mission to accomplish: helping children develop the ability to live in a social group. This indicates that there is a need to permeate the entire early childhood curriculum with experiences from social studies

and to transform the classroom into a social learning laboratory.

In the following sections we will explore the relationship of these three aspects to the development of the early childhood social studies curriculum.

Social Studies—A Multi-faceted Curriculum

One of the exciting features of social studies is its multi-faceted nature. Stemming from the realms of social sciences, humanities, and natural sciences, social studies mirrors all the aspects of human endeavor. A close look at the areas that comprise social studies is detailed in Figure 2–1. As you will see, each of the areas forming the social studies is one of several well-defined, individual disciplines, all emerging from and revolving around the study of human phenomena. Instead of examining reality from the perspective of one subject area (such as sociology or history) at a time, in social studies a reality is perceived through multiple disciplines. Thus, social studies represents a way to apply a multi-dimensional perspective to explore and explain people and their reality.

With so many different subjects forming social studies, many early childhood teachers will probably wonder what these individual disciplines examine. A close look at what each discipline entails is represented in Figure 2–2.

Encompassing the activities of human beings as well as their relationships and interactions, the so-

---

■■   **Let's Talk About . . . 2–2**

What is Your Definition of Social Studies?

You probably have your own ideas about how to define social studies. Before moving on, take this opportunity to write down your personal definition of social studies. Save it and compare it later with the definition given in this chapter.

FIGURE 2-1   The many areas of social studies.

Social Studies

Humanities	Social Sciences
■ fine arts	■ geography
■ literature	■ psychology
■ music	■ history
■ drama	■ economics
■ dance	■ sociology
■ philosophy	■ anthropology
	■ political science

of social competence that will provide "knowledge of and involvement in civic affairs" (NCSS, 1994, p. vii). These goals, in essence, represent the mission of the social studies. Crucial as they are for the survival of a democratic society, these social and civic behaviors begin their development in the early years. One realizes what social studies experiences offer to young children when considering that individual development and socialization of the child are among the goals of early childhood education.

■■ Social Studies and the Child
■■ with Special Needs

cial studies curriculum is aimed at helping to develop individuals who are capable of becoming effective citizens themselves. It promotes the acquisition of skills needed by each individual for successful membership in society. More specifically, social studies is targeted at fostering development

Social studies and social skills acquisition are of the utmost importance for children with developmental delays, whether the delay is physical, emotional, or mental. To alleviate the stigma often associated with having developmental delays and make it possible for these children to acquire citizenship

FIGURE 2-2   Subject areas that form the social studies and their content.

Subject Area	What Each Area Explores (Content)
Social Sciences	
■ *History*	Explores and helps us understand events from the past and present, and projects patterns or trends into the future. Helps to develop a sense of what people do and experience through time.
■ *Geography*	Studies people in terms of their relationships and interactions with space, location, natural phenomena, and natural resources.
■ *Sociology*	Studies how human groups react and relate to each other.
■ *Psychology*	Focuses on the study of human behavior. Examines the development of attitudes and emotional reactions.
■ *Anthropology*	Examines the role of culture in human life and how it influences human behavior.
■ *Economics*	Focuses on needs and wants and how people meet them.
■ *Political Science*	Examines the concept of governance and the decision-making processes followed by people to organize themselves into social units.
Humanities	
■ *The Arts*	Studies the different ways people use to represent and express ideas. Includes music, drama, dance, and the visual arts.
■ *Literature*	Examines the variety of ways people express ideas in writing. It reflects the reactions, feelings, and attitudes of people.
■ *Philosophy*	Describes the values people hold and their need to search for answers.

skills, they must be provided the opportunity to be educated with children of their own age in a regular classroom. Kronberg (1998) stated that making adaptations to accommodate each child, regardless of the stage of development, requires that the educator have information about the student. Teachers must be familiar with learning styles, strengths and weaknesses, and instructional support needs of the children with whom they work.

Meyen (1996) depicts the contrast between those children who experience delays in development and those who do not. He says that *maturation* is the primary contributor to the development of the non-disabled child, but that for the child with disabilities, it is the *educational process* itself that must account for a larger proportion of intellectual growth than maturation. For example, a child with a language delay may also experience a delay in social and cognitive development. Consequently, early childhood programs that emphasize social awareness must be made available to these exceptional children.

██ Goals of Social Studies Education

Specific goals outlined by NCSS and based on the perspective of developmentally appropriate practices (DAP) (see p. 35 and Chapter 1) help early childhood teachers fulfill the mission of the social studies. Essentially, there are *five key goals:*

1. **Individual development:** The social studies curriculum will foster the positive development of children as unique individuals. Development of a sense of oneself in relation to others is a related goal. Experiences will promote development of an effective decision-making ability that will enable the individual to make informed choices.
2. **Social and civic competence:** Children will develop appropriate knowledge, skills, and attitudes essential to an effective social life.
3. **Knowledge-based concept of social reality:** Classroom activities will provide opportunities for children to develop and acquire ideas about their social reality. These experiences will foster multiple ways to look at, value, and appreciate people and their behaviors.

> ## ██ Let's Talk About . . . 2–3
>
> **Goals of Early Childhood Social Studies Education**
>
> Consider the five goals of social studies education outlined below. Discuss them with your classmates or colleagues.
>
> 1. What is your opinion of the goals outlined by NCSS?
> 2. Do you agree with all of them? Why?
> 3. Are there any others you would add? Why?

4. **Appreciation and respect for human diversity:** Classroom experiences will promote a sense of equity toward others despite their characteristics. Individual differences and physical disabilities will be discussed early in a child's life. Opportunities to build and clarify attitudes necessary to live in a socially and culturally diverse society will be pursued through all classroom activities. An appreciation of different ideas, different physical appearances, different ways, and different behaviors will be fostered.
5. **Global citizenship:** Activities will lead to the development of a sense of being a part of the world. Children will acquire a sense of responsibility for their acts and for their impact on others.

Successful social studies experiences require teachers to have a thorough knowledge of the subject matter and of the needs of young children. Teaching and planning activities in such a comprehensive field demands clarity about the kinds of knowledge children need and can develop. Equally important for appropriate teaching is clarity of insight into the purpose of social studies.

Our ability to provide exciting and developmentally appropriate experiences in the social studies classroom depends upon our understanding of these five essential aspects:

1. What is the purpose of the social studies curriculum? Is it in consonance with the developmental tasks of early childhood?

■■ Let's Talk About . . . 2–4

Developmentally Appropriate Practices

Today the concept and philosophical statement called DAP (see pp. 12 and 35) is the nationally recognized framework for quality educational practices in early childhood settings. DAP fosters development by mandating the need to establish and design services and programs focused on the general and individual needs and characteristics of children. The concept of DAP has been expanded to include not only developmentally appropriate practices but also teaching practices that are developmentally and culturally appropriate—DCAP. These principles should guide educators in any curricular venture. Social studies embraces this philosophy, because it serves to nurture children and encourage them to develop as valuable individuals in society.

1. What do you think of the inclusion of DAP and DCAP in social studies?

2. In what ways do you think social studies responds to the mandates of this educational philosophy?

---

2. What is the content of the social studies? Where is it rooted?

3. What are the developmental characteristics and needs of young children, including those who experience developmental delays?

4. Which aspects of the social studies content are developmentally appropriate?

5. What kind of social studies teaching strategies are appropriate in the early childhood classroom?

Certainly, a key word in DAP and DCAP is *development*. A child's level of development is dependent upon several factors. Meyen (1996) believes that five influences dictate a child's rate and level of development: 1) instruction, 2) innate learner characteristics, 3) environment, 4) stability of support, and 5) wellness or illness. To the degree possible, educators of young children should play an active role

in making positive contributions in all of these areas for all children, including those who are developmentally delayed.

■■ Characteristics of an Effective ■■ Social Studies Curriculum

Selecting and designing experiences appropriate for young children is always a challenge. However, the challenge is even greater when it comes to social studies. Teaching young children about events, places, and things people do requires a solid understanding of developmental principles. Specific developmental characteristics and needs of children that impact the planning and teaching process will be explored in Chapter 3.

There are also several key descriptors that define good and sound social studies curricular experiences (Task Force on Standards for Teaching and Learning in the Social Studies, 1993; cited in Bredekamp & Rosegrant, 1995). Essentially, an *effective and appropriate* early childhood social studies curriculum is:

- meaningful
- integrated
- challenging
- based on knowledge, skills, and attitudes
- active

As you will see from the following explanation, these are not only curricular characteristics but also planning guidelines for the early childhood educator.

Guidelines for an Effective and Child-Appropriate Social Studies Curriculum

1. An effective and appropriate curriculum is *meaningful*. Any successful curriculum is characterized by its meaningfulness for children. This quality is achieved only when the content revolves around topics of interest and significance for the child. A sense of purpose emerges when children feel that there is value in what they are doing and when they find connections between the topics that are being examined and themselves. Central to this sense of

connection with the curriculum is the ability to match topics and activities in the classrooms with the interests of the children and their realities outside the classroom.

Meaningfulness is also achieved *when topics are worth learning* (Bredekamp & Rosegrant, 1995). Many times, early childhood curricula have been criticized for the low knowledge value they offer. It is important to remember that young children are in the process of building knowledge. For this reason, careful selection should be made of what they will spend their time exploring. The key here is to learn how to move away from "cute" and "trivial" topics that contribute very little and how to get into experiences where valuable learning will occur.

In the opinion of Bredekamp and Rosegrant (1995), meaningfulness is achieved when early childhood teachers:

■ are able to identify the disciplines from which the topic stems and to which it relates,
■ are familiar with basic key concepts,
■ have age-appropriate expectations, and
■ design individually appropriate activities.
(Bredekamp & Rosegrant, 1995, p. 19)

Also essential to a meaningful curriculum is the ability to select topics *at the level of what the child is able to process.* Developmental appropriateness is indispensable if true learning is our goal. Seefeldt (1997) points out the need to match content to the level of cognitive maturity exhibited by children. She also advises that, although it can be a challenging task, developmental match is more easily achieved if teachers remain current in their knowledge of recent child development principles and of policies issued by childhood organizations, such as NAEYC's position on developmentally appropriate curricular practices (DAP). Inherent in these principles is the need for teachers to ensure that the ways topics are chosen and presented respect children's cognitive abilities.

Good knowledge about the child is the best source of engaging and appropriate experiences. Awareness of individual needs, interests, and abilities will help you make sound curricular selections. Although the following topics are of interest to most young children, you will find that topics that are of keen interest to some individuals will hold little interest for other children.

Social Studies Topics of Interest to Young Children

Context	Topics
Home	family, family members, siblings, family roles and activities, family pets.
Neighborhood	places in the neighborhood, neighborhood composition and structure, types of dwellings found in the neighborhood, people living in the neighborhood, activities in the neighborhood.
Community	places, community services, community helpers, recreational areas, environmental issues and problems such as pollution and recycling.
Play (games, toys)	types of games, game objects, game rules, toys used by children in other places, old and new toys, songs and music related to games, play artifacts.
School/ classroom	children's roles and activities, classroom materials, equipment used, school members.

2. An effective and appropriate curriculum is *integrated.* Social studies itself is an integrated way to look at human phenomena. In early childhood education, fundamental to the appropriate teaching of social studies, experiences must provide a variety of views about a topic. Examination of concepts should offer opportunities to look at them from the perspective of the many disciplines comprised in the social studies (Figure 2–3). With young children, an integrated social studies curriculum occurs when:

■ experiences provide opportunities for children to view concepts from many angles, and from the perspective of different subject areas.
■ teaching transcends times, places, and cultures to offer children a sense of connection with things and events.

FIGURE 2–3   A sample integrated thematic plan for social studies.

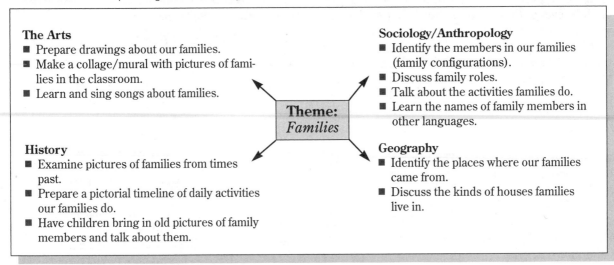

■ the curriculum integrates real-life experiences that are significant to the children in the classroom.

■ classroom experiences integrate a variety of sources of information and all kinds of learning tools, including technology.
(Task Force on Standards for Teaching and Learning in the Social Studies, 1993)

3. An effective and appropriate curriculum is *challenging.* Through the curriculum, social studies offer young inquisitive learners experiences that help them to become active, capable individuals. Well-designed classroom activities promote in children a sense of enjoyment, a desire for exploring, and ways of learning about themselves and others. Experiences are aimed at initiating the young learners in thinking and questioning skills, and in the ability to engage others in dialogue. These, in essence, are key characteristics of an effective citizen. The early childhood classroom is an active social laboratory in which a challenging social studies curriculum can unfold.

4. A challenging social studies curriculum is also characterized by the *knowledge, skills,* and *attitudes* and *values* it fosters.

■ **Knowledge:** Ideas and concepts about the social reality children live in are developed and discussed through the curriculum. Because young children are active knowledge-builders, opportunities to build on their own a sense of who they are and how they relate to their peers and their environment are an indispensable element of classroom teaching. Classroom experiences, drawn from the different disciplines and reflective of what is both of interest and age-appropriate, introduce children to events and ideas while clarifying personal views. The goal of these experiences is to provide and process information that results in the building and augmentation of knowledge schemes (NCSS Task Force on Early Childhood/Elementary Social Studies, 1988). The ways children build knowledge during their early years will be discussed further in Chapter 3.

■ **Skills:** To become effective learners and citizens requires the development of essential skills in four key areas (see Concept Box 2–2). Children should be encouraged to learn:
a. how to participate effectively in social groups.
b. how to think and inquire.
c. how to present and share their own ideas with others.
d. how to acquire and use information.

Opportunities to explore are an important part of the curriculum.

■ **Attitudes and Values:** All social groups are characterized by the values and attitudes they hold. **Attitudes** are defined as personal and group reactions and dispositions about an issue or subject. **Values** represent the desirable principles and standards people hold; these values guide their behaviors. Social studies is aimed at developing the democratic attitudes and values of the United States and other democratic societies. "The early years are ideal for children to begin to understand democratic norms and values (justice, equality, etc.)—especially in terms of the smaller social entities of the family, classroom, and community" (NCSS Task Force on Early Childhood and Elementary School Children, 1988, p. xiv).

Early childhood classrooms serve as the arena where children come to examine attitudes about themselves and others. The classroom is also the setting where these attitudes are clarified and selectively learned. Social interaction is, according to

Vygotsky (1978), essential for development of an individual who will be capable of effectively participating in the social group to which he or she belongs. Figure 2–4 identifies the attitudes and beliefs central to democratic life in our national and global societies.

5. An effective curriculum is *active.* The vision of social studies in the early childhood classroom would never be complete without this last descriptor: *active!* Embedded in the concept of any DAP program for children is the need to provide an environment where children have plenty of opportunities for active and direct participation. Because knowledge is actively and personally constructed, children need a setting where they can build ideas and concepts through direct interaction. As they interact with materials, ideas, peers, and adults, young children gain new and individualized insights about their realities. In the case of social studies, where children are in the process of developing knowledge about social phenomena, the optimal environment is a classroom that replicates society. In an active classroom environment, opportunities abound for children to look at reality through the classroom. In this setting, situations and issues—planned and unplanned—are introduced by the teacher or arise through the children's and adults' interactions, and time is available to explore these both individually and as a group (Katz & Chard, 1989).

A quality curriculum is characterized by its recognition of the role of active participation in children's knowledge construction. According to cognitive developmental theory, active participation in an environment leads each child to establish a personal and direct relationship with the concept being explored, thus building his or her own concept of that reality. In the case of social studies, active participation is central to building the key conceptual foundation of one's social realities. For teachers of young children, this translates into the need to create classrooms where concrete opportunities are constantly present. An active classroom is one in which children have an opportunity to choose and interact with an abundance of materials in a setting where teachers and adults provide children with support and encouragement (Hohmann & Weikart, 1995).

Concept Box 2–2   Essential Social Studies Skills for the Pre-K through Grade 3 Level

Social studies is targeted at preparing individuals with a set of essential skills that will enable them to function effectively and participate in society. A detailed look at the skills deemed important for the early childhood level is presented here. Based on the document developed by the NCSS Task Force on Scope and Sequence (1989), the skills shown here reflect expectations the authors of this book consider appropriate for children age five through eight. As you examine this list of skills, consider 1) their *appropriateness for the Pre-K through 3 level,* 2) how many of these skills are *shared with other disciplines,* and 3) how *children who have deficits in one or more areas of development* might be impacted.

Selected Key Social Studies Skills for the Pre-K through Grade 3 Level

At this level, children in a developmentally appropriate curriculum should be able to demonstrate the following skills:

Social participation—the child
- works in groups.
- takes turns.
- listens to others.
- shares ideas and materials.
- expresses opinions.
- has a positive sense about himself or herself.
- shows respect for others.
- uses "manners" words, such as "please" and "thank you."

Information—the child
- observes to gather information.
- knows where to look for information.
- asks questions to get information.
- uses a variety of information sources.
- is becoming aware of technology as a source of information.
- listens.
- follows directions.

Critical thinking—the child
- observes.
- asks questions to get information.
- shows interests in knowing more about events.
- organizes information (sorts, classifies, groups) according to characteristics.
- explores materials.
- finds solutions to simple problems.

Orientation in space—the child
- knows his/her address.
- uses points of reference to orient him/herself.
- gives directions to others using positional terms.
- knows how to trace a route to home, school, etc.
- uses blocks to describe spaces.
- is familiar with maps and globes.
- designs simple maps.

This same active learning process is what characterizes any appropriate environment for early childhood social studies education. Essentially, an active learning environment should include:

- *an abundance of carefully selected, age-appropriate materials:* Manipulatives, pictures and photographs, books, and artifacts are available for children to examine and use.
- *opportunities for manipulation:* The classroom is organized to encourage exploration through manipulation of a variety of materials. All children have an opportunity to participate; adaptations and specially planned activities are made for children with special needs. (Note: One of the easiest ways to include a special needs child is to have the child sit beside an adult who can help. Providing knobbed puzzles, squeeze-only scissors, bigger Legos™, giant crayons and pencils, and fatter washable markers are just a few adaptations that can easily be made to accommodate the special needs child.)

FIGURE 2–4 Learning about Democratic Rights and Beliefs in the Early Childhood Classroom

Democratic Rights and Beliefs	Rights and beliefs are learned when teachers:
Liberty Happiness Dignity Justice Security Privacy Tolerance Expression of ideas Participation Respect for others Compassion Respect for the property of others Freedom of religious beliefs	■ create activities and take advantage of "teachable moments" to discuss and demonstrate what each of the rights stand for. The class needs to read and discuss literature that portrays individual rights. Children need to learn to wait for one's turn and to respect the property of others. ■ establish an atmosphere where children can freely express their ideas. They should plan activities and encourage children to ask questions and to look for answers. They should plan activities that provide opportunities for children to discuss why others are entitled to hold ideas different from theirs and to have different preferences; this will help children develop a sense of tolerance. ■ provide opportunities to develop and refine prosocial skills. ■ use a guidance approach to foster development of self-control. ■ provide DAP experiences geared to helping children learn how to respect others and to helping children develop a sense about others (perspective-taking). ■ develop experiences that will enhance children's knowledge about the value of rules. ■ encourage children to share comments about rules at home and offer children opportunities to create classroom rules. ■ encourage the class to discuss why there are school and community rules and how they help safeguard people's rights.

Source: Adapted from Jarolimek, J, (1990). Social studies for citizens of a strong and free nation. In *Social studies curriculum planning resources.* Washington, DC: National Council for the Social Studies.

■ *many choices:* The classroom offers multiple choices. Children are encouraged to select those that closely respond and appeal to them. A menu of interesting and child-oriented experiences is carefully planned and reviewed.

■ *opportunities for language usage and for verbal interactions:* Children are encouraged to express their ideas and views about what is explored and experienced. Communication of personal experiences and ideas happens naturally among most children. (Note: For those language-delayed special needs children who may be in your classroom, encourage the use of oral language by requiring that those who are capable of speaking ask for items by name, rather than by just pointing. Items of interest can deliberately be put out of reach to encourage the use of oral language.)

■ *a circle of teacher/adult support:* Children find a circle of support and of interaction formed by teachers and other adults. This circle encourages children to present and communicate ideas
(Hohmann & Weikart, 1995, p. 38)

There are two other important factors contributing to an appropriate, active learning-oriented environment. An active classroom, where real learning happens, rests upon two central aspects: 1) *sound knowledge of child developmental principles* and 2) *good planning skills.* Knowledge about children provides the clues to the appropriateness of teaching strategies. It also offers guidelines for setting appro-

An appropriate curriculum provides opportunities for active engagement.

Knowledge about children and their development provides clues to the appropriateness of teaching strategies.

priate expectations for interactions among children, adults, and peers.

Developmental principles play a leading role in informing teachers about ways to design and organize both the classroom environment and experiences according to the needs of different ages and ability levels. Effective planning occurs when developmental knowledge is used to consider what children are capable of doing and experiencing.

A growing number of children with special needs are found in many preschools and child-care centers. These children have disabilities ranging from hyperactivity and attention deficit disorder to speech and language delays and physical impairments. Because of the **Americans with Disabilities Act** (PL 101-476), enacted in 1990, which provided civil rights protection to prohibit discrimination against persons with disabilities, regardless of age or disability, our society has had to become better equipped to accommodate these special children (Turnbull, 1993). However, not all early childhood educators have been trained to deal with these children. That's when developmentally appropriate planning becomes an absolute must. With the variety of concepts and ideas to explore through social studies, DAP always includes consideration of all

children's unique characteristics, abilities, and disabilities. Characteristics such as language differences, special developmental needs, and social traits must be taken into account in successful social studies planning. These concepts support quality services for children, also known as DAP. Social studies education for young children adheres to these practices, following them as guidelines for program planning and organization.

Key Considerations about the National Social Studies Standards

Standards define a level of achievement and excellence with regard to an activity or field. Specifically, curriculum standards are intended to "provide a vision of content and purpose" (NCSS, 1994, p. 14). During the 1980s and 1990s, education witnessed an increased interest in defining indicators for achievement in the different disciplines. In fact, DAP is a reflection of the standards movement. *Goals 2000* instituted the "development of national educational standards as a means of encouraging and evaluating student achievement" (NCSS, 1994, p. viii). These goals, outlined by the National Council for the Social Studies and sanctioned by the U.S. Congress, represent our national education agenda. They have served as a model to define similar performance expectations in most disciplines. Social stud-

Concept Box 2–3   Developmentally Appropriate Practices (DAP) and Social Studies Education

Central to an effective and child-centered social studies program is the application of the principles of quality early education. Today, those principles are embedded in the philosophy held by the NAEYC termed *developmentally appropriate practices (DAP)*, first described by Bredekamp in 1987 and revised by Bredekamp & Copple a decade later, in 1997. The DAP approach to teaching social studies will be discussed more fully in Chapter 3. These practices embody a set of nationally accepted descriptors for quality curricula in early childhood education. It is essential to know and follow these principles when planning social studies experiences for the young. Knowledge about DAP helps teachers to organize the curriculum in response to the children and their needs, rather than attempting to fit the children into the curriculum. As teachers of young children, it is important for us to understand that our commitment is to serve children in a developmentally appropriate and responsive manner. As DAP advocates, teaching responsively implies the need to recognize that today's classrooms are characterized by a diversity of ideas, cultural patterns, and ability levels, as well as social and linguistic backgrounds. Recognition of diversity is a fundamental part of the existence of social studies as a curriculum discipline.

Built around three pivotal points, DAP (Bredekamp and Copple, 1997) establishes the need to develop curriculum around different types of knowledge, all central to the teaching of social studies:

■ **Knowledge of child developmental processes**—current information about general developmental and learning characteristics.

■ **Knowledge of individual developmental characteristics**—specific needs, interests, and strengths.

■ **Knowledge of the children's social and cultural contexts**—including socioethnic characteristics, linguistic, and other diverse characteristics.

Quality social studies education for young children incorporates and follows the three main tenets of DAP. An appropriate curriculum reflects a DAP orientation when teachers are able to respond to the following concerns:

1. Do the strategies and activities reflect developmental learning theory? How? (knowledge about *child development*.)
2. Were individual needs and characteristics considered? How? (knowledge about *individual development*.)
3. Are adaptations made for children with specific physical, mental, or emotional needs? How? (knowledge about *individual development* as a guideline.)
4. Were the children's diverse characteristics considered and reflected in the curriculum? How? (knowledge about *social and cultural developmental contexts*.)

Preparing children for effective citizenship is a tremendous task. In it lies the essence of the future of society. DAP offers a way to achieve this task in a successful and child-responsive manner. Social studies early education teachers have a responsibility to familiarize themselves with the elements of DAP and their application in the classroom.

ies education joined the performance standards movement by publishing its curriculum standards in 1994. One of the central goals of the standards movement was to provide teachers with specific guidelines for the concepts and content targeted for children (Ravitch, 1995). This was accomplished in social studies with the formulation of the standards accompanied by a comprehensive conceptual framework for teaching social studies. Additionally, the social studies standards define with precision the areas of study and the concepts that should be included from the different disciplines forming the social studies.

In addition to the standards that now exist for the whole field of social studies, today there are standards for most of the individual disciplines included in the social studies—economics, history, geography, and so on. Each of these disciplines will be discussed in the corresponding chapters in Part II of this book. It is important to understand, however, that in spite of the existence of these individual standards, the general standards for social studies known as *Expectations for Excellence* offer a way to build a current and cognitively sound social studies curriculum. Today, these standards (see Appendix I, p. 271) serve as the basic framework for programs across the nation.

What the National Social Studies Standards Offer to Teachers

The NCSS *Expectations for Excellence: Curriculum Standards for Social Studies* (NCSS, 1994) set the levels of competence for social studies education throughout the early grades. However, the term *early grades* is unclear. In the absence of an official definition, educators have assumed that the "early grades" include kindergarten through fourth grade.

The standards (see Appendix I, p. 271) provide teachers with:

■ *comprehensive information about the social studies content.*
■ *a thematic content framework organized around ten thematic areas, or* **curriculum strands**:
   I. Culture
   II. Time, continuity, and change
   III. People, places, and environments
   IV. Individual development and identity
   V. Individuals, groups, and institutions
   VI. Power, authority, and governance
   VII. Production, distribution, and consumption
   VIII. Science, technology, and society
   IX. Global connections
   X. Civic ideals and practice
■ *grade-level expectations for student achievement within each thematic strand.* Expectations are es-

tablished for kindergarten through fourth grade. These expectations serve as guidelines for curriculum planning; however, to appropriately use the performance indicators, the developmental needs of children must be emphasized.
■ *suggestions for thematic integration of content strands, including detailed description of other themes that can be integrated in the curriculum design.*

Early childhood and social studies educators agree that the social studies standards for the primary grades represent one of the most significant educational achievements of recent years. The standards give early childhood teachers a comprehensive way to view the scope of the social studies curriculum and specific guidelines that can be used to shape a sound curriculum that corresponds to nationally accepted goals.

There are at least four ways in which the standards contribute to the development of an appropriate program:

1. The standards are a helpful source of information to build a *whole* and *pertinent* curriculum. They help teachers avoid falling into the trap of the curriculum based on trivial or "cutesy" topics.
2. The organization of standards in interrelated themes or strands provides early childhood teachers with helpful directions for development of integrated curricula.
3. The performance expectations broaden and clarify the scope and nature of each of the ten key themes.
4. The standards and performance indicators constitute a working curricular framework that establishes continuity of learning across age levels.

Although the standards are a valuable planning tool, some concerns regarding the content specified in the standards and the nature of young children must be kept in mind. *First,* it is imperative to understand the cognitive developmental characteristics of children. Because social studies consist of highly complex concepts, it is important to remember the limitations posed by the children's age. We know social concepts are developed and refined through time and with experience. Young children are, how-

Do the NCSS Social Studies Standards Apply to Three- and Four-Year-Olds?

Some teachers have expressed their concern about using the NCSS standards in designing the curriculum for three- and four-year-olds. Some have claimed it is not "DAP" to use "Expectations for Excellence" that were intended for grades K–4. Others have stated that it is too ambitious. Nonetheless, considering the thematic nature of the standards and the focus on integrating related strands we believe that, with good knowledge of the interests and the needs of children and through careful selection, the ten strands offer early childhood educators a pool of ideas for curriculum design. Used as a reference, the standards provide early educators with opportunities to build relevant experiences for young preschoolers. Educators need to dedicate time, however, to brainstorm and carefully examine each of the areas contemplated in the ten strands.

1. What are some strengths and weaknesses of the national social studies standards as they relate to young children?

2. Give examples of ways in which the NCSS standards can be used with children ages three and four.

ever, in the process of beginning to gain knowledge and experience about the social reality. The implications are clear: Content and concepts should be age-appropriate, as well as developmentally appropriate. This is accomplished only when teachers apply their knowledge of the different cognitive characteristics of young children and of the way they construct reality. The developmental needs of children should always be given primary consideration when developing curriculum. Concept development and the nature of children will be examined in Chapters 3 and 4.

Second, the ten strands in the NCSS standards are neither to be considered as a set of curricular units, nor are they to be followed sequentially. The standards should be used as guides for selecting integrated content according to the needs of children in the classroom. In fact, what they establish is a collection of pertinent topics to be used as key organizers.

Third, the standards are not to be used to isolate the study of each of the different disciplines in the social studies. Central to the philosophy of these ten strands is their holistic vision, one that corresponds with the way children acquire ideas about their realities. The standards serve as "an umbrella" leading to the development of integrative and inclusive experiences (NCSS, 1994, p.16).

Concept Box 2–4 Key Professional References for an Appropriate Social Studies Program

A child-appropriate curriculum requires teachers to apply knowledge of both curricular theory and child development principles. The following are sources of information to consult as you develop a child-appropriate social studies program:

Allen, K. & Marotz, L. (1993). *Developmental profiles: Pre-birth through eight.* Albany, NY: Delmar.

Atwood, V. (Ed.). (1991) *Elementary school social studies: Research as a guide to practice.* Bulletin 79. Washington, DC: National Council for the Social Studies.

Bredekamp, S. & Rosegrant, T. (1992). *Reaching potentials: Appropriate curriculum and assessment for young children,* Vol. 1. Washington, DC: National Association for the Education of Young Children.

Bredekamp, S. & Rosegrant, T. (1995). *Reaching potentials: Transforming early childhood curriculum and assessment,* Vol. 2. Washington, DC: National Association for the Education of Young Children.

Bredekamp, S. & Copple, C. (1997). *Developmentally appropriate practices in early childhood programs* (rev. ed.). Washington, DC: National Association for the Education of Young Children.

Jones, E. & Nimmo, J. (1994). *Emergent curriculum.* Washington, DC: National Association for the Education of Young Children.

Krogh, S. (1995). *The integrated early childhood curriculum.* New York: McGraw Hill.

Planning together is a good curricular strategy.

Addressing Teachers' Concerns About the Social Studies Curriculum

Teaching the social studies curriculum is a challenging experience because of its scope and breadth. A look at all of the areas included in the social studies may easily make some teachers feel overwhelmed. Competence in all of the disciplines converging into the social studies is an almost impossible expectation. Through the years we have heard teachers express their concerns about the social studies curriculum. From their comments, several issues were evident. On one hand, specific knowledge about curricular and conceptual frameworks is sometimes unclear. On the other, knowledge about child-appropriate curriculum requires clarification. The very idea of also having to plan for such a complex field as social studies can be overwhelming. With so many different programs and projects in the classroom, today's early childhood teachers feel there is no time to include additional areas of study. For instance, on one occasion, while one of the authors was discussing the national standards, a kindergarten teacher voiced her frustration, saying, "Do I also have to teach about democracy? *I don't have time for that!*" She calmed down when she was shown how those concepts can be threaded through the entire day and throughout the curriculum.

Teaching early childhood social studies should be a rewarding and exciting experience. However, teachers have many questions about how to teach social studies, how to organize instructional time, and what content to select. Here are some general guidelines to help address some of these concerns:

■ Review data about cognitive and psychosocial development and about their relationship to the ways children learn.

■ Become familiar with the concept of developmentally appropriate curriculum.

■ Talk to your colleagues. Sharing ideas among colleagues clarifies our views and builds a pool of curriculum options.

■ Review the NCSS social studies standards. Discuss them with your colleagues.

■ Look for information about the specific topics you have questioned. Use the professional literature to find suggestions and answers. The following journals are particularly recommended: *Social Studies and the Young Learner, Young Children, Childhood Education,* and *Social Education.*

■ Use the Internet to search for current information on social studies practices.* For example, visit the Web sites of the National Council for the Social Studies (http://www.ncss.org) and of the ERIC Clearinghouse on Social Studies (http://www.eric.org) Also, join an Internet discussion group. Questions about practices and strategies can be posed to an informal forum of national and international educators. There are several, one of which is ECENET, the Early Childhood Education discussion group (topics involving children ages birth through age eight) (ECENET-L @VMD.CSO.UIUC.EDU)

■ Attend workshops and in-service training sessions.

■ Lastly, remember that experience *is* what shows each of us what the best teaching strategies are for social studies education.

---

*Please note that Internet resources are of a time-sensitive nature and URL sites and addresses may often be modified or deleted.

A Vision for Social Studies Teachers in the Early Childhood Classroom

Whether children are able to build social studies concepts or not depends on many factors, the most important of which is the teacher. In social studies, effective teachers are those that know the difference between "covering topics" and actually leading children into experiencing and building knowledge. The powerful social studies teacher in the early childhood classroom is envisioned by us to have the following attributes:

1. The teacher has *current and practical knowledge* about child development. An effective teacher:
   - knows about general child development principles,
   - knows how to transfer child development concepts into the classroom, and
   - knows how to accommodate the child with special needs.
2. The teacher is *aware of the social reality* of children, of their families, and of their community. An effective teacher:
   - has current knowledge and an understanding of young children and their immediate environments and of the issues they face.
3. The teacher possesses *sound knowledge about curricular theory in early childhood.* An effective teacher:
   - follows the curricular tenets established by Developmentally Appropriate Practices (DAP) and
   - applies child development principles in the planning and design of experiences.
4. The teacher understands the process of *curricular integration.* An effective teacher:
   - is able to develop sound integrated experiences.
5. The teacher is knowledgeable about *the aims and purposes of social studies* in early childhood education. An effective teacher:
   - has an understanding of the mission and role of the social studies in early education.
6. The teacher understands the *diverse and global nature of society.* An effective teacher:
   - respects and acknowledges cultural diversity in the curriculum,
   - advocates for inclusion of all groups, and
   - fosters development of a sense of connection with our global community.

▪▪ Let's Talk About . . . 2–6

The Social Studies Teacher Children Need

In this section we have outlined our vision of an effective social studies educator. You may have a different perspective.

1. State your opinion of this teacher profile.
2. Do you believe you fit the profile? Why or why not?
3. Consider other descriptors you would add to this vision as well as those you would delete. Explain the reasons for your choices.
4. Discuss the profile with your colleagues or classmates, and draft your own version.

Bringing Ideas into Practice 2–2
Windows to Our Global Community: What Do We Celebrate in September?

In September, the calendar events highlight opportunities to learn about the following concepts:

■ Independence Day in different countries
■ key historical events related to the development of the United States
■ key celebrations enhancing social values

Global events and celebrations serve as interesting springboards for thematic studies and provide opportunities for children to develop a sense of connectedness with the global neighborhoods in which we live. As you share these events in the classroom, remember that young children require concrete experiences in order to be able to relate to the events and develop ideas about them. Always use pictures, related artifacts, or books, and have a globe the children can use to locate where the events are happening. Some recommended children's books are suggested on p. 42. Look for other appropriate children's literature to enhance the children's concepts of these events.

Here are some other suggestions for using the calendar and list of suggested readings in your classroom:

1. Select three holidays and plan how you would arrange your teaching around them.
   ■ Give your rationale for selecting those holidays.
   ■ Discuss specific skills you would target in the study of each holiday.
   ■ Make a list of resources you would need for each holiday.

September			
Cultural Celebrations	*National Celebrations*	*Birthdays*	*Other events*
■ Labor Day (U.S. and Canada, first Monday) ■ Children's Day (Honduras, 9/10) ■ Respect for the Aged Day (Japan, 9/15) ■ International Day of Peace (third Tuesday) ■ Native Americans Day (U.S., fourth Friday) ■ Grandparents' Day (U.S., first Sunday after Labor Day) ■ *Mayflower* ship sails from Plymouth, England to America (9/16)	■ Independence of Estonia, Latvia, and Lithuania (9/6) ■ Independence Day in Brazil (9/8), Belize (9/21), Central American countries (9/16), and Chile (9/18) ■ National Day in Mexico (9/15)	■ Booker T. Washington (U.S., 9/16) ■ Johnny Appleseed (U.S., 9/26) ■ Birthday of the *Star-Spangled Banner* (U.S., 9/14) ■ Christa McAuliffe (U.S., 9/2) ■ Confucius (Asia, 9/28)	■ Good Neighbor Day (U.S., fourth Sunday) ■ American Citizenship Day (U.S., 9/17)

ACTIVITIES

Keeping Track of What You Learn: Your Personal Activity Log

Here are more activities for your personal activity log (PAL).

A. Reflections

1. As students, we have personally experienced the social studies curriculum. Recalling those experiences, web those characteristics of social studies classes that you liked best. Write a statement describing why you still remember them pleasantly.

2. Based on your experiences, create your own definition of the concept *social studies*.

3. Visit at least three experienced early childhood teachers and ask them what their view of social studies is. Reflect on their comments and write a summary of their views. Include a commentary about how you feel about their answers.

4. As an early childhood educator, review the standards for social studies. Make a comment about them, stating your position and any concerns that you may have.

5. Answer the key questions at the beginning of this chapter.

B. Collections

1. Following the ten thematic strands in the NCSS standards, begin a thematic activity file. Use a box, a large accordion-type folder with pockets, or even several different boxes. Make sure you have plenty of room to accommodate props and other kinds of resources. Label each section accordingly with the ten themes. Begin to collect age-appropriate resources such as songs, pictures, titles of children's books, props, artifacts, newspaper clips, and similar items.

2. Social studies is part of the holistic classroom environment children experience. Visit several early childhood classrooms and observe the materials and resources they have. With permission from teachers, take pictures of the displays and centers. Include your comments and personal observations about each photograph.

3. The social studies standards are to be shared with parents and families. To share the standards with the parents in your classroom, develop a visual representation depicting the ten thematic strands for social studies.

C. Internet Resources*

Educators can find an unlimited number of valuable social studies resources in the World Wide Web. Suggestions about relevant Web sites are listed below. Remember that it is important to check these addresses periodically. Recommended Web sites:

■ **Carol Hurst's Children's Literature Site**

(http://www.carolhurst.com)

Features a monthly newsletter and information about appropriate children's literature. An index of subject-based activities is also provided.

■ **Children's Book Council (CBC) home page**

(www.cbcbooks.org)

An excellent source of children's literature, this Web site offers a selection of quality books for young children. You can search in this database by topic and age level.

*Please note that Internet resources are of a time-sensitive nature and URL sites and addresses may often be modified or deleted.

Recommended Children's Books

Bang, M. (1985). *The paper crane.* New York: Greenwillow.

Fox, M. (1985). *Wilfrid Gordon McDonald Partridge.* Brooklyn: Kane/Miller Book Publishers.

Greenfield, E. (1991). *Night on neighborhood street.* New York: Dial Books.

McKissack, P., & McKissack, F. (1991). *The story of Booker T. Washington.* Chicago: Children's Press.

Nodar, C. (1992). *Abuelita's paradise.* Morton Grove, IL: Whitman.

Nomura, T. (1991). *Grandpa's town.* Brooklyn, NY: Kane/Miller.

Ryland, C. (1985). *The relatives came.* New York: Bradbury.

References

Allen, K., & Marotz, L. (1993). *Developmental profiles: Prebirth through eight.* Albany, NY: Delmar.

Atwood, V. (Ed.). (1991). *Elementary school social studies: Research as a guide to practice.* Bulletin no. 79. Washington, DC: National Council for the Social Studies.

Bredekamp, S. (1987). *Developmentally appropriate practices in early childhood programs serving children from birth through age 8.* Washington, DC: National Association for the Education of Young Children.

Bredekamp, S., & Copple, C. (1997). *Developmentally appropriate practice in early childhood programs.* (rev. ed.) Washington, DC: National Association for the Education of Young Children.

Bredekamp, S., & Rosegrant, T. (1992). *Reaching potentials: Appropriate curriculum and assessment*, Vol. 1. Washington, DC: National Association for the Education of Young Children.

Bredekamp, S., & Rosegrant, T. (1995). *Reaching potentials: Transforming early childhood curriculum and assessment,* Vol. 2. Washington, DC: National Association for the Education of Young Children.

Hahn, C. (1991). Advocating early childhood social studies. In V. Atwood (Ed.). (1991). *Elementary school social studies: Research as a guide to practice.* Bulletin no. 79. Washington, DC: National Council for the Social Studies.

Hohmann, M., & Weikart, D. (1995). *Educating young children: Active learning practices in preschool and child care programs.* Ypsilanti, MI: High/Scope Press.

Jarolimek, J. (1990). Social studies for citizens of a strong and free nation. In *Social studies curriculum planning resources.* Washington, DC: National Council for the Social Studies.

Jones, E., & Nimmo, J. (1994). *Emergent curriculum.* Washington, DC: National Association for the Education of Young Children.

Katz, L., & Chard, S. (1989). *Engaging children's minds: The project approach.* Norwood, NJ: Ablex.

Krogh, S. (1995). *The integrated early childhood curriculum.* New York: McGraw Hill.

Kronberg, R. (1998). [on-line] www.agsnet.com/IDEA/idea4.asp

Meyen, E. L. (1996). *Exceptional children in today's schools* (3rd ed.). Denver: Love.

National Council for the Social Studies. (1994). *Expectations for excellence: Curriculum standards for social studies:* Bulletin 89. Washington, DC: Author.

National Council for the Social Studies. (1990). *Social studies curriculum planning resources.* Washington, DC: Author.

National Council for Social Studies. Task Force on Scope and Sequence. (1989). *Charting a course.* Washington, DC: Author.

NCSS Task Force on Early Childhood/Elementary Social Studies (1988/1991). Social Studies for early childhood and elementary school children: Preparing children for the 21st century. In V. Atwood (Ed.). (1991). *Elementary school social studies: Research as a guide to practice.* Bulletin 79. Washington, DC: National Council for the Social Studies.

Ravitch, D. (1995). *National standards in American education: A citizens' guide.* Washington, DC: The Brookings Institute.

Saxe, D. (1992). Framing a theory for social studies foundations. *Review of Educational Research, 62,* pp. 269–277.

Seefeldt, C. (1997). *Social studies for the preschool–primary child* (5th ed.). Upper Saddle River, NJ: Merrill.

Sunal, C. (1990). *Early childhood social studies.* Columbus, Ohio: Merrill.

Task Force on Standards for Teaching and Learning in the Social Studies (1993). A vision of powerful teaching and learning in the social studies: Building social understanding and civic efficacy. *Social Education, 57,* pp. 213–223.

Turnbull, H. R. (1993). *Free appropriate public education: The law and children with disabilities* (4th ed.). Denver: Love.

Vygotsky, L. S. (1978). In M. Cole, V. John-Steiner, S. Scribner, & E. Souberman (Eds.), *Mind and society.* Cambridge, MA: Harvard University Press.

CHAPTER 3

Getting Ready to Teach: Developmental Considerations

Each child carries his own teacher inside him.
They come to us not knowing that truth.
We are at our best when we give the teacher
who resides within each child a chance to go to work.

—ALBERT SCHWEITZER

Chapter Questions

After reading this chapter you should be able to answer the following questions:

- What are the basic concepts of developmentally appropriate practices (DAP)?
- What are the key developmental milestones during ages three to eight?
- What are the cognitive and social characteristics of children ages three to eight?
- What are thinking skills?

Key Terms and Concepts

concepts
developmental milestones
multiple intelligences
older preschoolers
operations
play
pretend play
primary-age children

psychosocial development
social and emotional development
social cognition
social competence
social skills
symbolic functioning
young preschoolers

Classroom Portrait: Lessons Children Teach Us about Planning

Mr. Ruwani is doing his teaching internship in a classroom with four-year-olds. Recently Ms. Ellison, his cooperating teacher, introduced him to thematic teaching. She emphasized the importance of developmentally and child-appropriate planning, as a key concept of this methodology. "Remember, real planning happens when you include the messages from the children into your instruction," she said on more than one occasion.

For almost two weeks the children have been noticing the ongoing road work near the school. Almost from the beginning, the children have expressed an interest in transportation and roads. This caused Mr. Ruwani to think that transportation might be a good thematic topic for discussion. He brought items such as brightly colored plastic cars, trucks, houses, and even wooden figurines of people and placed these props in the block center. In his lesson plan he wrote, "To enhance the block center with items and props about transportation; to foster discussion about the concept of transportation."

It didn't take the children long to notice the props in the block center. Mr. Ruwani observed, with pleasure, how a boy and a girl proceeded to build a road with houses along one side. "Just as I planned," he thought to himself. His smile faded, however, when he saw the girl pushing a big red car and heard her announce to the boy, "Move, or I'm gonna flatten you!"

Not missing a beat, the boy reacted, "Oh no, you won't!" as he proceeded to hit her car first.

As the verbal exchanges continued, Mr. Ruwani did not interfere; he hoped to see how the two children would resolve the problem. However, the squabble continued and even escalated:

"Get out of my way!" screamed the boy.

Gesturing, the girl yelled, "I'll hit you, I'll hit you!" As the voices grew louder and the children's words became harsher, they caught the attention of the rest of the children in the classroom. Everyone, including Mr. Ruwani, waited for Ms. Ellison to intervene. When she offered no help, Mr. Ruwani walked up to the children and demanded to know why they were fighting.

"We are not fighting," the children exclaimed in unison.

"That's how my uncle behaves in the car," said the girl.

"My sister screams and gets angry if the cars don't go fast," replied the boy, to Mr. Ruwani's disbelief.

Later, while discussing the experience with Ms. Ellison, Mr. Ruwani commented that he had never intended to cause such a scene with the materials he contributed to the block center. He said, "That's not what I planned. I wanted them to build roads and become interested in my thematic unit on transportation."

Ms. Ellison smiled, "I know, but what will you do now?"

Mr. Ruwani replied, "I'll take everything out of the center and let the children read books instead. That way they won't be disruptive and cause arguments."

Aware that this was the first time Mr. Ruwani had been faced with a change in a lesson plan, Ms. Ellison smiled and said, "I think bringing in the cars and other items was a great idea. It allowed the children to share their real experiences related to transportation. Did you plan to talk about courtesy and rules while driving? Or, about the feelings of drivers who are not in the car? Or, how people behave on planes and boats?"

"No, but . . . ," Mr. Ruwani began.

"Well, remember that teaching young children is closely associated with their development and their personal experiences. You just got a lesson in social development," said Ms. Ellison.

"I see it now," said Mr. Ruwani.

"How should we address the concept of driving courtesy with these four-year-olds? Do you have any ideas?" Ms. Ellison asked.

Mr. Ruwani paused, "Actually, I do! We could . . ."

■■ Planning Social Studies
■■ Experiences for Young Children

Early childhood is a unique time of growth, development, awareness, exploration, and preparation for the future. The early childhood social studies curriculum provides an exceptional framework for these experiences because of its diverse and rich nature. The best way to design an effective curriculum for young children is to base it on sound knowledge of child development (Bredekamp & Copple, 1997). Curricular appropriateness is achieved only when educators have a clear understanding of the developmental process and the role it plays in the early years. In this section we will explore how the knowledge of child development can be used to establish a basis for an exciting and child-appropriate social studies curriculum. Cognitive characteristics of the young child and their implications for classroom teaching will be also examined.

As teachers of young children it is important for us to remember that the early childhood years are a time of:

■ **wonder:** Children exhibit a desire to know about all that surrounds them, especially about themselves, about their family members and friends, about nature, and about their environments. They question how things are, how they work, and why they exist. Children also are very curious about social relationships.

■ **growth and development:** The early years are a time of rapid changes and developmental accomplishments. Through the eight years of the early childhood period, the most amazing **developmental milestones** occur. From a defenseless newborn, the child is transformed into an independent and capable individual who is able to ask questions, move, communicate, and socialize with others.

■ **preparation for the future:** Just as fertile soil gives seeds a boost and allows them to germinate into strong plants, the early childhood years serve as the foundation for the future development of the successful individual. During the early years, children acquire the social and cultural codes of their groups. They also begin to learn about the rules and patterns of acceptable behavior. Learning about their roles and responsibilities and about those of others in their families, communities, and school prepares children for future tasks.

■■ Knowledge about the Child—
■■ The Essence of Developmentally
Appropriate Teaching Practices

Anyone preparing to teach young children needs to be cognizant of the complexity of the developmental process and of the growth young children experience from birth through age eight. Knowledge about the dramatic changes and differences that occur during early childhood provides practitioners with the necessary tools to create *developmentally appropriate teaching* (Bredekamp & Rosegrant, 1995). Recognized as the foundation of responsive quality practices in early childhood education, the concept of developmentally appropriate practices (DAP—see Chapter 1) is grounded in the developmental changes and transformations experienced by children during the first eight years of life (Bredekamp & Copple, 1997).

The early years are a time of rapid changes and developmental accomplishments. Good teaching begins with sound knowledge of child development principles.

In the following statement, educator Lillian Katz describes the role of and need for developmental knowledge in classroom planning: "In a developmental approach to curriculum design, . . . what should be learned and how it would be best learned depends on what we know of the learner's developmental status and our understanding of the relationships between early experience and subsequent development" (Katz, 1995, p. 109).

Teaching in a developmentally appropriate way fosters children's optimum development. By providing an environment and experiences based on the children's general as well as unique individual developmental characteristics, teachers can make developmental appropriateness a reality (Bredekamp & Copple, 1997). Successful ways of addressing the needs of children occur when educators approach growth and development holistically. While there are many ways for teachers to learn how to do that, we strongly believe that knowledge about the developmental process evolves from training, practical experiences, and understandings acquired through daily interactions in the classroom. Combining ideas about children and about curriculum is what forms the basis for child-appropriate, developmentally sound teaching. A social studies curriculum that is developmental and appropriate will emerge as you blend your knowledge of children with your knowledge of content.

Learning about the Developmental Process: Valuable Sources

There are several sources that can help teachers learn about how children develop and grow during the early years. Some of these sources are discussed here.

1. **Training and In-service Programs:** Participating in courses on child growth and development is a professional requirement for early childhood educators. Workshops and professional conferences also provide good ways to learn about current issues and applied research in child development.

2. **Professional Journals:** Journal articles are an excellent source of information. They provide current research on innovative practices and other aspects of child development. Journals such as *Child Development, Childhood Education, Young Children, Journal of Early Intervention,* and *Early Childhood Education Quarterly* are among the many to read and consult.

3. **Observations:** Planned and unplanned observations provide a unique way to learn about children and their development. By observing children, teachers gain first-hand knowledge about each child's developmental patterns. When observations are made in a variety of settings, teachers get practical and realistic information about the role of the environment and its impact on the child's development as an individual.

4. **Experience:** There is no better source of information about how children grow and develop than direct experience. Whether in the classroom, at home, or in a special setting, the time spent working and interacting with young children is how professionals sharpen their knowledge and skills. This is where ideas and theories are tested and "witnessed."

Sharing Ideas with Colleagues and Other Early Education Professionals

Comments and observations exchanged with other teachers and professionals provide opportunities for clarification and learning about the developmental process. Informal and formal discussions about specific topics and issues from the classroom create opportunities for reflection and understanding of child development. Listserv or discussion groups available on the Internet also provide teachers opportunities to discuss and share observations about developmental issues. For example ECEOL-L, the Early Childhood On-Line mailing list (ECEOL-L @MAINE.maine.edu) and NCSS (http://www. ncss. com) are but two of the many discussion groups teachers may join.

■■ Key Developmental Milestones of ■■ Preschool–Primary Age Children

Although each child is a unique individual, from birth through age eight, all young children share a need for specially designed environments and programs that will foster their growth and development. Profound developmental differences can be observed among the three different age groups, **young preschoolers** (age three), **older preschoolers** (ages four to five), and **primary-age children** (ages six to eight). Various individual needs, defined by both their socio-cultural and biological characteristics, also make young children different from one another (Santrock, 1998). In this section you will find a review of the essential differences that early educators need to keep in mind as they plan the social studies curriculum. A summary of the overall typical developmental characteristics of children ages three to nine is found in Figure 3–1.

Developmentally Appropriate Practices for Teaching Children with Special Needs

Although the focus of this chapter is on the review and discussion of typical developmental characteristics, early childhood teachers also need to be aware of the needs of children who exhibit a different pattern of development. Knowledge of what constitutes average or typical development will help educators to become aware of the divergent characteristics of children with special needs. Early identification and intervention should be aimed at those children who exhibit language disorders and developmental delays, who do not perform well on tests of cognitive or motor skills, and who have had limited opportunity because of social and economic factors, or who are burdened by various medical problems.

New educators often wonder how one can teach children with both regular and special needs in the same class, but if you are now teaching, then perhaps you have already done so. Since many young, at-risk children have not been diagnosed, chances are that you have already had the opportunity to work with exceptional children (Deiner, 1983).

Consideration of children with special needs is essential to developmentally appropriate teaching. It is important to remember that special needs include a variety of specific developmental characteristics. For example, some children may have specific cognitive needs; others may have delays in motor, physical, or emotional development. These needs must be taken into consideration when planning a social studies curriculum. Fair and appropriate teaching happens only when educators provide experiences for *all* children.

Children who have handicapping conditions or at-risk conditions experience delays, deficits, and distortions, not only in developmental domains, but also in self-help and social skills. The interrelatedness of development is involved and complicated. For example, a response such as waving "bye-bye" extends beyond motor skills and includes communication and social skills as well (Meyen, 1996).

■■ Young Preschoolers: Working ■■ with Three-Year-Olds

Three-year-olds are the youngest members of the preschool group. No longer toddlers, they are entering a period of significant learning and development. More independent and physically, socially, and cognitively different from the toddlers, these children are in a period of developmental transition in which they swing back and forth between toddler and preschool behaviors. Providing carefully planned experiences that will encourage growth and development within the children's scope of possibilities is essential.

Three-year-old preschoolers appear to be more agile, and they are taller and slimmer than they were during toddlerhood. Three-year-olds have more control over their movements and coordination (see Concept Box 3–1), and they walk in an adult-like fashion. Young preschoolers enjoy being actively engaged in experiences that allow them to practice their physical skills. However, they do get tired and require rest periods.

Activities such as running, leaping, climbing, hopping, galloping, and jumping should be included

FIGURE 3–1   Facts About Child Development, Ages 3–10

Age 3–4 years

Physical Development
3 years: *Average size:* 32 lbs., 38 in. tall. *Sleep:* needs 12 hrs. per day. *Perception:* still slightly farsighted—easier to see distances.
4 years: *Average size:* 37 lbs., 40 in. tall.

Motor Development
3 years: rides tricycle, can walk on tiptoe, hops with both feet, runs smoothly, walks up and down stairs one foot on each step, buttons and unbuttons, pours from a pitcher, builds tower of 9 blocks and makes bridge with 3 blocks, tries to make the basic shapes (triangles, circles, and squares), catches ball, arms straight.
3½ years: uses basic shapes, scribbles to make designs, uses circles within circles, etc.
4 years: balances on 1 foot for 5 seconds, hops on 1 foot, can walk forward heel to toe, throws ball overhand, dresses self, catches small ball, elbows in front of body, does stunts on tricycle, descends short steps, alternating feet, hand preference nearly established.

Language Development
3 years: sentences contain many words with plural endings. Uses the declarative in a raised tone to ask questions. Sometimes uses nouns or other substantives with a negative word to express negation. A greater variety of emotions is now reflected in speech. Vocabulary is about 850 words. Can understand meaning of adult speech about events that have not personally been experienced. Easily repeats songs. Begins to use subordinate sentences. Most pronunciation correct except *r, l,* and the hissing sounds.
4 years: vocabulary of about 1500 words; most grammatical endings now known; deviation from adult speech more style than grammar. Begins to use future tense; two or more ideas are regularly expressed in complex sentences. Comprehends feelings (e.g., cold, tired) and prepositions; recognizes color names.

Cognitive/Piagetian Development
3 years: *Symbolic phase of preoperational stage* still in effect. *Imagination:* ability to pretend during play develops; engages in dramatic play. *Conservation:* beginning development of the conservation of amount. *Egocentrism:* reduction in the amount of egocentrism; more able to take other people's perspectives into account. *Classification:* objects are included in a particular class for personal reasons (e.g., "this makes a house"). *Time:* talks almost as much about the past and future as about the present; often pretends to tell time and talks about time a great deal; tells how old he is, what he will do tomorrow or on his birthday.
4 years: *Intuitive phase of preoperational stage* begins to operate; the thought processes begin to involve such things as a new understanding of relationships. *Motivation:* rewards continue to need to be fairly immediate and sensual; still very sensitive to praise and attention; *Time:* past and future tenses very accurately used; refinement in the use of time words; broader concepts expressed by use of month, "next winter," "last summer"; a much clearer understanding of daily sequence of events emerges.

Social Development
Attachment: by age 4, will accept temporary absence of mother without protest and will accept substitute attachment figures (Bowlby). *Play:* at 3 years, most children involve themselves in peer play; by 4 years, most involved in cooperative play. *Social skills:* at 3 years, washes, and dries hands and face; at 4 years, dresses with or without supervision. *Phallic stage:* both sexes have sexual fantasies about their parents for which they feel guilty; stage will last until age 6 (Freud). *Sex role and identity:* knows own sex but does not realize maleness and femaleness are permanent characteristics. *Moral development:* rules of a game are sacred and unchangeable but they tend to be applied in an egocentric manner.

Self Development
3 years: period of acute possessiveness and egocentrism. Capable of scanning and responding to inner states (e.g., identifying mood states and changes in one's own moods).
4 years: beginning to understand "mineness" and "ourness" and to see self as reflected in others. If told he is cute or devilish will include these characteristics in own self-concept. Adult responses to that image give him a positive or negative image about himself.

FIGURE 3–1 Continued

Age 5–7 years

Physical Development

5 years: *Average size:* 41½ lbs., 43 in. tall. *Sleep:* needs 11 hrs. per day. *Perception:* development has advanced so that child can scan and focus reasonably well. *Body changes:* brain development at 90% full adult weight; average body temperature at normal 98.6°F; fewer stomachaches, digestive system more regular, fewer ear infections, distance from outer ear greater, respiratory infections lessened due to a longer trachea.

6 years: *Average size:* 45½ lbs., 46 in. tall. *Teeth:* at 6½ years permanent upper and lower 1st molars and lower central incisors appear.

7 years: *Average size:* 53 lbs., 47 in. tall. *Teeth:* at 7½ years permanent upper central incisors and lower lateral incisors replace baby teeth.

Motor Development

5 years: catches bounding ball with elbows at sides, balances on 1 foot for 10 seconds, skips, descends large ladder, alternating feet easily, throws well, copies designs, letters, numbers, triangles, and squares, folds paper into double triangle, tries to form pictures of animals, people, and buildings.

6 years: can walk backwards heel to toe, running speed increases, jumping forms basis of many games and improves.

7 years: balance improves, more details are added to art work.

Language Development

5 years: language increasingly resembles adult models.

6 years: average vocabulary now 2500 words.

7 years: can recall grammatical sentences rather than strings of words and can make grammatically consistent word associations.

Cognitive/Piagetian Development

5 years: *Conservation:* beginning to understand the conservation of number. *Classification:* done largely on the basis of color.

6 years: *Classification:* done largely on the basis of shape discrimination using visual perception rather than touch. *Memory:* capacity is well developed and labeling aids greatly in recalling pictures.

7 years: beginning of *concrete operational period:* capable of certain logic so long as manipulation of objects is involved. *Classification:* uses definitions for grouping centering on one dimension, but still unable to use class inclusion. *Creativity:* drawings of the human are quite well defined and designs are very representative of reality.

7½ years: *Conservation:* understanding of conservation of length, seriation, and number. *Motivation:* rewards come from correct information; begins to adopt internal standards of performance. *Humor:* ability to understand riddles.

Social Development

Period of initiative vs. guilt: the family is the main human relationship; children freely engage in many adultlike activities, and parents' patient answering of questions leads to initiative; a restriction of activities and treatment of questions as nuisance leads to guilt (Erikson). *Latency period:* not a stage but rather an interlude when sexual needs are relatively quiet and energy is put into learning skills—will continue until age 11 (Freud). *Aggression:* physical fighting often used as a means of solving problems or defending one's image. *Sex role and identity:* at 6 years, realizes that sex is a permanent characteristic. *Moral development:* rules in games are important as codes that must be respected, but they can be changed; children are more able to cooperate and share because they are less egocentric and develop a characteristic way of responding to others.

Self Development

Understands that self is part of interrelated group of others (e.g., family, friends, kinships). Develops understanding that self is a sexual person and forms preferences for own sex. Perceives self as a moral person with goals for an ideal self. Understands self as initiator of novel and creative interactions.

FIGURE 3–1 Continued

Age 9–10 years

Physical Development

9 years: *Average size:* 68 lbs., 53 in. tall. *Sleep:* needs 10 hrs. per day. *Teeth:* permanent upper lateral incisors and lower cuspids. *Perception:* well-developed ability to read fine print.

10 years: *Average size:* males, 78 lbs., 58.7 in. tall; females, 77.5 lbs., 59.2 in. tall. *Teeth:* at 10 years upper and lower 1st bicuspids and upper 2nd bicuspids appear, total now 26 teeth. *Body changes:* females begin to have rounding of hips, breasts and nipples are elevated to form bud stage, no true pubic hair yet.

Motor Development

Increased gains in vigor and balance in motor control and coordination; manual dexterity increases; greater muscular strength develops; improvement in accuracy, agility, and endurance; girls continue to run faster than boys; throwing and catching are better; jumping and climbing are done with ease and assurance; eye-hand coordination is good.

Language Development

Acquires an average of 5000 new words in this age range. Knowledge of syntax fully developed. Has the ability to understand comparatives (*longer, deeper*), the subjunctive (*if I were a . . .*), and metaphors (*rotten egg, dirty rat*). Language has become a tool and not just words that refer only to objects. Specialized vocabularies develop for different situations (e.g., games).

Cognitive/Piagetian Development

9 years: *Concrete operation period* still in effect: logic and objectivity increase; deductive thinking begins to appear. *Conservation:* understands conservation of area. *Causality:* has a firm grasp of cause–effect relationships. *Humor:* begins to appreciate use of certain metaphors in joking because of an understanding of the incongruous elements.

10 years: *Conservation:* understanding of the conservation of substances acquired. *Classification:* elements classified using a hierarchical construct. *Space:* able to make or interpret simple maps and distances. *Memory:* memory tasks involve use of mnemonic devices.

Social Development

Period of industry vs. inferiority: has been ongoing since age 7; the neighborhood and school are now the main source of human relationships. Children are busy learning to be competent and productive using skills and tools, exercising dexterity and intelligence to gain praise for their accomplishments leading to industry. Limitation of activities, feeling inferior, criticism, and inability to do well lead to inferiority (Erikson). *Aggression:* reduction in physical fighting to defend self-image; verbal duels now become the tool. *Sex role and identity:* at 10 years, emphasizes social roles more than physical development, believing that "men should act like men and women like ladies."

Self Development

Develops a great variety of new skills and activities that lead to a sense of effectiveness.

---

as part of the classroom curriculum. With encouragement and practice, the three-year-old will soon master gross motor skills and related behaviors.

Three-year-olds are also able to grasp objects and manipulate them with more dexterity because they have gained more control of their fine motor skills. With greater fine motor maturity, they show more mastery in using crayons, brushes, and other writing and drawing instruments. Assembling one-figure puzzles and building with blocks are activities they particularly enjoy. However, they still require careful selection of appropriate materials and objects that will enhance their skills to use and practice hand and finger movements successfully.

Cognitive and Language Development

Development of the ability to think is perhaps the area that most concerns early childhood educators. Impacted by the overall forces surrounding an

---

Bringing Ideas into Practice 3–1   *Planning for Children with Special Needs*

Some curricular adaptations will be necessary when teaching children with special needs. These adaptations must be considered as part of the curriculum development process. Adaptations will depend upon the specific developmental needs exhibited by children.

- **Physical needs:** Consider the classroom arrangement, including the location of furniture, equipment, and materials; and the arrangement and type of learning centers. These should provide easy access for children in wheelchairs or with neurological or motor needs. Create a flexible space organization where furniture can be easily changed and moved. Materials that are easy to handle and manipulate, such as fat crayons and pencils, training scissors, and so on, should be available.

- **Cognitive needs:** Design activities with various difficulty levels. Use clear and easy to understand terms or vocabulary that is familiar to the child. Provide an abundance of hands-on opportunities. Include activities with a variety of sensory experiences. Use visual cues and prompts, such as pictures, labels, and color-coding. Use materials familiar to children, such as books, toys, songs, and so on.

- **Visual needs:** Select materials with large print and enlarged figures. Add materials in Braille if a visually impaired child is a member of the group. Provide materials with a variety of tactile characteristics. Include a variety of sensory experiences such as tasting, smelling, and listening.

---

individual, cognition is enhanced, we now know, by the quality of the experiences children find both at school and at home.

Language during the preschool years grows by leaps and bounds. The typical preschool child progresses from an average vocabulary of 250 words to almost 2,000 words. A variety of experiences related to play and opportunities to manipulate and act upon objects contribute to the rapid and amazing language growth during the preschool years (Bernstein & Tiegermann, 1993). The ways three-year-olds use language demonstrate how they represent ideas as well as how they perceive reality. In their own incredible way, children will use and create unique terms to describe their experiences. They use metaphoric languages to express their ideas. The desire to communicate and share what they have learned leads children at this age to use drawings and scribblings as expressive sources.

Cognitive development is directly related to the acquisition of key social concepts that are embodied in social studies education. Knowing the characteristics of the cognitive development of children is essential for implementing the Piagetian idea of *con-*

structivism—the process that individual children use to "build" knowledge through experiences.

According to Piaget, knowledge is developed through the process of *assimilation, accommodation,* and *equilibration.* This process occurs whenever an experience is encountered. Successful processing of the situation leads to the formation of new knowledge. The quality and the nature of prior

Teaching three-year-olds is an exciting experience.

Three-year-olds enjoy exploring their environments.

Implications of Physical Developmental Characteristics

Considering the physical characteristics and needs of three-year-olds,

1. What kind of experiences should the preschool curriculum include?
2. What elements should be incorporated in the classroom?
3. What kinds of social studies experiences would best fit the needs of these children?

experiences contribute to how successfully children build new concept knowledge. Building concept knowledge is the same as making sense out of what one encounters. As you see in Figure 3–2, children use the information already learned to process the new input. However, when one comes across things that are unusual or different, such as what the subject encounters in Figure 3–2, sometimes more than one encounter is required to build a complete new concept. Awareness of the knowledge-formation process helps educators to select appropriate activities and learning materials. It also helps teachers to

---

Concept Box 3–1   Typical Gross and Fine Motor Skills of Three-Year-Olds

Gross Motor Skills
A three-year-old:

■ walks in an adult-like fashion; child is able to walk by putting down alternating feet.
■ runs with more control of speed and direction.
■ climbs up and down with alternating feet and by using a handrail.
■ jumps off with better-coordinated movements; moves upper (claps) and lower (dances, stomps) extremities in a better-coordinated way, but does not exhibit a definite sense of movement direction yet.
■ engages in active play.

Fine Motor Skills
A three-year-old:

■ shows hand preference (handedness).
■ is able to hold and pour liquids with less spilling.
■ is able to unfasten buttons, fasten snaps, unzip, and to undress without assistance.
■ is able to pick, grasp, and hold objects like pegs and beads with fingers.
■ builds towers, works with puzzles, and represents objects with blocks.
■ is able to handle scissors.
■ begins to use drawing/writing tools such as crayons and markers with more control; is able to scribble.

Sources: Santrock, J. (1998). *Child development.* (8th ed.) Dubuque, IA: Brown & Benchmark; Berk, L. (1996). *Infants and children: Prenatal through middle childhood.* (2nd ed.) Needham Heights, MA: Allyn & Bacon.

Concept Box 3–2   Typical Cognitive and Language Characteristics of Three-Year-Olds

Cognitive Characteristics
A three-year-old:

- is able to represent ideas through drawings and during play.
- notices concrete characteristics of objects (color, form, size, shape).
- imitates behaviors of others.
- recognizes objects and names them.
- thinks about experiences from his or her point of view.
- attributes magical powers to certain objects and phenomena.
- focuses and centers attention on one characteristic at a time.
- shows an understanding about causal relationships.
- associates, sorts, and classifies objects logically based on one characteristic.
- knows his name.
- shows a beginning sense about time.

Language Characteristics
A three-year-old:

- communicates through language and has an increasingly intelligible speech.
- talks in sentences.
- expresses ideas, needs, and desires verbally.
- shares personally meaningful comments about stories.
- asks questions about places, objects, and natural phenomena.
- answers simple questions.
- engages in conversations with peers and adults.
- uses toy telephones and objects to "communicate" with others.
- recognizes and associates environmental and word sounds.
- uses noun phrases ("the big red ball").
- knows rhymes, songs, and enjoys singing.

Source: Adapted from Santrock, J. (1998). *Child development* (8th ed.). Dubuque, IA: Brown & Benchmark.

Concept Box 3–3   Piaget's Stages of Cognitive Development

- **Sensorimotor (ages 0 to 18 months or 2 years):** The child learns to use and rely on sensorial impressions as he or she moves to explore and discover the surroundings, which include objects as well as people.
- **Preoperational (ages 18 months or 2 to 6 or 7 years):** Child develops the ability to symbolize while relying on concrete objects to build concepts. At this age, children are easily deceived by appearances. Internal thought is developed, which helps them to formulate and solve problems. Logical thinking begins to emerge.

- **Concrete-operational (ages 7 to 12):** The child is able to think logically, but still requires concrete objects to build ideas. He or she is now able to deal mentally with abstractions, although still in a concrete manner. The child is able to move beyond appearances and can use mental operations to examine reality and solve problems.
- **Formal operations (age 12 to adulthood):** Logical thinking is achieved; the individual is now capable of dealing with abstractions and can perform mental operations.

Source: Forman, G., & Kuschner, D. (1983). *The child's construction of knowledge: Piaget for teaching children.* Washington, DC: National Association for the Education of Young Children.

FIGURE 3–2

Source: Wadsworth, B. (1971/1984/1989/1996). *Piaget's theory of cognitive and affective development: Foundations of constructivism* (5th ed.). New York: Longman Publishers USA. Reprinted with permission of Addison Wesley Educational Publishers, Inc.

Prior experiences help shape the way children build new concept knowledge—to make sense out of what they encounter.

Pretend play helps children to engage in symbolic representation. It is also an avenue to discover the influence of prior experiences. Courtesy of Fern Rothstein.

understand why helping a young child to acquire **concepts**—ways of organizing what is known—is something that demands careful preparation. It also requires patience, as well as good observation and listening skills!

Cognitive and Language Characteristics of Three-Year-Olds

Cognitively, young preschoolers are considered preoperational thinkers. Two of the major developmental milestones of this period are *their ability to use symbols* and *their ability to communicate through language*. In Piaget's theory, **symbolic functioning** is a substage of preoperational thinking that generally spans ages three to four. It describes "the child's ability to understand, create, and use symbols to represent something that it not present" (Zigler & Stevenson, 1993, p. 315). Observations of drawings, block constructions, toys, and manip-

ulatives are sources for children to symbolize their ideas about reality. Also symbolic in nature, language is extensively used by three-year-olds. In the classroom, they enjoy talking about themselves and others, making comments about experiences, and creating words to represent their own ideas. Three-year-olds use language to ask questions about anything that catches their attention. They enjoy holding conversations with peers and adults, thus expanding their ability to interact socially with others.

■■ Other Views about
■■ Cognitive Development

Recent studies have revealed that cognitive development can also be explained by different empirical observations and theoretical postulates. For educators, awareness of the existence of different ways

FIGURE 3–3   A Summary of Gardner's Multiple Intelligences

Intelligence	What it Means	Planning for Multiple Intelligences (MI): Classroom Applications
Verbal-Linguistic Intelligence	The ability to use language to communicate, express, and share one's ideas. The individual is able to memorize songs, stories.	Include a book corner with a variety of reading materials (books, magazines, newspapers); encourage oral expression. Create a listening center. Have a writing center with a variety of writing materials. Use questioning strategies to foster discussions. Create and display charts.
Logico-Mathematical Intelligence	The ability to calculate, estimate, quantify, use symbols, and use mathematical operations.	Have a math center with a variety of manipulatives (pattern blocks, objects with different shapes, color, sizes, textures). Plan measurement activities. Have a measurement and estimation center with items such as maps, graph paper, compass, thermometer, and a variety of other concrete objects available. Include time-related instruments and items (calendar, clock, timer, sand clock, sundial). Use charts to depict information.
Bodily Kinesthetic Intelligence	The ability to coordinate body movements and to manipulate objects and tools.	Include a variety of manipulatives (blocks, puzzles, modeling clay, art objects). Include a variety of tactile experiences. Have a classroom craft center. Provide role-playing and movement activities. Plan dancing experiences. Plan outdoor experiences.
Spatial Intelligence	The ability to perceive and discriminate the characteristics of space. The individual is able to visualize things and to imagine elements and can use and manipulate space creatively.	Set up an art center. Encourage graphic representation as a means of expression. Use walls and bulletin boards to convey information. Display pictures, posters, and use a variety of color, shapes, pictures to depict information.
Musical Intelligence	The ability to respond and listen to sounds and to create sound patterns.	Have a music center. Plan singing and dancing experiences. Encourage musical improvisation. Use background music regularly.

FIGURE 3–3 Continued

Intelligence	What it Means	Planning for Multiple Intelligences (MI): Classroom Applications
Interpersonal Intelligence	The ability to interact successfully with others and engage in social life. The individual is able to lead and organize others.	Use cooperative learning activities. Plan collaborative projects. Recognize leadership. Provide clear classroom rules and directions.
Intrapersonal Intelligence	The ability to understand oneself, to know one's strengths and weaknesses. The individual is able to set his or her own goals.	Encourage individual expression (art, journal writing, sharing time); give recognition. Provide time for reflection. Create quiet areas and "private zones." Engage children in planning and selection of activities.
Naturalistic Intelligence	An ability to relate to nature. The individual is able to identify a variety of species from the flora and fauna.	Have live animals in the classroom. Plan year-round (indoor-outdoor) gardening experiences. Plan field trips and nature walks.

Sources: Adapted from Gardner, H. (1983). *Frames of mind: The theory of multiple intelligences.* New York: Basic Books; Nelson, K. (1998). *Developing students' multiple intelligences.* New York: Scholastic.

and forms of cognition contributes to the effective planning and development of appropriate classroom experiences for children.

Fostering Cognitive Development: Gardner's Theory of Multiple Intelligences

Psychologist Howard Gardner's (1983) theory of **multiple intelligences** has revealed valuable data about how children learn. His theory contends that cognition is multi-fold, rather than unidimensional. Challenging the traditional view of intelligence, in which intelligence is considered as quantifiable and with definite attributes, his theory establishes the existence of a variety of human potential. According to Gardner, consideration of the existence of multiple intelligences is a fair and more accurate way to describe the many unique capacities individuals have. Depicted as a diverse range of abili-

ties, these multiple intelligences can be used as tools for learning, problem solving, self-definition, human interaction, and creativity. Gardner presented his theory in his book *Frames of Mind: The Theory of Multiple Intelligences* (1983). In this important book he identified seven intelligences and observed that perhaps many more also existed (see Figure 3–3). Later, he identified naturalistic intelligence as yet another form of cognitive potential. For early childhood education, Gardner's theory provides relevant guidelines to consider when planning experiences and designing the classroom environment.

Vygotsky's Socio-Cultural Theory

Lev Vygotsky, a Russian psychologist, also investigated the process of cognition. Like Piaget, Vygotsky proposed the existence and influence of more than one factor to explain how children build knowledge. He also believed development followed several stages. Despite these similarities to Piagetian theory, his essential theoretical postulates differ from those of Piaget. For Vygotsky, the role of interactions within one's social and cultural group is central to understanding how the child develops and learns. Because of his emphasis on the influence of culture and social interactions, his theory (1978) is described as the *socio-cultural theory.* In today's diverse society, his ideas provide important guidelines for both early childhood educators and social studies instruction.

Developmentally, young preschoolers are typically at the symbolic-function substage of the preoperational stage in Piaget's theory of cognitive development (see Concept Box 3–4 below). At this substage, which usually spans ages two through four, children generally tend to focus on appearances and rely on their perceptions to build ideas and concepts of reality (Berk, 1996). Relying on concrete and observable characteristics, they are easily impressed by sounds, physical characteristics, and elements in the environment. *Animism*—the perception that inanimate objects are alive—is commonly experienced by children during this period.

This helps to explain why they tend to assign magical powers to things they experience or do. Explanations such as "A monster came and ate it all!" are common among children of this age group. Toys, as well as television and story characters, become real-life persons. Story characters, such as the little bear named Corduroy (Freeman, 1968), are attributed human characteristics. Sylvester, the donkey who finds the magic pebble that transforms him into a rock (Steig, 1969), is totally believable to children of this age. Animism also extends into play activities. Very elaborate and cooperative play activities, where reality blends with imaginary and fantastic characters who perform incredible feats, are developed by young children (Santrock, 1998).

■■ Older Preschoolers: Working ■■ with Four- and Five-Year-Olds

Older preschoolers (ages four and five) undergo tremendous developmental changes during this period. Despite significant holistic developmental changes, these children have different needs from those of primary-age children (see p. 61).

Concept Box 3–4 Preoperational Thought	
According to Jean Piaget, preoperational thinking (ages two to seven) is characterized by the child's ability to use more symbolic activity; however, at this stage the child is not yet capable of engaging in **operations** (mental processes used to form ideas about a reality). The child's thinking is characterized by *egocentricity,* which is the inability to differentiate between the child's own perspective and that of others. Still unable to decenter, thinking evolves into using primitive reasoning and searching for answers to all that happens in the environment. This cognitive stage is divided into two substages:	1. **Symbolic function (ages two to four):** Children at this substage are able to do mental representations of objects that are not present. They are egocentric and animistic in their thinking. They engage in pretend play and use language to communicate ideas. 2. **Intuitive thought (ages four to seven):** Children at this substage use simple reasoning skills and appear sure of own knowledge. They exhibit a desire to know answers to all the things and phenomena in their environments. Their thinking is characterized by its centration.

Source: Singer, D. G., & Revenson, T. A. (1998). *A Piaget primer: How a child thinks.* New York: International Universities Press.

Bringing Ideas into Practice 3–2
Creating Opportunities for Pretend Play through Learning Centers

Young preschoolers require environments where **pretend play** is encouraged. Because of the value of pretend play as a source of social studies learning, learning centers emerge as a key instructional and developmental element in the classroom. Centers should foster both individual and group play. Pretend play is the most significant characteristic of three-year-old children, because of their ability to symbolize.

Pretend play also becomes a child's essential tool for learning about social realities. With their aptitude for symbolization, three-year-olds are able to create and represent things and experiences lived or read about in stories. Opportunities for sharing through play what they have experienced not only reveal the children's unique ways to interpret reality, but also foster further concept development. The three-year-olds' extraordinary ability to symbolize explains the need for involving children in the arts. Drawing, painting, singing, dancing, and scribbling activities become channels for representation. They are also vehicles for children to demonstrate their creative abilities.

The following play centers can be incorporated into classrooms for three-year-olds. Some of them can be used year-round; others can be added as children show an interest in specific areas. These suggestions all share the same goal—fostering pretend play.

- **Puppet Chest:** Fill a box or an old suitcase with a variety of hand and finger puppets. The types of puppets should vary according to the topics explored in the classroom or according to the children's interest.
- **Seasonal Sensorial Center:** Each season can be described according to what we learn through our senses. Capitalize on those things associated with each season: Use a box or a suitable container and include items that depict the season's characteristic

odors, flavors, touch sensations, and colors. Include a tape recorder to encourage children to "record" their sensations. Drawing paper and crayons can also be used. Have children share their impressions during circle time.

- **Repair Center:** This center is intended to foster knowledge of items commonly used in the home. A selection of replicas and actual samples of small appliances such as radios, blenders, small televisions, and similar safe objects that will engage children in pretend play. Items can be donated by parents and by community members. Be sure to check each item carefully to ensure that it is in good condition and safe to be handled by young children.
- **Fashion Design Center:** Symbolic play is enhanced when children have opportunities to dress-up, especially when they can create their own costumes. Include a variety of fabrics, fabric scraps, ribbons, hats, shoes, buttons (large), glue, and so on. Add materials to help children dress like characters they have read about in stories or have seen on television.
- **Block Construction Center:** Blocks are indispensable in early childhood. They are particularly well suited for social studies. Combine a variety of blocks—wooden, cardboard, plastic— along with people and animal figures to foster representations.
- **Baby Center:** A selection of objects used by or for infants, such as diapers, bottles, clothing, cribs, and toys, will offer opportunities for children to explore and express ideas about younger siblings and about life changes. Include the children's own pictures as infants, pictures of siblings and of other infants from the school or the community, as well as infant dolls to encourage pretend play.

Cognitive and physical changes occur rapidly in four- and five-year-olds.

Physically, four-and five-year-olds exhibit better motor control than younger preschoolers do. Older preschoolers' ability to coordinate their movements allows them to engage in more active experiences.

Increased fine motor coordination favors manipulation of smaller objects. Children can use writing and drawing tools with better coordination and the shapes and figures they draw can be recognized more easily by adults.

Cognitive and Language Characteristics of Four- and Five-Year-Olds

Those working with four- and five-year-olds know that this is the period when children exhibit remarkable progress, both linguistically and cognitively. With an expanded vocabulary, averaging 4,000 to 6,000 words by age four and 5,000 to 8,000 words by age five, children are now able to represent experiences and convey ideas in ways adults understand. The increased verbal abilities foster the children's inquisitiveness, and they are more eager to know the "what's," "why's," "how's," and "when's" of life's experiences. This inquisitiveness, coupled with marked language fluency, motivates four- and five-year-olds to actively explore their environments. More skillful at holding conversations, these children enjoy sharing experiences of telling and retelling stories, role-playing, and singing.

Concept Box 3–5   Gross and Fine Motor Characteristics of Four- and Five-Year-Olds

Gross Motor Development
A four- or five-year-old:

- shows an increased sense of motor coordination.
- walks on a straight line and up and down stairs alone.
- hops on one foot, jumps over objects, and climbs well.
- is able to cross legs when sitting on the floor.
- engages in active play and demonstrates a high energy level.

Fine Motor Development
A four- or five-year-old:

- drives nails and pegs more accurately.
- reproduces shapes, letters.
- pours more accurately.
- builds a tower with 9 to 10 blocks.
- uses scissors and cuts on line with increasing accuracy.
- demonstrates better control when using pencils, crayons, markers.
- throws and catches a ball.
- shows a predominant hand dominance.

Source: Adapted from Santrock, J. (1998). *Child development* (8th ed.). Dubuque, IA: Brown & Benchmark.

Let's Talk About . . . 3–2

Implications of Language Development of Four- and Five-Year-Olds

According to the principles of child development, older preschoolers have an increased ability to use conventional language because they possess a greater vocabulary. They also have the ability to learn a second language. The developmental differences will also become more noticeable because of the rapid linguistic development experienced during ages four and five. It is important to remember that variations are to be expected, because each individual follows a unique developmental pattern. Therefore, activities should include experiences that foster typical and atypical development.

The ability to learn a second language is among the distinctive traits of the four- and five-year-olds. Studies have shown that children's overall linguistic abilities are enriched when more than one language is learned (Hakuta & Garcia, 1989). Knowledge of languages has also been found to facilitate and promote understanding of other cultures later in life.

1. In what ways could social studies activities enhance and foster these abilities?

2. What considerations should early childhood teachers keep in mind when planning social studies experiences?

3. List your ideas. Collect additional ideas from your colleagues. Share your findings in class.

Implications for Social Studies Teaching: Key Cognitive Traits of Four- and Five-Year-Old Children

Cognitively, older preschoolers are characterized by their inquisitiveness. Eager to know and explore their environments, they show a more sophisticated level of thinking than younger preschoolers. According to Piaget (19xx), during this transition period, older preschoolers are capable of thinking about objects not physically present and about events that happened in the past and will occur in the future. The child begins to separate experiences into a simple time sequence of *now, then,* and *next* (Forman & Kuschner, 1983). The environment remains as a significant source of knowledge and a basis for concept building. Thus, there is a need to plan and prepare the environment not only to suit

---

Concept Box 3–6 Types of Knowledge Acquired by Children

According to Piaget (1952), children acquire the following types of knowledge:

■ **socio-conventional knowledge:** Refers to the information about relationships and daily life defined and accepted by society. It includes, for example, ways to address others, manners and acceptable behaviors, customs, linguistic connotations, and terminology used by one's group. This kind of knowledge is learned through social interactions.

■ **physical knowledge:** Includes learning the quality, structure, form, weight, and functions of objects. It is learned through direct interaction with various objects.

■ **logico-mathematical knowledge:** Logico-mathematical ideas are developed about the nature and relationships of objects. This type of knowledge represents mentally formed concepts about the properties of objects. Each individual develops his or her own set of ideas and uses them to group or classify things (Kamii, 1985).

Concept Box 3–7   Cognitive Characteristics of Four- and Five-Year-Olds

1. Children are concrete thinkers relying on observable and tangible traits (*concreteness*).
2. Thinking is centered on one element or characteristic at a time while ignoring other traits (*centration*).
3. Children assume others see and perceive things and realities as they do (*egocentrism*).

4. When reasoning things out, children presume their ideas are correct; however, their reasoning (*intuitive thinking*) does not follow the logical thinking used by adults.
5. After experiencing an activity, children at this age and stage of development will have difficulties mentally reversing the steps or actions (*irreversibility*).

Sources: Forman, G., & Kuschner, D. (1983). *The child's construction of knowledge: Piaget for teaching children.* Washington, DC: National Association for the Education of Young Children; Santrock, J. (1998). *Child development* (8th ed). Dubuque, IA: Brown & Benchmark.

---

the immediate needs of young children, but also to facilitate the formation of new knowledge.

Because the older preschoolers are still in the preoperational period, their thinking will have some limitations. Direct and hands-on experiences account for newly built and expanded knowledge. Focusing on concrete and observable elements, children will construct ideas guided by the perceived characteristics. These perceptions or concepts will transform as the child experiences objects and events in other contexts.

Children ages four to five also exhibit a tendency to establish cause and effect differently from adults. Causality is commonly based on their consideration of immediate events rather than on events that happened previously. Immediate association with a recent event prompts their assumptions about the situation. This characteristic has direct implications for teaching social studies concepts.

Thinking abilities of four- and five-year-old children can be described as having an additional limitation: the *inability to use rational thinking*. While children will seem sure of their ideas, they generally will not know why they know something. Extremely curious and anxious to make sense out of their realities, they will ask questions about almost everything. This inquisitiveness serves to rationalize and make sense of experiences.

Another important characteristic of five-year-old children is defined as *"the 5 to 7 cognitive shift"*

(Berk, 1997). Kindergarten teachers know that children often swing back and forth in the level of their thinking. As they transition from one cognitive level to the other, children will be able at times to function as more advanced concrete-operational thinkers. This cognitive unevenness further emphasizes the fact that development is individually based and also that some concepts are developed earlier than others (Zigler & Stevenson, 1993). Teachers need to be aware of this characteristic, because it helps to explain the apparent variety of children's cognitive responses.

■■ Primary-Age Children: Working ■■ with Six- to Eight-Year-Olds

Primary-age children are at the highest level of the early childhood period. Their advanced developmental characteristics set them apart from the younger children. Physically more mature than their younger counterparts, they are also more competent cognitively as well as linguistically. They demand classroom activities involving the use of both concrete and semi-abstract resources, because they are able to engage in more active and extended experiences. A brief sketch of the cognitive and linguistic abilities of primary-age children is presented in the next section.

These recommended books are either bilingual or contain words in other languages. Many of them are available at most public and school libraries. These books are good resources for promoting awareness of other languages. Also, they foster appreciation of languages spoken by classmates, parents, and families with linguistic differences. (See also Chapter 9.)

Dorros, A. (1991). *Abuela.* New York: Dutton. (Includes phrases in Spanish spoken by the *abuela*, or grandmother.)

Dorros, A. (1992). *This is my house.* New York: Scholastic. (Includes the phrase "this is my house" in several languages.)

Feder, J. (1995). *Table-chair-bear: A book in many languages.* New York: Ticknor & Fields. (Contains pictures of items in a child's room labeled in 12 different languages.)

Kissinger, K. (1994). *All the colors we are. [Todos los colores de nuestra piel.]* St. Paul, MN: Redleaf Press. (Bilingual)

Robinson, T. (1993). *Cock-a-doodle-do! What does it sounds like to you?* New York: Steward, Tabori & Chang. (Builds awareness of differences in sounds as perceived by people from different linguistic groups.)

During the primary years, children engage in a lot of physical activity.

stractions. Primary-age children still need to encounter concrete realities; however, they no longer totally rely on or are deceived by sensorial impressions (*decentering*). Use of concrete materials allows children to mentally manipulate objects (Forman & Kuschner, 1983; Trawick-Smith, 1997). They are now capable of understanding simple relations between objects because they can think symbolically. For instance, primary-age children know that objects will remain the same even if they are placed in a different container (*reversibility*). Unlike their younger counterparts, six- to eight-year-olds are now able to understand how one's actions cause things to happen (*causality*).

Of importance to social studies educators is the fact that by ages six to eight, children have developed a more mature concept of space and time than that of preschoolers. By the time they reach age six, children typically know the difference between left and right, as well as the difference between things happening in the immediate present, past, and future.

Children between the ages of six to eight use language to communicate ideas more effectively, verbally and in writing. Their vocabulary and linguistic ability is almost adult-like by age eight. Primary-age children easily engage in conversations with both children and adults. The use of humor and knowledge about different word connota-

Cognitive and Language Characteristics of Six- to Eight-Year-Olds

Teachers working with children ages six to eight know these children are capable of more complex linguistic and cognitive performance. When compared with younger children, primary-age children have the ability to conserve ideas. By age six to eight, children have developed the following abilities: *decentering, causality,* and *reversibility.* These three mental operations have significant implications for social studies instruction.

More proficient thinking abilities allow primary-age children to solve problems using mental ab-

---

Concept Box 3–8   Physical and Motor Characteristics of Six- to Eight-Year-Olds

Slower but steady growth continues during this period.

Children exhibit a lanky look as extremities enter a rapid growth phase.

Baby teeth are lost as permanent teeth emerge.

Facial characteristics become more adult-like.

Children exhibit increased motor strength and dexterity.

Children engage in active physical activity such as jumping, climbing, hopping, kicking balls.

Children show better control of fine motor skills.

Children use scissors, pencils, and markers with increased dexterity.

Children show increased eye-hand coordination when writing, reproducing, copying, drawing.

Sources: Adapted from Santrock, J. (1998). *Child development* (8th ed.). Dubuque, IA: Brown & Benchmark; Bredekamp, S., & Copple, C. (1997). *Developmentally appropriate practice in early childhood programs* (rev. ed.). Washington, DC: National Association for the Education of Young Children.

---

tions afford children opportunities to expand their social interactions (Bredekamp & Copple, 1997).

■■ Social and Emotional Development ■■ During the Early Years

We have intentionally left the topic of **social and emotional development** to be addressed last. Erik Erikson's theory of **psychosocial development** (1963) is a helpful framework for understanding emotional development. According to his theory, individuals go through a lifelong process of emotional development that he described as occurring in eight stages. Each stage represents a variety of needs that individuals must fulfill in order to attain positive emotional development. The first four of Erikson's stages depict development during the early childhood years. Maturity and the quality of the interactions and experiences in the environment directly influence how individuals evolve from one phase to the other (Figure 3–4).

What are the implications of Erikson's ideas for the social studies classroom? First of all, they tell us that practices and decisions must be geared to fostering positive emotional development of children.

Concept Box 3–9   Cognitive and Language Characteristics of Primary-Age Children

Cognitive Characteristics
At this age, children:

■ are not easily deceived by physical appearances (able to decenter).

■ are able to mentally retrace the steps in a process or in a situation (able to reverse).

■ are able to understand that actions cause things to occur, or lead to an effect (causality).

■ are able to use symbolic representations.

■ have a more mature understanding of the concepts of *time* and *space*.

Linguistic Characteristics
At this age, children:

■ are able to engage in conversations.

■ use words with a variety of connotations.

■ use grammar, pragmatics, and syntax that are expanded and more refined.

■ are able to make more precise statements to express ideas.

■ are able to communicate ideas in writing.

■ are able to read.

■ show greater understanding of more complex oral and written linguistic structures.

FIGURE 3–4   Stages of Emotional Development During the Early Childhood Years, Based on Erikson

Stage	Age	Description
Trust vs. Mistrust	Birth to 18 months	A sense of trust in the adults and caregivers who provide basic needs, safety, affection, and care develops. If unable to trust, a sense of mistrust of others emerges.
Autonomy vs. Shame and Doubt	18 months to age 4	With improved motor ability, children develop a sense of independence from adults and believe they are capable of taking actions on their own. When restricted, child may develop a sense of shame and doubt about himself.
Initiative vs. Guilt	4 to 6 years	During this period, children need to have freedom to decide what to do, act, explore, and create. If ideas and actions are limited and rejected, child develops a sense of guilt.
Industry vs. Inferiority	6 to 12 years	Children develop a sense of self-competence in those skills considered valuable by the social and cultural group. These skills include the ability to make friends and to be considered important by peers and adults. Children who are often told they are not capable will feel inferior to others.

Source: Adapted from Berk, L. (1997). *Child development* (3rd ed.) Needham Heights, MA: Allyn & Bacon.

Awareness of the negative emotional effects when needs are not met helps teachers understand why developmental knowledge must be paired with educational practices. It also alerts educators to the significant role they play in the child's affective development. Secondly, Erikson's stages imply the need to adapt teaching to the child's emotional stage. An emotionally appropriate classroom is created when the teacher plans activities based on developmental information and in consonance with what each age group and individual child require.

The preschool years are also critical for the positive socialization of children. During this formative period, children recognize and define themselves as individuals and learn about others and the ways to relate to them. Effective socialization (see p. 3) is one of the major goals of both education and the social studies curriculum. Socialization happens as children interact with peers and the older generation, such as parents, family members, other adults, and teachers. A great deal of this process is enhanced by the school and the classroom activities.

Learning the existing codes of social interaction is another one of the tasks of the preschool and primary years. Essentially, during the first eight years of life, children are expected to develop knowledge about the social norms and customs deemed accept-

Socialization spurs learning of gender roles and behaviors.

■■   **Let's Talk About . . . 3–3**

Fostering Socioemotional Development

Transferring theory into practice is not always easy. Here is a brief questionnaire to help you determine if your teaching reflects Erikson's ideas. The questions are grouped by age level.

Preschoolers (ages three to six):

1. Is time allowed to listen to what children say and suggest?
2. Do children know their ideas are welcome? How?
3. Are children allowed to freely select the centers where they want to be?
4. Are children's ideas considered as valid suggestions?
5. Are children encouraged to pursue their interests and test their ideas?
6. Is the classroom schedule flexible enough to accommodate the children's needs (i.e., allowing additional time to work on a project; reading a book instead of napping, and so on)?
7. Are children involved in curriculum planning?
8. Is the classroom reflective of ideas suggested by children (i.e., is there a sign that explains the classroom arrangement was suggested by a child)?
9. Are the achievements of individual children recognized?
10. Are children tactfully led to see why their ideas might not be the best option?

Primary-age children (ages six to eight):

1. Is time periodically allocated to observe and discover the skills and abilities of children? Is this knowledge used to build the curriculum?
2. Does the classroom environment encourage children to make and do things?
3. Is the curriculum flexible enough in order to accommodate individual interests?
4. Do the activities foster the children's interests?
5. Are opportunities offered for individual children to demonstrate their competencies?
6. Are activities created to enhance the abilities of individual children?
7. Are children offered opportunities to fortify their sense of responsibility? (Example: Classroom "Helping Hands" chart, showing what classroom tasks are and which children are in charge)

---

able by the groups to which they belong. This **social cognition** and **social competence** is achieved through the children's interactions with different social environments like the family, the classroom, and the community. What social studies and early childhood teachers are able to contribute in this task is invaluable.

Play: A Means to Positive Social and Emotional Development

There is no better teaching strategy for children to develop social competence appropriately than

play. Play is the child's own way of developing and learning. Play is an excellent vehicle for development across developmental domains. Social skills are particularly enhanced and fostered through play activities. As Arnaud (1971, p. 5) has noted, ". . . when shared with other children, play is a major vehicle for constructive socialization, widening empathy with others, and lessening egocentrism." Life codes, tasks, and realities are learned during the many hours children spend at the housekeeping center and many other classroom centers. Arranging the classroom to foster play is central to both appropriate child development and effective social studies

Dramatic centers contribute to social development.

the kind of play in which the child voluntarily participates along with his or her peers (Smilansky, 1971). Sociodramatic play is one of the key strategies to consider when applying developmental ideas in the classroom. Smilansky's extensive play research has led to the identification of six key components of sociodramatic play (see Concept Box 3–10). They are helpful guidelines for the teacher as activities are planned. They are also a good tool for conducting observations of what actually happens at the various learning centers. It is important to note that sociodramatic play is a way for children to reflect on and rehearse the **social skills** they have learned from their environments. It brings into the classroom the variety of cultural and social formulas present in our society.

Awareness of the social concepts of the children's various cultural groups must be incorporated into role-playing. In fact, sociodramatic play is an excellent way to introduce children to diversity and tolerance.

Planning for appropriate social development in the classroom depends on the use of play as a central strategy. In building the curriculum, teachers

education. It is also the way to use what comes naturally to children: *knowing how to play.*

Much of what children learn about social relationships is learned through *sociodramatic play*—

Concept Box 3–10   Smilansky's Elements of Sociodramatic Play

Smilansky (1971) has identified six characteristics that differentiate sociodramatic play:

1. *Role-playing:* A make-believe role is assumed by the child. Through his or her actions, the child engages in imitative behavior and/or verbalizes the role (for example, feeding a doll while pretending to be a mother).

2. *Make-believe with objects:* Real objects are used to represent a make-believe one (for example, sitting inside a cardboard box and using it as a bus).

3. *Make-believe with actions/situations:* A situation is announced by the child, followed by actions (for example, a child pretending to be the father says, "It's raining, children; come inside!")

4. *Verbalizations:* Verbal expressions are related to the play episode (for example, a child playing a pilot says: "Fasten your seat belts! We are landing.")

5. *Social interaction:* At least two players are engaged in the play episode. Their actions follow the play framework (for example, when two children are pretending they are shopping, one child take things out of the cart while another child demands payment).

6. *Persistence:* The play episode engages children for more than five minutes (for example, the child pretending to be the toll-gate agent continues in that role, demanding payment for almost 15 minutes).

Sources: Smilansky, S. (1971). Can adults facilitate play in children? Theoretical and practical implications. Washington, DC: National Association for the Education of Young Children.; Berk, L. (1997). *Child development.* (3d ed.). Needham Heights, MA: Allyn & Bacon.

should plan activities targeted at the myriad of social tasks, codes, and knowledge that can develop while children are engaged in play. Planning and selecting developmentally and culturally appropriate objects and props to incorporate into the classroom activities are central to effective socialization. Sources for age-appropriate materials are listed in Appendix III (p. 282).

Connecting Development and Social Studies Teaching

The social studies curriculum complements the developmental process in several ways: First, it fosters the development of social knowledge that will help children to understand the world and its patterns of accepted ideas (physical and socioconventional knowledge—*cognitive development*). Second, it opens doors to learning about oneself and about others (*social and emotional development*). Third, it promotes appreciation of the individual's creative and expressive abilities (*creativity and cognitive development*). Fourth, it involves children in direct experiences (*physical and motor development*).

Achievement of these milestones is only possible when teachers combine knowledge about child development with knowledge of social sciences. Throughout the following chapters you will find ideas and suggestions targeted at the development of an appropriate and developmentally sound early childhood social studies curriculum.

ACTIVITIES

Keeping Track of What You Learn: Your Personal Activity Log

In this chapter, we have discussed many important ideas. Here are some additional activities for your personal activity log (PAL).

A. Reflections
1. Based on the ideas presented in this chapter, explain in your own words why early childhood teachers need to be current about child development.
2. Define in writing your views about the role of child development and social studies education in the lives of young children.
3. Create a web describing the characteristics of developmentally appropriate social studies teaching.

B. Collections
1. Plan to visit one or two early childhood classrooms, and observe for at least fifteen minutes. Based on the age group observed, find examples of development representative of each domain: *physical, cognitive, language,* and *socioemotional.* Share your findings with your classmates.
2. Working with children of diverse cultural backgrounds helps you understand how culture establishes developmental differences. Interview a family from a cultural background different from yours and find out about their child-rearing practices. You may want ask questions about feeding, care, who is responsible for the upbringing, dressing, and so on.
3. With the parent's/guardian's permission, take pictures of children at play. Use Smilansky's play typology to explain what each picture represents.

ACTIVITIES continued

C. Internet Resources*

These are suggestions for Internet Web sites about developmental theories. Once you visit them, you may want to add them to your bookmarks.

■ **Child Development Theory**

(http://www.ecdgroup.harvard.net)

This Web site is a source for relevant information about the different developmental characteristics.

■ **Developmental Theories**

(http://www.wpi.edu)

Descriptions of Piaget's stages and other developmental theories.

■ **I Am Your Child**

(http://www.iamyourchild.org)

A database containing information about development from birth through age three.

■ **Project Zero**

(www.pzweb.harvard.edu)

A source of information about Project Zero, a project targeted at researching the cognitive processes of children. Includes links to the project researchers, including Howard Gardner.

*Please note that Internet resources are of a time-sensitive nature and URL sites and addresses may often be modified or deleted.

References

Arnaud, S. (1971). Introduction: Polish for play's tarnished reputation. In National Association for the Education of Young Children. *Play: The child strives toward self-realization.* Washington, DC: Author.

Berk, L. (1996). *Infants and children: Prenatal through middle childhood* (2nd ed.). Needham Heights, MA: Allyn & Bacon.

Berk, L. (1997). *Child development* (3rd ed.). Needham Heights, MA: Allyn & Bacon.

Berns, R. M. (1994). *Topical child development.* Albany, NY: Delmar.

Bernstein, D., & Tiegermann, E. (1993). *Language and communication disorders in children* (3rd ed.). New York: Merrill.

Bredekamp, S., & Copple, C. (1997). *Developmentally appropriate practice in early childhood programs.* (rev. ed). Washington, DC: National Association for the Education of Young Children.

Bredekamp, S., & Rosegrant, T. (1992). *Reaching potentials: Appropriate curriculum and assessment for young children,* Vol. 1. Washington, DC: National Association for the Education of Young Children.

Bredekamp, S., & Rosegrant, T. (1995). *Reaching potentials: Transforming early childhood curriculum and assessment,* Vol. 2. Washington, DC: National Association for the Education of Young Children.

Castorina, J. (1996). *El debate Piaget-Vygotsky: La búsqueda de un criterio para su evaluación* [The debate about Piaget-Vygotsky: In search of a criteria for its evaluation]. In J. Castorina, E. Ferreiro, M. Oliveira, & D. Lerner, *Piaget-Vygotsky: Contribuciones para replantear el debate* [Piaget-Vygotsky: Contributions to restate the debate]. Buenos Aires, Argentina: Editorial Paidós.

Deiner, P. L. (1983). *Resources for teaching young children with special needs.* New York: Harcourt Brace Jovanovich.

Dorros, A. (1991). *Abuela.* New York: Dutton.

Dorros, A. (1992). *This is my house.* New York: Scholastic.

Erikson, E. (1963). *Childhood and society* (2nd ed.). New York: Norton.

Feder, J. (1995). *Table-chair-bear: A book in many languages.* New York: Ticknor & Fields.

Forman, G., & Kuschner, D. (1983). *The child's construction of knowledge: Piaget for teaching children.* Washington, DC: National Association for the Education of Young Children.

Freeman, D. (1968). *Corduroy.* New York: Puffin Books.

Gardner, H. (1983). *Frames of mind: The theory of multiple intelligences.* New York: Basic Books.

Hakuta, K., & Garcia, E. (1989). Bilingualism and education. *American Psychologist, 44,* 374–379.

Kamii, C. (1985). *Young children reinvent mathematics: Implications of Piaget's theory.* New York: Teachers College.

Katz, L. (1995). *Talks with teachers of young children: A collection.* Norwood, NJ: Ablex.

Kissinger, K. (1994). *All the colors we are.* [Todos los colores de nuestra piel.] St. Paul, MN: Redleaf Press.

Meyen, E. L. (1996). *Exceptional children in today's schools* (3rd ed.). New York: Love.

Nelson, K. (1998). *Developing students' multiple intelligences.* New York: Scholastic.

Piaget, J. (1952). *The origins of intelligence in children.* New York: International Universities Press.

Robinson, T. (1993). *Cock-a-doodle-do! What does it sound like to you?* New York: Steward, Tabori & Chang.

Santrock, J. (1998). *Child development* (8th ed.). Dubuque, IA: Brown & Benchmark.

Singer, D. G., & Revenson, T. A. (1998). *A Piaget primer: How a child thinks.* New York: International Universities Press.

Smilansky, S. (1971). Can adults facilitate play in children?: Theoretical and practical implications. In National Association for the Education of Young Children. *Play: The child strives toward self-realization.* Washington, DC: Author.

Steig, W. (1969). *Sylvester and the magic pebble.* New York: Simon & Schuster.

Trawick-Smith, J. (1997). *Early childhood development: A multicultural perspective.* Upper Saddle River, NJ: Merrill.

Wadsworth, B. (1971/1979/1984/1989/1996). *Piaget's theory of cognitive and affective development: Foundations of constructivism* (5th ed.). New York: Longman Publishers USA.

Vygotsky, L. (1978). *Mind in society.* Cambridge, MA: Harvard University Press.

Zigler, E., & Stevenson, M. (1993). *Children in a changing world: Development and social issues* (2nd ed.). Pacific Grove, CA: Brooks/Cole.

PART II

*Creating an Early Childhood
Social Studies Curriculum*

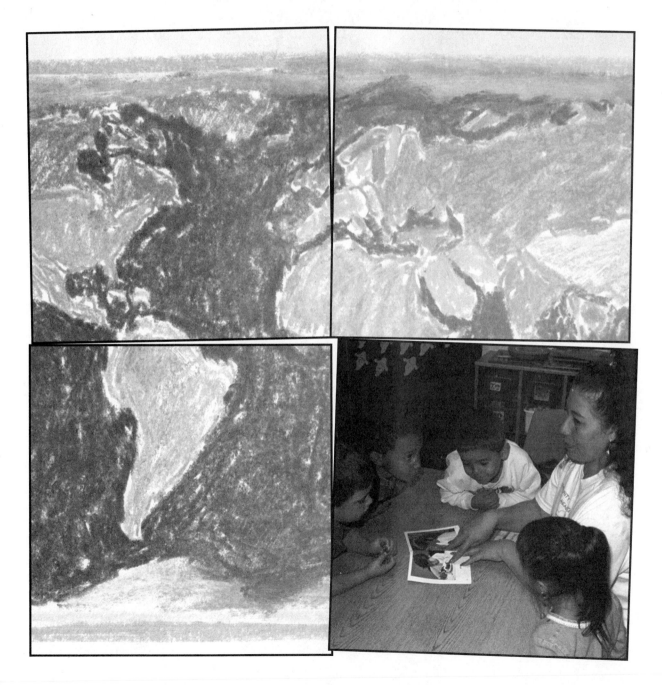

CHAPTER 4

Planning Developmentally Appropriate Social Studies

Teachers develop, refine, and use a wide repertoire of teaching strategies to enhance children's learning and development

—S. Bredekamp and C. Copple (1997)

Chapter Questions

After reading this chapter you should be able to answer the following questions:

- What are the key elements of appropriate curricular practices?
- What are the essential elements of a good social studies curriculum?
- What considerations should be taken into account in planning DAP social studies experiences?

Key Terms and Concepts

affective objectives
behavioral objectives
concept maps
curriculum
developmental planning
goals
learning centers
lesson planning

performance objectives
project approach
teaching strategies
teaching techniques
thematic teaching
unit planning
webbing
webs

Classroom Portrait: **Planning, planning . . .**

How many times have we planned for children to learn about a concept, and then to our surprise, they come out with a totally different idea? Many times! And the more it happens, the more one learns that teaching young children requires good planning. More so, it demands that we plan with an awareness of *what children already know* and knowledge about *their social reality,* and about *where they are,* in terms of their development. Read what happened to a new teacher who forgot those central planning elements:

A recently appointed kindergarten teacher was sharing with a colleague an incident from the morning class. In hand, he had a story about community helpers. He had felt confident that by choosing such a simple topic and by sharing the book with the children, by now they would have a sound knowledge about "community helpers." After the story was read, the children were all looking at him attentively. The group sat in a circle right next to the book center where the teacher had a display of pictures of community helpers—a doctor, a police officer, a postal employee, and firefighters. These were all the usual pictures to set up the ideal

setting for children to learn about community helpers, or at least that was what the teacher thought. However, as he explained to his colleague, he found out that he had missed an important piece: "As I closed the book, I noticed some very serious faces. So I asked, 'Well, who wants to be a community helper?' "

"Then a child seated at the center of the circle asked me, 'If I'm a community helper, will I have to wear funny clothes?' I didn't even have a chance to answer when a girl jumped up and said, 'I want to be a helper. I'm gonna make pretty nails. Mommy says it makes people feel good.' "

"They all surprised me," commented the teacher.

Both teachers looked at each other and laughed. The more experienced teacher then said, "You know, they are right. Well, I guess you now know that it takes more than just having the right materials. You have to think the way children do, and you ought to know about their experiences."

"Yeah, you're right," the kindergarten teacher said. "Next time, I'll keep in mind what they know already!"

■■ Planning and Teaching Appropriate ■■ Social Studies Experiences

Teaching social studies is a way to bring life into our classrooms. With the many concepts and ideas to explore and share, it is important to consider how we translate those into meaningful experiences for young children. Five essential aspects characterize a successful social studies program—not only a **curriculum** that is worthy to be learned, but a responsive, developmentally sound, social studies program:

■ Time is set aside to carefully plan experiences.
■ Professional knowledge about children is applied and followed to make curricular and instructional decisions.
■ Teaching strategies are age-appropriate.

■ Materials and activities are reflective of the children's characteristics.
■ Adaptations are made to accommodate individual children's needs.

(National Association for the Education of Young Children, 1997)

Teaching young children about their social world is an exciting, demanding task. As you read the five points above, you probably identified those you or fellow colleagues already follow. Perhaps you also thought about those you do not totally agree with. Because as educators we are always striving to create the best learning environment for young children, this chapter will help you to clarify these five essential areas. In the process, you will also explore what is embodied in developmental teaching.

Exchanging ideas among colleagues helps to build meaningful experiences.

■■   **Let's Talk About . . . 4–1**

Is Planning Really Important?
Lessons from the Field

The importance of planning is best gleaned by checking with practitioners. To emphasize the need for good planning, we recommend that you visit a sample of classrooms and interview teachers. Simply ask them the questions below. Remember to review their answers and summarize your findings. Share them in class.

1. How important is planning for you? Why?

2. How much time do you spend planning? When do you plan?

3. What *three* things would you suggest to make planning more effective?

Toward Effective Social Studies Teaching: Planning Child-Appropriate Classroom Practices

Planning is an essential step in effective and child-appropriate programs. Whether it is done informally or formally, the planning phase is central to any successful activity. Working with young children requires that we pay specific attention to how we decide what experiences they will participate in. The impact of our choices—effected on children by the materials, characters, and objects they interact with—should never be considered lightly. Being in a rapid knowledge-formation period makes children more susceptible to what is presented in a classroom. Words, as well as images used and brought in by teachers, are thought of by children as authoritative ideas. Many times people tend to believe that because they are working with young children, any activity will be good for them. Little or no time is sometimes used to decide what to do and how to do it on a given day. However, experiences from classrooms tell us that simplifying concepts like those in social studies (*families, rules,* and *the neighborhood*) is actually a very difficult task. As you read in the opening vignette to this chapter, the ways children process ideas can surprise us if we do not take the time to examine our targeted topics from the perspective of children!

Professional educators spend time considering and selecting the **curriculum**—what young children will experience in the classroom. Actually, educators spend lots of time not just deciding what to teach, but in preparing and finding the specific artifacts and materials that will trigger children's desire to discover and learn. A visit to any classroom will reveal how much time most teachers have invested in the planning of activities. Besides the action-packed environments, the children's faces and expressions will depict how effective the planning efforts have been.

The Two Dimensions of Developmental Planning

Planning is a necessary process for the success of any endeavor. In education, it "is used for the purpose of ensuring that overall program aims are accomplished" (Eddowes & Ralph, 1998, p. 107). Professional educators know nothing happens without putting time aside to foresee what will be offered or what can happen in the children's classroom. Then, what are the steps for effective planning?

First of all, there are "no magic formulas" (Jones & Nimmo, 1994). However, there are essential factors to consider and to reflect upon as the planning process begins. As Jones and Nimmo state, "No teacher invents curriculum from scratch; we borrow from every possible source" (1994, p. 5). In this section we will discuss two important planning dimensions: first, the knowledge about the audience we teach and, second, the purpose guiding our teaching.

The *first dimension* for effective **developmental planning** entails the general and specific knowledge we have about children. When planning, it is important to always consider *who your audience is.*

1. **Knowing your audience—who are the children we teach?** Knowing your audience requires teachers to learn about children's general developmental characteristics, as well as about the particular elements that define an individual child in a group. Because of the special nature of the topics explored through social studies, it is of the utmost importance to learn about the children's cultural and social realities. Besides the knowledge children will build, social studies is also aimed at empowering the individual child. This objective is accomplished only when classroom experiences offer opportunities for children to identify with. This also happens when children find activities that relate in some way to their own realities. Suggested questions that will help define your audience appear in Figure 4–1.

The *second dimension* for effective planning is knowledge about the *purpose or goal* you are pursuing. Early childhood years are a precious time for children. As educators we must guarantee time spent by children in activities is indeed necessary and valuable. The time spent in social studies is crucial, because it should help children develop essential social concepts about themselves and others (see Chapter 3).

Many times social studies activities have been criticized because they do not lead children to acquire any knowledge. Consider the child whose first-grade class was engaged in preparing paper-bag puppets. When a visitor inquired what they were doing, the child said, "We are doing faces." Questioned further about why they were doing them, the child shrugged and replied, "I don't know. Teacher told us to." Obviously, in this case, the product, instead of the process and the purpose for engaging in the experience, was what was being emphasized. In cases like this, the experience communicated to children is that their thinking or special way of doing something is not what is valued (Isenberg & Jalongo, 1997). Remember that clarity about the purpose of activities also validates the curricular choices you have made.

FIGURE 4–1 Planning for success— who are the children I teach?

- Where are the children I teach, developmentally speaking?
- Which children will need to be challenged differently?
- What modifications will be required?
- What do the children in my class experience in their environment outside the classroom?
- Do they share the same environment?
- What cultural patterns do they belong to?
- What are their interests?
- How familiar are they with this topic?
- What experiences have they had with this topic?

Planning Social Studies Experiences

Planning is central to any effective social studies program. With its exciting and profusely conceptual content, social studies offers a wide array of ideas and issues from which to select. Even for the experienced teacher who is deciding what and how to teach, planning a social studies curriculum is quite a challenging task. When teaching young children, time taken to examine how to design sensible and developmentally sound activities is fundamental. Because of the unique characteristics defining chil-

---

Concept Box 4–1   Key Developmental Planning Considerations

General considerations:
- Content must match children's developmental age levels.
- Curriculum needs to respond to the needs of the individual child.
- Experiences need to reflect the cultural characteristics of both children and their communities.

Specific considerations:
- Curriculum is established by teachers for the children being taught.
- Design is made through the careful analysis of assessment findings.
- General curricular scope is designed around what children can learn, rather than what they did not learn.
- Experiences are built to foster continuous developmental progress.

- Curriculum is planned around child-appropriate teaching strategies.
- Strategies emphasize learning processes (learning how to) rather than content.
- Curricular strategies are planned considering the variety of gifts children have.
- Strategies accommodate the many ways in which children learn.
- Curricular framework is built around skills and concepts relevant to children.
- Curricular content must be worth learning. It must reflect academic integrity.
- Curricular content is built around the idea of ongoing challenge and success.
- Curriculum design is flexible; it adapts to the realities and needs of children.
- Plans to evaluate the curriculum both during the implementation (formative stage) and at its conclusion (summative stage) are established.

Sources: Bredekamp, S. & Copple, C. (1997). *Developmentally appropriate practices in early childhood programs.* (rev. ed.) Washington, DC: National Association for the Education of Young Children; Bredekamp, S. & Rosegrant, T. (Eds.). (1992). *Reaching potentials: Appropriate curriculum and assessment strategies for young children,* Vol. 1. Washington, DC: National Association for the Education of Young Children; Feinburg, S. & Mindess, M. (1994). *Eliciting children's full potential: Designing and evaluating developmentally based programs for young children.* Pacific Grove, CA: Brooks/Cole.

---

dren during the preschool and primary years, social studies experiences must be carefully chosen and planned. Social studies activities must match not only what children are able to learn, but the activities should also be in accordance with the ways children learn: through doing, touching, seeing, hearing, and experiencing.

Curricular decisions should never be made hastily or at random. They require careful planning, using knowledge about what children need to learn to establish well-informed directions in classrooms (Krogh, 1995). Good planning is the keystone to effective and developmentally appropriate teaching. In fact, planning is central to any professional activity. As Seefeldt and Barbour (1998, p. 170) point out:

. . . Planning is essential. Without planning, chaos reigns. And under conditions of chaos, children's learning is up to chance. *No one can take the chance that a single child will not learn and experience success* [emphasis added].

Because social studies is understood by many to occur throughout the entire curriculum (and indeed it does!), many times people relegate its formal planning to a lower priority. According to many teachers, more time is spent planning for math and language arts, areas in which teachers feel they are more accountable for achievement than they are in social studies. At other times social studies is taught incidentally, by letting it just "happen." This idea was confirmed in an informal study conducted by one of

Let's Talk About . . . 4–2

Is It Easy to Plan Social Studies Experiences?

Some people contend that planning for social studies is often relegated to a lesser role in the curriculum because of the highly complex and abstract nature of social studies concepts. They believe that teaching young children about concepts such as *interdependence* and *conflict* requires a sound understanding of what they entail. In fact, teachers who believe so add that lack of effective teacher training in this field is to be blamed for the lesser importance assigned to it.

Do you agree with this statement? Why?

Well-planned activities engage children.

the authors. This study revealed that despite the renewed interest in social studies education, many early childhood educators still consider it is not necessary to formally plan for it (Robles de Melendez & Ostertag, 1997). The reason most frequently given (74%) was that "It would happen anyway" (i.e., through incidental teaching). While it is true that social studies occurs throughout the curriculum, it is equally important to understand that development and acquisition of key social concepts require careful and thorough planning.

Planning a Quality Curriculum That Is "Worthy of Learning"

What makes a social studies curriculum a quality one depends upon several elements. According to the NCSS (1989), a quality curriculum:

■ possesses *consistency* and leads to the *cumulative* and *systematic* study of people and their interactions;

■ has *depth* in the content and themes treated;

■ possesses *relevancy* and is of interest for the students;

■ is well *balanced* (in its coverage of local-national-global issues); and

■ is developmentally appropriate.

(NCSS, 1989, p. 12)

To this list we add one key characteristic: *flexibility*. The children's curriculum must provide for the many teachable opportunities that will easily happen. Incidental experiences abound that will motivate children to learn more about them. The birth of a sibling, a trip to a visiting circus, a natural event, or a new child who just enrolled in the class are all incidental happenings that will trigger the children's curiosity to know more about them. Such instances must be grasped and maximized. Nothing is more accurate than to say that we learn best when things are of our interest.

Planning is the key to an early childhood social studies curriculum that possesses the characteristics identified by the NCSS. Taking time to think about the issues to be explored, the materials and strategies to be used is what leads to the quality of experiences. Whether you follow a mandated (district- or school-decided) curriculum or your own, it is indispensable to outline formally what children will explore.

Concept Box 4–2   Essential Characteristics of Quality Social Studies Curricula

- **Consistency:** Children build concepts upon knowledge already developed. Each concept studied serves as a step for further knowledge development.
- **Cumulative and systematic learning:** Ideas learned by children expand concepts and skills they already possess. Content follows a logical and coherent examination of ideas and concepts.
- **Depth:** Content examined allows opportunities for a detailed and thorough study and analysis.
- **Relevancy:** Content has validity and pertinence for the children in terms of their social reality and interests.

- **Balance:** Curriculum provides opportunities for the analysis of ideas from the children's personal, local, national, and global reality.
- **Developmental appropriateness:** Content is delivered through modalities that are appropriate for the children. Procedures and activities are consistent with the needs and characteristics of the children being taught.
- **Flexible:** The curriculum is easily adaptable to allow for newly emerged interests or special events.

■■ Do We Know Why Children Are ■■ Doing What They Do?

Deciding what children will learn is at the heart of what teachers do in the classroom. As you get ready to create social studies experiences, clarity about your intended purposes is central to effective teaching. Knowing what the expected outcomes are contributes to successful teaching.

Establishing Social Studies Goals and Objectives

Important to the planning process is to identify the outcomes pursued. As you design your curriculum, goals and objectives serve as the "steering wheel," helping you to define why you have selected certain experiences. They also establish the outcomes children will exhibit.

Writing Goals

Central to the process of planning is to have a clear understanding of the goals to achieve. **Goals** are broad statements describing the general learning intentions. They communicate the general, rather than the specific, knowledge children will derive from a unit or a lesson plan. These goals are im-

portant, for they clearly set the directions of your teaching. Sample goals are:

- to enjoy working in small groups;
- to learn about people in our community;
- to understand that we are alike;
- to know about other countries.

Performance Objectives

Objectives define the specific kind of knowledge, whether it is a concept or a skill, children will acquire. Unlike goals, objectives require the use of action verbs (such as *assemble, write, draw, cut, paste, describe,* and so on) that clearly define the observable behavior children are expected to demonstrate. Typically, cognitive, affective or social, and physical developmental behaviors are targeted through classroom objectives. To help teachers know how much progress a child has made, specific behavioral or performance objectives are established.

Behavioral or performance objectives are those which state with a degree of specificity what children have learned. A performance objective defines the kind of behavior the child is expected to exhibit and establishes the expected level of performance teachers will observe. Behavioral objectives answer the question, "What behavior should children engage in during this activity?"

Writing performance objectives requires use of behavioral verbs. In the example below you will see how these verbs outline with specificity the observable behaviors children are to exhibit.

- Children will build a tower
- Children will sing with emphasis
- Children will share their crayons
- Children will pour the liquid
- Children will estimate the distance
- Children will collect soil samples

Cognitive and Social Performance Objectives

Social studies experiences primarily revolve around cognitive and social objectives. Cognitive objectives describe those highlighting the development of knowledge concepts and skills. Because knowledge is built when the child acts and reflects upon his actions and/or relationship with an object or an event, cognitive objectives emphasize thinking processes (Forman & Kuschner, 1983; Bloom, 1984). According to Bloom, thinking processes occur with different degrees of complexity. He established a system or taxonomy for classifying thinking processes in the cognitive domain.

A summary of Bloom's taxonomy, indicating cognitive performance behaviors by levels, appears in Figure 4–2. According to his taxonomy, the first and simplest level of cognitive processing is defined as *knowledge building*. The most sophisticated level and the highest is called *evaluation*. Bloom's taxonomy is a helpful planning tool. It reminds teachers of the different and challenging directions classroom experiences can take. Knowledge about the different levels of thinking processes helps teachers to design activities aimed at fostering development of essential thinking processes. It keeps teachers aware of the fact that children, if taught appropriately, can perform at higher thinking levels. As you examine the list of behaviors defining each of Bloom's six thinking levels, you will see how classroom activities can easily be planned around them. A sample list of action verbs describing the cognitive domain appears in Figure 4–3.

Development of thinking processes is of utmost importance in social life. Because all of life's actions are based on the decisions that individuals make, the ability to apply the appropriate process becomes critical for individual success. Opportunities for development of thinking processes occur throughout the entire social studies curriculum. For instance, discussion of story characters, decisions children make at the playground, consideration of classroom

---

FIGURE 4–2   A Summary of Bloom's Taxonomy of Cognitive Processes

6. **Evaluation:** Children make value judgments about an event, opinion or concept: (Actions:* argue, conclude, judge, decide, select, evaluate, justify)

5. ↑ **Synthesis:** Children rearrange ideas to create new concepts or views: (Actions:* combine, arrange, create, formulate, rearrange, construct, plan, produce, constitute)

4. ↑ **Analysis:** Children separate information into its parts to determine its relationships (Actions:* identify, divide, outline, compare, contrast, discriminate)

3. ↑ **Application:** Children apply what was learned (Actions:* apply, develop, modify, design, relate, use)

2. ↑ **Comprehension:** Children demonstrate understanding of the information obtained (Actions:* select, estimate, expand, interpret, classify, generalize, infer, describe)

1. ↑ **Knowledge:** Children recognize and recall information (Actions:* observe, touch, note, describe, define, list, name, identify)

*The observable actions that reveal the cognitive process the child is using are listed in parentheses.

FIGURE 4–3   Sample List of Action Verbs Describing the Cognitive Domain

to ask	to classify
to arrange	to choose
to assemble	to catch
to attempt	to collect
to act	to change
to agree	to construct
to accept	to color
to analyze	to check
to build	to cut
to bring	to compliment
to compile	to discuss
to contrast	to defend
to compare	to distinguish
to communicate	to group
to display	to identify
to dance	to plan
to draw	to sing
to read	to volunteer
to organize	to gather
to locate	to define
to list	to suggest
to aid	to demonstrate
to graph	to verbalize
to estimate	

How many other action verbs can you add?

FIGURE 4–4   Sample Action Verbs for Stating Affective or Social Behavior Objectives

demonstrate empathy	talk
share	help
work along with	answer
accept	interact
compliment	smile
contribute	praise
greet	participate
volunteer	help
express	cooperate
show forgiveness by . . .	admit
join	thank
laugh	discuss
follow	express
show respect for by . . .	disagreement
use manners	verbalize

and school rules, and selection of activities are all situations where thinking processes are applied.

Social or **affective objectives** are frequently used in social studies. Affective objectives, which define emotions and feelings that children will develop and exhibit, are central to the development of values and attitudes (see Chapter 3). Although affective objectives are more subjective in nature, a careful selection of verbs will allow teachers to observe progress in this dimension. A sample list of verbs describing affective behavior appears in Figure 4–4.

Advantages of Using Performance Objectives

One of the advantages of using performance objectives is that they allow teachers to "see" what the child has learned. A performance objective answers the following questions:

1. What will motivate children? (teacher-initiated activity)
2. What will children do? (specific classroom tasks)
3. How will I know what they have learned? (level of progress)

Development of performance objectives entails a three-step process. Each step defines the experiences and roles of both teacher and children. According to Maxim (1989), the three basic elements are: 1) input process, 2) description of children's behavior, and 3) level of performance. In the example below, you can see how each step helps to establish, with precision, what will happen in the classroom and which outcomes are expected. You will also see how each step answers the three main questions discussed above: What will motivate children? What will children do? How will I know what and how much they have learned?

1. **Input process:** Initial activity provided by the teacher. This serves as a motivator for the child to engage in the experiences to come.

Example: A visit to the post office. (Answers the question: What will motivate children?)

2. **Description of children's behavior:** States the experiences and the behaviors children will exhibit. Defines the process and kind of activities used to engage children.

    Example: After a visit to the post office, *the children will name . . .* (Answers the question: What will children do?)

3. **Level of performance:** Indicates the *minimum level of behavior* children are expected to exhibit. This is the element that allows teachers to assess the progress achieved by children (Maxim, 1989, pp. 448–449).

    Example: After a visit to the post office, *the children will name at least two* of the tasks postal employees do. (Answers the question: How will I know what they have learned?)

■■ Objectives Are Important,
■■ but *Children* Are the Reason
for Teaching

Although it is true that knowing what children will learn is very necessary, the essential key to appropriate early childhood education is to place your emphasis on the process through which children come to accomplish the listed objectives. It is in the process, not the product, that early educators need to place their attention (Maxim, 1989; Kamii, 1991; Bredekamp & Rosegrant, 1992). What the child is capable of performing is more important than the actual targeted outcome. Child-based teaching happens when activities are planned based on what the children will come to experience.

Sources of Learning Objectives: Starting with the Children

In early childhood education, learning objectives emanate from two main sources: first, and most important, the children, and, second, the already-established objectives in a school subject.

The first and most important source of curricular objectives is found in the children we teach. Be-

cause social studies is about people, your best reference to what is appealing, novel, or at stake in the children's families and in the community is found in what happens in the classroom. A prerequisite of successful teaching is for all early childhood educators to be excellent observers and listeners. By observing *what* children do, as well as *when* and *where* they do it, teachers can get to know children and the environment in which they live and participate. Your interactions with children in the classroom and in other school areas offer you many valuable details. Discussions in class, comments made after an activity, reactions to materials and objects, responses to stories and events will all lead you into the day-to-day world of each child. Communication with their parents and families also reveals important details about what they consider interesting and relevant. A good observer and listener will notice the things children feel attracted to and the topics they enjoy talking or even arguing about. By jotting down your observations, you will see the social studies curriculum unfold and come alive.

How to Use the National Social Studies Standards as a Curriculum Source

The most important curriculum source is always what is officially defined as the knowledge base for a subject area. In the case of social studies, the *Expectations for Excellence: Curriculum Standards for Social Studies* (1994), discussed in Chapter 2 and reprinted in Appendix I of this book, define the knowledge expectations for each education level. In addition to the national standards, there are individual state mandates as well as goals and objectives established by the local school districts. Early childhood educators must determine how to include all of these requirements in a social studies curriculum that will be appropriate and meaningful for young children. In trying to accomplish this difficult task, teachers need to remember that the children are the reason for our profession, and that the goals and objectives of any curriculum must respond to their needs first.

Standard 1, Culture, of the *Curriculum Standards for Social Studies* is an example of goals and

---

■■ Let's Talk About . . . 4–3

What Should Teachers Observe in the Classroom for Curricular Planning Purposes?

If you plan to build a child-based social studies curriculum, you will want to observe:

- general developmental characteristics. Look for individual developmental differences.
- what individual children do at the learning centers.
- words children use to describe events in and out of the classroom.
- the songs they sing.
- role-playing (especially in the housekeeping and block centers).
- how they interact with their peers (large and small groups).
- their comments about events or situations happening in the community.
- their reactions and comments about such key concepts as families, community, or neighborhood.
- their comments about what other children and adults say, do, or wear.
- their play. Notice what kind of play children engage in.
- their reactions to stories shared.

You will also want to interview children, individually, about their preferences and listen and talk to their parents and families. Also, observe the children's reactions while they are with their parents/families.

---

objectives that can be used as a framework for classroom activities:

General Goal:
  Social studies programs should include experiences that provide for the study of culture and cultural diversity.

Objectives/Performance Expectations:*
  1. <u>Explore</u> and <u>describe</u> similarities and differences in the ways groups, societies, and cultures address similar human needs and concerns.
  2. <u>Give examples</u> of how experiences may be interpreted differently by people from diverse cultural perspectives and frames of reference.
  3. <u>Describe</u> ways in which language, stories, folktales, music, and artistic creations serve as expressions of culture and influence behavior of people living in a particular culture.
                    (NCSS, 1994, p. 33; emphasis added)

*The underlined words represent specific behaviors.

Engaging Parents in the Planning Process

Parents and families play an important role in the process of curriculum development. An important source of information, they provide valuable data that helps us learn about their expectations, as well as about the things they consider relevant. Learning what the parents and families value as important gives teachers a source they can use to tailor the curriculum to the needs of the children in their classroom. In social studies, information about parents' preferences and opinions about given topics contributes to the development of relevant and pertinent experiences for the children served. Including the perspective of families and parents helps them to know their ideas are valued. It also helps teachers to adapt the curriculum to the reality in which children live. Parents' views about a topic can be easily gathered through informal questionnaires or personal interviews. An example of an informal questionnaire appears in Figure 4–5. Involving parents in the curriculum planning process also offers an opportunity for them to collaborate more directly on what happens in the classroom. Although this type of outreach requires making additional efforts, it will certainly be worthwhile when you find that your resources and possible areas to be explored have doubled.

The Community as a Curricular Source

The community is a valuable source of current and socially relevant information for teachers. Plan-

FIGURE 4–5 Involving Parents in the Planning Process: Sample Informal Questionnaire

Dear parents/family of (child's name): _____

Our class will soon be studying the following topic: _____

We would like to hear your opinion about this topic. Please share some of your ideas by answering the questions below. Your collaboration is very valuable. Please cut along the dotted lines and return the answered questionnaire with your child. Thank you for taking the time to answer.

Cordially,

(Teacher)

✂ ···

Family of _____ (Write your child's name)

1. What do you know about _____ ?

2. What do you consider most important about this topic?

3. What would you like children to learn about this topic?

4. Do you have any resources or experiences related to this topic that you would like to share with the class? If yes, please describe.

ning of an effective social studies curriculum requires inclusion of what takes place in the community. As the setting where the children live, the community provides a wealth of interesting topics to explore. Pertinence is a central characteristic of any child-appropriate curriculum. Classroom activities are relevant when they are based on what happens in daily life. Knowledge about key community issues allows early childhood teachers an opportunity to design a curriculum based on real-life experiences. First-hand knowledge about a community is usually the best source of information. In decades past, teachers often lived in the communities where they taught. However, today many teachers are not residents of the community where they teach.

There are several ways to gather formation about a community:

1. Visiting the community.
2. Interviewing or talking with parents, families, and other community residents.
3. Talking with other colleagues and school staff who are residents of the community.
4. Reading the community newspapers.
5. Talking with community leaders such as church members and members of civic organizations.
6. Talking with the school's community liaison person.
7. Visiting the local library (community affairs and events are usually advertised on the bulletin board).
8. Listening to what children say about their community.

The topics that will emerge from the community will depend on the age level of the children taught and on the community itself. Rather than assigning a one-time opportunity to talk about the community in the classroom, community topics should be integrated throughout the year. If proper planning takes place, current events and issues from the community that will be of interest to children can be easily fit into the curriculum. Undoubtedly, the place where they live always appeals to children, particularly when a special event has taken place. A list of suggested age-appropriate, community-based topics follows:

- houses and buildings
- community businesses
- playgrounds and parks
- construction sites
- places to eat
- typical food in our community
- languages spoken
- important places in the community
- services and agencies
- local government
- contests and competitions
- community sports
- keeping the community beautiful
- community holidays
- pets living in the community
- community symbols and landmarks
- people in the community

How many others can you add?

Lesson Plans and Units

Planning can be done daily, weekly or over a longer range, as in the case of units or projects. Planning can be done individually, or it can also be done by a teaching team.

- **Lesson planning** involves choosing short-range programmed experiences for children. Like a menu, a lesson plan establishes the activities and strategies that are scheduled to happen throughout a day or a week. In lesson plans, teachers design activities that are usually organized around a topic, skill, or concept. Lesson plans indicate the specific objectives, materials, process activities, and evaluation experiences teachers will use.
- **Unit planning** entails a long-range study of a central theme and related topics. In planned units, children are engaged in a variety of interdisciplinary experiences, extended over a period of time ranging from a week to up to a month. The amount of time they will spend is determined by the children; teachers should observe their demonstrated level of interest.

Lesson and unit plans have several elements in common. Essentially, they both include:

- a theme or area of study (topic, skill, concept)
- outcome objectives
- modifications/adaptations (alternate ways to provide for children with special needs, children with linguistic differences, and/or children of different cultural backgrounds)
- materials and resources
- activities
- evaluation activities

Concept Box 4–3   Sources for Appropriate Social Studies Curricula

Formal sources:

- State-specified goals
- School district goals and curriculum
- Professional organizations such as:
  National Council for the Social Studies
  National Association for the Education of
    Young Children
  Association for Children Education
    International

- What teachers deem relevant based on professional knowledge

Informal sources:

- What children like and express interest in
- What the parents and families consider relevant
- What the community considers important
- Local, national, and global events and incidents
- What is culturally and socially valued

Let's Talk About . . . 4–4

The Cycle of Teaching and Learning

Bredekamp and Rosegrant (1992) identified the process for teaching young children as a cycle of teaching and learning behaviors. They stated four essential behaviors children and teacher perform. The cycle is a helpful instrument to plan and design child-appropriate experiences. As you examine the four behaviors, think about the behaviors you and your class exhibit.

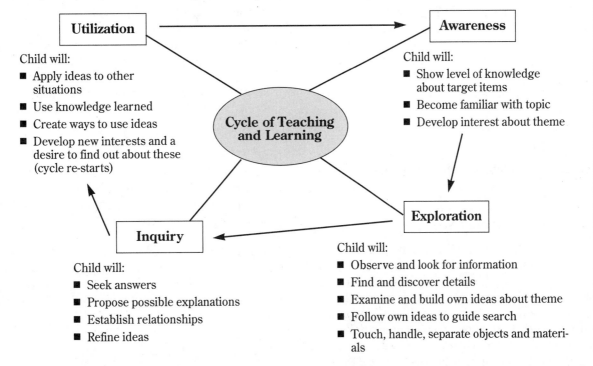

Utilization

Child will:
■ Apply ideas to other situations
■ Use knowledge learned
■ Create ways to use ideas
■ Develop new interests and a desire to find out about these (cycle re-starts)

Awareness

Child will:
■ Show level of knowledge about target items
■ Become familiar with topic
■ Develop interest about theme

Cycle of Teaching and Learning

Inquiry

Child will:
■ Seek answers
■ Propose possible explanations
■ Establish relationships
■ Refine ideas

Exploration

Child will:
■ Observe and look for information
■ Find and discover details
■ Examine and build own ideas about theme
■ Follow own ideas to guide search
■ Touch, handle, separate objects and materials

Source: Adapted from Bredekamp, S., & Rosegrant, T. (Eds.) (1992). *Reaching potentials: Appropriate curriculum and assessment for young children* (Vol. 1). Washington, DC: National Association for the Education of Young Children, p. 33.

Because of its long-range targets, unit planning differs from daily planning in several ways. Units are based on specified goals that serve as the framework for what children will experience. Unlike lesson plans, unit plans list a range of *suggested* activities rather than the specific activities found in daily plans. There are two main reasons for this. One is the fact that it is hard to predict what activities will actually be needed a week or two later. When teaching young children, nobody can predict the exact direction a thematic study will take! A second reason is that it is difficult to predict the children's level of interest. Because the success of a unit study depends on the interest of children and on its flexibility to incorporate other dimensions, teachers can only outline general activities that will likely happen. Needless to say, that flexibility also needs to exist when planning daily experiences. Resource and materials indicated in units are usually not as specific as in a lesson plan. Again, many other resources can be added or needed as the unit unfolds. Also, when planning units, teachers commonly include a list of

Concept Box 4–4 Key Differences Between Daily Lessons and Units	
Daily Lessons	**Units**
short range	long range
topic- or skill-based	theme-based
implicit goals	specific goals
specific objectives	specific objectives
specific activities	suggested activities
specific materials	suggested materials
adaptations	suggested adaptations
specific evaluation activities	specific evaluation activities
no bibliographical list	list of bibliographical resources

references and bibliographical materials pertaining to the area of study.

Selecting a Planning Strategy

The selection of which planning strategy to use is, in fact, a very personal decision. Some teachers prefer daily or weekly planning. With the emphasis on thematic teaching (organizing several lessons around a theme), many teachers like to plan units. A word of caution, though, when planning units. Best practices tell us that when working with young children, it is best to set your targets no more than two weeks ahead.

Knowledge about children's learning styles reminds us that there are times when a topic will certainly spur their interest for an extended period of time. However, there are other times when, despite the apparent child-appropriateness of a topic, their interest might extinguish much sooner. This commonly happens when analysis of the topics chosen is seen from only one point of view.

To avoid falling into the trap of choosing topics children will lose interest in, early childhood educators Elizabeth Jones and John Nimmo (1994), authors of the *Emergent Curriculum,* recommend considering the perspective of both teachers and children. We suggest adding the perspectives of the

community and the children's families, too. Keeping in mind that there are many sources for building a good curriculum, Jones and Nimmo find it is important to consider what each side values as relevant or interesting. When teachers look at a topic from a variety of perspectives, a series of important areas will emerge. Skills and key concepts will be identified by teachers, as well as possible subtopics related to the main topic chosen. By using **webbing** as a key planning tool to brainstorm different areas and possibilities that exist, teachers can find a variety of learning avenues to take (Jones & Nimmo, 1994).

Although a child-appropriate curriculum emerges from both teachers and children, responsibility for the selection and planning, as well as for setting directions about what it is to be examined, remains in the teachers' hands (Katz & Chard, 1989; Jones & Nimmo, 1994). As a professional, the teacher has the responsibility of guiding children in exploring what is deemed valid and worth learning.

Good planning requires teachers to know with precision what their prior knowledge and opinions are about the topic or theme selected. Remember, *how you feel* about a topic and *how much you know* about it will directly affect your approach to it. Once your perspective as a teacher has been established, consideration of how children would look at the

---

Bringing Ideas into Practice 4–1
Planning for Success

As you get ready to teach about a particular topic, consider:

■ How much do I know about the topic or concept?

■ Have I taught it before?

■ What do I know (factually) about it?

■ Do I have any direct or related experiences with this topic or concept?

■ How do I personally feel teaching about it?

■ What resources do I have?

■ Do I know where to find information and related materials?

topic comes next. How children feel and what they know about it determines the way to approach its exploration in class. Considering the teacher's and the children's views about a topic in advance provides a more realistic outlook. It also leads to a more meaningful selection of experiences.

Webbing the ideas children have about a topic offers a good profile of the ways children perceive the topic and ideas related to it. It also establishes the prior knowledge they have in reference to what is proposed to be learned (Gamberg, Kwak, Hutchings, Altheim, & Edwards, 1989). When these ideas are melded together, a realm of valid possibilities to explore can be discovered (see Figure 4–8, p. 92).

Lesson planning can take many other formats besides webbing. Some teachers prefer a detailed lesson plan in which specific information about objectives and materials is presented; others prefer more simple ways. Although planning is a very personal activity, less experienced teachers tend to benefit from more detailed planning. In the next section, suggestions for planning and organizing social studies activities will be discussed.

■■ Getting Ready to Plan
■■ Social Studies Experiences:
   Using the DAP Perspective

Developmentally appropriate practices (DAP) (NAEYC, 1997) is the concept (see Chapter 3) that defines the paradigm of quality in early childhood programs today. Conceptualized to serve as a set of guidelines for programs, DAP outlines and recommends practices for teaching and working with young children from birth to age eight. The DAP philosophy and approach apply to all areas of services for children. In curricular areas, DAP defines the principles to follow as learning experiences are planned (Bredekamp & Rosegrant, 1995; Bredekamp & Copple, 1997).

As you get ready to plan social studies experiences, it is essential to review the key tenets of DAP. They will serve as guideposts for your planning.

**Effective Developmental Planning
Happens When There Is . . .**

Knowledge about children's
developmental characteristics
(*what they are ready for developmentally*)

+

Knowledge about children's interests
(*what children enjoy exploring and learning about*)

+

Knowledge about what is both pertinent
and culturally relevant
(*what is sound and worth learning;
what is significant in their environment*)

+

Knowledge about appropriate instructional
practices and strategies
(*what helps to convey ideas and engage
children in learning*)

Central to the concept of DAP is the role of development as a key characteristic of the early childhood years. According to Bredekamp and Copple, "developmentally appropriate practice is based on the knowledge about how children develop and learn" (1997, p. 9). Knowledge about child development informs all levels of services geared toward children. Across a broad range of programs, from instructional programs to food and nutrition programs, DAP delineates *what to expect*. DAP expectations and practices are based upon three key types of knowledge about children:

1. **Knowledge about general child development and learning principles.** Universal child developmental milestones such as the ones listed in Chapter 3 describe approximate age-based expectations in the different developmental domains. Appropriate expectations can be used to help predict age-related characteristics and behaviors (physical, social, cognitive, linguistic) as well as needs of children.

2. **Knowledge about the individual child.** Specific developmental information about individual

children informs educators about the unique characteristics and factors embodied by each child within the group.

3. **Knowledge about the social and cultural environments of the child** defines and recognizes the influence of the immediate worlds children live in. This knowledge informs teachers and other professionals about the variations in experiences and ideas children have and acknowledges the importance of families and the culture in development.

(Bredekamp & Copple, 1997, p. 9)

DAP dimensions are directly related to the goals of social studies programs. In fact, the key tenets of the DAP philosophy are embedded in effective social studies experiences. Meaningful learning occurs only when consideration of what is specifically unique and characteristic of children, along with acknowledgement of their cultural milieu, is added to general developmental knowledge.

Applying the DAP Dimensions to Classroom Planning and Teaching: General Considerations

Planning social studies with a DAP perspective requires educators to consider the three knowledge dimensions as instructional decisions are made. A DAP perspective on planning contributes to quality child-centered experiences. It also outlines the need for educators to apply professional knowledge in day-to-day classroom practices and to become fully cognizant of the children they teach. As teachers get ready to implement a DAP perspective, it is important to remember two important aspects: *First,* knowledge about child development is constantly evolving, which implies a need to keep ourselves abreast of new research in the field. *Second,* family and social characteristics are dynamic, thus what is known about a child's environment today may not hold true tomorrow.

Familiarity with general developmental milestones is central to well-informed instructional decisions. Keeping a list of milestones handy (see Chapter 3) will help teachers clarify appropriate ex-

---

■■ **Let's Talk About . . . 4–5**

Guidelines for Decisions about Developmentally Appropriate Practices

According to the NAEYC (Bredekamp & Copple, 1997), there are five interrelated points defining quality in early childhood practices. As you read them, keep in mind that they also reflect the aims of teaching in early childhood social studies classrooms:

■ A caring and inclusive community of learners.

■ Teaching with the purpose of enhancing development and learning.

■ Development and use of an age-appropriate curriculum.

■ Use of assessment to foster development and learning.

■ Positive interactions and relationships with families.

Consider the following:

1. How many of these characteristics already define your teaching?

2. Which of these characteristics are directly related to social studies education?

3. Visit a classroom or two and see how many of these elements are easy to observe. Report your findings in class.

---

pectations. It will also serve to alert us to individual variations.

It is equally important to profile the families and the community where we teach. This information will prove essential as we try to establish meaningful and valuable learning experiences.

There are many ways in which teachers can apply the three DAP knowledge dimensions into classroom planning. You are encouraged to develop your own. For your reference, a sample *DAP Thematic Planning Grid* is presented in Figure 4–6. Essentially a questionnaire, the grid applies the essence of DAP to the planning process. The questionnaire helps to establish activities that are engaging and

FIGURE 4–6 DAP Thematic Planning Grid

Theme: _____   Age level: _____

1. **How do I know that children are ready to learn/explore this theme? What experiences would engage them in learning?** (*General development/learning dimension*)

   Comments:

2. **What will children gain from this topic?**

   Comments:

3. **What adaptations do I need to make?** (*Individual dimension*)

   Adaptations (List the materials, activities):

4. **In what way does the theme reflect the children's cultural and social environment? How can it be made more meaningful culturally?** (*Social/Cultural dimension*)

   Adaptations/Changes (Materials, activities)

"worth learning" for children. As you will see, it takes into account the three knowledge dimensions as a theme is selected. Decisions are made based on consideration of the general characteristics of children, yet accommodations for individual variation are also made.

Selecting Strategies for Teaching Social Studies

Effective learning depends on the proper selection of teaching strategies and techniques. **Teaching strategies** are essentially ways to bring the content of any discipline into the classroom in an engaging and child-appropriate manner. A teaching strategy defines a long-range approach aimed at helping children build knowledge around a specific topic. You probably have learned that **teaching techniques** are also used to engage the class in studying a topic. Techniques are the "day-to-day teaching activities" (Welton & Mallan, 1976, p. 159) teachers use to present the content. Essentially,

teachers select strategies as they make long-range plans for teaching a specific theme or topic; they also select techniques as they plan what will happen daily in the classroom.

Role-playing experiences are central to social learning.

FIGURE 4–7 A conceptual scheme for a progression from non-directive to directive teaching strategies

NON-DIRECTIVE ↕	**Recognize** (needs, interests, abilities)
	Model (behaviors, concepts, skills)
	Facilitate (learning)
MEDIATING ↕	**Encourage** (provide support)
	Scaffold (learning)
	Participate (collaborate with learners)
DIRECTIVE	**Present** (concepts, skills)
	Guide (learning)

Source: Adapted from Bredekamp, S., & Rosegrant, T. (1992). Teaching continuum. In *Reaching potentials: Appropriate curriculum and assessment for young children,* Vol. 1. Washington, DC: National Association for the Education of Young Children, p. 21.

from the directive to the non-directive style. Decisions about when to use a style in the continuum are based on teachers' observations of what children are already capable of performing.

Deciding what strategy to use starts with what we know about children. Knowledge about how children learn tells us that young children are essentially in three cognitive stages (Piaget, 1952): *sensorimotor, preoperational,* and entering into the *concrete-operational stage* (see Chapter 3, p. 54). Although children are in three different stages, here the element in common is the need to offer concrete experiences and opportunities to interact with what is explored.

There are many strategies and techniques available to introduce children to curricular content. In the social studies in particular, the menu of strategies is quite abundant. However, when teaching social studies to young children, determination of *which methods* to use demands special attention. It is important to point out that to select and rely on the use of a single teaching strategy is not an appropriate decision (Bredekamp & Rosegrant, 1995).

Appropriate practices establish the importance of using a variety of teaching strategies and techniques, all based on what best suits children at specific times. Bredekamp and Rosegrant (1995) identified a spectrum of developmental teaching techniques, defined as a *continuum of teaching behaviors* (p. 21). Figure 4–7 illustrates a list of possible teacher/student roles as teaching progresses

---

■■ Let's Talk About . . . 4–6

Sample Teaching Strategies and Techniques

When it comes to deciding how to interest children in a topic, there are many ways to do it. A list of commonly used strategies and techniques for sharing content with children appears below. Place a checkmark next to those you already know and use:

■ **Techniques (daily activities)**

___ role-playing   ___ group discussions
___ games   (small and large)
___ simulations   ___ field trips

■ **Strategies (long-range approaches)**

___ whole language   ___ individualized
      instruction   instruction
___ learning centers   ___ large group
___ thematic teaching   instruction
___ projects   ___ cooperative learning

1. How many other strategies and techniques could you add?

2. Are the ones listed here appropriate for young children?

3. From this list, which ones do you prefer/like the least? Why?

Selection of appropriate strategies and techniques must be based on the cognitive characteristics of children. It is also based on the individual knowledge teachers have about children. In this section we will explore and discuss some of the issues entailed in the process of building an appropriate and successful social studies curriculum.

A Sampler of Appropriate Teaching Strategies

Teaching social studies to young children is both an exciting and demanding challenge. Because of the unique characteristics of children at this age level, classroom teaching strategies need to be specially selected. Three key developmentally appropriate strategies will be described in this section: 1) integrated/thematic teaching, 2) the project approach, and 3) learning centers. There are many other strategies that also apply when teaching young children. They will be explained throughout the book. You are encouraged to explore them as well.

■■ Thematic Teaching: ■■ The Key Strategy for Child-Appropriate Social Studies Classroom Experiences

Someone once said the social studies curriculum includes "everything that exists and relates to people." If we believe that statement is true, there are endless themes to explore and learn about. It also means that the only way to explore everything related to people is by looking at events as a whole. Needless to say, social studies offers ample opportunities to engage children in truly interesting, real-life experiences. **Thematic teaching** is a strategy used to reflect the integrated view of life that people have. In the early childhood classroom, thematic teaching offers opportunities to build a child-appropriate curriculum around integrated topics from a variety of subject areas and experiences. Best practices in childhood education endorse the use of inte-

grated teaching practices, the heart of thematic teaching.

Why Social Studies Teachers Should Use an Integrated Approach

Why use an integrated curriculum? Developmentally appropriate practice (Bredekamp, 1987; Bredekamp & Rosegrant, 1992; Bredekamp & Copple, 1997) establishes the use of an integrated curriculum as the responsive strategy when teaching young children. In the revised edition of *Developmentally Appropriate Practice in Early Childhood Education Programs,* Bredekamp and Copple state that a child-appropriate curriculum is based on integration of subject matters:

> Curriculum includes a broad range of content across disciplines that is socially relevant, intellectually engaging, and personally meaningful to children. . . .

> Effective curriculum plans frequently integrate across traditional subject-matter divisions to help children make meaningful connections and provide opportunities for rich conceptual development.
> (Bredekamp & Copple, 1997, p. 20)

The key to appropriate teaching is the emphasis on the integrated nature of the social studies—the aspect that responds to the way children learn and build ideas about their world. It is important to remember that young children do not build knowledge in isolated pieces, but rather as the result of their total participation in a meaningful experience (Bredekamp, 1987). Simply stated, this means children will not learn about any of the disciplines embedded in the social studies if they are taught in isolation. In the early childhood classroom, activities are not planned solely on one area such as history or geography. In fact, it is inappropriate to design a curriculum for young children in which learning is segmented into separate subjects (Bredekamp & Copple, 1997). Appropriate developmental practices demand integrated planning and teaching. This same principle applies to the teaching of the social studies curriculum. An integrated, developmentally

---

Bringing Ideas into Practice 4–2
Effective Teacher Behaviors for Successful Integrated Teaching in the Early Childhood Social Studies Classroom

1. Teachers possess current knowledge about child development principles and about the content and purposes of the social studies curriculum.
2. Teachers are cognizant of current events in the community, nation, the world. They look for opportunities to integrate current events into the classroom.
3. Time is dedicated to *learning and reflecting* about:
   - the interests and needs of children,
   - the characteristics of children's families, and
   - the characteristics of the community/neighborhood.
4. Teachers select topics that address and respond to areas of interests to children.
5. Teachers constantly search and review their materials and resources.
6. Teachers assess children's responses and reactions to what is explored and keep track of their progress.

---

appropriate approach to teaching history and geography will be explored in the next two chapters.

Integrated teaching is aimed at responding to the nature of children's learning. When teaching young children, the challenge of building a good curriculum rests on reminding ourselves that our efforts are intended to serve children, and not to just cover a list of topics. As Jones and Nimmo (1994) say, we must remember that *"in early childhood education, curriculum isn't the focus; children are"* (emphasis added, p. 12).

Elements of Thematic Teaching

Thematic teaching is an excellent strategy teachers can use to build an interesting, challenging, and meaningful curriculum. The most important characteristic of integrated or thematic teaching is that it helps children to "make sense of their world" (Mitchell & David, 1992, p. 145). Carefully selected themes will engage an entire class in short- and long-term, productive explorations. Thematic teaching is a flexible strategy that uses a variety of sources to build the curriculum. Various kinds of knowledge are considered by teachers when building thematic curricula:

- knowledge about the social studies
- knowledge from the different subject areas
- knowledge about child how children develop and learn
- knowledge about children and their families
- knowledge about the community and neighborhood
- knowledge about daily classroom, school, and life experiences

How do we engage in thematic teaching? There are several elements:

1. The first element is for teachers to be fully aware of the children's needs and interests—what will spark their interests and what will benefit them. A good way to start is to list possible themes children would enjoy exploring. A list of themes can be built from the following sources: *age-appropriate knowledge, themes defined by school curricula,* and *community and culturally related themes.* (See Concept Box 4–3, p. 82.)
2. Selection of the theme to be studied is a crucial element. Successful selection of a theme is at the heart of successful experiences. Roberts and Kellough (1996) recommend critiquing the themes before making a final decision. They suggest six different criteria themes should comply with:
   a. **Length of time:** Is the theme broad enough to be studied over a period of time?
   b. **Value:** Is the theme worth studying? What will children gain from it?
   c. **Application to life:** Does the theme provide for a broad application and for application in real life?
   d. **Teacher knowledge about the theme:** Is this theme related to my experiences?

e. **Active learning/child-appropriateness:** Does this theme provide opportunities for active learning? Will the theme hold its interest for children?

f. **Resources:** Do I have an abundance of materials and resources to support its exploration? (Roberts & Kellough, 1996, p. 35)

3. Clear determination of how much interest and how much children know about the theme is the next element. Before making a final selection of a theme, take time to prepare a web or concept map. **Concept maps** or **webs** are a helpful way to get a pictorial description of what children know and want to learn about (Mitchell & David, 1992). Concept maps are formed through informal discussions in which children present the knowledge, graphically, they have about the theme. Roberts and Kellough (1996) suggest saving concept maps built before the theme is explored. According to these authors, concept maps should be revisited periodically during each unit as well as at the end. Periodic checks offer ways to determine children's progress and the directions that the concepts being built will take.

Thematic teaching also demands that teachers know themselves—their own interests, knowledge about subject matters, and experiences. This knowledge helps develop teaching activities based on the teacher's strengths. It also alerts teachers to what they need to learn about a theme before teaching it. (See "Planning for Success," p. 84.)

4. Identifying the opportunities for integration each theme offers is central to thematic teaching. This is where the real value of thematic and integrated teaching is found. Once a theme has been chosen, it is important to know what subject matter, as well as which developmental domains, the theme incorporates, in order to plan related experiences (Figure 4–8).

5. Selection of resources and materials available is essential for the successful implementation of thematic learning. An inventory of resources available will prove helpful in planning specific experiences. It should include a variety of instructional resources and materials (e.g., dolls, books, maps, blocks, artifacts and costumes). People are also an excellent resource. Consider those individuals from the school, parents, and other members of the family and community who are familiar with the theme and include these people among your resources. Technology, such as Internet and multimedia resources, should also be considered as sources of quality teaching materials.

6. Outline an appealing introductory experience as well other possible experiences. A tentative plan of activities helps teachers to set initial directions. As children become immersed in the theme, observations of what they enjoy exploring will lead into the specific experiences. Rather than following a pre-established set of activities, observe and respond to the children's interests when planning classroom experiences. In thematic teaching, there are many times when interests will deviate into areas perhaps not even imagined by teachers (see Classroom Portrait, p. 71). Remember, flexibility is a key characteristic of thematic teaching.

7. Involvement of parents and family members in what children are exploring is an important element to bear in mind. Communications can be sent home describing what children will be engaged in. Periodic notes can be sent home to share how each child's interest and activities are progressing. Class work can be exhibited in the classroom for parents to see as they visit the school. Samples can be sent home with children.

8. Keeping track of progress is essential. A journal can be used to record activities as they unfold. Portfolios of children's work also document their progress.

9. Evaluation of the process and the progress accomplished by children is an indispensable element. Ongoing assessment should take place. Use of checklists, anecdotal records, photographs, and samples of children's work helps to track the course of the theme being studied. Culminating experiences should be planned. An example of a culminating experience is to build a

FIGURE 4–8 A Sample Web of Integrated Topics

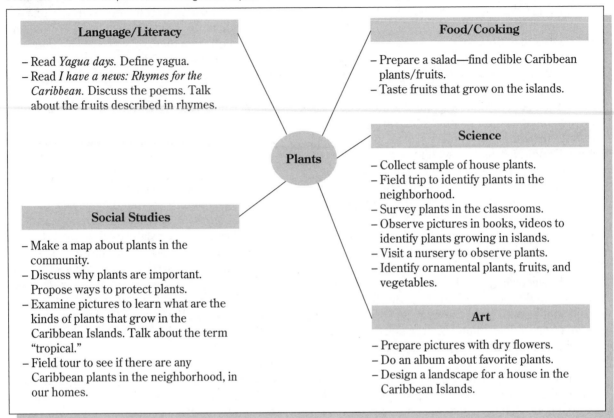

Language/Literacy

– Read *Yagua days*. Define yagua.
– Read *I have a news: Rhymes for the Caribbean*. Discuss the poems. Talk about the fruits described in rhymes.

Food/Cooking

– Prepare a salad—find edible Caribbean plants/fruits.
– Taste fruits that grow on the islands.

Plants

Science

– Collect sample of house plants.
– Field trip to identify plants in the neighborhood.
– Survey plants in the classrooms.
– Observe pictures in books, videos to identify plants growing in islands.
– Visit a nursery to observe plants.
– Identify ornamental plants, fruits, and vegetables.

Social Studies

– Make a map about plants in the community.
– Discuss why plants are important. Propose ways to protect plants.
– Examine pictures to learn what are the kinds of plants that grow in the Caribbean Islands. Talk about the term "tropical."
– Field tour to see if there are any Caribbean plants in the neighborhood, in our homes.

Art

– Prepare pictures with dry flowers.
– Do an album about favorite plants.
– Design a landscape for a house in the Caribbean Islands.

new concept map that will graphically demonstrate knowledge acquired. A comparison of concept maps made at the beginning and at the end contributes to an objective assessment of the progress achieved.

Advantages of Thematic Teaching

Thematic teaching has many advantages. One advantage is the opportunity it provides to accommodate the different needs of children. It particularly provides for children with special needs and those with linguistic and cultural differences. Adap-

tations required for children with specific physical and developmental needs are easily made. For instance, for children with visual impairments, books in Braille, recorded on audio tapes, or with large print can be added to the classroom materials.

Themes selected can also be used to explore the ways and behaviors of children's cultures (see Chapter 9). Opportunities for culturally and linguistically different children to share their knowledge abound through thematic teaching. An analysis of each theme selected will tell teachers how to incorporate experiences from the different cultures represented in their classrooms. Children can share and guide their peers as they learn words, phrases, songs, and dances from their cultures and languages.

The Project Approach

The **project approach** is another child-appropriate teaching strategy. Based on the early ideas of Dewey and Kirkpatrick (cited in Roopnarine, 1992), this strategy organizes teaching around children's expressed interests. These interests are shared by children and identified by the teacher, who helps children transform their initial areas of interests into projects extending over a period of time. A project is defined as "an in-depth study of a particular topic that one or more children undertake" (Katz & Chard, 1989, p. 2). According to Katz and Chard, projects are one of the most child-appropriate teaching strategies. They claim the appropriateness of the project approach stems from the opportunities it provides for children to engage in personal and meaningful learning. Simply stated, "[The project approach] emphasizes children's active participation in their own studies" (Katz & Chard, 1989). Open to the ideas and questions children have, projects serve to build a flexible curricula, based on children's experiences with the real world.

Projects respond to the interests of all children. Activities can engage a whole class, a small group, or individual children. Projects can extend over time periods ranging from as short as one week to as long as several months (Chard, 1998). Typically, in a class following the project approach, one or more projects are explored at a same time. Serving as facilitators, teachers support children's interests and help to organize their interests into viable investigations. Teachers also help to identify materials and resources pertinent to each topic being explored. Constant interaction between teachers and children helps children to clarify doubts and set new directions.

A project can begin as a result of the expressed interests of a child or a group of children, or it can also combine the interests of both children and teachers. An example of a project started out of the interests of children is the *Pet Project* (Keller, 1998). Describing how she got the idea for the project, Keller says, "I observed the children discussing pets. The children would initiate the topic almost daily. I decided there was a definite interest in pets" (p. 1). Having observed their interests, Keller encouraged her group of four- to six-year-olds (in which six of the 12 children had developmental delays) to undertake the project. For five weeks, her class shared experiences about their own pets, made a list of animals they would like to have as classroom pets, visited a pet store, set up a fish tank, and talked about death after one of their fish died. Sharing her thoughts about the class experiences, Keller says, "I have enjoyed going through the journey with my class. I was amazed at how much they would remember from week to week. Also, [at] how their excitement continued to build" (p. 3).

Similar in some aspects to thematic teaching, projects begin with the selection of a key topic. Selection of appropriate topics is made by both children and teachers. A good topic is usually chosen when the following areas are considered (Katz & Chard, 1989, pp. 65–66):

1. activities and experiences familiar to children
2. the local community
3. current events
4. places near and far
5. things related to natural phenomena
6. topics suggested by children

Determining the best criteria for choosing an appropriate topic is a key concern in the project approach. Dearden's four criteria (cited by Katz & Chard, 1989, p. 68) for the selection of topics emphasize paying attention to the following aspects:

■ What is the immediate applicability of the topic to children?
■ How will the topic contribute to a balanced school curriculum?
■ How will the topic help to build relevant lifelong knowledge for children?
■ What is the importance of studying this topic in the classroom?

Projects are developed in three phases (Katz & Chard, 1989; Chard, 1998). *Planning and getting started* is phase one. Here teachers do their preliminary planning and set the rationale for what is about to become a project.

Projects in progress is phase two. Here children are introduced to the topic. For example, in *The School Building Project* (Wilson, 1998), teachers took second graders to visit different places in their school. They also visited the school bus and interviewed its driver. They looked at an old school yearbook, where they learned how their school had been built fifteen years earlier.

Reflections and conclusions is the last phase. At this point, the objective is to culminate the project, both for the group and for individual children. Application of what has been learned depends on the group's age level. Katz and Chard (1989) state that for younger children, ages three through five, culminating experiences include project constructions and role-playing.

An example of a culminating experience with a group of four- and five-year-olds is reported by teacher Paddi Towne (1998). Working with a project around the grocery store, children concluded their project by building a grocery store in their classroom. Towne says the store the children built reflected what they had learned. Through their role-play at the store, the group re-enacted the series of events they had experienced. Reflecting on the children's and her own experience, Towne (p. 2) concluded, "Most importantly, we learned to share, cooperate, listen, and be creative."

This "classroom restaurant" promotes learning of economic concepts.

velopmentally appropriate way to organize and arrange the classroom (Bredekamp & Copple, 1997). A social studies learning center can be defined as "a child-centered, exploratory way to get children involved in self-directed, autonomous behavior" (Ellis, 1995, p. 100). Each center is aimed at representing a different and child-meaningful aspect of life (Isbell, 1995). When appropriately designed, centers offer unlimited opportunities to engage children in direct exploration of life itself. A classroom arranged in centers is like an attractive menu that children can examine. Freedom to choose what to explore and discover is what also

■■ Learning Centers:
■■ A Creative Approach
to Social Studies Learning

Learning centers are an effective and child-appropriate strategy. In essence, learning centers are areas in the classroom specifically designed to meet the needs of young children and encourage them to acquire independent understanding of concepts (see Concept Box 4–5, p. 96). They are a de-

---

Bringing Ideas into Practice 4–3
Learning Centers—a Concept with Many Names

At times people get confused about learning centers. They might believe someone is following a different teaching strategy just because the term used is different. We have found that there are at least four terms used to designate learning centers:

- learning areas
- interest areas
- learning stations
- centers

makes this strategy a child-appropriate one (Ellis, 1995; Bredekamp, 1987).

Types of Learning Centers

Social studies learning centers are known for being a very creative way to develop essential social studies knowledge. A variety of materials can be used to build new centers. Learning centers can be designed around numerous themes and include a wide and imaginative variety of materials:

- **Reference Centers:** informational books, atlases, maps; informational materials such as brochures and magazines; computer programs, computers with Internet access
- **Travel Center:** pictures and posters of different places; used airplane, train, bus tickets; different types of clothing according to climate; suitcases; diaries; postcards from different places; souvenirs from other countries
- **What's New? Center:** newspapers; clippings about recent local, national, and world events; magazines; pictures about people in the news; videos; books related to current events
- **Neighborhood/Community Places Center:** a bank, restaurant, or a grocery store
- **Before and Now Center:** artifacts such as cooking pots or implements; replicas of old cars, ships; photographs of parents and relatives when they were younger; old photographs of means of transportation, schools, houses, or other places in the community; old pieces of clothing and accessories
- **Geography Center:** maps, world globe, reference books, posters, photographs of places, measurement tools, drawing and graph paper, replicas of famous places, cameras
- **Around the World Center:** world map and globe, signs in different languages, books about other countries, dolls representing different ethnicities, tape player and cassettes with music from other places, stamps from different parts of the world, writing materials to create messages and letters for other children
- **Seasonal Centers:** transitional centers organized around events and the expressed interests of children

Organizing effective learning centers depends on two essential elements: 1) knowledge about the children and 2) knowledge about the purposes of centers in the classroom. As in other types of preparation, planning a learning center begins by reviewing what we know about the group of children one teaches. Developmental levels and specific characteristics, such as impairments, cultural differences, and community characteristics, must be considered. It is also important to keep in mind the interest level and meaningfulness the center will have for the class. Together, these elements serve as the framework for the center to be.

The next consideration is clarity about the purposes to be pursued through the center. Successful learning centers happen when objectives are set. Although learning centers are aimed at encouraging children to explore and respond to materials, their existence depends on the general and specific objectives established by teachers. Once a theme for a learning center has being identified, objectives are defined (see p. 76). Knowledge about the objectives pursued helps early childhood teachers know what materials to select and include, as well as to set appropriate expectations. Clarity about a center's purposes guides teachers in what to observe as chil-

Learning centers are based on various themes.

Concept Box 4–5   Learning Centers

Learning centers are specified areas set up for children where children can become involved in activities designed to encourage independent understanding of concepts. According to Van Lue (1996), through activities in a learning center, children:

- learn skills emphasized through error-free activities.
- practice skills at an individualized level.
- discover, explore, and investigate with concepts and alternative problem-solving strategies.
- learn by doing.
- are encouraged to express feelings and ideas.
- demonstrate their creativity and divergent ways of thinking.
- think well of themselves when their ideas and ways are appreciated by others.
- learn each person has different ideas and methods of expression and problem solving.
- develop social skills, including self-control and learning to work cooperatively with others.
- are encouraged to elaborate on concepts and themes.
- are supported through encouragement and engagement.
- integrate and transfer learning from other content areas.
- have opportunities to develop necessary prerequisite skills.

Source: Van Lue, E. (1996, September). *Interest areas: Who, what, where, how, and why?* Paper presented at annual conference of the Early Childhood Association of Florida, Orlando, FL.

---

dren respond and react to materials. Through informed observations, teachers monitor the progress achieved, both individually and as a group. Observations also allow teachers to detect the existing level of interest the center still evokes from children.

Advantages of Learning Centers

Among the many advantages to using learning centers, it is important to highlight their value for individual and social development. In social studies, the use of learning centers provides opportunities for both individual and group work. Different children can satisfy their own interests while using the same objects and materials. Primarily, this is a strategy that benefits the individual child. Designed to serve as an area where children are challenged as individuals, the learning center values the ideas children have. Learning centers emphasize ways children can express their own approaches and solutions, free from the risk of competition with others. Children learn that their ideas are accepted and considered; this fosters a sense of self-value.

Careful selection of materials and activities in learning centers encourages individual and divergent responses. In this way, centers provide for the many individual and valuable ways of learning children have (Gardner, 1993).

Centers also encourage development of social skills by inviting social interaction and providing opportunities for small group participation. As children work in pairs or in small groups, they can develop many essential social skills, such as cooperation, sharing of materials, taking turns, listening to others, working together to complete a task, and respecting the ideas of others.

Another advantage of learning centers is the opportunity they offer to balance and enliven the menu of classroom activities. When some centers have a rotating character, classrooms can be transformed as the children's interests change. Knowledge about both children and social studies purposes will guide teachers to make decisions about what kind of centers to include in the classroom.

Still another advantage of learning centers is their adaptability to the characteristics of the children served. Modifications to learning centers can be easily made to accommodate and include children with special needs. For example, in classrooms that include children with visual impairments, books with large print, tape-recorded books, or books in Braille can be added to the reference center.

■■ Technology in the Classroom

Today, modern technology is recognized as a valuable and essential educational resource. Technology provides teachers with the means to add new strategies to their teaching repertoire. The educational technology resources now available are especially important in the social studies curriculum. This is especially true of the latest interactive inventions that can be brought into the classroom.

Technology is an especially valuable resource for young children. When materials are carefully selected and used with the collaboration and interaction of adults and children, television, computers, and cybercommunication provide an almost endless number of sources that can expand the child's learning experiences.

Television

Television is one of the more commonly used technologies in the classroom. Television is a window to society and to the world that almost everyone in this country watches, including young children. Unfortunately, television programming often includes negative and violent portrayals of events and individuals. As a result, it is not unusual to observe children imitating the behaviors and responses of characters in the media, whom they also use as role models. This dangerous trend has caused advocates for children like the NAEYC to issue position statements about the effects of television on young children and its proper use (NAEYC, 1990).

Nonetheless, despite criticism, television provides many benefits for young children. When adults carefully select what children will view and when adults view television programs together with children, the benefits are optimal (Levin & Calsson-Paige, 1994).

For example, the Public Broadcasting System (PBS) provides several age-appropriate children's series, some of which are suitable for preschoolers. The Discovery Channel and the History Channel also provide interesting children's programs. Documentaries and special programs produced by organizations like the National Geographic Society, often transmitted by several different stations, can also be of interest and value to students in the primary grades.

To foster child-appropriate use of television, teachers should:

■ Become familiar with the local television programming for children. Take time to watch these programs and identify those with content relevant to curricular experiences.
■ Keep a schedule of selected programs that relate to classroom topics.
■ Regularly send notes ("Special Programs on TV") to parents about recommended programs they can watch together with their children. Include suggestions for questions and activities to guide the viewing. This practice contributes to the meaning and the value of the experience.
■ Provide parents and family members with a description of the ratings for television programs.
■ Provide parents with suggested ways to use television at home.

Computers and the Internet

Computers have brought the global society into the information age. Having permeated business, governments, and industry, computers are becoming a common part of many households in our country and around the world. The dramatic increase in home computers has resulted in exposing young children to this technology very early in life. Use of a computer is recognized not only as an instructional element but as a necessary skill for all learners to master.

According to the International Society for Technology in Education (ISTE), successful social participation in the twenty-first century requires individuals to be technology literate. ISTE states that

FIGURE 4–9 Profile of the Technology-Literate Student (Pre-K through Grade 2)

A technology-literate student:

1. uses input and output devices to operate computers, videocassette recorders, audiotape players, and other electronic equipment successfully.
2. uses a variety of media and technology resources for direct and indirect learning activities.
3. communicates about technology using developmentally appropriate and accurate terminology.
4. uses developmentally appropriate multimedia resources (software, interactive books).
5. collaborates with others (i.e., shares materials, cooperates in activities) when using technology.
6. exhibits positive social behavior when using technology.
7. demonstrates responsible use of technology.
8. uses technology to create products (i.e., drawings or cards) with the support of the teacher, family, and peers.
9. uses technology materials for problem solving, communication, and to share and illustrate ideas.
10. uses technology (i.e., E-mail) to gather information and to communicate with others with the support of teachers, family members, and peers.

Source: International Society for Technology in Education (ISTE). (1998). *Profile for technology-literate students: Performance indicators* (Grades Pre-K through 2). Available on-line* at http://www.ISTE.org

*Please note that Internet resources are of a time-sensitive nature and URL sites and addresses may often be modified or deleted.

technological literacy begins during the early years (1998). ISTE has established student profiles specifying the performance behaviors for each grade from Pre-K through 12. Figure 4–9 describes the profile of a technology-literate student for grades Pre-K through 2. The profile provides guidelines teachers can use to select technology-related experiences to incorporate in the early childhood classroom. However, decisions as to what to select and include should always take into consideration the needs and characteristics of children. Appropriate practices suggest that use of computers should not become a substitute for concrete experiences. Good knowledge about each child will establish the best way to use computers. We would like to emphasize that it is important to assess what the child already knows about computers. Though many children are already familiar with computers, teachers should make provisions for those students who have had little or no experience with computers.

Computers in the classroom provide opportunities to learn and practice a variety of concepts. Many companies have produced play-based software and programs covering the different disciplines. With proper guidance from and interaction with adults, these programs can benefit children. Software should be selected carefully, especially when it is intended to be used with preschoolers. Several organizations offer suggestions for good age-appropriate software. Among these, Teacher Source (a section of PBS OnLine at http://www.pbs.org) has a detailed inventory of appropriate software for different subject areas, including social studies.

Computer-based instruction is now considered viable, but it is the impact of technology in the area of communications that has transformed society. Many different forms of telecommunications provide effective ways to keep in contact with the world. Use of the Internet has opened up opportunities to participate and collaborate with children and teachers anywhere in the world. Properly used, telecommunications is an exciting way to foster the concept of the "global village" to which we all belong.

ACTIVITIES

Keeping Track of What You Learn: Your Personal Activity Log

In this chapter, we have discussed many important ideas about curriculum planning and teaching strategies. To review and ponder what was discussed, here are some additional activities for your PAL.

A. Reflections

1. Based on the information in this chapter, list the most important attributes of an effective and relevant social studies curriculum for young children.
2. Review the national standards for social studies and contribute your own notions to them. You can make a whole new list or delete and add to the existing one.
3. Visit a school in an inner city and another one in an affluent suburb in your area and compare what the children in the same early grade are learning. Write an anecdotal record of it and include your conclusions.
4. Design an effective way to include the input from the community into the curriculum. Identify who could help you and how you would go about including them in curriculum planning.
5. Think of ways you could provide for individual and special needs of some children in teaching a thematic unit. Write your ideas down and add them to your resource file.

B. Collections

1. Design your ideal learning center, using a shadow box, storyboard, or a collage.
2. Make a big book of different concepts that may appeal to your children and have them review it and select what they want to study.

C. Internet Resources*

1. **Web Page of the National Child Care Information Center** (http://www.ericps.ed.uiuc.edu/nccic/nccichome.html) provides information about child development issues of interest to teachers and families. It has links to the ERIC database and to the *Child Care Bulletin,* which can be read on-line.
2. **American Forum for Global Education** (http://www.globaled.org) provides information about curricular projects and materials. The *Global Reporter* is an on-line forum where teachers can exchange ideas.
3. **ERIC Clearinghouse for Social Studies/Social Sciences CHESS** (http://www.indiana.edu/~ssdc/eric.chess.html). ERIC is the Educational Resources Information Center. This database about social studies resources and materials includes multiple links to key social studies organizations.
4. **International Society for Technology in Education.** (1998). Profiles for technology-literate students. Grades Pre-K through 2. Available at http://www.ISTE.org.

*Please note that Internet resources are of a time-sensitive nature and URL sites and addresses may often be modified or deleted.

References

Bloom, B. S. (Ed.). (1984). *Taxonomy of educational objectives. Book I: Cognitive domain*. White Plains, NY: Longman.

Bredekamp, S. (Ed.). (1987). *Developmentally appropriate practice in early childhood programs, serving children from birth through age 8*. Washington, DC: National Association for the Education of Young Children.

Bredekamp, S., & Copple, C. (1997). *Developmentally appropriate practice in early childhood programs*. (rev. ed.). Washington, DC: National Association for the Education of Young Children.

Bredekamp, S., & Rosegrant, T. (Eds.). (1992). *Reaching potentials: Appropriate curriculum and assessment for young children*, (Vol. 1). Washington, DC: National Association for the Education of Young Children, p. 33.

Bredekamp, S., & Rosegrant, T. (Eds.). (1995). *Reaching potentials: Transforming curriculum and assessment* (Vol. 2). Washington, DC: National Association for the Education of Young Children.

Chard, S. (1998, January 17). *Projects*. [On-line].* http://www.ualberta.ca/~schard.htm.

Eddowes, A., & Ralph, K. (1998). *Interactions for development and learning: Birth through eight years*. Upper Saddle River, NJ: Merrill.

Ellis, A. K. (1995). *Teaching and learning elementary social studies* (5th ed.). Boston, MA: Allyn and Bacon.

Feinburg, S., & Mindess, M. (1994). *Eliciting children's full potential: Designing and evaluating developmentally based programs for young children*. Pacific Grove, CA: Brooks/Cole.

Forman, G., & Kuschner, D. (1983). *The child's construction of knowledge: Piaget for teaching children*. Washington, DC: National Association for the Education of Young Children.

Gamberg, R., Kwak, W., Hutchings, M., Altheim, J., & Edwards, G. (1989). *Learning and loving it: Theme studies in the classroom*. Portsmouth, NH: Heinemann.

Gardner, H. (1993). *Frames of mind: The theory of multiple intelligences* (2nd ed.). New York: Basic Books.

International Society for Technology in Education. (1998). *Profile for technology-literate students: Performance indicators* (Grades Pre-K through 2). [On-line].* http://www.ISTE.org.

Isbell, R. (1995). *The complete learning center book*. Beltsville, MD: Gryphon House.

Isenberg, J., & Jalongo, M. R. (1997). *Creative expression and play in early childhood* (2nd ed.). Upper Saddle River, NJ: Merrill.

Jones, E., & Nimmo, J. (1994). *Emergent curriculum*. Washington, DC: National Association for the Education of Young Children.

Kamii, C. (Ed.). (1991). *Achievement testing in the early grades*. Washington, DC: National Association for the Education of Young Children.

Katz, L., & Chard, S. (1989). *Engaging children's minds: The project approach*. Norwood, NJ: Ablex.

Keller, K. (1998, January 17). *The pet project*. [On-line].* http://www.ualberta.ca/~schard/petfish.htm

Krogh, S. (1995). *The integrated early childhood curriculum* (2nd ed.). New York: McGraw-Hill.

Levin, D., & Calsson-Paige, N. (1994). Developmentally appropriate television: Putting children first. *Young Children, 49*(5), pp. 38–44.

Maxim, G. (1989). *The very young: Guiding children from infancy through the early years* (3rd ed.). Columbus, OH: Merrill.

Mitchell, A., & David, J. (Eds.). (1992). *Explorations with young children: A curriculum guide from the Bank Street College of Education*. Mt. Rainier, MD: Gryphon House.

National Association for the Education of Young Children (1990). NAEYC Position statement on media violence in children's lives. *Young Children, 45*(5), pp. 18–21.

National Association for the Education of Young Children. (1997). *Teaching and working with culturally and linguistically different children*. Washington, DC: Author.

National Commission on Social Studies in Schools. (1989). *Charting the course: Social studies for the 21st century*. Washington, DC: Author.

National Council for the Social Studies. (1994). *Expectations for excellence: Curriculum standards for social studies*. Bulletin 89. Washington, DC: Author.

Piaget, J. (1952). *The origins of intelligence in children*. New York: International Universities Press.

Roberts, P. L., & Kellough, R. D. (1996). *A guide for developing an interdisciplinary thematic unit*. New York: Merrill/Prentice Hall.

Robles de Melendez, W., & Ostertag, V. (1997). *Teaching young children in multicultural classrooms: Issues, concepts, and strategies*. Albany, NY: Delmar.

Roopnarine, J. L. (Ed.). (1992). *Approaches to early childhood education*. Upper Saddle River, NJ: Merrill.

Seefeldt, C., & Barbour, N. (1998). *Early childhood education: An introduction* (4th ed.). Upper Saddle River, NJ: Merrill.

Towne, P. (1998, January 28). *The grocery store*. [On-line].* http://ualberta.ca/~schard/grocdc.htm

Van Lue, E. (1996, September). *Interest areas: Who, what, where, how, and why?* Paper presented at annual conference of the Early Childhood Association of Florida, Orlando, FL.

Welton, D. A., & Mallan, J. T. (1976). *Children and their world: Teaching elementary social studies.* Chicago, IL: Rand McNally.

Welton, D. A., & Mallan, J. T. (1992). *Strategies for teaching social studies.* Boston: Houghton Mifflin.

Wilson, K. S. (1998, January 18). *The school building project.* [On-line].* http://ualberta.ca/~schard/school. htm

*Please note that Internet resources are of a time-sensitive nature and URL sites and addresses may often be modified or deleted.

CHAPTER 5

Learning about the Past and the Present: History and the Young Child

Historical memory is the key to self-identity, to seeing one's place in the stream of time, and one's connectedness with all of humankind.

—NATIONAL CENTER FOR HISTORY IN THE SCHOOLS (1994)

Chapter Questions

After reading this chapter you should be able to answer the following questions:

- What is the child's concept of time?
- What does developmental theory say about the child's ability to understand time?
- What is history?
- What are DAP strategies for teaching history in the early childhood classroom?

Key Terms and Concepts

artifacts
change
chronological thinking
chronology
dramatic activities
historical fiction
historical thinking

historical understanding
history
history education
oral history
recent past
time

Classroom Portrait: What Does It Mean to Be Old?

Ms. Lane's kindergarten class brought in old pictures today. Everyone was anxiously waiting to talk about his or her family and friends. All of a sudden Ms. Lane heard the sound of crying coming from the art center. As Ms. Lane approached the three children, she also heard a loud voice.

"That's not true!" Jimmy was shouting.

Yvonne was crying, while Viveca was getting ready to shove Jimmy. "Her daddy is not a little baby. I know him and he is very big!" said Viveca, in a very frustrated voice.

Jimmy looked at her, puzzled. "How come Yvonne says this is her daddy? This is a picture of a baby," he protested. "I have a baby sister and she is small like that."

By now Yvonne was trying to explain: "We have pictures in my house of my grandma, when she was also a baby. And Aunt Kathy has a picture of her on a bicycle just like mine."

"If you are small like us, you can't be a daddy or a mommy," argued Jimmy.

"You can, too! I have two Barbies, and I am their mommy," Viveca countered, in a belligerent voice. "And next week Shavon and I are getting married," she continued.

"You can't get married," protested Yvonne. "Only big people can get married."

"That's what I mean," said Jimmy. "This can't be your daddy; this is a baby."

Ms. Lane realized that the upcoming lesson about time was going to be very interesting.

■■ Developing a Sense of History

> Social studies programs should include experiences that provide for the study of the ways humans beings view themselves in and over time.
>
> (NCSS, 1994, p. 22)

We are sure that, like the children in the opening vignette, you have spent time looking at old family pictures. *"Is this really me?" "What are they wearing?" "Who is that?" "What are they doing?"* are the questions all of us have asked on these trips to nostalgia. Memories of good and not-so-happy events come to mind when we look back. Examining and remembering the past allows us to examine the present and gain a sense of who, what, and why we are. As each of us recalls various events of time past, we engage in history. **History** is the study of *what* and *why* people have achieved and done in the past (Hoge, 1996). History helps us to understand the reasons for the actions and the decisions made in the present. History also helps people learn about their roots and origins, about the ways of other people close and far away, and about the deeds that have transformed our lives and the lives of others.

History is one of the main areas of social studies education. Because history reflects all of what humanity has accomplished, it is one of the best exam-

Pretend play facilitates the development of the concept of time periods.

■■   **Let's Talk About . . . 5–1**

"You Mean We Have to Teach History?"

For many people, history is their least preferred subject. Many social studies and history educators contend that the problem stems from a lack of understanding of what history is. They point out that very few teachers recognize history as an active field, even define it as an area of little relevance to daily life. This may be one reason why inappropriate classroom approaches are often used in teaching history. Before you continue reading through this chapter, take time to think about your own perception of history. Talk to your colleagues or classmates regarding their experiences with and opinions of history, and find out what their views on teaching history are as well. Discuss the relevance of history to young children and how history could be integrated into the early childhood curriculum.

ies, arts, and even math. History lends itself to learning about life as a series of interrelated episodes, in which all elements directly affect one another. This is similar to what best practices state about the way young children learn: They see things as a whole, not just as bits and pieces (Bredekamp & Rosegrant, 1992). Chapters 5 through 10 will take a closer look at the ways these interrelated content areas can be brought into the social studies curriculum for young children.

The Need for History Education

You are a part of history—and you've already left many clues about yourself for the future.
                                    —Ira Wolfman (1991, p. 3)

Historical knowledge is essential to the survival of our society. "Without history, a society shares no common memory of where it has been, what its core values are, or what decisions of the past account for present circumstances" (National Center for History in the Schools [NCHS], 1994, p. 1). Knowledge about the past helps children to understand and interpret the present. When history is presented as an integrated field and not as a rote study of dates and facts, the events and patterns from the past become an exciting area to explore.

ples of integrated knowledge and a very special source for the curriculum. For example, the discovery of the Americas integrates a variety of subject areas, such as geography, sociology, cultural studies

■■   **Let's Talk About . . . 5–2**

Engaging Children in Historical Understanding

Social studies educators contend that young children can be successfully led to develop an understanding of the past and its link to the present. The key lies in selecting child-appropriate historical topics and effective teaching strategies. For instance, having children use old objects or old clothes for a "history show and tell" is very effective in developing the understanding of history (Barton, 1997). Meaningful discussions and inquiries easily emerge as these personal artifacts from earlier times are examined and discussed by the children. Unfortunately, hands-on activities with a historical theme are not commonly encoun-

tered in young children's classrooms. According to many social studies educators, this accounts for the lack of interest in and understanding of history.

1. What is your opinion of this?

2. What was your experience with the study of history as a young child?

3. What may be some reasons why historical experiences are not commonly built into early childhood activities?

4. Share your comments with your colleagues and classmates.

Bringing Ideas into Practice 5–1
Resources Teachers Can Use to "Do History" with Young Children

The need for active learning is the central tenant of developmentally appropriate practices (DAP). Simply put, children learn best when they play a part in what they are learning. When doing history with children, consider the following resources for involving your young students in developmentally sound, real historical adventures:

■ **Time Warp Center/Mystery Center:** A permanent center dedicated to a variety of historical themes will stimulate interest and create curiosity about how things were in the past. Have a "mystery box" and periodically include unusual artifacts (i.e., an old hand beater, alarm clock, or a telephone) for children to explore.

■ **Visual resources:** Posters and old photographs are visual bridges to the past. Family photographs of the children are always exciting to exhibit and discuss. A bulletin board titled "Now and Before" will help to establish the sense of the past and the present.

■ **Pictorial books:** Include books with pictures and photographs of people and activities from the past. Especially appropriate are those resources depicting children and their activities. Two excellent titles are: *Glorious children: A celebration of children* (Myers, 1995) and *Brown Angels: A book of pictures and verse* (Myers, 1993). Awareness of change and the passing of time in our country and around the world is presented particularly well in *Glorious children.*

■ **Art/Paintings:** Art is an excellent visual display of life in various time periods (see Chapter 8). Paintings from many of the great masters were inspired by events from daily life, such as farming, wedding celebrations, play time, and so on. Include reproductions of paintings depicting life scenes, and take time to talk about what they show. Calendars and art journals are particularly good sources of art reproductions.

■ **Oral history/Story time:** Storytelling is an ideal source of historical knowledge from the perspective of people. **Oral history**—an account of human experiences and events preserved as tales that are shared orally—provides life perspectives as well as insights into events from the human perspective. Stories about personal experiences also help children to gain a sense of what happened "before." Community members, parents, and family members are all excellent resources. As guest speakers, they can share special "stories" with the class. Recordings of people telling their experiences are also a good resource of oral history.

■ **Periodic demonstrations:** Inviting people to show their skills with fashioned crafts, old instruments, and simple home or office appliances creates interest and helps children see evolution and change in a tangible manner.

History education is a study of the past intended to help children develop a sense of understanding about events, actions, and decisions made by individuals and groups in the past. History education also fosters an understanding and an appreciation of the existing conditions in life, one's roots and culture, as well as the origins of others. When approached this way, history education can be a voyage into many different worlds. As such, history appeals to all, and especially to children.

In the early childhood classroom, history is not memorized or read about. It is experienced. We *"do*

history" with young children. By searching through their neighborhoods and their homes, by examining various artifacts, and by interacting with different people, children recognize the essence of history.

The teacher's understanding and perception of history as an active, dynamic field is central to the successful engagement of children in meaningful historical explorations. Diane Ravitch, a specialist in social studies education, believes that when history is "properly taught, it awakens youngsters to the universality of the human experience; encourages the development of intelligence, civility, and a sense of perspective; [and] leaves its students with cultural resources on which they may draw for the rest of their lives" (1985, p. 17). Cooper (1995, p. 3) states that "history is not only appropriate for young children; it is essential." History makes links between the child and the home, between the school and the wider community, between the past and the present.

"The past coming alive in the classroom" is perhaps the best way to view the true nature of history education. This phrase defines history as a *process* students follow as they walk through time to discover the *content* found in history. Use of critical thinking skills, inquiry, and constructive criticism defines the process children use as they replicate the tasks of the historians. The many topics and themes examined in the classroom define the historical content, which actually emerges from the many questions and interests of children. Thus, children gain meaning from the study of the past.

Why Study History in the Early Childhood Classroom?

What children of this age need is rich food for their imagination, a sense of history, how the present situation came about.

—Bruno Bettelheim

To many, history education is out of place in the early childhood classroom. The truth is that when history is looked at only as a series of dates and names, it is not appropriate at any age level. However, when it is recognized as an opportunity to gain an understanding of our diversity and of who we are, history becomes an exciting and meaningful field. There are many arguments to support the appropriateness of exploring historical themes with young children:

■ History education responds to and is consistent with the children's innate curiosity. Through historical themes, children find answers to their many questions. The need to know why and how is satisfied and encouraged as they explore items related to the past. An inquisitive attitude, an ideal attitude, is fostered in the examination of

events and people close to and of interest to children.

■ Exploration of historical themes provides children with a sense of the real-life individuals and events shaping their lives. It immerses children in the adventures and day-to day experiences of people and families from the past and the present.

■ Historical content in the early years is intended to promote an understanding of one's culture and of the cultures of important people. The main purpose of historical content is to target thinking about people's decisions, accomplishments, and their effects (NCSS, 1994). It is also a source of information children can use to build what Piaget described as knowledge about society and about its conventions (see Chapter 3).

■■ **Let's Talk About . . . 5–3**

What Is Your Position Regarding History Education and Young Children?

Educator Diane Ravitch has called the social studies "tot sociology" (1996, p. 1). She claims elimination of historical content from the curriculum and introduction of topics centered around the immediate family, the neighborhood and the environment has left it a "sterile" and "vacuous" curriculum that has little meaning or relationship to the children's reality. In her opinion, young children are able to learn about historical themes when appropriate teaching strategies are used. She proposes a curriculum for young children rich in historical themes such as heroic adventures, biographies, and folktales from our country and from the other parts of the world.

1. What is your reaction to this view? Do you agree or disagree? Why?

2. How does this differ from the way history is usually taught in the early childhood classroom?

■ In a world of diversity, learning who we are and how others are is essential to promoting positive social relationships. Much of what we know about others and ourselves is learned through the study of human experiences. This is the goal of history education (Ravitch, 1996).

■ Through history, children gain an appreciation for their culture and the cultures of others. Cultural and global identities are fostered through folk stories, traditions and customs that are learned and shared (Banks, 1993). Learning about the cultural heroes and about the events behind local, national, and global celebrations help young children to value their culture and those of others (see Chapter 9). Learning about different cultures also leads to a stronger sense of global identity.

■ Seeing life through a historical perspective makes one aware of the paths traveled by others, their struggles, and their legacies. Who we are, where others came from, knowledge of names and places, and appreciation for the events of the past are among the concepts children can learn through history education (National Council for History Education, 1998; NCHS, 1994).

■ For young children who are beginning to discover themselves, the world, and its society, understanding about who they are and about what surrounds them is indispensable (NCHS, 1998).

Opportunities for children to identify with the people and the heroes from the past and present promote positive self-esteem and self-concept.

Using Developmentally Appropriate Historical Content to Respond to the Children's Needs and Interests

The historical content for young children does not follow a set plan. It emerges from the children's interests and is integrated into the rest of their classroom experiences. The study of the past in the early childhood classroom centers on the present and moves into the past. Children's own curiosity leads them to discover why things are as they are. Meaningful learning occurs as children search through history to satisfy their own curiosity (Bredekamp & Rosegrant, 1995).

Teachers can also create curiosity and interest in the past. Best practices remind us that when items such as artifacts and appealing photographs are brought into the classroom, children will generally be attracted to them. It will not take long before a thousand questions will start to pour out. This is an effective way to engage the children in historical topics.

Sensible and practical selection of historical content to explore in the classroom is important for successful learning. Paying attention to what children

---

Bringing Ideas into Practice 5–2   *Developing a Literature Bank to Build Historical Concepts*

Children's literature is one of the most effective social studies resources. Children's books are also excellent for dealing with historical concepts. Throughout this chapter, titles will be suggested to help you build a literature bank appropriate for young children. The recommended titles are categorized in four different groups: personal and family history, American historical events, concept of time (p. 111), and general historical/cultural events. Share these titles with your colleagues and add others to the list.

Personal and Family History
■ Curtis, L. H. (1996). *Tell me again about the night I was born.* New York: Harper.
■ Dorros, A. (1991). *Abuela.* New York: Dutton.
■ Knight, M. (1994). *Welcoming babies.* Gardiner, ME: Tillbury House Publishers.
■ Say, A. (1994). *Grandfather's journey.* Boston, MA: Houghton Mifflin.
■ Say, A. (1999). *Tea with milk.* Boston, MA: Houghton Mifflin.

Concept Box 5–1   Thematic Teaching: Exploring Household Items from the Past and the Present

Theme: What household items did people have in the past? Did our parents and grandparents use the same objects as we do?

Areas integrated: Science, math, and literature

Centers: Science (testing starch; finding ways to "iron" (smooth out clothes) without an iron);

Questions to explore:

■ *How did people iron clothes in the past?*

1. Did they have irons? What did they look like? What other instruments did they use? What were they made of? How long did it take to iron a piece of clothing? Can we "iron" without an iron? How?

2. What is starch? Was starch used in the past? How many different kinds of starch are there? Do our families use starch? What kind do they use?

■ *How were clothes washed?*

1. Did people have washing machines in the old times? What did people in the past use to wash their clothes? Did early washing machines look like ours? Do all families have washing machines? Do they all look alike?

2. What are the different places we can wash clothes? Where were clothes washed in the old times? What is a laundromat? How does it work?

Books to share and to use as references:

Hutchins, P. (1983). *You'll soon grow into them.* New York: Greenwillow.

Perrault, C. (1981). *The glass slipper: Charles Perrault's tales of times past.* New York: Four Winds.

San Jose, C. (1994). *Cinderella.* Honesdale, PA: Boyds Mills.

Ziefert, H. (1986). *A new coat for Anna.* New York: Knopf.

---

ask and what catches their interest will reveal the content to be explored. For example, the keen observation of the teacher of four-year-olds led to an interesting study of household items used in the past. After a girl told the class that her mother had a "cordless iron," children became interested in learning whether people in the past also used irons. Rather than simply answering "Yes," the teacher encouraged the children's curiosity by letting them explore the topic. First, the children looked at picture books and examined different clothes, specifically to determine whether people of the past had irons. "The dresses look neat," said one little girl, pointing to the pictures of Pilgrims in *Wyeth's pilgrims* (San Souci, 1991) and in *Felicity* from the American Girls Series (Tripp, 1995). Next, families of the children were interviewed, and it was determined that they all had and used irons. This led some families to share some of their old irons with the class. One grandmother, who was a collector of irons, brought in samples dating back to the nineteenth century. That, in turn, provided an opportunity for children

to discover why these objects were called "irons." An ironing center was also created, where children could examine and try out modern and old irons, under the teacher's supervision. Ironing materials like spray starch, liquid starch, and cooked starch were also tested and tried out. Soon the children's attention moved to washing machines (*How did people wash their clothes? Did they have washing machines?*), which led to another exciting historical exploration.

■■ Exploring Key Elements of History ■■ in the Early Childhood Classroom

Working with history in the early childhood classroom requires teachers to know what history represents. History is about life experiences recorded by people. In any historical experience, four distinctive elements are found: *time, people, space/ places,* and *events/changes.* These elements are defined in Figure 5–1. As topics and themes are se-

FIGURE 5–1 Selecting Developmentally Appropriate Historical Themes

Time:
When does it happen? Can children relate to that time period? How?
Space/Place:
Where does it take place? Are children familiar with that location/setting? Are there any links to the children's reality?
People:
Who are the characters involved? What qualities/attributes makes them appealing to the group? Any links to the children's realities?
Events:
What is the human experience in this event? How does it relate to the children's lives? What should they know in order to understand its meaning? How significant is the event to the group? What child-meaningful elements are contained in the theme?

lected, educators should remember that, as a rule, prior experiences and familiarity with a topic plays a major role in how the child will process ideas. On the other hand, it is important to remember that each of the elements represents a concept that is not always easily grasped by children. Teachers need to keep in mind that of these four elements, the concepts of *time* and *space/place* are usually difficult for children to understand. The concept of time will be further discussed in the next section; "space/place" is explained later on. As the interest in historical themes emerges, teachers should carefully select strategies to present these themes to children in appropriate ways. Figure 5–1 lists a series of suggested questions to guide teachers in selecting appropriate historical themes for each age group.

Time: A Key Concept in History Education

Time, a universal social convention, defines both the *duration* and the *sequence* of an event

(Charlesworth & Lind, 1995). It is a way to measure the distance that separates us from an action. Time also establishes the **chronology,** or order of events, followed in an experience and the changes that take place.

During the early childhood years, learning how to think historically requires awareness of "the passing of time" and its effects. Knowing what steps were taken to build a block tower, or to cook a snack, or to retell the story read the day before, leads to the development of the concepts of time and change and introduces the children to **chronological thinking.** When children think chronologically, they differentiate between what happens in the past, in the present, and in the future. Appreciation and valuing what an event stands for depends on the understanding of the time context in which it happened. By itself, time is an abstract concept that requires more advanced thinking, which explains why very young children have difficulty grasping it. By the age of eight, however, children generally develop a functional concept of time (Timberlake, 1986; Chancellor, 1992). Teachers of young children know and recognize the special challenge this creates for teaching history in the early childhood classroom. A list of books teachers can use to help develop the concept of time appears on p. 113.

Children's Ideas of Time

Time is a social concept that is acquired gradually by children. Young children typically experience difficulty in conceptualizing events within a conventional time frame. Research indicates that typically children in the preoperational and early concrete operational stages of development possess an intuitive and subjective sense of time (Cooper, 1995). Perception plays a major role in how children interpret time. Easily impressed by appearances, children assign meaning based on what they perceive as significant. Conventional use of time labels such as hours, minutes, or years carries no meaning for young children. Unlike adults, children perceive and understand time in their own fashion: They use their own referents to define time lapses. For exam-

Concept Box 5–2   Elements of History and Young Children

TIME

Time is an abstract and conventional concept that is central to the study of history. The period when an event took place can be perceived as occurring at one of two different levels: *recent* or *distant* past. Cognitively, children have difficulties manipulating things that happen in a time frame that is different than theirs. With children, the **recent past** includes things that have taken place in a span of time as short as a class period. The distant past involves things that have happened as long as a year or more ago, or beyond the child's life span. Key to learning about time is the development of the concept of *change* (see p. 111) and of its effects.

Suggestions:
■ Keep a visible schedule of activities at school and home.
■ Exhibit pictures of the class to record how they change throughout the school year.
■ Use time instruments (clock, wristwatch, sand clock, timers, alarms).
■ Plan field trips.
■ Add infant and adult items to the housekeeping area.
■ Keep a class time line, diary, or a journal.
■ Observe and talk about artifacts, old pictures, etc.
■ Contrast what the children like to do *now* with what they liked to do *before*.
■ Use time words frequently (*now, before, later, after, yesterday, tomorrow*).

PEOPLE

People are the actors and characters of an historical event. Young children are attracted to people who have some relationship to them, or to those whose heroic characteristics make them stand out. Characters representing peers from times past as well as patriotic and folk heroes usually attract children.

Suggestions:
■ Use biographies of patriotic heroes and cultural leaders.

■ Include stories about children and heroes from the distant and recent past.
■ Display pictures and photographs of key historical characters and people in the community.
■ Invite/interview grandparents, community leaders, and others.

SPACE/PLACES

The location where an action happens is essential to understanding any historical event. Linking places to events helps children to explore and inquire about why things happen and why people were involved. As with the concept of time, children exhibit difficulties relating to places distant from their realities. Concrete experiences facilitate younger children's understanding of distant locations. (For more about integrating geography in the curriculum, see Chapter 6.)

Suggestions:
■ Display maps and globes and encourage children to use them.
■ Prepare maps of places visited by the children.
■ Create a map of the classroom and make changes as they occur.
■ Use geographical terms.
■ Use atlases and other reference materials to look up geographical places.
■ Share and read story books with geographical content.
■ Display pictures of different places and countries.

EVENTS/CHANGES

Actions taken by people and other human experiences form the core of history. Events also establish changes—alterations of people, attitudes, and other phenomena—that lead to the understanding of cause-and-effect relationships. Life incidents are of interest to children when they relate to their own realities, or when they are inherently exciting adventures. Cultural events and accomplishments also contribute to ways children can identify with their culture.

Concept Box 5-2   Continued

Local and national identity is fostered and built in the early years as children engage in learning about the historical episodes of their town, state, and the nation.

Suggestions:
- Keep a calendar of events in the community and other places.
- Read folktales describing significant events.
- Develop a calendar of important local or state events.

- Read stories and discuss the events behind major holidays.
- Display pictures of places and heroes related to key events.
- Prepare and display symbols representative of an event.
- Read and discuss events from other countries (see Chapter 9). Invite people from other countries to share their experiences.
- Learn songs, poems, and rhymes about key national and local events.

---

ple, in the toddler classroom, children show their sense and understanding of time when they start to pick up the blocks as they hear their teacher sing the clean-up song. In the kindergarten classroom

Concept Box 5-3   Using Books to Help Develop the Concept of Time

The following books help to develop the concepts of sequence and chronology:
- Anno, M. (1978). *Anno's journey.* New York: Philomel.
- Carle, E. (1971). *The grouchy ladybug.* New York: Crowell Books.
- de Paola, T. (1978). *Pancakes for breakfast.* San Diego, CA: Harcourt Brace Jovanovich.
- Flournoy, V. (1978). *The best time of day.* New York: Random House.
- Fox, M. (1989). *Night noises.* San Diego, CA: Harcourt Brace Jovanovich.
- Hutchins, P. (1993). *The doorbell rang.* New York: Scholastic.
- Isadora, R. (1991). *At the crossroads.* New York: Greenwillow.
- Rockwell, A. (1985). *First come spring.* New York: Crowell Books.
- Thomas, A. (1993). *Wake up, Wilson Street.* New York: Henry Holt & Company.

some children will use time words to talk about the trip they made the day before (*"Yesterday, when we went to the park . . ."*) and what they will do in the future (*"Next weekend we will go to the beach."*). Primary-age children will look at their watches or at the wall clock when it is time to go out to the playground. Even the children's emotional reactions and attitudes exhibited throughout the day will reflect their own understanding of time. However, because young children do not perceive time as adults do, their ability to see the distance between themselves and the characters in a historical story or event is not always accurate.

Relating Change to Time

Like time, **change** is also an abstract and subjective concept. There are two different kinds of changes: tangible and intangible. *Tangible change* usually refers to physical, visible change in people, objects, or events; *intangible change* is internal and covert in nature. Children grasp tangible change more easily because of its concreteness. Visible physical differences such as human growth, change of hair color, or an increase in weight are tangible changes children can grasp. However, an internal transformation like a change of opinion is not easily understood by young children. When dealing with intangible change, teachers need to provide opportunities for discussion and clarification.

■■   Let's Talk About . . . 5–4

Children and the Concept of Time

Educators and developmentalists agree that time is one of the hardest concepts for children to understand. They also agree that children do not lack a sense of time but that their grasp of time is not adult-like. To gain a sense of how children perceive time, interview a sample of children of different age-levels (toddler; kindergartner, primary age). The following set of suggested questions will help you find out their ideas about time. Feel free to add other questions. Remember to share your findings in class.

1. When is your birthday?
2. How old are you?
3. How long ago did you celebrate your birthday?
4. Are you the oldest in your house? Who is?
5. Will it be long before the night comes?
6. When do we say "Good morning" or "Good night"? Why?
7. What did you do yesterday in school? What will you do tomorrow?
8. How long does it take to go from your house to school?
9. Tell me what you do at school. What is the first thing you do? What is the last thing? What do you do after lunchtime?

Knowing how to take advantage of a "teachable moment," along with the use of good questioning strategies, contributes to timely and child-based opportunities for clarifying the concept of change. For example, in one pre-kindergarten classroom we found an appealing exhibit of infant items. According to the teacher, the exhibit evolved after sharing a book about birth. The teacher indicated that after

---

■■   Let's Talk About . . . 5–5

Children's Perception of Change

Many times children are unable to perceive changes. For example, young children do not easily grasp reaching the age to marry or to drive a car. In the vignette that follows, a parent is faced with trying to have a child understand why a story character is old enough to get married. As you read it, consider the following:

1. What is the child's idea of being "old"?
2. Do you agree with the explanation offered by the father? Why?
3. How would you explain what "old" means?
4. What would you do if this incident were to happen in your classroom?

Opening the book of *The tale of the flopsy bunnies* (Potter, 1995), Julie's father read: "When Benjamin Bunny grew up he married Flopsy, Peter Rabbit's sister."

Four-year-old Julie quickly interrupted him: "He married Flopsy? Children don't get married."

"That's right, they don't," her father answered, "but Peter Rabbit is big now and big people get married."

"I'm big too; can I get married to Jimmy?" Julie persisted.

"No, you are not big enough, honey," replied the father with a smile, continuing to read while Julie looked puzzled.

Bringing Ideas into Practice 5–3   *Planting: A Way to Learn about Time and Life Cycles*

Young children's perception of time is affected when they observe life changes. Nature's life cycles, such as the growth of plants, provide excellent opportunities for hands-on classroom activities that reinforce the relationship between time and change. The following are several planting activities that can be replicated in the classroom:

■ *Planting sprouts:* Bean sprouts are fast-growing plants that provide children with opportunities to observe a plant's life cycle in a short period of time. Select red beans, alfalfa, or watercress. Have children observe the seeds, and encourage them to talk about the way they look and feel. Guide the children to place the seeds they selected into a clean container and fill it up with room temperature water, just enough to cover the seeds. Let the seeds soak overnight away from the sunlight. Next day, help the children plant the seeds by spreading them on damp cotton and placing them in plastic trays or milk cartons. Remind the children that they must spray (mist) the seeds to ensure they are kept moist at all times. Sprouting will occur between 2–10 days, depending on the seeds. If alfalfa seeds are planted, enjoy the sprouts in a salad. Discuss the growth and the change process with the children.

■ *Flower seeds:* A classroom garden is also an excellent way to observe the life cycle of plants. Good choices for flowers to plant include marigolds, zinnias, sunflowers, and coleus. Select a spot on the playground and have the children prepare the soil. (If space outdoors is not available, plant the seeds in pots and place them on a sunny windowsill.)

Talk about the seeds and plant them. If more than one kind of seed is planted, assign each kind to a different group of children, and make each group responsible for labeling those seeds, taking care of them, and recording the growth process. Have regular discussions with the children about their observations.

■ *Cut flowers:* Observing and discussing how long flowers last after they are cut is another way of developing a sense of time and change. Any kind of cut flowers can be used. (Remember to talk about safety measures first, since some flowers may cause allergies.) Check the flowers every day, and have the children keep a record of how they look. Encourage the children to make drawings and a chart to help keep track of how long the flowers look fresh and alive. Once the cut flowers are wilted, you can also talk about ways to preserve dried flowers. (If you plan to dry flowers, it is best to do so before they wilt.) This will help the children to understand the concept of artifacts.

Share books about plants and the life cycle, such as:
Gibbons, G. (1984). *The seasons of Arnold's apple tree.* San Diego, CA: Harcourt Brace.
Krauss, R. (1945). *The carrot seed.* New York: Harper & Row.
Leslie, S. (1977). *Seasons.* New York: Platt & Munk.
Pringle, L. (1995). *Fire in the forest: A cycle of growth and renewal.* New York: Atheneum.
Silvestein, S. (1964). *The giving tree.* New York: Harper & Row.
Wiesner, D. (1992). *June 29, 1999.* New York: Clarion.

reading *Tell me again about the night I was born* (Curtis, 1996), she engaged the class in a discussion about how they were "before." "Were you babies at one time?" she asked the class. All the children laughingly replied, "Sure!" "How do you know that you're not a baby now?" the teacher went on. "I don't have a Pamper!" a boy said quickly. Soon

after the discussion the children started bringing to school baby photographs and an array of baby clothes and other objects (rattles, baby bottles, shoes) for a display. The teacher's own infant gown was put up. When the teacher told the class she wanted to wear it, the answer was a unanimous "No." The children proceeded to give various rea-

> **Concept Box 5–4   Books About the Concept of "Change"**
>
> Baker, J. (1991). *Window.* New York: Greenwillow Books.
>
> de Paola, T. (1996). *Strega Nona: Her story.* New York: Putnam.
>
> Gerrard, R. (1996). *Wagons west!* New York: Farrar Straus & Giroux.
>
> Goodall, J. (1987). *Story of a main street.* New York: Macmillan.
>
> Hutchins, P. (1971). *Changes, changes.* New York: Macmillan.
>
> Johnson, A. (1992). *The leaving morning.* New York: Orchard Books.

sons, all of which focused on the changes in the teacher herself.

As children learn that change can be caused by the passing of time, the idea of causality—the relationship between cause and effects also emerges. Successful historical thinking enhances the importance of knowing that behind a fact or an event, something has been responsible for its happening (NCHS, 1994). Young children's ideas about change are linked to either their own direct action or those of someone or something else (Piaget, 1970; Berk, 1996). Listening to a child's explanation of an event reveals his or her sense of causality (see Chapter 3). Generally, children perceive themselves or others as the actors responsible for what has occurred. Their ability to deal with causality is fostered through classroom experiences. When related to events at their level, children enjoy examining the actions that have led to changes related to life milestones or other events at home, at school, and in the community.

Children's literature is a particularly effective way to explore change and causality, because it encourages the use of inquiry skills to determine the reasons, facts, causes, and effects behind a change (Cooper, 1995). A list of suggested titles appears in Concept Box 5–4.

Fostering Concrete Experiences with Time and Change

Children see time through the meaningful events in their lives. The passing of time is understood by the concrete changes it brings. Teaching children time concepts begins by focusing on what they consider important, because young children's ideas about time and change are linked to what takes place in their life.

Through interactions at home and in the classroom, children gradually acquire a conventional sense of time. The key to building this concept lies in the many opportunities teachers offer children to "experience" time directly.

Charlesworth and Lind (1999) suggest experiences based on three kinds of time children can relate to more easily: personal experiences, social life/activities, and cultural time. *Personal experiences* include all those a child considers relevant and of which he or she has a recollection. For example, children will demonstrate their personal sense of time when they describe themselves as big now and having been a baby before (Charlesworth & Lind, 1999). They will also show their understanding of time when describing changes that have happened in their families ("We have a doggie now.") or neighborhoods ("The road is getting bigger this week.").

Birthdays help children relate to the passing of time.

Concept Box 5–5   Helping Children Build Time Concepts: Using the Language of Time

- **General words:** time, age, era, generation, and epoch
- **Specific words:** morning, afternoon, evening, night, day, noon, midday, midnight
- **Relational words:** soon, tomorrow, yesterday, early, late, a long time ago, once upon a time, new, old, now, when, sometimes, then, before, present, while, never, once, next, always, fast, slow, speed, first, second, third
- **Specific duration words:** clock and watch (minutes, seconds, hours); calendar (date, names of the days of the week, names of the months, names of seasons, year, century, millennium).
- **Special days:** birthday, vacation, holiday (Christmas, Passover, Kwanzaa, Easter, Thanksgivings, etc.), wedding, school day, weekend

Each young child has a *social life/activities* defined by the routines followed at home and at school. Typically, a day's activity represents a variety of predictable sequenced events that occur both at home and at school. For instance, a teacher of three-year-olds noticed that her class knew the day and the time the music teacher came and would form a circle minutes before he came into the classroom. Taking advantage of this awareness, she showed the children where the "music time" fit on the wall clock. By the end of the year, the children knew where the hands of the clock would be when it was time for the music class.

The third kind of time children relate to is *cultural/conventional time,* which is described as time "fixed by clocks and calendars" (Charlesworth & Lind, 1999, p. 204). Young children usually learn how to recognize and use time instruments by the time they reach the concrete-operational level (see Chapter 3). A calendar of activities in the classroom helps them to recognize the "calendar," as well as to

use time language (months, days, yesterday, today, tomorrow, etc.). It is not, however, until children reach the formal operations period (in Piaget's view of cognitive development) that a full sense of the concept of time is achieved (Seefeldt, 1997).

Helping Children Develop Quantitative and Qualitative Concepts of Time

Piagetian research emphasizes the role of relevant and day-to-day experiences in concept formation. Learning happens "through the interaction between the objects in the environment and the knowledge that the subject brings to the situation" (Kamii & DeVries, 1980, p. 180). According to Piaget (1970), time is both a *quantitative concept* (defined by conventional labels such as hours, minutes, etc.) and a *qualitative concept* (based on what is experi-

---

■■ Let's Talk About . . . 5–6

What Activities/Resources Do Teachers Use To Develop Time Concepts?

There are many ways to help children build the concept of time. To find out more about how teachers address the concept of time, talk to your colleagues, visit and observe classrooms, and ask experienced early childhood teachers. To guide your interviews and observations, keep in mind that DAP principles indicate that children's activities and resources are more likely to succeed if they are *age-appropriate, hands-on, meaningful,* and *responsive to the special needs of children* (see Chapter 3).

1. Describe your findings in a short report and highlight those activities and resources you found that met the DAP criteria. Share them with your colleagues and classmates.

2. Select the activities and resources you consider the most appealing and child-appropriate.

**Concept Box 5–6   Building Concepts about Time:
Children's Literature about Birthdays and Holidays**

One of the best ways to teach the concepts of time is through literature, because most children delight in discussing and planning special holidays and birthdays. Here are some children's books that will help you teach about time through literature. For additional books you can use to develop concepts of time, see p. 113.

Birthdays:

Cummings, P. (1994). *Carousel*. New York: Simon & Schuster.

Feldman, E. (1995). *Birthdays: Celebrating life around the world*. New York: Bridgewater.

Freeman, D. (1985). *Corduroy's birthday*. New York: Viking.

Hoban, R. (1994). *A birthday for Frances*. New York: Harper & Row.

Jeram, A. (1998). *Birthday happy, contrary Mary*. Cambridge, MA: Candlewick Press.

MacKinnon, D. (1996). *Cathy's cake: A first "lift the flap" book. (Surprise, surprise)*. New York: Dial Books.

Mora, P. (1992). *A birthday basket for Tia*. New York: Macmillan.

Ryland, C. (1991). *Birthday presents*. New York: Orchard.

Tafuri, N. (1995). *The barn party*. New York: Greenwillow.

Fall holidays:

Ancona, G. (1993). *Pablo remembers: The fiesta of the day of the dead*. New York: Lothrop.

Cowley, J. (1996). *Gracias, the Thanksgiving turkey*. New York: Scholastic.

Nerlove, M. (1995). *Thanksgivings*. New York: Putnam.

Packard, M. (1996). *Fall leaves*. New York: Scholastic.

Rose, E. (1993). *Pumpkin faces*. New York: Scholastic.

Swamp, Chief Jake. (1995). *Giving thanks: A Native American good morning message*. New York: Scholastic.

Winter holidays:

de Paola, T. (1987). *An early American Christmas*. New York: Putnam.

de Paola, T. (1989). *My first Chanukah*. New York: Putnam.

Hegg, T. (1995). *Peef: The Christmas bear*. Minneapolis, MN: Waldeman House.

Mendez, P. (1989). *The black snowman*. New York: Scholastic.

Porter, Q. L. (1991). *Kwanzaa*. Minneapolis, MN: Carolrhoda Books.

Van Allsburg, C. (1985). *The polar express*. Boston, MA: Houghton Mifflin.

Waters, K. & Low, M. (1991). *Lion dancer: Ernie Wan's Chinese new year*. New York: Scholastic.

Spring holidays:

Bartoletti, S. (1997). *Dancing with Dziadzu*. New York: Harcourt Brace.

Dorros, A. (1991). *Tonight is Carnival*. New York: Puffin.

Friedrich, P. & Friedrich, O. (1983). *The Easter bunny that overslept*. New York: Morrow.

Hall, D. (Ed.). (1997). *Celebrate in Central America*. New York: Lothrop.

Kindersley, B., & Kindersley, A. (1997). *Celebrations*. UK: DK Publishing.

Nerlove, M. (1994). *Purim*. Morton Grove, IL: Albert Whitman.

Zalben, J. (1990). *Happy Passover, Rosie*. New York: Holt.

---

enced during a period of time). For young children, time becomes meaningful when its qualitative character its realized. Sharing what happened in the morning or describing what they did as they built a block tower reveals the children's qualitative knowledge of time. Conventional labels describing the

FIGURE 5–2 A Classroom Pictorial Holiday Timeline

| **August** Friendship Week | **September** International Literacy Day | **October** Halloween | **November** Thanksgiving | **December** Winter Solstice | **January** Chinese New Year | **February** Valentine's Day |

quantitative nature of time are meaningless unless they are related to a personally significant experience.

Names of days, months, and seasons, among others, are learned as social knowledge, but are not fully understood by children until a meaningful event is associated with that point in time (Van Scoy & Fairchild, 1993; Piaget, 1970). For instance, a kindergarten teacher reported that a group of five-year-olds showed an understanding of "July 4" as a special day when it was associated with the day of the fireworks for "America's birthday." In another case, when children were talking about their favorite time of year, "winter" was mentioned by a four-year-old who said that this was the time of year for him "to go on an airplane." When the teacher asked how he knew it was winter, he did not hesitate to say, "That's when it's cold!"

Research has established that what we know today about time was learned as we directly experienced and attributed meaning to life events. This applies directly to children's ability to learn about time. Children learn about time when concrete objects and or meaningful experiences are attached to learning (Van Scoy & Fairchild, 1993). Successful learning of the concept of time depends on appropriate classroom practices. This point is highlighted by Van Scoy and Fairchild (1993, p. 21), who comment that one of the difficulties children face when learning about time is that classroom activities usually fail "to

help them develop an understanding about the passing of time." Activities that involve rote memorization of calendar dates are often used in the classroom. These activities can help children learn the conventional time labels used to depict time (such as the names of days, months, and of seasons). However, actual understanding about *what time is* is not always emphasized. It is important to attach concreteness and special meaning to activities for children to acquire the abstract meaning of time. A pictorial timeline, such as the one shown in Figure 5–2, is an effective and appropriate way to accomplish this.

The Many Worlds of History

The study of history is the study of many facets of the human experience. Many historians and social studies educators agree that there are many kinds of history. Because the study of history entails things close and distant, there are four essential types of historical frameworks: *personal, community and neighborhood, state and national,* and *world/global.* In early childhood these four areas represent a wealth of different themes to explore (see Concept Box 5–7). Each of these many history themes is an opportunity to see how life unfolds. Hands-on explorations in each of these areas offer appropriate ways for children to see themselves as a part of these different worlds.

FIGURE 5–3   Daily Schedule

8:00 A.M.–8:30 A.M. Breakfast	
8:30 A.M.–9:00 A.M. Playtime Outdoors or in Gym	
9:00 A.M.–9:15 A.M. Group Meeting	
9:15 A.M.–10:30 A.M. Center Activities	
10:30 A.M.–10:45 A.M. Snack	
10:45 A.M.–11:15 A.M. Playtime Outdoors or in Gym	
11:15 A.M.–11:45 A.M. Story and Language Development Group Activities	

FIGURE 5–3 Continued

11:45 A.M.–12:00 Wash Hands, Go to Lunch	
12:00–12:30 P.M. Lunch	
12:30–1:00 P.M. Playtime Outdoors or in Gym	
1:00–2:00 P.M. Rest	
2:00–3:00 P.M. Art, Music, Writing, Reading	
3:00–3:30 P.M. Clean-Up Prepare to Leave or Go to Extended Day	

Bringing Ideas into Practice 5–4
Suggested Classroom Experiences to Help Young Children Learn about Time

For the child learning to understand life in terms of time sequences, the classroom plays an instrumental role. Here are some appropriate activities for building the concept of time:

■ *Classroom routines:* Following predictable routines is important for creating a healthy and stable environment. Routine activities such as the morning and afternoon circle time, hand washing before lunch, snack times, clean-up times, and others help children to organize their day. Routines also help to develop the skill of *sequencing,* which is significant for the development of historical thinking.

■ *Pictorial classroom schedule:* Displaying and using a schedule of activities is another essential instructional time element. A properly laminated schedule should be mounted at the children's eye level, where both the children and teacher can see it. Teachers should use the schedule while the morning routines are reviewed. When children ask such questions as *"What are we doing now?"* or *"When are we going to the zoo?"* they should be encouraged to look at the schedule. Helping children find out by themselves when it is time to go to the various centers emphasizes the functional nature of the schedule and the way time defines activity periods (Charlesworth & Lind, 1996). With younger children, teachers can use photographs and drawings to identify the different daily activities and to help children learn what will happen during each time period (see Figure 5–3). Blending words and numbers with pictures makes the schedule an appropriate and useful reference for the children.

■ *Calendar:* A calendar should be kept and used as part of the classroom routine. A review of the activities that have already happened, those that will take place next, and others that are planned for the next day contributes to a sense of different time levels (past, present, future). A routine review of the calendar can enhance time concepts when teachers ask the following questions:

☐ What are we doing today?
☐ What day is today? Show me on the calendar.
☐ What do you remember from what we did yesterday?
☐ When will we go to (*place*)?

■ *Wall time lines:* Keeping a time line of the classroom events helps to reinforce the concepts of *now* and *before.* Personal time lines can also be developed to learn about the changes that are caused by the passing of time. Time lines foster the development of sequencing skills. They can be created as a group activity (such as a field trip) is planned and carried out.

■ *Celebration of birthdays and holidays:* Time becomes meaningful to children when it is attached to people and events they consider relevant. Research shows children use their birthdays and preferred holidays and family celebrations as time referents (see p. 118). Celebrations of the children's birthdays are valuable learning experiences. A birthday time-line prepared at the beginning of the school year allows children to see when their birthdays will take place. Periodic review of this time line helps children to identify upcoming birthdays to be celebrated and those already observed. The use of words like *soon, far, tomorrow, next, first, last, older than,* and *younger than* in connection with birthday celebrations builds time concepts.

Holidays are also meaningful time-related concepts. The special days and cultural and patriotic celebrations families observe throughout the year engage children in concrete time-based activities. A display of pictures with symbols of their favorite holidays or a monthly calendar of holidays will help children to learn about sequence and time as the factors closely linked to their lives. Use of rhymes and songs about holidays also provides opportunities to continue building a sense of time.

Bringing Ideas into Practice 5–4   *Continued*

Children relate easily to special holidays.

■ *Classroom time instruments:* A wall clock, clocks of various kinds, timers, wristwatches (toy and old watches), and sand clocks should be available in the classroom. Modeling how to use them plays an important role in learning about time and how it is conventionally defined.

■ *Classroom history book:* A history book about the class will help children to look at activities they have engaged in throughout the year. This will help to reinforce ideas about "what happened before" and "the things we did."

■ *Cooking experiences:* Cooking helps children understand the changes happening over time as well as the effect of the passing of time on concrete objects. Cooking experiences help in developing a sense of chronology and sequencing skills.

■ *Literature:* Selection of appropriate literature (see lists throughout this chapter) helps children learn about the concepts of time and change in meaningful contexts. Biographies and titles about familiar experiences that take place in other times further the ideas about how things were in the past. Titles with these concepts should be periodically incorporated into the story-telling segment.

■ *Musical cues:* Use of music, whether it is a holiday song or a tune that signals the next class segment, contributes to the perception of time in a meaningful way. When children respond to the teacher's singing of the "clean-up song," they show their understanding of the upcoming new event and the closing of the current activity.

■ *Use of "time language":* Time language needs to be constantly used in the classroom. Frequent verbal interactions and expressions will help to clarify the meaning and appropriate use of time concepts and terminology (Vygotsky, 1996). Visual labeling also helps to acquire the language of time. Consider including charts labeled: "Today's Activities are . . ." "Tomorrow's Activities," "Things We Will Do Soon," and wall charts depicting "Before and After" events and sequences.

Concept Box 5–7   Thematic Teaching: A Variety of Historical Themes to Choose From!

The personal history world:
- *Individual/Personal Topics:*
  All about Me, The Day I Was Born, Celebrating Birthdays, Growing Up, The Place Where I Was Born, Things I Like to Do Now, Games I Play Now, My Favorite Pet, Places I Like and Know.
- *Family, School, and Friends Topics:*
  My Family, Knowing Our Grandparents, Things We Do in My Family, Our Ancestors, Family Celebrations, My Family Now and Then, My Friends, Friends from Here and There, Games I Play with My Friends, My School Now and Then, School Friends, Friends from Other Places and Other Times.
- *Oral History/Cultural Topics:*
  Traditions, Celebrations at Home, Our Favorite Holidays, Folk Stories We Know, Traditions at Home, Traditional Songs We Know, Traditional Games, Cooking for the Holidays.

The world where I grow up (community):
- *Community/Neighborhood History Topics:*
  Knowing Our Neighborhood, Friends and People in Our Neighborhood, Places in Our Community, Historical Places in Our Community, Preserving Our Community, Artisans and Crafts from Our Community.

The world around me/us:
- *Current Events Topics:*
  Daily News, Sharing Daily Stories, Happenings at School, News about Myself and My Family.
- *State and National History Topics:*
  People in Our State, Famous People, State Heroes, Places in Our State, Holidays and Festivals, Our State Long Ago, Meet the Presidents, People in Other States, Customs across the State/Country.

The world I/we live in:
- *World/Global Topics:*
  Friends and People from Other Places, Famous People from Around the World, Traditions from Other Countries, Folktales from Other Cultures, Celebrations, Famous Places, Traveling around the World.

■■ Connecting History Education with the National Social Studies Standards
■■

History education provides opportunities to integrate the social studies standards developed by the National Council for the Social Studies (NCSS) into the curriculum. The standards for the primary grades are reprinted in Appendix I at the back of this book. Although all of the standards are reflected in different themes (called curricular strands) that recur through history, strands I (culture), II (time, continuity, and change), and III (people, places and environment) are particularly related to this area. Consider what the NCSS standards state about these curricular themes or strands:

Strand I: Culture
Social studies programs should include experiences that provide for the study of culture and cultural diversity. . . . Culture helps us to understand ourselves as both individuals and members of various groups. Cultures are dynamic and ever-changing.
(NCSS, 1994, p. 21)

Strand II: Time, Continuity, and Change
Social studies programs should include experiences that provide for the study of the ways human beings view themselves in and over time. Human beings seek to understand their historical roots and to locate themselves in time. Such understanding involves knowing what things were like in the past and how things change and develop.
(NCSS, 1994, p. 22)

Strand III: People, Places, and Environments
Social studies programs should include experiences that provide for the study of people, places and environments. The study of people, places and human-environment interactions assist learners as they create their spatial views and geographic perspectives on the world . . . Geographic concepts become central to learners' comprehension of global connections as they expand their knowledge of diverse cultures, both historical and contemporary.

(NCSS, 1994, p. 23)

Through the first three themes or strands, sensible and logical history experiences are built. Essentially, the standards state that the study of history depends upon the child's ability to understand the passing of time and its effect upon both people and their environment. Cultural changes are directly related to historical experiences. There are many ways children can explore these themes in the classroom. The following questions suggest ways to incorporate them into the curriculum:

Strand I: Culture

■ How did my family come to this community?
■ What were the activities that my grandparents used to do?
■ What other languages were spoken in our community?
■ What traditions did people follow in the past?
■ What activities did children do in other communities, countries?
■ How were holidays observed in the past?
■ Who were the people who lived in my community before?

Strand II: Time, Continuity, and Change

■ What songs or music did children like in the past?
■ What games did children from other countries play in the past?
■ What activities did I used to do when I was little?
■ What things can I do now that I could not do before?
■ How has my house changed?
■ How were houses built in other communities in the past?

■ How has our community changed?
■ What are the names of people who built our community?

Strand III: People, Places, and Environments

■ Where did my family come from?
■ Where do my friends live?
■ How has our community changed?
■ What are the characteristics of our community?
■ What activities do people do in other places?
■ What are houses like in other places?

NCHS History Standards for Early Childhood Education

Selecting themes and establishing content priorities is one of the hardest tasks of curriculum development. Early childhood educators can get help in selecting the appropriate historical content by using the history standards defined by the National Center for History in the Schools (NCHS, 1994). The standards outline the key purposes of historical knowledge and suggest specific areas of study as guidelines for teachers of grades K through 12.

A separate set of eight standards for the K through 4 level (see p. 127) was developed based on the belief that young children can develop historical understanding and thinking. Although the NCHS standards do not include three- and four-year-olds, they serve as a good resource and a valuable reference for teachers of the very young. The NCHS standards are valuable for several reasons. First, although they do not prescribe a content or an approach, the *National Standards: History for Grades K–4* (1994) outline the goals of history and suggest key topics and concepts to highlight in the classroom. Second, selection of the topical content and organization of the curriculum is left in the hands of teachers. Third, the standards are flexible enough to accommodate the characteristics and needs of children. Fourth, the standards foster curricular integration, a characteristic of developmentally appropriate (DAP) curricula. Fifth, the standards also recommend the integrated acquisition of both historical thinking skills and of historical understanding. **Historical thinking** is defined as the ability "that enables children to differentiate the past, present, and future time; raise questions; seek and evaluate evidence; compare and analyze historical stories, illustrations, and records from the past; interpret the historical record, and construct historical narratives of their own" (NCHS, 1994, p. 2). **Historical understanding** is "What students should know about the history of their families, their communities, states, nation, and the world" (NCHS, 1994, p. 2).

The eight standards recommended for grades K through 4 by the NCHS are based on the following six basic principles that relate history to young children:

1. Young children can build historical content when it makes use of their innate curiosity and imagination.
2. Despite their conceptual difficulties, children can learn to differentiate time concepts when presented as "the time present, time past, and time long, long ago."
3. History is alive and becomes interesting when it revolves around people (families, extraordinary and common people, people from their state, country, and other parts of the world).
4. Use of stories, myths, and biographies serves to entice and attract children into historical feats and events.

::   Let's Talk About . . . 5–7

What is Your Opinion about Teaching History to Young Children?

Review the NCHS history standards and form your own opinion by:

1. identifying those points you agree with and explaining why you are in agreement;
2. adding any points you consider missing; and
3. writing down your own set of principles for historical teaching in your classroom.

---

5. Hands-on resources—artifacts, manipulatives, regalia, visits to museums and historical places—help develop interest in and the understanding of historical content.
6. Good questioning skills foster the use of thinking skills and reflection on historical content. Opportunities to question and offer ideas should abound in the classroom.

(NCHS, 1994, p. 3)

The eight history standards are embedded in four major topical areas (see Figure 5–4). In each area, the opportunities for integration of both historical thinking and understanding are reflected.

Developing a History Curriculum with DAP Themes

A successful curriculum engages the children's curiosity and leads them into meaningful and productive experiences. Curiosity, the children's intrinsic learning characteristic, is easily activated through the careful selection of topics and themes. Meaningful and productive experiences are accomplished when three key sources are integrated:

1. *Children's interests:* What the children want to learn should be considered as one of the essential sources for building a child-based curriculum. Knowledge about their interests will guide the selection of key themes to explore.
2. *Knowledge of the children's developmental traits and needs:* The successful curriculum is one that takes into account the characteristics of the learners. Both the content and the strategies are developed based on the specific needs of the group. Curricular content challenges children according to their cognitive and social characteristics. Materials and support resources are chosen to satisfy the physical, motor, and cognitive needs of each child (see Chapter 3). When necessary, adaptations are made to the materials to include all children.
3. *Consideration for diversity issues:* An appropriate curriculum reflects the variety of cultural and social characteristics of the group and of the society (see Chapter 9).

FIGURE 5-4 Topical Summary of the NCHS History Standards (K–4)

Topical Area #1: Living and working together in families and communities, now and long ago

NCHS Standard 1: Family life now and in the recent past; family life in various places long ago.
NCHS Standard 2: History of students' local community and how communities in North America varied long ago.

Topical Area #2: The history of the students' own state and region

NCHS Standard 3: The people, the events, problems, and ideas that created the history of the their state.

Topical Area #3: The history of the United States: democratic principles and values and the people from many cultures who contributed to its cultural, economic, and political thinking

NCHS Standard 4: How democratic values came to be and how they have been exemplified by people, events, and symbols.
NCHS Standard 5: The causes and nature of the various movements of large groups of people into and within the United States, now and long ago.
NCHS Standard 6: Regional folklore and cultural contributions that helped to form our national heritage.

Topical Area #4: The history of people of many cultures around the world

NCHS Standard 7: Selected attributes and historical developments of various societies in Africa, the Americas, Australia, and Europe.
NCHS Standard 8: Major discoveries in science and technology; their social and economic effects, and the scientists and inventors from many groups and regions responsible for them.

Developing Global Awareness through the History-based Curriculum

Through history we find endless opportunities to build ideas about our global community. Global awareness is developed as children examine the incidents, the characters (both real and fictitious), and the daily life experiences of adults and children from other times and other places. More specifically, children build connections with the world as they engage in:

1. learning about the deeds of common people in other places. For example, children can expand their connections by reading about characters from other times, or by reading fairy tales, which are a source of historical and global information.
2. singing songs and learning riddles about historical events. Discussions of the lyrics and the characters in songs and in literature serve as bridges into the past.
3. learning about the experiences of heroes and notable people from the past and from other cultures (e.g., Marco Polo; Simon Bolivar; Henry the Navigator; Leif Ericsson).
4. exploring the traditions and customs from the past in other countries (e.g., holiday celebrations in other countries; daily life in the middle ages).
5. reading about important global historical moments (e.g., discovery of the Americas; travels of the Vikings; invention of the telegraph).
6. investigating ways of life in the countries their families and other immigrants came from.
7. reading and discussing legends and folk stories from other countries (e.g., Grimm's fairy tales; African *Pourquoi* folktales, which try to give answers to interesting situations).

Bringing Ideas into Practice 5–5
Developing a Literature Bank to Build History Concepts

More titles appear here to continue your literature-based history curriculum.

American historical events:

Adler, C. (1986). *A picture biography of Benjamin Franklin.* New York: Holiday House.

Bates, K. (1995). *Oh beautiful, for spacious skies.* (Based on the song *America*)

Burleigh, R. (1992). *Flight: The journey of Charles Lindbergh.* New York: Philomel Books.

Cohn, A. (Ed.). (1993). *From sea to shining sea.* New York: Scholastic.

With illustrations from Caldecott winners, this is a collection of stories and songs about all periods of American history.

Deustch, E. (1995). *The early people of Florida.* New York: Atheneum.

A reference book about early life in Florida.

McCully, E. A. (1996). *The ballot box battle.* New York: Knopf.

A story based on the life of Elizabeth Cady Stanton, leader in the struggle for women's rights.

A careful analysis of historical themes helps teachers distinguish those that are suitable for building global connections. Both the children's interests and the topics suggested by the history standards help to identify possible historical and global themes (Figure 5–5).

Curricular Integration: Creating Developmentally Appropriate History Experiences through the Arts

The arts—music, dance, theater, and the visual arts—provide one of the most exciting sources of historical knowledge. Like written documents, the arts reveal the ideas, feelings, events, and trends of the past eras. Because every culture creates and expresses itself though the arts, the opportunities to learn about the past and to establish global connections are abundant. The arts serve "to connect each generation to those who have gone before, equipping the newcomers in their own pursuit of the abiding questions: Who am I? What must I do? Where am I going?" (Consortium of National Arts Education Association, 1994, p. 5).

The arts are a fascinating and an appealing window into the past. The ideas, beliefs, and values held by people from times past are shared through the many artistic forms they have left behind. As an artistic piece is explored, children are led to appreciate and enjoy the arts. Because of the variety of interpretations and representations, the arts are also a way for children to learn about the diversity of ideas and artful expressions of the people from other places and times.

The arts are a rich source of developmentally appropriate experiences, particularly because of their highly sensorial and interactive characteristics. As you will see in Chapter 8, the opportunities for young children to learn about the past and other themes from the arts are endless. Here are some suggestions:

a. Music

Use classical music to depict the times described in fairy tales and folktales. (Examples: Tchaikovsky's *The Sleeping Beauty, The Nutcracker, Swan Lake*)

■ Learn and sing childhood songs grandparents and parents know.

■ Listen to musical pieces to explore how people felt about key historical events. (examples: the national anthem of France and United States; the *1812 Overture*)

■ Learn about the contributions of the great European musicians (Mozart, Brahms, Schumann, and Chopin). Listen and react to some of their works. (examples: Brahms' *Lullaby* or Schumann's *Dreaming*)

FIGURE 5–5 Using the NCHS History Standards to Build Global Connections

Suggested themes

Topical Area #1: Living and working together in families and communities, now and long ago:

- Family life in other places and other times
- Relatives from long ago
- Where did we came from? (immigration)
- Jobs from the past

Suggested children's books:

Bunting, 1989. *How many days to America.* New York: Clarion.

Levinson, 1985. *Watch the stars come out.* New York: Dutton.

Polacco, 1989. *The keeping quilt.* New York: Simon & Schuster.

Pomerantz, 1993. *The chalk doll.* New York: Harper.

Say, 1993. *Grandfather's journey.* Boston, MA: Houghton Mifflin.

Topical Area #4: The history of people of many cultures around the world:

- Travelers and explorers from long ago
- Inventors from other places
- Important people from long ago
- Children from other times and places
- Legends and myths from other places
- Celebrations and holidays in olden times

Suggested children's books:

Aardema, 1981. *Bringing the rain to Kapiti plain.* New York: Dial.

Adler, 1993. *A picture story of Anne Frank.* New York: Bantam.

Cheng, 1976. *The Chinese new year.* New York: Holt.

CIDCLI, 1988). *Cristobal Colon* [pop-up book]. Columbia: Carvajal.

Coerr, 1993. *Sadako.* New York: Putnam.

de Paola, 1980. *The legend of old Befana: An Italian Christmas story.* San Diego, CA: Harcourt Brace.

Krull, 1994. *Maria Molina and the days of the dead.* New York: Macmillan.

Lattimore, 1987. *The flame of peace: A tale of the Aztecs.* New York: Harper.

Lock, Kelly and Rivers, 1995. *Xochiquetzal.* Australia: Martin International.

Nickly, 1982. *The emperor's plum dress.* New York: Greenwillow.

Polacco, 1993. *Babushka Baba Yaga.* New York: Philomel.

Steptoe, 1987. *Mufaro's beautiful daughters: An African tale.* New York: Lothrop.

Wild, M. *Let the celebrations begin!* New York: Orchard.

- Listen to holiday music from other time eras, and respond to it with body movements. (examples: traditional and contemporary Christmas music)

b. Dance

- Learn current folk dances and those from the times of the children's grandparents.
- Create a dance or use movement to represent a particular time or historical event.
- Learn traditional dances from other countries. (examples: waltz, polka)

c. Visual Arts

- Observe and discuss paintings depicting family activities from past eras. (examples: selections by Grandma Moses, Norman Rockwell, Rembrandt, and other masters)
- Use paintings to compare and contrast activities and objects in the different eras. (examples: children's toys, clothing, household items, means of transportation, meals, and farm animals)
- Explore the concept of change by observing cities and landscapes in selected paintings.

■ Use different art media and techniques to express ideas about an event in the recent or distant past.

■ Learn about the people represented through statuary. (examples: statues in the community parks, schools, local museums)

d. Theater

■ Create dialogues and action scenes about what a historical character would say and do.

■ Role-play characters from the past.

■ "Interview" selected characters from a story or event.

■ Prepare and design the stage to represent a historical episode.

■ Select and prepare outfits depictive of a historical period for classroom dramatizations.

Using Museums to Learn about the Past

Museums are places where the heritage of humankind and the record of the natural world are kept. A visit to a museum can be a journey into the realm of many human achievements and natural wonders. Museums are also the places where our heritage and the memories of our past are zealously preserved. Museums are ideal places of learning for young children. The many exhibits at a museum trigger young children's innate imagination and curiosity. Today, museums offer activities and educational programs specially created for the young. Many have interactive and hands-on exhibits designed to fit the needs of children.

Types of Museums

There are many kinds of museums. They all offer multiple ways to learn about the past. Your community may have many of the following kinds of museums (Greene, 1998):

■ **Art museums** (see Chapter 8) house collections of artistic works from the present and the past. They usually have programs with special traveling exhibits, which offer opportunities to experience prized historical works.

Concept Box 5–8   Developmentally Appropriate Practice: Learning about the Lives of the Maestros

Research findings about brain development suggest children benefit from an early exposure to a stimulating environment (Shore, 1997). According to research, music, when played regularly during the early years facilitates the development of brain connections. Besides enhancing brain development, music also reinforces the appreciation for the legacies of the past. Children can learn to appreciate the work of some of the music *maestros* when they learn about their lives.

Young children will enjoy listening to the stories in the collection *Famous Children* (Aladdin Books, 1993) by Ann Rachlin. Portraying musical geniuses when they were child prodigies, Rachlin includes sketches from the lives of the following gifted composers: Chopin, Bach, Brahms, Handel, Haydn, Mozart, Schumann, and Tchaikovsky. As children learn about the incidents in the musicians' lives, their music becomes more significant.

■ **History museums** are dedicated to preserving artifacts, documents, and objects of historical interest. They preserve the past and also make it come alive for the present generations.

■ **Natural history museums** house collections of natural specimens that help us learn about how our world has changed through time.

■ **Historic houses** are restored residential places that offer an opportunity to learn about how families lived in other times. A visit to an historic house is like a journey into the past.

■ **Cultural heritage museums** are dedicated to specific cultural groups, such as African-Americans, Asian-Americans, or Native Americans.

■ **Special interest** museums focus on a single topic or house collections such as cars, toys, quilts, and birds, etc.

Museum Resources in Our Community

Have you visited a museum or historical site lately? Do you know how many there are in your community? If you answered "yes" to these questions, you already know that there are many exciting ways to help children learn about the past. Every community has museums and places where historical and interesting objects are preserved. Knowing what these resources offer helps in designing lively and exciting learning experiences.

■ Identify the museums in your community, visit them, and learn about what they offer to young children.

■ Create your own list of the museums and places suitable for young children to visit.

■ List museums and other exhibits in other places you have visited and list the special opportunities they provide for learning about the past.

Create a resource file from this information you can share with your colleagues and classmates.

■ **Children's museums** are designed to provide hands-on and interactive experiences for children. Most cities have a children's museum.
■ **Restored areas,** such as Colonial Williamsburg in Virginia and the nineteenth-century Hacienda Buena Vista in Puerto Rico, are sites of historic importance where you can visit settings and living environments that have been recreated as they were in the past.
■ **On-line museums** have been created through the magic of modern cybercommunications. You can visit exhibits and bring virtual museums into your classroom just by clicking on their Web page on the computer. Visit the Smithsonian (Washington, DC), the Field Museum of Natural History (Chicago), and the Metropolitan Museum of Art (New York). Travel to the Louvre Museum (Paris, France), and the Prado Museum (Madrid, Spain), all of which are already on-line.

To make the most of a visit to a museum, always plan ahead what questions to ask the children. According to Greene (1998), questions help children to focus on what they are observing. Museum visits are also an exciting way to involve the family in learning about the past. To enhance your class's visit to a museum, Greene suggests listening to what children ask at the museum and then engaging them in extended conversations. Questions similar to the ones recommended in Figure 5–6 below will lead to lively conversations and help build important concepts.

Children's Literature: A Journey into the Past

Literature is one of the best bridges to the past. The past is brought alive in creative and appealing ways through all the literary genres: biographies,

FIGURE 5–6 Visiting the Museum: Suggested Focus Questions

What is a good name for this?
What does this remind you of?
What do you think will happen if _____?
What words would you use to describe this _____?
What do you think this is made of?
What do you think they made it for?
When do you think this was used?
What do you think they used this for?
How does it make you feel?
Can you imagine if you were _____?

Source: Adapted from Greene, W. P. (1998). *Museums and learning: A guide for family visits.* Washington, DC: Office of Educational Research and Improvement and the Smithsonian Office of Education.

Bringing Ideas into Practice 5–6   *Using Artifacts to Learn about the Past*

By definition, **artifacts** are objects that characterize the customs, ideas, and trends of an historical period. For example, photographs of antique cars, objects such as antique cameras, and garments worn in the past are all considered artifacts. Like documents, artifacts are sources of information about the past and the present. Whether relics, heirlooms, or antiques, artifacts provide children with hands-on opportunities to know what it was like to live in the past. Although it is true that some artifacts are difficult to obtain, replicas of old objects are also a valuable sources of information.

Finding artifacts is both a matter of having a keen eye and knowing where to look. Many of the artifacts and replicas we use in the classroom come from our own home, or from the children's homes. A search of the attic or the basement will probably result in an interesting collection of artifacts you can use in the classroom. As you search, consider the following household objects:

family relics and heirlooms	tools (kitchen, garden, etc.)
photographs	school materials (books, supplies)
postcards	sports memorabilia
old toys	
children and adult garments	

Thrift stores, garage sales, and flea markets are also places where a variety of artifacts can be found.

Family, friends, and community members are also valuable sources of meaningful and interesting artifacts. Knowing who the collectors are in your community and what they collect can be another source of rare and unique pieces. Also, there are many local museums that lend artifacts and replicas for classroom use. In some cases, museums offer on-site exhibits that they will bring to schools. These activities require advance reservations. To find what services are available in your community, check your local telephone book and contact the museum curators. They will provide details about the artifacts and exhibits available for young children.

---

historical fiction, and folktales. Biographies help children learn about the lives of important people. Good biographies offer accurate portrayals of key incidents in the life of a person. For young children, biographies are a way to learn about values and human qualities. Well-written biographies are also a way for children to meet real-life characters they will come to consider as "personal friends" (Norton, 1995, p. 646). *Rosa Parks* (Greenfield, 1973); *Sacajawea* (Jassen, 1973), and *Happy birthday, Martin Luther King* (Marzollo, 1993) are a few of the many biographical books appropriate for young children.

Historical fiction takes children to "live" in the past, together with all the emotions and conflicts of a particular period. As children meet characters and analyze the various situations, they "discover that in all times, people have depended upon one another and that they have had similar needs" (Norton, 1995, p. 505). Historical fiction is characterized by the presentation of a realistic story that is set in the past with characters that are either historical or fictional. The presentation of facts that are accurate is the most essential element of good historical fiction (see criteria in Concept Box 5–9). In this literary genre children are offered the opportunities to live vicariously the conflicts of other times. Historical fiction allows them to gain a sense of being a part of society in the past.

Drama in the Classroom: A Developmentally Appropriate Way to Make History Alive

Early childhood educators recognize the child's dramatic ability as an important learning strategy. Dramatic experiences happen daily in the classroom. They take place as children engage in pre-

---

Concept Box 5–9 Criteria for Evaluating Historical Fiction

_____ Are characters appropriately described?
_____ Is the setting accurately described?
_____ Does the plot help to understand the event or the contribution made by the character?
_____ Are events historically correct?
_____ Do illustrations provide an accurate portrayal of the historical period?

Source: Adapted from Huck, C., Hepler, S., Hickman, J., & Kiefer, B. (1997). _Children's literature in the elementary classroom_ (6th ed.). Madison, WI: Brown & Benchmark.

■■ Let's Talk About. . . 5–9

Creating a Resource Bank of Folk Stories and Folk Songs

You can build your own resource bank based on the folklore of your community. There are many sources for folk stories and songs. Begin by writing those passed on to you by your family: stories, songs, characters, proverbs, and so on. Try to recall the stories, the songs, and the games you and your friends enjoyed during your childhood. Families and community members are an excellent source for culturally meaningful and unusual folk stories and songs. Libraries are also a good place to look for traditional stories and songs. Among the books you may want to look for are: _The acorn tree and other folktales_ (Rockwell, 1995) and _The adventures of spider: West African folktales_ (Arkhurt, 1992).

Record and save your findings. And, of course, share them with children in the classroom!

---

tend play, as they role-play a favorite part from a story, and as they create imaginary play partners. Children use drama not only as an avenue for self-expression but also to communicate their views about reality through their creative interpretations of events. Informal and spontaneous dramatic representations commonly spin out of a variety of activities—stories shared in class, a field trip, a community event, a visit from a resource person. Coody (1997) points out that despite the unstructured nature of children's dramatic interpretations, "they take their roles quite seriously" (p. 54). Children will spontaneously respond dramatically to a story, a personal experience, or to something they witness in or out of the classroom. They will add their own movements and words to share what impressed them the most. Valuable learning emerges as children "act out." The acting-out experiences offer valuable opportunities to build critical reflection, problem-solving skills, prosocial behavior, and understanding of others.

There are many ways to encourage and nurture the children's need for **dramatic activities.** A drama center with props and materials always triggers the children's role-playing based on imaginary

and real situations. Puppets also contribute to dramatization. (For more ways to use drama to integrate different themes in the curriculum, see Chapter 8.)

Puppets allow additional "characters" to come alive and participate in the children's representations. A first grade teacher working in an inclusion classroom has found puppets to be successful tools for all children (Brea, 1998). She keeps a variety of puppets in her classroom in an old chest, named "The puppet home" by the children. In her opinion, puppets provide opportunities for all children—including those witih special needs—to participate in different dramatic roles. As an example, she mentions a child in a wheelchair who commonly uses puppets to describe his perceptions about actions and movements while another child helps to move his chair around. She also reports that children with Down's syndrome have successfully used hand puppets to participate in dramatizations.

Concept Box 5–10   Sources for Quality Children's Literature

Several professional organizations publish lists of appropriate children's literature for social studies. You may want to contact them.

■ *National Council for the Social Studies (NCSS)* and the *Children's Book Council (CBC) Joint Project.*

NCSS and CBC have a joint annual project to select the best trade books in the field of social studies. A not-for-profit organization, CBC fosters the use and enjoyment of children's literature. The list of recommended titles is published in the April issues of the *Social Education* and *Social Studies and the Young Learner.* Inquiries about the annual list of best trade books should be sent to:

Children's Book Council
568 Broadway, Suite 404
New York, NY 10012

Inquiries about NCSS should be sent to:
National Council for the Social Studies
3501 Newark Street, NW
Washington, DC 20016

■ *The International Reading Association (IRA)*

In conjunction with CBC, IRA sponsors the *Children's Choices* project. The project publishes an annual list of newly published books best liked by children (throughout the U.S.) in the fall issue of the *Reading Teacher.* You can obtain a copy of the list from IRA for a nominal fee.

International Reading Association
Dept. EG
800 Barksdale Road
P.O. Box 8139
Newark, DE 19714–813

The advantages of dramatic experiences are many. Through drama activities, children interpret and reflect upon actions and their consequences as encountered in stories, role-play characters from other times, express their understandings of customs and beliefs, and explore the many intricacies of life (Consortium of National Arts Education Association, 1994).

Teachers can plan dramatic experiences to help children build ideas about the characters and concepts to be explored. After a story is shared, prompts such as *"Imagine that _____ is here,"* *"What if _____ ?"* and *"Oh, look, Mr. _____ is here"* serve as invitations for dramatic play. It is easy for the whole class to participate by singing a song or by reciting repetitive phrases. Encouraging children to use improvised dialogue provides opportunities to interpret an event and to visualize themselves as the characters. Dorothy Heathcote (Van Hoorn, Nourot, Scales, & Alward, 1999), a drama educator who has developed drama techniques around social and historical themes, suggests that to successfully participate in the children's dramatic plays, teachers

should guide and support the children's actions indirectly. In the beginning, teachers can introduce the situations and the characters to help children expand their drama scripts; however, once the play is established, teachers can retire to the background, assuming the role of a conscious observer who will intervene only occasionally. When teachers "scaffold" dramatic actions, either by providing support or by helping the play event to unfold, children are led to express and expand their knowledge to the fullest (Van Hoorn et al., 1999).

While dramatic activities commonly occur at the drama centers, a special place in the classroom can be designated where children can "stage" their interpretations of scenes from stories, events from daily life, or reenact holiday celebrations. A chest or a box with a variety of materials and props placed at the designated area will engage children in dramatization (see Concept Box 5–11). Materials for costumes help children to "become" the characters of their choice. As they pretend to become people from the past, historical learning takes place in developmentally meaningful ways.

Concept Box 5–11   Materials for Dramatic Play

Three-year-olds	*Preschoolers (ages 4 to 5)*	*Primary-Age Children (ages 6 to 8)*
realistic material puppets	realistic objects	hats
hats	housekeeping props	scarves
masks	puppets	costumes
scarves	clothing	regalia
toys	accessories (hats, shoes,	transformational items
regalia and artifacts	bags)	
costumes	dolls	
adult clothing	toy animals (stuffed, plastic)	
transformational items	transformational items	
(blocks, boxes, cardboard)		

Recommended Children's Books

There are many good examples of stories with historical characters. Examples of fictional characters are Felicity (Tripp, 1991), a girl living during the Revolutionary War and Addy (Porter, 1994), an African-American character from 1864. Both characters are in the *American Girls Collection,* a series portraying the life of girls in different time eras. Although this series is written for elementary children, the stories can be adapted for younger children. Characters from the stories by Laura Ingalls Wilder are also appealing to young children. The series, adapted for young children, include stories appropriate for ages 3 through 8. Titles such as *Bedtime for Laura* (Wilder, 1997) and *County fair* (Wilder, 1998) provide opportunities to learn about family and community life in the past.

There are also many stories set in historical times to choose from. Among them are *Sweet Clara and the freedom quilt* (Hopkinson, 1993), *The drinking gourd* (Monjo, 1970), *An early American Christmas* (de Paola, 1987), *Let the celebrations begin!* (Wild, 1991), and *The ballot box battle* (McCully, 1996). These and other appropriate titles can be found in the listing of *The Notable Children's Trade Books in the Field of Social Studies,* published annually by NCSS and the Children's Book Council. This publication is an excellent source. The list includes a selection of the best historical fiction titles, including their reading levels.

Folktales and *folk songs* offer children a rich and colorful sense of the past. Because folktales are characteristic of cultures around the world, they represent a way to discover the stories passed on through generations in our global society. Folklore is not only a popular repository of traditions, but also an account of historical events as seen through the eyes of the people who witnessed or participated in them.

Legendary characters like Johnny Appleseed and Paul Bunyan, incredible animals like Croojaw the whale, adventurous cowboys and ingenious ladies from colonial times, and people searching for freedom through the Underground Railroad form a part of our national historical tradition. Folk stories also serve to establish global connections. Chinese folktales about dragons, European fairy tales, and stories about characters such as Babushka (Russian), Anansi (West African, Jamaican), and Juan Bobo (Puerto Rican) give children historical glimpses of life in other countries and in other times.

ACTIVITIES

Keeping Track of What You Learn: Your Personal Activity Log

In this chapter we discussed some of key ideas relating to history education for young children. Here are some additional activities for your PAL.

A. Reflections

1. Based on what you have learned about teaching history to young children, formulate your own philosophy of history education for kindergarten through fourth grade.
2. Plan a lesson about the concept of time, using some of the information and resources in this chapter, and either present it to your classmates or teach it to your class.
3. List 10 activities you could use to teach the relationship between time and change to the primary grade level of your choice.

B. Collections

1. Compile a resource list of books and objects that can be used in teaching history to young children and add it to the school library. You can also use it as start of a more extensive reference guide that your colleagues and classmates can contribute to.
2. Create a bank of hands-on materials to foster development of the concepts "old" and "new."
3. Develop an inventory of nursery rhymes, fingerplays, and songs to help children develop time concepts.

C. Internet Resources*

Your Internet bookmarks keep growing! Here are some additional sites you will enjoy visiting. They provide rich historic information you will want to share with children.

1. Noah Webster House Museum in Hartford

Web site: http://www.ctstateu.edu/~noahweb/noahwebster.html

Information about the life of Noah Webster, author of the first American dictionary, including descriptions of life in colonial America. Of particular interest is the description of children's games and toys in colonial times.

2. The Smithsonian Institution

Web site: http://www.si.edu

This is an interesting web site that offers an online visit to the Smithsonian. Teachers will find information about exhibits and educational materials.

3. The Learning Page

Web site: http://memory.loc.gov/ammem/ndlpedu/index.html

A source for historical pictures and photographs as well as activities, this site is part of the American Memory Internet project. The photograph and picture collection covers various aspects of American cultural life. Children will enjoy observing the portraits of presidents and first ladies.

4. Teaching with Historic Places

Web site: http://www.cr.nps.gov/nr/twhp/home.html

This exciting Web site offers ideas for classroom activities as well as information about key historical places across the country. The section called *Adventures* offers children an opportunity to travel through time. Drawings about a variety of historical places can be downloaded and colored by children. The site sponsored a gallery with selected illustrations colored by children. A teacher's guide is available. This site is sponsored by the National Park Service, the National Register of Historic Places, and the National Trust for Historic Preservation.

*Please note that Internet resources are of a time-sensitive nature and URL sites and addresses may often be modified or deleted.

References

Anno, M. (1978). *Anno's journey.* New York: Philomel.

Adler, D. (1993). *A picture book of Anne Frank.* New York: Bantam Doubleday.

Arkhurst, J. (1992). *The adventures of spider: West African tales.* New York: Little Brown.

Banks, J. (1993). *Multicultural education: Characteristics and goals.* In J. Banks & C. Banks (Eds.). *Multicultural education: Issues and perspectives.* (2nd ed.). Boston, MA: Allyn & Bacon.

Barton, K. (1997). History—It *can* be elementary. *Social Education, 61*(1), 13–16.

Berk, L. (1997). *Child development.* (3rd ed.). Needham Heights, MA: Allyn & Bacon.

Brea, E. (1998). Personal communication.

Bredekamp, S., & Rosegrant, T. (Eds.). (1992). *Reaching potentials: Appropriate curriculum and assessment for young children.* (Vol. 1). Washington, DC: National Association for the Education of Young Children.

Bredekamp, S., & Rosegrant, T. (1995). *Reaching potentials: Transforming early childhood curriculum and assessment.* (Vol. 2). Washington, DC: National Association for the Education of Young Children.

Carle, E. (1971). *The grouchy ladybug.* New York: Crowell Books.

Chancellor, D. (1992). Calendar mathematics: Time and time again. *Arithmetic Teacher, 39*(5), pp. 14–15.

Charlesworth, R., & Lind, K. (1999). *Math and science for young children* (3rd ed.). Albany, NY: Delmar.

Charlesworth, R. (1996). *Experiences in math for young children* (3rd ed.). Albany, NY: Delmar.

Cheng, H. (1976). *The Chinese new year.* New York: Holt.

CIDCLI. (1988). *Cristobal Colon.* Bogota, Colombia: Carvajal.

Coerr, E. (1993). *Sadako.* New York: Putnam.

Consortium of National Arts Education Association (1994). *Dance, music, theater, visual arts: What every young American should be able to do in the arts.* In *National Standards for Arts Education.* Reston, VA: Author.

Coody, B. (1997). *Using literature with young children.* (5th ed.). Madison, WI: Brown & Benchmark.

Cooper, H. (1995). *History in the early years.* London, UK: Routledge.

de Paola, T. (1978). *Pancakes for breakfast.* San Diego, CA: Harcourt Brace Jovanovich.

de Paola, T. (1987). *An early American Christmas.* New York: Holiday House.

Flournoy, V. (1978). *The best time of day.* New York: Random House.

Fox, M. (1989). *Night noises.* San Diego, CA: Harcourt Brace Jovanovich.

Greene, W. (1998). *Museums and learning: A guide for family visits.* Washington, DC: Office of Educational Research and Improvement and the Smithsonian Office of Education.

Greenfield, E. (1973). *Rosa Parks.* New York: Crowell Books.

Hoge, J. (1996). *Effective elementary social studies.* Belmont, CA: Wadsworth.

Hopkinson, D. (1993). *Sweet Clara and the freedom quilt.* New York: Alfred A. Knopf.

Huck, C., Hepler, S., Hickman, S., & Kiefer, B. (1997). *Children's literature in the elementary classroom.* (6th ed.) Madison. WI: Brown & Benchmark.

Hutchins, P. (1993). *The doorbell rang.* New York: Scholastic.

Isadora, R. (1991). *At the crossroads.* New York: Greenwillow.

Jassen, K. (1973). *Sacajawea: Wilderness guide.* New York: Troll.

Kamii, C., & DeVries, R. (1980). *Group games in early education: Implications of Piaget's theory.* Washington, DC: National Association for the Education of Young Children.

Levinson, R. (1985). *Watch the stars come out.* New York: Puffin Books.

Lock, K., Kelly, F., & Rivers, S. (1995). *Xochiquetzal.* Sydney, Australia: Martin International.

Marzollo, J. (1993). *Happy birthday, Martin Luther King.* New York: Scholastic.

McCully, E. A. (1996). *The ballot box battle.* New York: Alfred A. Knopf.

Monjo, F. N. (1970). *The drinking gourd.* New York: Harper & Row.

Myers, W. D. (1993). *Brown angels: An album of pictures and verse.* New York: HarperCollins.

Myers, W. D. (1995). *Glorious children: A celebration of children.* New York: HarperCollins.

National Center for History in the Schools. (1994). *National Standards: History for grades K–4.* Los Angeles, CA: Author.

National Center for History in the Schools. (1998). *U.S. National Standards for United States History K–4.* Available on-line:* [http://www.ucla.edu/nchs/usk4ch.1.html]

National Council for History Education. (1998). *Reinvigorating history in U.S. schools.* Available on-line:* [http://www.oce.org/nche/recommend.html]

National Council for the Social Studies. (1994). *National Standards: History for grades K–4*. Los Angeles, CA: Author.

Nickly, M. (1982). *The emperor's plum dress*. New York: Greenwillow.

Norton, D. (1995). *Through the eyes of a child: Introduction to children's literature*. Englewood Cliffs, NJ: Merrill.

Piaget, J. (1970). *The child's conception of time*. New York: Basic Books.

Porter, C. (1994). *Addy*. Middleton, WI: Pleasant Company.

Potter, B. (1995). *The tale of the flopsy bunnies*. In *Treasury of stories*. Lincolnwood, IL: Publications International.

Rachlin, A. (1993). *Famous children*. London, UK: Aladdin Books. (Series includes: Chopin, Bach, Brahms, Handel, Haydn, Mozart, Schumann, and Tchaikovsky).

Ravitch, D. (1985, Spring). The precarious state of history. *American Educator, 9*(1), p. 17.

Ravitch, D. (1996, December). What happened to history in the grade schools? Tot sociology. *History matters! Online edition.** Available on-line: [http://www.oce.org/nche/archives/dec_news .html]

Rockwell, A. (1995). *The acorn tree and other folktales*. New York: Greenwillow.

Rockwell, A. (1985). *First come spring*. New York: Crowell Books.

San Souci, R. (1991). *Wyeth's pilgrims*. San Francisco, CA: Chronicle Books.

Say, A. (1993). *Grandfather's journey*. New York: Houghton Mifflin.

Seefeldt, C. (1997). *Social studies for the preschool–primary child* (5th ed.). Upper Saddle River, NJ: Merrill/Prentice Hall.

Shore, R. (1997). *Rethinking the brain: New insights into early development*. New York: Families and Work Institute.

Thomas, A. (1993). *Wake up, Wilson Street*. New York: Henry Holt & Company.

Thornton, S. (1997). First-hand study: Teaching history for understanding. *Social Education, 61*(1), pp. 11–12.

Timberlake, P. (1986). Time concepts in the classroom. *Dimensions, 15*(1), pp. 5–7.

Tripp, V. (1991). *Felicity*. Middleton, WI: Pleasant Company.

Van Hoorn, J., Nourot, P., & Scales, P. (1999). *Play at the center of the curriculum* (2nd ed.). Upper Saddle River, NJ: Prentice Hall.

Van Scoy, I. J., & Fairchild, S. H. (1993). It's about time! Helping preschool and primary children understand time concepts. *Young Children, 48*(2), pp. 21–24.

Vygotsky, L. (1996). *Thought and language*. Cambridge, MA: The MIT Press.

Wild, J. (1991). *Let the celebrations begin!* New York: Orchard Books.

Wilder, L. I. (1997). *Bedtime for Laura*. New York: HarperCollins.

Wilder, L. I. (1998). *County fair*. New York: Harper Trophy.

Wolfman, I. (1991). *Do people grow on family trees? Genealogy for kids & other beginners: The official Ellis Island handbook*. New York: Workman Publishing.

---

*Please note that Internet resources are of a time-sensitive nature and URL sites and addresses may often be modified or deleted.

CHAPTER 6

Learning about Where We Live: Geography and the Young Child

The study of geography has practical value through the application of a spatial view to life situations.

—NATIONAL GEOGRAPHIC JOINT COMMITTEE (1994)

Chapter Questions

After you read this chapter you should be able to answer the following questions:

- What is geography?
- How do children learn about geography?
- What are children's ideas of spatial relationships?
- How can we organize the classroom to help children learn about geography?

Key Terms and Concepts

cognitive mapping
geographic literacy
geographic processes
geography
macro-environmental cognition
map

perspective
position and orientation
scale
space
symbols
visual literacy

Classroom Portrait: Exploring Geography with Children

In Mrs. Campbell's classroom, pre-kindergartners were busy getting ready to start the new day. On this particular morning, instead of having the children choose the song of the day, the teacher made a suggestion: "What if we sing *'The Wheels on the Bus'*?"

An energetic "Yeah!" resounded from the children.

"Before we sing, let's play a game. Let's imagine I'm the bus driver," Mrs. Campbell said, putting on a cap, "and I want all of you to ride on my bus. So, where do you need to be to get on the bus?"

"At the bus stop," said the girl in the blue dress.

"You need to wave, or the bus won't take you," said the tall boy who was gesturing in the back of the classroom.

"I don't wave and the bus always stops to bring me to school," a little girl commented, puzzled.

"Why is that? Does anyone know why?" Mrs. Campbell asked.

It did not take long for the children to decide that there are different kinds of buses. "Buses can take you to many places—to downtown, to school, to the mall," the children concluded.

"Well, let's pretend that the classroom is our city and that I'm driving a bus that goes downtown, and you want to go there. So, let's see where the bus stops are where you can get on the bus," Mrs. Campbell an-

nounced. The children quickly created four BUS STOP signs, and placed them throughout the classroom.

"Now we are ready to sing 'The Wheels on the Bus.' Remember to be at one of the bus stops," Mrs. Campbell reminded the class.

Taking their places, the children started to sing and to get on the bus. A simple change to the lyrics was suggested by one of the children:

> *The wheels on the bus go round and round*
> *Round and round,*
> *Round and round.*
> *The wheels on the bus go round and round*
> *All around the* classroom!

After several trips around the classroom and a change of bus drivers, the class arrived at their destination. Now it was time to review some important ideas. "Let's talk about our trip. Which way did the bus go in our classroom?" Mrs. Campbell asked. "Who can show me the direction the bus took?" she inquired. Soon the class was engaged in a discussion about the different "places" along the bus route and about the distances from one stop to another.

"Tomorrow," Mrs. Campbell announced, "we are going to ride the bus on the playground. So, be ready!"

■■ Geography in the Early
■■ Childhood Curriculum

"Oh, the places you will go!"
                                    —Dr. Seuss

One of the best ways to describe young children is to say that they are natural explorers. Children begin to discover the world around them as soon as they are born. In their eagerness to learn the intricacies of their environment, children display inclinations and skills similar to those used by geographers. Relying on their senses and curiosity, children learn about major geographical concepts like space, place, distance, time, and representa-

tions. These experiences and innate behaviors make children predisposed to geography education.

The Nature of Geography

Geography is the science of space in all of its dimensions, from the general characteristics of the world at large to the personal places where we live. Geography also examines how people interact with each other and with natural resources. It is "[t]he study of people, places, and the environments and the relationships among them" (National Geographic Society, 1994, p. 1). Knowledge about local, national, and worldwide geography helps people gain "a sense of place and of their relationship in

---

Concept Box 6-1   Children's Expanding Sense of Space

Infants (Birth through age 1)
Personal Space

Explore themselves; acquire a sense about their body image; become familiar with physical characteristics of their immediate environments like the crib, home, childcare facility; recognize important people.

Toddlers
(age 18 months through 3 years)
Personal Space
Local Space

Expand exploration of immediate environments such as classroom, playgrounds, neighborhood, homes of friends and relatives; acquire images of other places from media, storybooks, and notions about distances.

Preschoolers (ages 4 to 5)
Personal, Local, National;
Beginning Ideas of the Space Far Away

Continue to develop and refine ideas about personal space; gather ideas about local space through direct interaction with environment and with people; build mental images of people and objects in the local space (neighborhood, shopping areas, recreational places); experience space through family outings, visits to relatives and friends, and classroom activities based on spatial relationships; develop notions about national space through the media, music, and children's literature (i. e., books about rain forests, animal life, polar zones, and ocean floor).

Primary-Age Children
Personal, Local, National;
Far Away/Global Space

Continue to refine ideas about personal space; expand concepts about local, national, and global space through media, school experiences, friends, and adults.

---

time to historical and current events" (NCSS, 1989, p. viii). This broad and exciting field plays an important role in the growth and development of children.

Understanding the concept of **space**—the area where human and natural activities take place—is essential to the study of geography. Space can be explored at different levels: *personal, local, national,* and *global.* Research shows that children begin to conceptualize space very early in life. Through the media and through personal experiences, they learn about the characteristics of space.

Teaching geography in the early years is an active process built upon the experiences and the interests of children. Space can be transformed by the actions of people and by changes caused by natural phenomena such as floods, earthquakes, and volcanoes. Far from merely teaching facts about places, geography education in the early childhood classroom is based on an engaging, active hands-on curriculum (Palmer, 1994). The opportunities to design

an effective curriculum can be found in the children's field trips, visits to local and familiar places, and walks around the neighborhood.

The Geography of the World around Children: Explorers from Birth

In the early years, geography takes the form of the expanding personal and local space surrounding young children. Their active explorations include self-exploration as well as the exploration of the people and objects sharing their world. From infancy, young children display a desire to learn about the things around them. Observe infants in their cribs as soon as they are born, and see how they begin touching, pulling, and grasping their bodies as they initiate the process of self-exploration and discovery. As they grow, they soon begin to explore the faces of people who are holding them such as parents, friends, and caregivers. These common behav-

Children are explorers from birth.

■■ Let's Talk About . . . 6–1
Children's Natural Instinct to Explore
To learn more about how children explore their environments, observe what children do in different settings. Look for behaviors indicative of exploration, such as touching and examining objects, taking objects apart, or examining a large object or piece of furniture. Observe children at home and see which of these behaviors they demonstrate.
Visit an early childhood center, and observe the children's actions during center time and on the playground. Look for exploratory behaviors in these settings. Record your findings in an anecdotal record such as your personal activity log (PAL). Remember to share your findings and comments with your colleagues.

iors are ways of learning about the geography around them. As children mature, their interests in exploring the more remote spaces emerge. Learning about the places where relatives, friends, famous persons, and imaginary characters live causes young children to examine the characteristics of environments away from their immediate surroundings.

The Need for Geography in the Early Years

Educators agree that the study of geography complements the developmental patterns of young children. The innate curiosity; the exploratory behaviors; the understanding of space, place, and distance; as well as the ability to understand symbolic representations make geography a developmentally appropriate field for young children. There are several reasons to support geography education in the early years.

1. An understanding of space provides the foundation for well-informed individual decisions later in life.
2. A person who is aware of the spatial relationships acquires a sense of personal control over the environment.
3. Knowledge about geographic space fosters in children an appreciation and sense of the places and things, near and away.

4. Geography education also promotes a sense of responsibility towards the environment. Promoting positive attitudes towards the protection of our resources and conservation of the environment are essential because the world's landscape is seriously at risk.
   (National Geographic Joint Committee, 1994)

Engaging in child-appropriate activities that promote awareness of other people and foster an interest in their environments is one of the best ways to build geographic knowledge. Early childhood educators should remember that developing awareness of essential geographic elements should be based on the experiences of the individual child (Palmer, 1994).

Geography—the Spatial Context for History

Long, long ago, the land now known as Mexico was a green and fertile place where plants and animals flourished. At this time the Aztec people lived in harmony with their land. Gods and goddesses lived in the mountains and valleys and the greatest of all Aztec gods was the Great Mother Earth.
   —*Xochiquetzal* (Lock & Kelly, 1995)

When learning about history, phrases like "Long, long ago *in a far away place* . . ." set the stage for many adventures. Knowledge about the setting—the *geography* where events take place—not only establishes the mood for what is to be experienced but also defines the relevance of the actions. For example, the passage that introduces this section provides a rich setting for children listening to the story of *Xochiquetzal*. Events throughout the story will become significant as children imagine them in the lush natural setting described in the beginning passage.

As children learn about the events of the past, an understanding of the settings (geography) contributes to their appreciation of the significance of those events. Geography helps children to see how the environment influences human actions. It also helps them to visualize the different challenges they and other people face. When seen in the context of geographic information, the feats of people in the past take on a new perspective. For example, the challenges faced by the knights of the medieval times amaze children largely because of the environments where the events took place.

■■ Fostering Geographic Knowledge

One of the main goals of education is to provide learners with many different tools for successful participation in society (see Chapter 7). Knowledge of geography helps people understand the connections between the human, animal, and plant life along with other elements of the environment. Such knowledge is essential for sound decision making in the society. This is one of the reasons geography is emphasized in the national education agenda and why geography is an important area of the curriculum. Developing knowledge of geography in young children begins with the understanding of the concept of *space*.

Developing a Concept about the Space Around Us

Appropriate understanding of spatial concepts occurs as children begin to grasp the active and evolving nature of space. This occurs as children observe the impact of the two key **geographic processes** that transform our world—*natural forces* and *people*.

A knowledge of how natural forces alter our communities promotes the children's understanding of the climatic processes that alter the face of the Earth. Discussions of stories like *The year of no more corn* (Ketterman, 1993), *Hurricane* (London, 1998), and *Flood* (Calhoun, 1997) evoke comments about natural events taking place. In addition there are opportunities for children to share personal experiences of rainstorms and other events caused by natural forces.

A knowledge of how people transform the environment at different levels—from community playgrounds to artificial ocean reefs—builds the children's understanding of the relationship of humans to their environments. Field trips to local places and discussions of stories like *The great kapok tree* (Cherry, 1990) and *Someday a tree* (Bunting, 1997) are examples of developmentally appropriate ways to foster understanding about how humans impact the environment.

Seeing the results of these processes makes children understand the effects of space on people and their environments. It also helps the children see themselves as a part of this evolving change process.

Becoming Geographically Literate

Learning how to interpret information about the environment and our relationship with it as humans is essential for making well-informed decisions. **Geographic literacy** starts with getting a sense of where we are and where others live; as we become more literate in this area, we recognize the impact of geography and the environment on our lives and world events. Learning how to read geographic messages and understanding their significance is one of the main goals of geography education.

One of the skills a geographically literate individual has is the ability to use space and its elements appropriately. The acquisition of this skill starts at birth. Infants begin to develop geographic literacy

Bringing Ideas into Practice 6–1
Sources for Thematic Teaching:
Planning Activities about Geographic
Processes in Action

Natural Processes
Weather changes:
- rain
- droughts
- lightning
- wind (hurricanes, storms, tornadoes)

Water changes:
- oceans
- rivers, streams

Earth movements:
- earthquakes
- landslides
- volcanoes

Animal migrations and
Vegetation changes:
- forests
- rain forests
- deserts

Processes Caused by Human Actions
Changes in Earth's surface through construction of:
- human communities
- roads, dams
- recreational areas

Deforestation
Farming
Pollution
Environmental protection

FIGURE 6–1   Children's Comments about the Characteristics of Their Environments

- "Grandma lives in a house with big feet." (Alexia, age 3, referring to a house on stilts)
- "I'm talking to my aunt. She lives with Mickey Mouse." (Barbara, 29 months, referring to her aunt, who works in Disneyland)
- "Let's go over the hill to McDonald's" (Bertito, age 4, referring to an overpass on a highway)
- "I can see the sea jumping over the bridge!" (Crystal, age 4, sharing her observations about the seacoast)
- "You sleep and sleep again, and then you are there." (Brittany, age 4, describing her sense of distance while traveling on an airplane)

as they explore the space around their cribs and play areas. An awareness of the characteristics of their environment helps young children to visualize themselves as a part of it and to see the roles of others. Knowing how to read the elements and patterns in their surroundings provides a sense of place and belonging for children. For example, the comments made by preschoolers in Figure 6–1 show how keenly aware they are of the myriad of characteristics in their environments and how they perceive themselves and others in a particular space. This early sense of geographic literacy provides the foundation for the more complex tasks of understanding the interrelationships between people and their environments. One of the goals of geography education in the early years is not only to create opportunities for children to read the clues in their immediate space, but to expand their knowledge of the world beyond their surroundings.

■■ Building Global Connections ■■ through Geography

Proficiency in geography will prepare children to live in the increasingly global society that has been transformed by modern telecommunications and transportation. Technology has bridged the distances among all people and created a more compact world. Technology has made the acquisition of all knowledge—including geography—almost instantaneous. More important, it has brought the world into the lives of young children. One prekindergarten teacher reported that during the 1998

Olympic Games her class followed the various competitions at home and in the classroom. She noticed that not only did the children realize that the Games were far from where they live, they also knew that people from other countries were attending the events (Fisher, 1998). Following up on the children's interests, the teacher embarked on a two-week thematic unit about the Olympics. The children located the countries represented in the Games, found the home states of the leading American athletes, and talked about ancient Greece, where the Olympic Games originated. Another teacher had a similar experience with her class during the celebration of the 1998 World Soccer Cup in France. With families and the whole community following the games, the children were provided with a rich setting for learning about the world. Helping children to develop a sense of the location of their global neighbors is an important part of early education.

■■ Let's Talk About . . . 6–2

Are We Preparing Children to Live in a Global Society?

Since the 1980s, several studies have revealed that American students were graduating from high school and even the institutions of higher learning without achieving competence in geography. The response to this problem has been to include geography education in *Goals 2000,* and to develop the national geography standards (see p. 149). In spite of these significant efforts, some educators still feel that geography is a subject unsuitable for young children.

1. How can we educate teachers about the value of geography in the early childhood curriculum?

2. Do you find the geography standards to be appropriate for young children? Why or why not?

Developing an Awareness of Global Society in Young Children

Early childhood educators know that young children bring to the classroom an awareness of things and people in other places. Their ideas, though "blurred" and incomplete, still reveal a knowledge of the world beyond their neighborhoods (Palmer, 1994). Much of this knowledge, built through "personal contacts, holidays, films, television, and other media . . ." (p. 59) consists of powerful images of the places far away from their communities. These perceptions mark the beginning of children's awareness of global connections.

Building an Accurate Vision of Our Global Society: Avoiding Biased Images

Most of us have been amazed at the ways children conceptualize places around the world. As they acquire images from many different sources, children tend to build mental glimpses of far-away places that often lack accuracy (Figure 6–2). They also express views about people that are often stereotypical and biased. Some of these stereotypes gained in childhood are potentially dangerous, for they lead to negative attitudes and inaccurate views of the world. Teachers should take a lead in promoting fair images about others as a goal of global education. (See Chapter 9 for more on multi-cultural education and diversity.) Helping young children to develop an awareness of and an appreciation for diversity is one of the fundamental goals of healthy social development (NAEYC, 1997).

"Evidence from research suggests that children absorb prejudices and negative attitudes from the media and social discourse well before they learn accurate information" (Palmer, 1994, p. 96). Teachers need to be aware of this, so they can correct early biases that may hinder the establishment of positive global connections among the new generations. There are several ways to promote accurate information about places away from the children's immediate surroundings:

1. *Listen to what children say and respond to their comments.* Create an inviting environment where

FIGURE 6–2 Children's Images of the World

A four-year-old talking to a visitor from Brazil:
Child: "Do you live in a rain forest?"
Adult: "No, I live in the city. Rain forests are far away from my house."
A six-year-old referring to the desert:
Child: "Your house must be all dusty."
Adult: "Why?"
Child: "You said you live in the desert, and deserts are sandy! They are full of sand and no water."
An adult talking to a four-year-old:
Adult: "Tell me about Australia."

Child: "They have kangaroos."
Adult: "And what else?"
Child: "Oh, big alligators and koalas. I know one."
Adult: "You do?"
Child: "Yeah, Koala-Lou."
Group of children browsing through a book about Africa:
Child 1: "It's all wild, see?"
Child 2: ". . . and where are the people?"
Child 1: "Oh, they live in mud houses."
Child 2: "Yeah."

children can freely discuss what they think and know about life and people in other places. Take opportunities to clarify the children's ideas during the conversations. This can also be accomplished through individual and group thematic explorations.

2. *Provide an accurate portrayal of places and people.* Select a broad spectrum of current and ac-

Concept Box 6–2   Ways to Depict Distant Places and People Appropriately

Be sure that what is presented shows:
■ a variety of people: gender, race, religion, and social background.
■ a variety of occupations.
■ a variety of images of people reflecting changes over time (past and present).
Present a variety of geographical contexts:
■ an assortment of natural contexts and landscapes.
■ an assortment of social contexts.
■ a variety of ways in which space is used.
■ contrasting lifestyles and population configurations (small towns, cities, rural areas).
■ an accurate portrayal of the racial and ethnic groups living in a place.

curate visual materials about places and people from other countries. Include information and artifacts related to a variety of human tasks, occupations, settlements, and landscapes (urban and rural, including countryside, fields, farms, and wildlife).

3. *Select literature that depicts a variety of places and people.* Children's literature should provide opportunities to learn about different perspectives and places. Select books that show environments, lifestyles, and cultures very different from and similar to theirs. Provide examples that are representative of all parts of our planet.

■■ What Children Should Learn about
■■ Geography: Themes and Skills

Several things need to be considered when planning an effective and meaningful curriculum for young children. First, we must remember that any successful curriculum begins with an appropriate selection of the content. Learning about the world and its many characteristics encompasses a rich variety of topics. Second, developmentally appropriate practices (DAP—see Chapters 1 and 3) state that children's knowledge and their interests are essential for building *worthy-to-be-learned* experiences. Teachers must be able to obtain and assess chil-

---

▪▪ Let's Talk About . . . 6–3

Are We Ready to Teach Geography?

Many of us think that geography is a very interesting and complex subject. Some of us also feel that we are not equipped to teach it. This is understandable, because geography was not a required subject for most of us, unless we majored in it. This lack of knowledge of geography can be a serious obstacle to the most dedicated teacher.

1. What academic preparation do you have for teaching geography?

2. What recommendations do you have for enhancing your knowledge of geography?

3. What resources would you suggest to sharpen your geography skills?

Concept Box 6–3 Where to Obtain Information about Geography Education

■ **National Geographic Society**
Geographic Education Program
1145 17th Street NW
Washington, DC 20036
(1–800-NGS-LINE)
Web site:
http://www.nationalgeographic.com*

Provides a source for information about teaching practices and strategies. An important source for appropriate geographic materials. The National Geographic Society also offers teacher workshops.

■ **National Council for Geographic Education**
Indiana University of Pennsylvania
Indiana, PA 15705
Publishers of the *Journal of Geography*

■ **Educational Resources Information Center (ERIC)**
Clearinghouse for Social Studies/
Social Science Education
Indiana University
2805 East 10th Street
Bloomington, IN 47408

ERIC offers a searchable database of research and journal articles about education, available at http://www. indiana.edu/~ssdc/eric.chess.html*

■ Local affiliates of the National Council for the Social Studies (NCSS). For a list of affiliates, check NCSS's Web site at:
http://www. ncss.org*

---

*Please note that Internet resources are of a time-sensitive nature and URL sites and addresses may often be modified or deleted.

---

dren's prior knowledge and interests accurately in order to include them in the curriculum. Third, the teacher's knowledge level about the content should also be considered. Competency in geography is essential for designing an academically sound and relevant curriculum.

In an effort to provide a framework for geography education, a joint committee of the National Geographic Society (1994) developed the *National Geography Standards.* The standards identify the key geography themes and skills to be taught from kindergarten through twelfth grade. It is important to understand that the skills and themes addressed in the standards do not represent a "stand-alone" curriculum. Rather, the national geography standards identify the concepts to be "incorporated throughout the curriculum" (1994, p. 255). They represent a source of information as well as helpful guidelines teachers can use to build appropriate child-based experiences. This approach to the standards is particularly appropriate for teaching young children who do not respond well to direct instruction.

The Many Facets of Geography: Five Fundamental Themes

"I know a place not very far away
Where we can dance with crawfish and play
'Alligator—Keep Away!'
We can fish on the bayou *and climb the live oak trees.*
I'd be very pleased to show you, if you'd like to come
with me."

—*Welcome to Bayou Town* (Schadler, 1996)

The *Guidelines for Geographic Education* (Natoli et al., 1984) identify five fundamental geography themes: *location, place, human-environment interactions, movement,* and *regions.* These themes can be used as frameworks for planning the curriculum (Figure 6–3). A close look at each of these major themes reveals a broad spectrum of interrelated concepts and ideas for thematic projects. Activities built around these themes will help children understand the active and changing nature of geography.

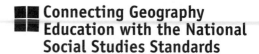

Connecting Geography Education with the National Social Studies Standards

The standards developed by the National Council for the Social Studies (1994) identify ten key social studies concepts that are essential to include in the curriculum. These national standards, including

---

FIGURE 6–3   Five Fundamental Geography Themes

■ **Theme 1: Location**
Description: The position of people, places and objects on the Earth's surface.
Concepts and Topics: Identifying one's absolute position (knowing one's own place, or its exact position); identifying one's relative position a "geographic context of the relationships among the locations of people, places, and events" (Hardwick & Holtgrieve, 1996, p. 50); using maps; creating simple maps; building models; estimating distance.

■ **Theme 2: Place**
Description: Unique human, cultural, and physical traits that distinguish a place.
Concepts and Topics: Recognizing natural or physical characteristics such as land forms, water forms, vegetation, animal life, climates; identifying the human characteristics of an area, such as language, cultures, people, settlement patterns (urban, rural); transportation and communication; recreational activities (sports, parks, and so on).

■ **Theme 3: Human-Environment Interactions**
Description: The context in which actions and

events occur, emphasizing the relationships between people and their environment.
Concepts and Topics: Personal places (home, school, and playgrounds); people and the community; other locations where people live; animal habitats; usage of environmental resources; pollution; environmental protection.

■ **Theme 4: Movement**
Description: Movement of people throughout the world and how they interact with each other in the new places where they move.
Concepts and Topics: Immigration; family origins; transportation; communication; movement of products and other resources; moving goods to markets.

■ **Theme 5: Regions**
Description: The study of change in human and land areas.
Concepts and Topics: Natural areas in the community; animal habitat; people habitats; land use in the community.

Source: Natoli, S. J., Boehm, R., Kratch, J., Lanegran, D., Monk, J., & Morill, R. (1984). *Guidelines for geographic education: Elementary and secondary schools.* Washington, DC: Association of American Geographers and National Council for Geographic Education.

the performance expectations and recommended child-appropriate themes, are reproduced in Appendix I (p. 271). *Fostering geographic knowledge* is the goal of the third theme, or curricular strand, of the social studies standards (NCSS, 1994). Strand III—*People, Places and Environments*—establishes how geography influences and affects individuals. It also defines the ways individuals alter the environment. Development of the knowledge about the interactive nature of geography is crucial. Today, effective social and civic participation requires individuals to become aware of their responsibilities towards their environments.

Along with Strand III, Strand IV—*Global Connections* (see p. 276)—provides another way to address geographic and environmental knowledge. Understanding the interrelationships that exist among people and their environment, near and far, is critical in today's global society. Realization of how events and circumstances happening in other places affect people across the street and around the world contributes to building a sense of shared responsibilities. In the classroom there are many opportunities to help children build these concepts.

Teachers can integrate a variety of themes from Strands III and IV into their curriculum planning. Suggested classroom topics include the following:

- Learning to locate our community
- Mapping the places where we live
- Using geography tools (maps and globes)
- Exploring the physical characteristics of the community
- Studying recreational places in our community
- Visiting places where animals live
- Learning to take care of plants and animals
- Learning about plants and animals from other places
- Exploring the places where food comes from
- Helping to keep the environment clean
- Learning about rain forests
- Discovering what geographers do
- Learning about crops people grow in other places
- Exploring what people in other communities and in other countries wear
- Studying how houses are built in other places

- Learning about children's games and activities throughout the seasons

Essential Geography Skills

According to the Geography Education Standards Project, the acquisition of five key geographic skills provides children with the ability to form perspectives about their space and the space of others. "The skills enable them [children] to observe patterns, associations, and spatial order" (1994, p. 45). The target skills for children in grades K through four appear in Figure 6–4. They provide teachers with valuable information and guidelines for building the curriculum and fostering the development of these skills in young children. We have included some examples of what constitutes developmentally appropriate behaviors and expectations for each of the five skills. As you review the essential geography skills, notice how closely they resemble critical thinking skills. Use "what children do" to plan meaningful geography experiences.

Planning Geography Experiences

All successful classroom experiences, including geography activities, depend on good planning. Good planning includes discovering relevant and meaningful ways to integrate the knowledge and experiences of children into the curriculum. As you get ready to plan your activities, ascertain what ideas the children already have regarding the skills and concepts you plan to introduce. This is especially important in geography education, because in the early years, geography-oriented experiences do not follow a pre-established curriculum: Rather, they originate from the child. Through appropriate questioning techniques and by listening closely to the children's comments, teachers can assess the emerging geographic concepts and skills the children already possess.

In spite of having some basic knowledge, young children generally are not ready for formal teaching of such an abstract field as geography. According to Piagetian principles (see Chapter 3), preoperational

FIGURE 6–4   Geographic Skills in the Early Childhood Classroom

1. **Learning to ask geographic questions**
   What children do:
   - inquire about the location of objects and areas at home, classroom, and school.
   - ask questions about the homes of peers, relatives, and their own homes.
   - ask questions about places described in stories.
   - inquire about where relatives and peers live.
   - ask questions about places where pets and animals live.
   - ask questions about places discussed in the media (news stories, programs).
   - show an interest in landforms and water forms.
   - identify geographic characteristics of places in stories and in the news.
   - inquire about distances and means of transportation.
   - ask questions about roads and routes people use.
   - inquire about land use in the community.

2. **Acquiring geographic information**
   What children do:
   - explore the space (home, classroom, and playground) to discover its characteristics.
   - manipulate objects within an area to gather information.
   - visit places to collect information (i.e., the museum, a zoo, and a farm).
   - observe photographs and pictures to gather information about a particular area.
   - look through books to collect information.
   - examine models and simple maps.
   - observe changes over a period of time and record the information (i.e., weather; birds coming to the feeder).
   - take photographs of places visited.
   - record information in drawings, tape recordings, journal entries.

3. **Knowing how to arrange geographic information**
   What children do:
   - use blocks or objects to describe and display information gathered through direct experiences.
   - make drawings to represent what was observed.
   - cut pictures from magazines and other sources to describe information about a place.
   - keep daily records of weather changes, changes in the landscape during building or road construction, clothing people use according to weather.
   - prepare simple maps (floor or table maps).
   - construct tables and pictographs to display information.

4. **Analyzing geographic information**
   What children do:
   - visit places and share impressions about their characteristics.
   - look at illustrations from stories and books and interpret them.
   - observe photographs and pictures and interpret them in terms of traits, relationships.
   - use a layout of the school to determine the distances between their classroom and other areas.
   - use a map to determine the distance between their location and the place where story characters live.
   - look at a map of their community to find out where they or their friends live.
   - look at a pictograph and interpret its meaning.
   - observe the globe and maps to compare distances, size of countries, and water masses.

5. **Answering geographic questions**
   What children do:
   - use points of reference to describe where they live.
   - share information about a place seen in the news and media.
   - recognize familiar places in pictures and photographs.
   - describe the location of objects and people with details.
   - create models with blocks or other objects to describe a place or objects within a space.
   - make drawings to share impressions about a place.
   - use simple maps to find a route.

Source: Adapted from National Geographic Joint Committee (1994). The five sets of geographic skills. In *Geography for Life: The National Geography Standards*. Washington, DC: Author, pp. 46–49.

Bringing Ideas into Practice 6–2   *Selecting Books to Promote Knowledge of Geography*

Children's books provide child-appropriate ways to learn about geography. There are many good ones that foster the development of geography skills and concepts. As you look for titles, check the list published annually by the NCSS in a joint project with the Children's Book Council (CBC). CBC also has a similar project with the National Science Teachers Association. Your school and public library also have many valuable resources. When searching for books, keep in mind the following suggestions:

1. Before you begin your search, review the five themes of geography described in Figure 6–3. Use them as a reference to organize your search.
2. Choose books with good illustrations. Consider the details and how the geographical elements are depicted.
3. Before making a selection, take time to read the story. Check the language (terminology, clarity of descriptions) and determine if it is appropriate for the age group you teach.
4. Consider all genres. Poetry and folktales are good sources for learning geography. Folktales like *Abiyoyo* (Seeger, 1986), *The Egyptian Cinderella* (Climo, 1989), *Anansi the spider: A tale of the Ashanti* (McDermott, 1987), and *Johnny Appleseed*

(Lindbergh, 1990) bring alive a variety of rich and colorful environments.
5. Do not discard any stories. Book titles might be deceiving. Always read them carefully, and check to see what geographical elements are included. Fairy tales, for example, are a child-appropriate source of geographical information about the environment in the past.
6. Consider song picture books. They offer an active and an appealing way for learning geography. Suggested books about popular and traditional songs are listed below:

Aliki. (1974). *Go tell Aunt Rhody.* New York: Macmillan.
Bullock, K. (1993). *She'll be comin' 'round the mountains.* New York: Simon & Schuster.
Child, L. (1974). *Over the river and through the woods.* New York: Coward.
Kowalski, M. (1989). *The wheels on the bus.* New York: Trumpet.
Langstaff, J. (1974). *Oh, a-hunting we will go.* New York: Atheneum.
Raffi. (1987). *Down by the bay.* New York: Crown.
Rounds, G. (1989). *Old MacDonald had a farm.* New York: Holiday House.
Thiele, B. & Weiss, G. (1995). *What a wonderful world.* Littleton, MA: Sundance.

and early concrete-operational thinkers tend to have difficulties dealing with representations and abstract concepts. Piagetian research in cognitive development indicates that it is not until ages 11 to 14 that children are fully capable of dealing with mental representations (such as maps) that are found in geography.

Today, studies conducted with preschoolers have demonstrated not only their awareness of different places, but also an ability to deal with simple representations at an early age. For example, a study conducted with four-year-olds showed that they were capable of identifying places on an aerial map (Sowden, Stea, Blades, Spencer, & Blaut, 1996).

Other studies have demonstrated young children's ability to represent their neighborhoods by drawing simple maps (Boardman, 1990) and their ability to grasp information from symbolic instruments (Uttal & Wellman, 1989). These findings point to an emerging sense of spatial cognition and a budding ability to deal with symbols (see p. 161). Observations of children in a variety of settings would confirm these findings. In the experience of the authors, some young children can demonstrate a spatial sense as early as age three. While visiting some friends, one of the authors observed a three-year-old child busily drawing with chalk on the patio floor. What the adults had described as "scribbles" turned out to be a detailed sketch of the neighborhood, when described by the child. On another occasion, a child who had just turned four described to one of the authors the way to her house by mentioning signs and landmarks on the road. She included body movement to indicate the number of turns to her street: "You first turn here [she turned her body to the left] and then you stop [she halted] and call and the gate opens!"

Assessing Prior Knowledge of Geographic Concepts

There are several informal ways to assess prior geographic knowledge of young children. All of the techniques require good listening, observation, and interpretation skills on the part of the teacher. Conversations with children about purposefully selected topics provide clues about the children's ideas regarding some major geographic concepts. For example, comments about current topics in the news can provide hints about the way that children per-

ceive space. Discussions and responses to stories with geography related topics could reveal additional perspectives about the environment.

Puppets and objects can set the mood for children to talk about symbolic representations. Animal puppets can be used to encourage children to talk about their personal experiences with animal life. In one classroom, a puppet of an airplane used by the teacher led three- and four-year-old children to share their knowledge about how land looks from above. The teacher's question, "Tell me what you see from the airplane," spurred the group to vividly describe landforms as "little colored spots."

Effective questioning techniques are the key to assessing the children's prior knowledge of geography. For instance, the use of a questioning script, like the one in Figure 6–5, which is built around the five geography themes (see p. 148), helps teachers assess the children's pre-existing notions and ideas. Analysis of the answers will indicate to the teacher not only what the children know, but also how to plan child-appropriate activities that will continue to build upon the children's existing knowledge.

FIGURE 6–5   A Questioning Script to Identify Children's Existing Knowledge of Geography

Location:
■ Where is the _____ (name of places)?
■ What things do you find at _____ ?
■ Have you been to _____ ?
■ How do you get to _____ ?
■ How far is _____ ?
Place:
■ What is a _____ ?
■ How would you describe the place where you live?
■ Who lives in _____ ?
■ What did you see during your visit?
■ What do people do at _____ ?
■ Where do _____ animals live/plants grow?
■ How do places where _____ live look?
■ How do you know that?
Relationships within places:
■ Why do we have farms?
■ Why do people live in communities?

■ How is land used in our community?
■ How can we protect the environment?
Movement:
■ How do you get to school?
■ What way does the bus go to your house?
■ How does your family travel to work?
■ Can you walk to _____ ?
■ How do you communicate with _____ (your friends, family); people in other places?
■ Where do we get our _____ (food, clothes, etc)?
■ How does our food and clothing get to the store?
Regions:
■ Where does _____ live?
■ Where do they grow _____ ?
■ Where do people wear _____ ?
■ What do people wear in _____ ?

Concept Box 6–4   Items to Keep on Your Professional Bookshelf

DAP curriculum:

- Bredekamp, S., & Copple, C. (1997). *Developmentally appropriate practice in early childhood programs.* (rev. ed.). Washington, DC: National Association for the Education of Young Children.
- Bredekamp, S., & Rosegrant, T. (Eds.) (1992). *Reaching potentials: Appropriate curriculum and assessment for young children.* (Vol. 1) Washington, DC: National Association for the Education of Young Children.
- Jones, E., & Nimmo, J. (1994). *Emergent curriculum.* Washington, DC: National Association for the Education of Young Children.

Geographic education:

- Geography Education Standards Project. (1994). *Geography for life: National geography standards.* Washington, DC: National Council for Geographic Education.

Professional journals:

- *Social Studies and the Young Learner.* Washington, DC: National Council for the Social Studies.
- *Young Children.* Washington, DC: NAEYC.
- *Childhood Education.* Olney, MD: Association for Childhood Education International.

Magazines for children:

- *Faces* (Cobblestone)
- *World* (National Geographic Society)
- *Ranger Rick* and *Your Big Backyard* (National Wildlife Federation)

Assessing the children's existing knowledge is a highly critical and subjective task. It is also an important step in the process of creating a child-based and academically sound curriculum (Bredekamp & Copple, 1997). According to Palmer (1994), two conditions determine the success of the assessment process in the preplanning stages of the geography [or any] curriculum:

1. *The teacher's knowledge of geography and geography education.* There is no substitute for expertise and competence in the subject matter. It influences the way teachers perceive and analyze the children's feedback. It also establishes the basis for the proper selection of the content and provides direction for curricular integration.

Suggestion: It is important to state that, although not formally, we all possess practical geographical knowledge. Whenever you follow directions or use a map to get from one place to another, you are using geography. When you describe the location of items inside your house, you are also using geography. However, if you or other teachers do not feel competent in geography education, there are several things that can be done. Consult with the social studies

teacher in your school. Ask for suggestions and help in identifying relevant experiences and content. Propose a team-teaching effort and offer to assist the social studies teacher with an area in which you have more expertise. Learn more by reviewing traditional and Internet resources in geography education. (Suggested Web sites appear at the end of this chapter.) Subscribe to appropriate professional journals. Participate in workshops about geography. Read journals and magazines with geographical information. For example, the *National Geographic* is an excellent journal with easy-to-understand geographic information. *Social Education* and the *Journal of Geography* provide professional information about classroom strategies and related research.

2. *The teacher's knowledge of curriculum development and developmentally appropriate practices.* Designing a successful curriculum depends on the teacher's experience and mastery of curricular principles (see Chapter 4). The psychological and pedagogical theories and principles of curriculum development should guide teachers in their selection of models, teaching strategies, and learning activities. Additionally, knowledge of human development

(discussed in Chapter 3) is also essential. An engaging and child-appropriate curriculum depends upon the teachers' awareness of what is developmentally appropriate for young children.

Suggestion: Engage in discussions about DAP with your colleagues. Clarify with them what is termed as *appropriate* for the age group you work with. Review the literature to keep yourself abreast of current views, and consult with others as necessary. Become a member, and participate in the National Association of the Education of Young Children (NAEYC), and read their by-laws and other guidelines. Attend conferences and workshops about early childhood curriculum design and/or child development.

Creating an Appropriate Geography Curriculum

An appropriate geography curriculum begins with consideration of the key principles embedded in the concept of DAP. These principles were discussed in Chapters 3 and 4. To ensure the developmental appropriateness of classroom experiences, always ask yourself the following questions:

■ Are children developmentally ready (physically, cognitively, socially) to embark on this experience?
■ Are children's individual needs (cultural needs and exceptionalities) met and reflected in the curriculum?
■ Are these classroom activities based on familiar and meaningful experiences for children?

Appropriate geography education in the early years also takes place through curricular integration. An important part of the integration process involves the inclusion of the five geography themes discussed previously (p. 148): location, places, human-environmental interactions, movement, and regions. Discussions and analyses of the curriculum plans with colleagues will provide clues to pedagogically sound ways to integrate those fundamental themes into the learning experiences. A thorough analysis of the curriculum content will

also allow you to exclude activities that offer few or doubtful opportunities for knowledge building (Alleman & Brophy, 1993). Another important element of the integration process is the inclusion of themes that are meaningful and of interest to children. Focusing the learning experiences on their interests and building on the children's existing knowledge will ensure that the curriculum is developmentally appropriate and relevant.

Geography-oriented Materials

Active exploration of space and spatial relationship requires the use of hands-on materials. Several items are essential for creating an environment that fosters these skills. A list of suggested materials is presented in Figure 6–6. Teachers should remember to give special consideration to children with special needs. For example, relief maps, books in Braille, and books recorded on tape are essential when teaching children with visual needs. A table with adjustable legs for block play is recommended for children in wheelchairs. Placing and securing a plastic tablecloth or an old blanket on the table helps to reduce noise levels.

Using Literature in DAP Geography Education

Literature is a rich and child-appropriate source for developing children's interests in geography. It is also an essential planning tool for the integration of geographical concepts and themes into the curriculum. Adding children's literature to the curriculum makes geographical activities more meaningful (Stremme, 1993). The five themes of geography—location, place, human-environment interactions, movement, and regions—provide a good way to organize the curriculum while infusing it with geographical ideas. Developing your own inventory of suitable titles for each of the themes will facilitate appropriate curricular integration. The selection of children's books on p. 158 is intended to get you started in developing your own reference list. For other Recommended Children's Books, see p. 169.

Bringing Ideas into Practice 6–3

To help you enhance your young students' desire to discover the classroom space, consider the following suggestions:

1. Avoid a flat design. Instead, design a stimulating layout for your classroom, with a variety of areas and types of spaces (open, semi-open, and private spaces).
2. Wherever possible, elevate some of the classroom areas and include crawling tunnel areas (easily made with crates and planks). For example, a ramp could lead to a play area, or a loft could serve as the reading center. Make sure the access is sturdy and safe for children at this age level.
3. Design a series of paths in the classroom. Use the furniture and other elements to create different path shapes (open spaces, circular, U-shaped, curves, corners). For instance, a series of cubbies or cardboard boxes could be used to create curved paths.
4. Use the ceiling to suspend plastic strips or ribbons that will serve to demarcate an area.
5. Use rugs or colored tape to define areas and to develop a sense of boundaries. For example, a rug or a comforter in the block center will alert children that it is the place to work with block sets. A colored tape or a set of symbols on the floor will establish the boundaries for the large meeting area.
6. Revisit your classroom design and make changes. Periodically, remove some items and define new areas. Discuss the changes with children.
7. Develop a classroom "map." Together with the children, "map out" the classroom and post the map in a visible area. Use the map frequently as a reference when talking about an area.
8. Plan to include a block center. (It's a must for building spatial knowledge in young children!) Use a variety of blocks (wooden, plastic, cardboard). Enhance the center with props and figurines or puppets.
9. Include in the classroom environment a variety of textures (soft, semi-soft, hard).
10. Build in a sense of ecology inside the classroom. Add plants and live animals to the classroom.
11. Create a visually stimulating space, including an area where you can display posters, pictures, and photographs of a variety of landscapes and spatial elements. Change the images periodically.
12. Consider the windows and doors as a way to extend the classroom space. Include exit doors and window in the general layout. A door opening into the playground provides a transition into a different landscape. Windows provide a source of constant visual input into the surrounding and outside space (weather, physical changes, and objects).
13. Label the classroom areas with signs. If you are teaching younger children, use pictorial labels. Labels and signs help children to develop a sense of direction and of spatial orientation.

Centers can be easily created with common materials.

■■ Let's Talk About . . . 6–4

Children's Sense about Things Near and Far

Some people believe that young children have a limited sense of places far from their environment. Other educators and psychologists claim that from early on, children show a rudimentary sense of spatial relationships. The best way to form your own opinion is by listening to children's own clues regarding their understanding and sense of places *near* and *distant*.

1. Visit an early childhood classroom, and interview the teacher to find out what his or her perceptions are about the children's sense of space.

2. Observe the children and listen to what they say. Engage them in conversations and look for the references made to places distant and near.

3. Share your findings in class.

FIGURE 6–6   Suggested Materials to Foster Geographic Knowledge

When you are organizing the classroom, consider including the following resources:

- a display with photographs and pictures of familiar and distant places
- blocks (different textures such as cardboard, wood, and foam blocks, which are especially good for the younger children)
- figures of people, animals, transportation vehicles, traffic signs
- orientation signs (cardinal points, left, right, north, and south)
- measuring tools (yarn, rope, ruler, measuring tape)
- digging tools (hoes, shovels)
- geography instruments (compass, magnifying glass)
- maps and globes (Maps of the school, neighborhood, and town are a must! Also include state, national, and world maps)
- cameras (preferably a Polaroid™)
- map-making materials (drawing paper, crayons, pictures, modeling clay, dough—see recipe in box below)
- reference materials (atlases, books with road maps, informational books)

Concept Box 6–5   Recipes for Dough (to Build Relief Maps)

Common dough

4 cups of flour	1 tablespoon of oil
1½ cups of water	food coloring
½ cup of salt	

Mix the dry ingredients first. Slowly add water and oil. If the dough is too sticky or dry, add more flour or more water. Knead well and form a ball. Keep the dough in an airtight container or in a plastic bag. Use the dough to form shapes.

Cornstarch cooked dough*

2 cups of boiling water
2 cups of baking soda
1 cup of cornstarch

Mix all the ingredients. Cook over low heat, stirring constantly until the mixture thickens. Form a ball. Color dough with food coloring, if desired.

Sawdust dough

2 cups of sawdust
3 cups of wheat flour
water, as needed

Mix wheat flour with water and make a paste. Add the sawdust and mix well. More water can be added as needed.

*Requires the help of an adult.

Bringing Ideas into Practice 6–4   *An Integrated Geography Activity Packet*

Teacher Linda Renicks developed this sample activity packet for her kindergarten class. Notice how she integrated geography in a child-appropriate manner.

Theme: Learning about Far-Away Places: Australia
Age group: 5 years
Social studies standard: People, places, and environments
Target area: Geography—how the environment affects people

Integration:
1. *Language Arts:*
   ■ Read and discuss the poem, *The zoo in the park* (adapted to animals of Australia).
   ■ Read and discuss the story *Koala Lou* by Mem Fox.
   ■ Discuss the phrase "down under."
   ■ Observe selected photographs and pictures depicting different geographic features in Australia. Discuss and share their impressions about the pictures. (For example: What would you see if you were on top of Ayers Rock?)
2. *Math/Science:*
   ■ Make a class graph about the children's favorite animals from Australia.
   ■ Locate Australia on a world map and on the globe and visually compare the size of Australia with the United States and other countries.
   ■ Use yarn to estimate the distance between the United States and Australia.
3. *Art:*
   ■ Prepare a collaborative mural about Australia.
   ■ Have children draw their favorite Australian animal. Make their favorite animals using clay.

Source: Adapted from Renicks, L. (1998). Sample social studies integrated activity packet. Course assignment. Ft. Lauderdale, FL: Nova Southeastern University, Graduate Teacher Education Program.

Preparing the Classroom Environment to Foster Learning about Geography

Early childhood educator Lucy Sprague Mitchell, who dedicated a part of her life to research about geographic learning in the early years, believed that it was essential for young children to learn about the things that surround them. She firmly maintained that geographic knowledge started "unofficially at birth" (Mitchell, 1934/1991, p. 21). For Mitchell, geography was a dynamic and appealing field, integral to the lives of developing children. Today, research corroborates her ideas. Not only are children predisposed to learning geography, but also they actually enjoy it, especially when it presents dynamic opportunities to explore the environment. Fostering in children the desire for exploration of their space depends upon a well-planned and well-equipped environment.

Using Maps in the Early Childhood Classroom

A **map** is a way to represent space. Of all the tools geographers use to define and describe space symbolically, maps are the most important. Cartographers—people who are experts in cartography, the science and art of map making—develop maps. Maps have *five basic elements* (National Geographic Joint Committee, 1994; Palmer, 1994; Bale, 1989):

1. **Perspective** is a way of presenting the characteristics of objects from various positions, including what an observer sees when looking from a "bird's-eye view." Suggestions for introducing children to the concept of perspective include:

   ■ tracing common classroom objects (like a pencil or a cup) on a piece of paper and recognizing that drawings of their shapes represent them.

Bringing Ideas into Practice 6–5
Selected Children's Literature about the Five Geographic Themes

1. *Location*

Dorros, A. (1992). *This is my house.** New York: Harper-Collins.

Grimes, N. (1995). *C is for city.* New York: Lothrop.

Morris A. (1995). *Houses and homes.* (Around the World Series). New York: Mulberry.

Reiser, L. (1996). *Beach feet.* New York: Greenwillow.

Thomas, A. (1993). *Wake-up, Wilson Street.* New York: Holt.

Young, R. (1991). *Daisy's taxi.* New York: Lothrop.

2. *Places*

Angelou, M. (1994). *Kofi and his magic.** New York: Clarkson Potter.

Anno, M. (1978). *Anno's journey.** New York: PaperStar.

Baer, E. (1990). *This is the way we go to school: A book about children around the world.* New York: Scholastic.

Bate, L. (1989). *How Georgina drove the car very carefully from Boston to New York.*

Greenfield, E. (1991). *Night on neighborhood street.* New York: Puffin.

McLerran, A. (1991). *Roxaboxen.* New York: Lothrop.

3. *Human-Environment Interactions*

Adoff, A. (1991). *In for winter, out for spring.* New York: Harcourt.

Angelou, M. (1993). *My painted house.** New York: Clarkson Potter.

Anno, M. (1986). *All in a day.** New York: PaperStar.

Cocca-Leffler, M. (1996). *Clams all year.* New York: Yearling.

Keegan, M. (1991). *Pueblo boy: Growing up in two worlds.* New York: Cobblehill.

Kellogg, S. (1984). *Paul Bunyan.* New York: Morrow.

Krauss, L. (1996). *The marvelous market on Mermaid.* New York: Lothrop.

Polacco, P. (1988). *Rechenka's eggs.** New York: PaperStar.

Spier, P. (1980). *People.** New York: Doubleday.

Ryland, P. (1982). *When I was young in the mountains.* New York: Dutton.

4. *Movement*

Bunting, E. (1996). *Train to somewhere.* New York: Clarion.

Bunting, E. (1993). *Fly away home.* New York: Clarion.

Crews, D. (1996). *Freight trains.* New York: Mulberry.

Crews, D. (1989). *Flying.* New York: Mulberry.

Levinson, R. (1985). *Watch the stars come out.* New York: Penguin.

Pinkney, G. (1992). *Back home.* New York: Dial.

Say, A. (1992). *Grandfather's journey.* San Diego, CA: Harcourt Brace.

Sharmat, M. (1980). *Gila monster meets you at the airport.* New York: Simon & Schuster.

5. *Regions*

Ardeema, V. (1989). *Bringing the rain to Kapiti Plain.* New York: Dial.

Bunting, E. (1996). *Secret place.* New York: Clarion.

Bunting, E. (1995). *Dandelions.* New York: Harcourt Brace.

Dann, C. (1992). *The animals of Farthing Woods: Fire!* London, UK: Random House.

de Paola, T. (1983). *The legend of the Bluebonnet: An old tale from Texas.* New York: PaperStar.

de Paola, T. (1984). *The legend of the Indian paintbrush.* New York: PaperStar.

Gerrard, R. (1996). *Wagons, west!* New York: Farrar Strauss.

Lewin, H. (1984). *Jafta—The town.** Minneapolis, MN: Carolrhoda.

*These titles also foster global awareness.

- having children pretend they are birds, or that they are flying in an airplane. Standing on their seats or on a table, children can look at objects on the floor and describe what they see.
- examining and discussing photographs of themselves or of others.
- reading appropriate literature. Two good books are:

  Dorros, A. (1991). *Abuela*. New York: Harper-Collins.

  MacLachlan, P. (1991). *Three names*. New York: Harper & Row.

2. **Scale** is defined as a way to represent the size of real objects accurately in proportion to other objects on maps. It helps to establish the relative size of objects represented on a map. Scale is a very difficult concept for children to grasp. Here are some suggestions to foster development of this concept:

- playing with manipulatives representative of people and common objects (Bale, 1989).
- having children draw on a piece of paper or on the easel what they see in the classroom or what they noticed on a field trip.
- constructing things with blocks.
- structuring activities with figurines and other materials.

3. Position and orientation define the relationships between objects in an area and the points of reference describing their locations. **Position** answers the question "where." **Orientation** establishes the specific location of an object, using the cardinal points (north, south, east, west) as descriptors. Some suggestions to foster knowledge about position and orientation are:

- using directional labels (i.e., *north, south, east, west*) and signs (i.e., *front, back, left, right*) in the classroom.
- with younger children, using references to key objects on each side of the room.
- integrating directional phrases ("in front of the window"; "behind the door"; "forward") into the teacher's conversation.

- building structures with blocks and having children draw different classroom locations and places they have visited.
- reenacting of scenes from storybooks and focusing on the relative positions of storybook characters.
- using maps to find places in storybooks, objects in the classroom, and places in the school, as well as places in the community.

4. Cartographic **symbols** represent the elements and objects in the area depicted on a map. A key explains to the reader what each symbol represents. Classroom practices like the ones described here will foster understanding and use of map symbols:

- using pictorial maps introduce young children to the use of colors and shapes to represent what they see in a space.
- discussing the weather by using drawings or cutouts to represent the weather pattern each day.
- encouraging children to learn to "read" and distinguish symbols (in a map key or legend) used to represent capital cities and airports.
- preparing maps about common symbols found in the community. This will help children understand the purposes and needs for symbols.
- having children create their own symbols. This also promotes the understanding of the meaning and role of symbols.

5. **Content and purpose.** Maps are made with a purpose or goal. The *purpose* of the map is defined by its *content*. Maps are used to depict a variety of places and things: bodies of water, urban and farming areas, roads, buildings, etc. Here are some suggestions for helping children understand the purposes of different kinds of maps:

- Discussions about particular maps can give clues about their nature and meaning. To encourage discussion, ask children: "Why do you think they call this a road map?" "What information can we find on the map of our neighborhood?" "What kind of a map would you use to find information about Disney World?"

■ Planning a field trip also offers an opportunity to identify the purposes of maps.

Stages of Mapping

Young children have difficulty understanding and using maps, because mapping requires an ability to understand abstractions and representations. The ability to understand symbols is typically developed later on in the elementary and middle school years. Research reveals, however, that young children are capable of beginning to form cognitive maps, which they often use to interact at home and in the classroom. **Cognitive mapping** develops in three stages (Palmer, 1994):

■ **Stage 1: Topological mapping (preschool years).** Children produce pictorial maps in preschool. They are able to map places by using drawings, pictures, and block constructions. These early maps show children's ideas about the elements in their immediate environment (familiar topography). Drawings and block constructions show their knowledge of real and imaginary places. Young children's maps are usually egocentric in nature and reveal their knowledge of their immediate environments. The absence of map elements (such as direction or

perspective) is characteristic. Relevant experiences, such as creating a map of their neighborhood and their house, build their sense about what exists in the environment.

■ **Stage 2: Semi-abstract mapping (primary years).** Maps include more details, and symbols are used to depict elements. Although typical maps are not totally accurate, the inclusion of such elements as perspective, scale, and orientation shows the children's ability to represent environmental objects and their relationships in the particular space.

■ **Stage 3: Abstract mapping (elementary years).** Children's use of symbolic representations is typically found in the elementary grades. The maps are accurate and include detailed information. Map elements are also present.

Fostering Early Mapping Abilities

Young children are able to relate real objects to those represented in pictures and maps (see p. 151). This is an important ability because it is essential for understanding maps. Research has shown that preschoolers are able to form early cartographic images (Bale, 1989; Trifonoff, 1998). This refers to children's ability to identify and represent objects in

---

Concept Box 6–6 Fostering Geographic Knowledge: Essential Classroom Materials	
Basic materials	**Basic mapping tools**
Set of wood unit blocks	Map of the United States
Set of hollow blocks (wood, cardboard carton)	World map
Set of giant foam blocks	State map
Set of architectural blocks	Neighborhood map
Boxes of different sizes	School map
Set of wood international signs	Classroom map
Manipulatives (people, animal figurines)	Globe (raised-relief)
Sand and water table	Camera
Easel	A variety of map puzzles
Paints	Pictures about different landforms
Modeling clay	

a given setting. A study conducted by Spencer, Blades, and Morsley (1989) evidenced the ability of children ages four to six to recognize the elements and symbols in an aerial map. Using a plastic car, researchers (Sowden et al., 1996) found that four- to six-year-olds were able to trace the route a car would follow on an aerial map. Research findings, based on conversations with children, reveal an early ability to map places mentally. This ability is also revealed through children's drawings and block constructions (see Stages of Block Building below).

The evidence from observations and research findings reinforce the need to include mapping experiences in the early childhood classroom. Classroom experiences can help foster the development of cartographic abilities. For example, teachers can include a set of plastic transportation figurines and a play mat representing a community to encourage pretend play. Children can be encouraged to find places on the play mat and trace routes using the figurines. Play mats are commercially available. They can be also made from a piece of canvas. Many fabric stores carry one-yard stamped pieces represent-

---

Bringing Ideas into Practice 6–6   *Stages of Block Building*

Knowledge of spatial relationships is appropriately fostered when teachers are aware of the representational process experienced by children. According to Harriet Johnson (cited by Hirsch, 1974), young children experience seven stages of block building. Teachers are encouraged to use the block stages as guidelines for assessing children's developing awareness of spatial relationships.

Stage 1: Children, particularly younger ones, carry blocks around but do not use them for construction.

Stage 2: Onset of the building process. Typically, children will make horizontal rows or vertical stacks.

Stage 3: Children typically perform *bridging*—connecting two blocks with a third one to create a bridge. This type of construction represents an early attempt to solve technical building problem.

Stage 4: Children will build enclosures by placing blocks so as to create an enclosed area. Together with bridging, enclosures are also an early method of solving a technical building problem.

Stage 5: As mastery in using blocks develops, constructions appear more symmetrical and are more likely to be adorned with decorative patterns. Buildings may have names assigned to them.

Stage 6: Constructions are named and are used in dramatic play. Use of other materials (i.e., people figures, transportation vehicles, animals, sticks, traffic signs) adds to the complexity of children's structures and constructions.

Stage 7: More complex structures appear. Constructions represent and symbolize familiar structures. Dramatic play develops using structures as an element of it.

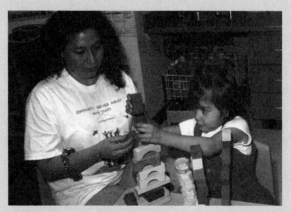

Blocks help children develop spatial concepts.

Source: Adapted from E. Hirsch (Ed.). (1974). Appendix 1: Stages in block building. *The block book.* Washington, DC: National Association for the Education of Young Children, pp. 101–104.

Concept Box 6–7   Good Sources of Maps for the Classroom

- *National Geographic Association:* This is an excellent source for a wide array of accurate and interesting maps and globes. Issues of the *National Geographic* magazine include colorful maps of specific locations around the world. Although the maps are very detailed and go beyond what young children can understand, they serve to familiarize them with different types of maps.
- *Rand MacNally:* Known for their excellent maps and globes, they also have a variety of geographic materials appropriate for children, such as books, inflatable globes, collections of stones, and so on.

- *American Automobile Association (AAA):* Although their services are available to members only, they are a good source of U.S. road maps. They will provide maps for specific point-to-point routes (e.g., Orlando, Florida, to Helena, Montana) on request.
- *Newspapers:* Weather maps are included in most papers. Particularly good is the colorful daily weather map in *USA Today.*
- *United States Geological Service (USGS):* Maps can be obtained through this federal agency by calling 1–800-USA-MAPS.

---

ing state maps as well as world and U.S. maps. These cloth maps can be easily sewn and turned into handy and affordable "map play mats."

Fostering Pre-Mapping Skills

Adults are able to use maps effectively, because they have already acquired two essential skills: 1) they have a sense of what exists in the physical world; and, 2) they know how to represent things. These two skills are essential for understanding maps and developing **visual literacy.** Before children become visually literate, they must first develop *pre-mapping skills.* These skills involve interpretation of symbols and representations from the very simple to the more complex levels. As young children acquire pre-mapping skills, they progress in their ability to visually discriminate and identify the physical elements found in their environment. Pre-mapping skills are initial stages of the visual literacy process that will lead to the development of the children's macro-environmental cognition about the world. The acquisition of **macro-environmental cognition,** or knowledge about the environment, allows children to perceive the elements as well as the changes in their particular settings.

Pre-mapping skills include the following (Maxim, 1995; Palmer, 1994; Bale, 1989):

- *Developing knowledge about the physical characteristics of the world:* Becoming cognizant of the natural elements (i.e., mountains, valleys, rivers, canals), man-made elements (i.e., farms, parks, roads, airports), physical objects (buildings, bridges, statues, schools, hospitals, churches), and of human elements (people, residential areas).
- *Developing an awareness of representations and symbols used throughout the children's environments:* Recognition of symbols such as traffic lights, traffic signs, commercial symbols (i.e., recognizing McDonald's by seeing its symbol), and sounds (i.e., fire alarms, ambulance sirens, police cars).
- *Building knowledge about the environmental elements commonly found in the children's space:* Recognition of elements such as natural resources, building materials, agricultural areas, recreational places, recycling areas, and so on.
- *Becoming aware of the Earth:* Fostering an initial sense about the Earth and some of its overt characteristics, such as the force of the wind and of water; recognizing that water and soil make up

Let's Talk About . . . 6–5

Working With Map Experiences

The formal teaching of map skills to young children is not considered an appropriate practice (Bredekamp & Copple, 1997). However, encouraging children to build upon what they find in their surroundings is considered child-appropriate. Observing and listening to children will reveal their early cognition of their environment. For example, the three-year-old who suddenly talks of food as he sees a fast food sign is demonstrating the ability to recognize symbols and to interpret what they represent. The remarks of first-graders touring the beach who can name the elements such as "sand," "dogs running," "swimming pool," "people in bathing suits," "boats," and "a lot of heat" show children's understanding of the physical world.

1. Describe five other settings where children are able to display their understanding of the physical environment.

2. What are some other ways you have observed children's awareness of the physical environment?

the Earth; learning about the weather and about climatic changes; recognizing the globe as a representation of the Earth; becoming aware of shadows and of the existence of night and day.

■ *Developing knowledge about the characteristics of the environments in other places:* Recognizing the existence of settings such as rain forests and deserts; learning about animal life, plants, and people in or near human settlements in other places.

■■ Helping Children Build Knowledge ■■ about the Physical Environment

Knowledge about the physical world develops gradually. Children begin the process by first making sense out of the elements in their immediate space and then interacting with them. In her seminal work in the 1930s, educator Lucy Sprague Mitchell identified the developmental stages of geographic or environmental awareness. According to Mitchell (1934/1991), children gradually expand their ideas about the environment. Mitchell's developmental stages help to explain the way children progress in their perception and cognition of their surroundings. According to Mitchell, a beginning step in developing a sense of the world is the development of the child's cognition of his own physical characteristics. As the child builds the concepts about his own body, gradually his attention is drawn to the significant elements in the immediate world. Colors, sizes, textures, and people all become part of the early mental map the child creates. This mental map will expand as the child interacts with and explores other environments. According to Mitchell (1934/1991), active and direct exploration is central to the children's continued development of cognition about the environment.

Field Trips and Young Children

One of the best ways for children to build concepts about the physical world is through field explorations (Natoli, 1989). Field trips are indispensable in providing direct information about the characteristics of specific areas of the Earth. A well-planned field trip sparks the interests of children and prompts them to observe the prominent features of a place (see Figure 6–7). To make the most out of a field experience, children need to be aware of the purpose of the activity. Establishing the objectives for the outing in advance will keep the children focused during the field trip. A set of questions will also help children to notice and analyze the various elements of the new setting.

Teachers of preschoolers and teachers of three-year-olds in Florida (personal communications) have suggested that sensory field trips are particularly helpful in learning about physical characteristics of the environment, such as the textures, aromas, colors, shapes, and sizes of different objects

Concept Box 6–8   Summary of Mitchell's Stages of Spatial and Environmental Knowledge Development (Birth through Age Six)

Approximate Developmental Age	*What a Child Does at This Age*	*How the Child Builds Spatial Knowledge*
Infant (Birth through 14 months)	Experiments with and explores his or her own body; explores physical characteristics such as size, color, texture, distance of immediate surroundings (i.e., crib, play area, room, house)	Uses senses to build ideas. Manipulation, tasting, smelling provide input to get an idea about elements in physical settings. Locomotion expands opportunities to explore and learn. Play is used to explore. Sees space as related to self and non-self.
Toddler (14 months to 3 years)	Continues to discover own body and build self-image. Motor development affords means to explore the qualities of objects and people in the the environment.	Uses sensorial experiences and play as tools for exploration. Motor abilities increases child's ability to investigate settings. Recognizes position of objects in familiar spaces (room, home, and classroom).
Preschooler (Ages 3 to 4)	Still interested in self, focuses on the home and familiar environments like the classroom, neighborhood, and homes of friends and relatives. Exhibits a sense of direction about familiar places.	Uses senses and manipulation of objects as means for building concepts about space. Constant investigation of familiar areas. Block play is used to explore objects and their relationships. Language is used to gather details about the characteristics of the environment. Uses simple symbolic representations.
Kindergartner (Age 5)	Explores familiar places (street, neighborhood, home, and school). Associates objects in space according to various functions, characteristics	Uses block and dramatic play to continue building concepts of space. Uses language to obtain information and expresses spatial knowledge through language. Recognizes and uses simple symbolic representations.

Source: Adapted from L. S. Mitchell. (1934/1991). *Young geographers: How they explore the world and how they map the world.* (4th ed.). New York: Bank Street College of Education.

and places. Among the sensory field visits their groups enjoy are trips to the bakery section at their local grocery store (especially because they get to sample what they smell!), the flower shop, the fish market, the school playground (after the rain), and a baseball field (after the grass is cut). The Florida teachers agree that sensory field trips make children perceive familiar places in new and more complex ways.

In another case, a third grade teacher used a questionnaire we designed based on the five themes of geography mentioned previously: location, place,

FIGURE 6–7 Guidelines for Field Trips with Young Children

In selecting a site for a field trip, a teacher should consider:

■ *Children's interests:* As a teacher listens to what children say, the questions they ask, and their dramatic play, she becomes aware of the knowledge and attitudes they gain and the values they place on certain types of experiences.

■ *Community resources:* In a walk around the building and the playground, a teacher might discover many places of interest. A survey of the neighborhood can reveal additional places and activities that might be of interest.

■ *Time needed to reach destination:* Although there are exceptions, a teacher should plan for no more than 20 minutes of travel each way.

■ *Mode of transportation:* Walking is usually the best means of travel. When private motor transportation is needed, attention must be given to the competence of the driver, insurance coverage, and safety seats for children. If public transportation is to be used, a teacher must know procedures, cost, and arrival and departure schedules.

■ *Number of children taking the trip:* Where possible, the group should be small enough so that each adult has only three or four children to supervise.

■ *Supervision:* When three-year-olds leave the premises, each adult should be responsible for no more than two children. With four- and five-year-olds, one adult should be available for every four children.

■ *Safety:* A teacher needs to determine the safest route. The teacher needs to feel confident that the group can be controlled and that he or she can cross streets with them and help them on and off conveyances. A teacher should always carry a small first-aid kit.

■ *Length of visit:* For most young children, 20 minutes at the site is enough. If more time seems appropriate, the trip can be repeated.

■ *Nature of visit:* A teacher needs to take the trip first and be sure that anyone else involved understands the purpose of the trip. There should be only one focus for a trip. Too much stimulation defeats the purpose of the trip and causes disruptive behavior.

human-environmental interaction, movement, and regions. She found that the specific questions encouraged the children to pay attention to details of places they visit. She also sent a copy of the questions to the children's homes so it could be used on family outings as well (Figure 6–8).

Creating Appropriate Map Experiences

Helping children refine map skills in the classroom requires active, hands-on experiences. Visits to places in the school, walks around the neighborhood, and field trips are essential. Identifying interesting places for field trips and outings in the community is a good way to start planning appropriate geography activities (see Figure 6–9). Field trips are also a good way to create thematic experiences that

incorporate the five themes of geography (described on p. 148).

Young children develop mental maps of familiar places as part of their growth process. Early mapping experiences begin with activities related to such familiar places as the home, the classroom, the school, the playground, and homes of friends and relatives. Experiences such as those suggested in Figure 6–10 contribute to the child's emerging sense about what is found in the environment.

When planning mapping experiences, teachers need to include time to discuss the elements in the children's drawings. Such discussions about familiar places stimulate the development of geographic knowledge. Drawings will usually lead to the children's use of blocks, another way for young children to use and strengthen their representational lan-

FIGURE 6–8   A Questionnaire to Foster Knowledge about the Physical Space

Location:
    What did you visit?
    Can you describe how to get there?
Place:
    What did you see that attracted you the most?
    What are some special things you saw during the visit?
    What did you expect to see?
Relationships with places:
    Were there any people?
    What were the people doing?
Movement:
    How did you get there?
    What road did you take?
Regions:
    Was that place similar to where you live?
    Can you make a drawing of the place you visited?

FIGURE 6–9   Incorporating the Five Themes of Geography into Field Trips—Suggested Places to Visit

Visits to the places suggested below are an opportunity for young children to learn actively about the geographic themes listed after the suggestions. (See also discussion of these themes on p. 148.)

■ *School:* playground, school facilities (e.g., lunchroom, cafeteria, auditorium, other classrooms). Geography themes: location, place.

■ *Neighborhood:* grocery stores, public services, residential areas, construction sites, roads, recreational areas. Geography themes: location, place, movement, and relationships with places.

■ *Town or city:* buildings, roads, means of transportation, parks. Geography themes: location, place, region, and movement.

■ *Farm areas:* production, plants and animals, learning about what people do to produce our food. Geography themes: place, location, and relationships with places, regions, and movement.

■ *Zoo:* types of animals, learning about their habitats in nature, countries where they come from. Geography themes: location, place, and relationships with places.

guage. Mapping skills can also be encouraged through the use of photographs, which allows the children to view various perspective and scale elements from different angles.

Becoming Aware of the Earth

Early geography experiences include the emerging awareness of the Earth. Children gradually acquire some notion about our planet as they become aware of its more concrete characteristics. The presence of night and day, the changes in the seasons, and references to places beyond their immediate environment such as deserts, mountains, or lakes, create an awareness of something much larger that exists outside the child's immediate world. Today, the media and technology that provide instantaneous information about places far from our immediate surroundings outside accelerate this process. The characteristics of the Earth listed below offer opportunities for appropriate learning experiences for young children (National

Geographic Joint Committee, 1994; Charlesworth & Lind, 1999). For more about incorporating environmental education in the early childhood classroom, see Chapter 10.

■ **Awareness of day and night:** A chart of activities children do during the day and night helps to establish awareness of changes based on the Earth's rotation around the sun. The charts can have titles such as "When the sun is shining we . . ." and "When the moon is away, we . . ." Children's literature is another excellent way to make children aware of day and night and about the rotation of the Earth. Try the following titles:

FIGURE 6–10 Topics for Initial Mapping Experiences with Young Children

1. Maps of "familiar geographies" (Bale, 1989): These include the home, the place where the child was born, places where the child has lived before, places where he goes on his own (i.e., to homes of neighbors, friends), and places where the child goes on vacation. Maps also offer good opportunities to engage parents and family members in activities with children.
2. Maps of the classroom (Siegel & Schadler, 1981): Siegel and Schadler recommend mapping the classroom, because in many cases it is the place where the child spends most of his or her time.
3. "Child-centered [maps] . . . emerging from what children show an interest in" (Palmer, 1994): Palmer suggests that mapping experiences should follow what interests children. For example, start with places the children are familiar with through stories, or with real places they are related to (home, school, child-care center, and neighborhood).

Aylsworth, J. (1995). *Country crossing.* New York: Aladdin.

Ghazi, S. H. (1996). *Ramadan.* New York: Holiday House.

Karman, S. (1997). *Wake-up, groundhog!* New York: Golden Books.

Schnett, S. (1995). *Somewhere in the world right now.* New York: Dragonfly Books.

Thomas, A. (1991). *Wake-up, Wilson Street!* New York: Holt.

■ **Water and landforms:** Walks around the neighborhood (especially where there are different land formations such as lakes, rivers, canals, the sea) help establish the concepts about different water and landforms. The water and sand table in the classroom and the sandbox or a garden on the playground are particularly important. They provide opportunities for experimentation with landforms such as islands, as well as with water forms, such as changes in water volume. Manipulatives such as plastic boats, cars, figurines of people, photographs, maps, and globes are important in helping children grasp the concepts of land and water forms. Music and children's literature are also valuable resources.

Child, L. M. (1999). *Over the river and through the woods.* New York: Henry Holt.

McDonnell, F. (1995). *I love boats.* Cambridge, MA: Candlewyck.

Otteson, P. (1996). *Kids who walk on volcanoes.* Santa Fe, NM: John Muir Publications.

Yolen, J. (1992). *Letting swift river go.* New York: Little, Brown & Co.

Young, R. (1991). *Daisy's taxi.* New York: Orchard.

■ **Shadows:** All children are attracted to shadows. Tracing their own shadow patterns is a favorite activity of young children. Observing shadows at different times of the day builds knowledge about the sun and its movement. A record can be kept of the direction of shadows and the times of day when they are formed. A sundial also provides ways to observe the passing of shadows and to learn about the concept of time.

■ **Weather patterns:** A weather center in the classroom helps to track weather elements such as the wind, the rain, the clouds, and so on. Keeping a daily weather record alerts children to weather changes and to their effects on people. Suggested titles include:

Barrett, J. (1992). *Cloudy with a chance of meatballs.* New York: Aladdin.

Polacco, P. (1990). *Thunder cake.* New York: Philomel.

Yashima, T. (1999). *Umbrella.* Topeka, KS: Sagebrush Learning Resources.

■ **Types of soil:** Field observations help to build knowledge about different kinds of soil and the contents of each type. Digging tools help in exploring and discovering what the Earth's soil is like and what it hides. Suggested titles are:

Baylor, B. (1975). *The desert is theirs.* New York: Scribner's.

Lasky, K. (1990). *Dinosaur dig.* New York: Morrow.

McPhail, D. (1985). *Farm morning.* San Diego, CA: Harcourt Brace.

Pulutsky, J. (1988). *Tyrannosaurus was a beast: Dinosaur poems.* New York: Greenwillow.

■ **Changing of the seasons:** Children already have perceptions about the seasons by the time they begin school. Teachers have many opportunities to refine the children's ideas about seasonal changes and their impact on the world. For example, experiences such as observing people's clothing, charting the weather patterns, recording animal behaviors, charting the changes in plant life and people's activities, and observing the changing length of the day are activities that can help establish concepts about the seasons. Some suggested titles are:

Adoff, A. (1991). *In for winter, out for spring.* San Diego, CA: Harcourt Brace.

George, J. (1993). *Dear Rebecca, winter is here.* Cambridge, MA: HarperCollins.

Using World Globes Appropriately with Young Children

In teaching geography to the young, the use of a globe is essential. An inflatable globe is easy for children to manipulate, and for younger preschoolers, fabric globes are especially good. Frequent references to the globe help in developing the concept of the Earth as the place where people and natural life coexist. Use of the globe in the classroom contributes to building all the essential geographic skills such as representational knowledge, recogni-

tion of perspective and scale, and use of symbols. It is important to keep in mind that the globe is a representation and that as such, it is difficult for young children to understand what it stands for. Young children, and especially those of ages three through five, require use of concrete and meaningful experiences. Meaningful experiences are those that deal with topics familiar to children. Appropriate ways to use globes include:

■ locating places where families came from.

■ locating the setting where stories or a current event takes place.

■ establishing the distance from their state to that of a place where a story/event takes place. (A piece of ribbon or yarn can be used to help children visualize the distance.)

■ locating and marking distinctive topographical features, landforms such as mountains, rain forests, deserts, oceans.

■ creating symbols to represent places on the globe (i.e., green ribbon to mark the rain forests).

■ identifying and referring to it as the Earth or the place where people live.

The purpose of teaching effective geography skills is to facilitate in children the building of ideas and connections with people and environments around the world and to allow children to incorporate accurate geographic information into decision making. The skills, principles, and experiences discussed in this chapter are intended to build those two major goals. As we enter the twenty-first century, knowing the impact of geography on the human, animal, and plant life of our planet will facilitate greater understanding of events that take place. This knowledge will allow for more effective and, hopefully, more compassionate solutions to problems and conflicts that will arise in the future. Young children we teach today will have the responsibility of making this goal a reality.

Recommended Children's Books

Aardeema, V. (1991). *Borreguita and Coyote*. New York: Knopf.

Albert, B. (1991). *Where does the trail lead?* New York: Simon & Schuster.

Andrews, J. (1986). *Very last very first time*. New York: Atheneum.

Angelou, M. (1996). *Kofi and his magic*. New York: Clarkson Potter.

Best, C. (1994). *Taxi! Taxi!* New York: Little, Brown.

Heide, F., & Gilliland, J. (1990). *The day of Ahmed's secret*. New York: Lothrop, Lee & Shepard.

Joosse, B. (1995). *Snow day!* New York: Clarion.

Peterson, P. (1997). *Farmer's market*. New York: Orchard.

Schertle, A. (1995). *Down the road*. San Diego, CA: Harcourt Brace.

Skurzynski, G. (1992). *Here comes the mail*. New York: Bradbury.

Tresselt, A. (1990). *Wake up, city!* New York: Lothrop, Lee, & Shepard.

ACTIVITIES

Keeping Track of What You Learn: Your Personal Activity Log

In this chapter we discussed some key ideas relating to geography education for young children. Here are some additional activities for your PAL.

A. Reflections

1. Write your ideas about the value and importance of geography for children.
2. Using baseball's World Series as a theme, design a unit that incorporates the major, geographic elements discussed in this chapter. The World Series theme has endless possibilities. It can provide opportunities for mapping experiences, globe explorations, symbol recognition, role of the environment, study of scale and perspective, and other important topics.
3. Design two activities about each of the five geographic themes discussed on p. 148: location, place, human-environmental interaction, movement, and region. Use materials from the past and the present such as old and new photographs, and utensils to also give a sense of history to the activities.
4. Write specific directions of how you would have young children create a topography map using simple pictures as models. List the various materials for construction of rivers, mountains, streets, cars, etc. Write procedures that could be replicated by others. Share them with your colleagues, and try them out with a group of children.
5. Create a game that would teach children about the rotations of the Earth, the sun, and other planets. Use some of the literature resources suggested in the chapter to help you.

B. Collections

1. Collect pictures of different landscapes from magazines such as the *National Geographic*. Use the pictures to teach about the Earth's topography and various environments.
2. Make a collection of simple maps children can replicate. Pay particular attention to symbols and make a set of flash cards from them to use with children.
3. Identify a group of guest speakers from the various parts of the world who are willing to come to speak to the children about their countries. Ask them to bring artifacts, clothing, pictures, and other objects indigenous to their region that will enhance their presentations. Make your resource list with a short biography sketch available to other teachers and caregivers.

C. Internet Resources*

There are many resources about geography education on the Internet. The ones listed here are a few we found to be particularly appropriate and helpful for early childhood classrooms.

■ Commission on Student Learning

Web site: http://www.csu.wednet.edu

The site originates in Washington state and offers the state geography standards along with other information that can be used in teaching young children.

■ National Geographic

Web site: http://www.nationalgeographic.com

A wonderful resource that offers a geography pen-pal network as one of its features. Once you visit this site, you'll be hooked!

---

*Please note that Internet resources are of a time-sensitive nature and URL sites and addresses may often be modified or deleted.

References

Alleman, J., & Brophy, J. (1993). Is curriculum integration a boon or a threat to social studies? *Social Education, 57*(6), pp. 287–291.

Bale, J. (1989). *Didáctica de la geografía en la escuela primaria. [Geography in the primary school].* Madrid, Spain: Ediciones Morata.

Boardman, D. (1990). Graphicacy revisited: Mapping abilities and gender differences. *Educational Review, 42*(1), pp. 57–64.

Bredekamp, S., & Copple, C. (1997). *Developmentally appropriate practice in early childhood.* Washington, DC: National Association for the Education of Young Children.

Bunting, E. (1997). *Someday a tree.* New York: Clarion.

Calhoun, M. (1997). *Flood.* New York: Morrow.

Charlesworth, R., & Lind, K. (1999). *Math and science for young children* (3rd ed.). Albany, NY: Delmar.

Cherry, L. (1990). *The great kapok tree.* San Diego, CA: Harcourt Brace.

Fransecky, R., & Ferguson, R. (1973, April). New ways of seeing: The Milford visual communication project. *Audio-Visual Instruction, 45.*

Geography Education Standards Project. (1994). *Geography for life: The national geography standards.* Washington, DC: National Council for Geographic Education.

Hardwick, S., & Holtgrieve, D. (1996). *Geography for educators: Standards, themes and concepts.* Upper Saddle River, NJ: Prentice Hall.

Hirsch, E. (1974). *Appendix 1: Stages in block building: The block book.* Washington, DC: National Association for the Education of Young Children.

Ketterman, H. (1993). *The year of no more corn.* New York: Orchard Books.

Krogh, S. (1994). *The integrated early childhood curriculum* (2nd ed.). New York: McGraw Hill.

Lock, K. (1995). *Xochiquetzal.* Australia: Aubrey Press.

London, J. (1998). *Hurricane.* New York: Lothrop.

Mayesky, M. (1998). *Creative activities for young children* (6th ed.). Albany, NY: Delmar.

Maxim, G. (1995). *Social studies and the elementary school child* (5th ed.). Englewood Cliffs, NJ: Merrill.

Milson, A. (1998, September–October). Mental mapping: Today my home, tomorrow the world! *Social Studies and the Young Learner, 11*(1), pp. P1–P2.

Mitchell, L. S. (1934/1991). *Young geographers: How they explore the world and how they map the world.* New York: Bank Street College of Education.

National Geographic Joint Committee. (1994). *Geography for life: The national geography standards.* Washington, DC: Author.

National Association for the Education of Young Children. (1997). *Teaching and working with culturally and linguistically different children: Position statement.* Washington, DC: Author.

Natoli, S. J., Boehm, R., Kratch, J., Lanegran, D., Monk, J., & Morill, R. (1984). *Guidelines for geographic education: Elementary and secondary schools.* Washington, DC: Association of American Geographers and National Council for Geographic Education.

Natoli, S. (Ed.). (1989). *Strengthening geography in the social studies.* Bulletin no. 81. Washington, DC: National Council for the Social Studies.

National Council for Social Studies. (1989). *Charting a course: Social studies for the 21st century.* Washington, DC: Author.

Nickell, P. (1995). Thematically organized social studies: A solution to the primary education dilemma. *Social Studies & the Young Learner, 8*(1), pp. 1–17. (Pull-out feature).

Palmer, J. (1994). *Geography in the early years.* London, UK: Routledge.

Robles de Melendez, W., & Ostertag, V. (1997). *Teaching young children in multicultural classrooms: Issues, concepts and perspectives.* Albany, NY: Delmar.

Schadler, M. (1996). *Welcome to Bayou Town.* New York: Pelican Publications.

Siegel, A. W., & Schadler, M. (1981). The development of young children's spacial representations of their classrooms. In E. M. Hetherington & R. D. Parke (Eds.), *Contemporary readings in child psychology* (2nd ed.). New York: McGraw Hill.

Spencer, C., Blades, M., & Morsley, K. (1989). *The child in the physical environment.* UK: John Wiley & Sons.

Sowden, S., Stea, D., Blades, M., Spencer, C., & Blaut, J. M. (1996). Mapping abilities of four-year-old children in York, England. *Journal of Geography, 95*(3), pp. 107–111.

Stremme, R. (1993). Great geography using notable trade books. In M. Zarnowski & A. Gallagher (Eds.). *Children's literature & social studies: Selecting and using notable books in the classroom* (pp. 12–15). Dubuque, IA: Kendall-Hunt.

Trifonoff, K. (1998, September–October). Introducing thematic maps in the primary years. *Social Studies and the Young Learner, 11*(1), pp. 17–22.

Uttal, D., & Wellman, H. M. (1989). Young children's representation of spatial information acquired through maps. *Developmental Psychology, 25*(1), pp. 128–138.

CHAPTER 7

Becoming Socially Responsible Citizens in a Democratic Society

I know of no safe depository of the ultimate powers of the society but the people themselves.

—THOMAS JEFFERSON (1820)

Chapter Questions

After reading this chapter you should be able to answer the following questions:

- What are the main characteristics of effective citizenship?
- Why do we need to foster a sense of global citizenship in young children?
- How do children acquire a sense of social responsibility?
- How do positive social skills relate to good citizenship?
- What kind of classroom experiences help foster social development?

Key Terms and Concepts

citizenship
civic responsibility
community
cooperative learning
internalization
moral thinking
perspective taking

political socialization
prosocial skills
role model
social responsibility
social skills
"teachable moments"
values

172

Classroom Portrait: **A Moral Dilemma**

"Today was a bad day," thought eight-year-old Jordan to himself while riding home on the school bus. During circle time he kept hitting Loretta with a pencil. Ms. Barrett told him to stop, but he kept at it, and she sent him back to his seat for a "time to reflect." On the playground he got into a fight with Selena and Joel, and the teacher blamed him for it. "If you misbehave one more time, Jordan, I am sending a note to your mom." Sure enough! He tore up Derek's picture in the afternoon, and here he was riding the bus home with a note to Mom in his lunch box.

Jordan knew he was in trouble. He also remembered the last time his second grade teacher sent the note home. Mom got very angry with him. She made him go to his room and wait for Dad to get home. After a long talk, most of which Jordan did not understand, Dad cut off all television and computer games and did not let him eat any ice cream for three days. Those were the worst three days!

"Well, here I am again. Only this time I am in more trouble," Jordan thought. "I could throw away the note, or tear it up and not say anything." He remembered that Billy did that, got caught, and was in even more trouble because he had to go to the principal's office with his father. Jordan knew his options did not look good either way. If there was a way of not getting punished, he sure wanted to find it. As Jordan was considering his options, the bus stopped in front of his house.

■ Building a Community

A **community** is defined as the coming together of people who are bound by their sense of belonging and mutual responsibility, and who seek the well-being of themselves as individuals and of the group. Communities influence the social lifestyles of people. They range in size from a country like the United States to a classroom filled with young children. Becoming a member of a community is a process that begins at birth and continues throughout our lives. Acquiring a sense of community is essential to the survival of individuals, of our country, and of the world. It is also a major goal of education (Elias et al., 1997).

The combined efforts of family members, educators, and child-concerned people lead to the building of a sense of community in children. During the early years, as children interact with people and explore their environments, they experience the skills and behaviors of social life. It is through these incidental and formal interactions that young children begin to construct ideas about what it means to be a member of a social group. Successful membership in a social group requires knowledge about oneself; participatory and decision-making skills; and a sense of social responsibility and caring for others (Committee for Children, 1992; Berman, 1997; Elias et al., 1997). These characteristics are also related to the expectations of good citizenship.

Becoming Good Citizens

The civic nature of education strives "to prepare informed, rational, humane, and participating citi-

The classroom is a special community.

Bringing Ideas into Practice 7-1   *Classrooms as Communities*

Children develop a sense of community life by experiencing different environments. One of those major settings is the classroom. Organizing the classroom as a community is considered a developmental strategy. The key traits of a classroom as a democratic community are listed below. Use them as guidelines to determine how closely your classroom and others you visit reflect these concepts.

Creating a Classroom Community Context:
A Checklist

Check (√) those items present in your classroom or observed during a visit.

Physical environment:

____ The classroom can be described as an orderly, inviting, and attractive place.

____ The classroom is organized into a variety of spaces:

    ____ Individual

    ____ Small group space

    ____ Large group space, or group meeting areas

____ Children and adults together decide on the arrangement of the space.

____ Children help to keep the physical environment orderly.

____ There are announcements about events, samples of activities and projects, and labels that describe the social life of the classroom.

Social/emotional environment:

____ A warm, inviting, and socially active atmosphere exists.

____ A variety of activities take place: children are engaged in quiet, active, individual, and group experiences.

____ There are opportunities for a variety of social interactions:

    ____ Adult/children

    ____ Child/child

    ____ School staff and children

    ____ Community members and children

    ____ Senior people and children

____ Opportunities for dialogue between children and adults are observed.

____ Children are encouraged to ask, share ideas, and pose questions.

____ Children are given options when selecting learning activities.

____ Adults listen attentively to children and other adults.

____ Children and adults respond to each other in a respectful way.

____ Children and adults with differences (cultural, linguistic, special needs) are treated with respect and given equal opportunities.

____ Children and adults participate in establishing the classroom rules.

____ Children participate in problem solving and decision making.

____ Participation of both children and adults is encouraged.

____ Children exhibit a sense of being valued and trusted.

____ Emotions and feelings are expressed in positive ways.

____ The classroom atmosphere makes children feel safe.

____ Group exhibits a spirit of collectivity (e.g., showing pride about themselves as a class; displaying pride about their school; etc.).

____ Group action is taken to share and support others during moments of need (e.g., collecting goods for needy people; sending cards to friends when they are sick; etc.).

zens committed to the values and principles of American constitutional democracy" (Center for Civic Education, 1994, p. v). Success in this endeavor is essential for the success of our global society. The process of acquiring the tools of effective citizenship begins at birth and continues throughout our lives. Whether on the subway, in a community park, or on a voyage down the Amazon River, the skills and attributes of good citizenship are demonstrated on a daily basis. For young children, the

---

⬛⬛   Let's Talk About . . . 7–1

Mirroring Community Life in Our Classrooms

1. What elements are most important for creating a mirror image of a community in the classroom?

2. What other areas would you add to the checklist in addition to the physical and social/emotional elements?

3. What resources are needed to create a mirror of our community in the classroom?

4. How would you involve other significant groups like parents, community members, other teachers, and special guests in creating a community in your classroom?

---

initial exposure to the good citizenship skills begins in the classroom and at home.

Citizenship is defined as the sense of belonging to a nation whose social and political values and rights one follows and defends. Citizenship also establishes living under the political protection of a country, which, in the case of the United States, is a democracy. Effective citizenship is observed when people know the rights and responsibilities of civic life. The classroom is one of the first places where future citizens are nurtured and where children experience what being a good citizen means. Discussing various characteristics of good citizenship is a starting point for building more complex notions about that concept.

There are many ways to define citizenship. Learning about the attributes of good citizens provides a way to understand this concept. Good citizens:

■ exhibit a sense of social responsibility.
■ recognize they have rights and responsibilities.
■ participate in deciding issues about the present and the future of their group, town, states, nation, and of the world.
■ know and follow rules and laws.
■ recognize and respect the rights of others.

Bringing Ideas into Practice 7–2   *Exploring the Concept of Citizenship*

Citizenship, a very abstract concept, is difficult for children to grasp. However, through discussion and through familiar examples, they are able to relate to it. To start a discussion, begin by finding out the children's ideas about citizenship. Sharing a list of characteristics also encourages children to elaborate on their ideas. The suggested examples, intended to define citizenship, can also serve as thematic organizers.

Topic: Good Citizenship

We demonstrate good citizenship by . . .
■ acting as responsible individuals.
■ being caring members of our families.
■ being cooperative members of a classroom.
■ being good friends.
■ keeping our neighborhood clean.
■ respecting others.
■ helping in our community.
■ participating in the events in our community.

■ helping others.
■ being proud of our country.
■ respecting the rights of others.

Suggested Activities:

1. Create a web about the ways we demonstrate our citizenship. Discuss each idea and have the children give specific examples.

2. Have children select those characteristics of citizenship they consider most important and draw examples of them.

3. Look through magazines to find pictures that illustrate the specific civic characteristics selected by children. Conduct a "show and tell" of the pictures of each of the characteristics and ask the children to explain the reasons for the selections.

4. Share stories about positive civic actions and discuss them with the group.

- realize others have a right to dissent and to have different ideas.
- exhibit open- and critical-mindedness.
- show concern for the well-being of the group, community (at the state and national level).
- display a sense of compassion toward those in need.
- display a sense of patriotism and stand by the ideas and values of American democracy.

(Center for Civic Education, 1994, pp. 35–40)

Teaching Children about Citizenship

Some of the characteristics of citizenship may seem too sophisticated for young children. Early childhood educators need to be able to simplify the ideas by putting them into simpler frames of reference that are more familiar to young children. For example, showing compassion toward others can be as simple as discussing how a child would empathize with a friend whose pet bird died. Following rules and laws can be easily understood in the context of the classroom, where children follow the rule of lining up to go to the playground.

Use of puppets is also an effective and child-appropriate strategy for teaching children about citizenship. Establishing several puppet characters as part of the classroom community provides a helpful channel to learn about citizenship skills. Early in the year teachers can introduce these characters to the class. Each puppet can have a very unique personality, which teachers can then use to present specific social and citizenship skills. Assigning puppets to a particular center or place in the classroom contributes to establishing their identity. In one classroom visited by these authors, "Matt" and "Alinne," two puppets the teacher had made, shared the library and housekeeping corner along with the children. Each puppet had a name given by the children, and a very unique personality. "Matt," for example, was a very compassionate and a law-abiding "puppet-person." He did not always agree with "Alinne," who occasionally forgot to share things or to help others. Exciting discussions would emerge every time the teacher brought to the group's atten-

Let's Talk About . . . 7–2

Defining Citizenship

Citizenship is a complex concept because it consists of many different elements. Make up your own definition of citizenship and compare it to the one provided in this section. Look for the commonalities and differences between your definition and ours. Discuss the meaning of citizenship with your colleagues or classmates and build a group definition.

tion what these puppets were doing. Regular participation of puppets in classroom activities, incidents, and events enhances their presence as characters and contributes to creating a sense of them as members of the group. Specific situations can be designed for the puppets based on the events and things happening in the classroom and in the community. Whether the puppets are teacher-made or commercially produced, they are recommended as a teaching resource and strategy. Suggestions for making your own puppets appear in Figure 7–1.

Becoming a Citizen of the World

They had made a new flag.
Showing the blue white marble of earth,
Traveling silently through the blackness of space.
                    —*The day the earth was silent*
                            (McGuffee, 1996, p. 2)

As members of a global society, there are skills and values we must develop to achieve personal and group success in the world community. Life in the twenty-first century demands practical and sensible solutions regarding the ways people affect each other and the environment. Our global society already has ways of collaborating on common issues and challenges that affect us.

One example of global collaboration is the movement to protect the environment. A common con-

FIGURE 7–1 Ideas for Making Your Own Puppets

Paper-Bag Puppets

Materials

paper bags, scissors, crayons or marking pens, paste, yarn or paper scraps, and paint (if desired)

Construction procedure

1. Making paper-bag puppets is quick and easy. Give each child a small paper sack. (A no. 6 bag works well.)
2. Show them how the mouth works and let them color or paste features on the sack.
3. You may wish to have them paste a circle on for the face. Paste it on the flap part of the bag and then cut the circle on the flap portion so the mouth can move again.
4. Many children will want to add special features to their paper-bag puppets, for example, a tail or ears.

Stick Puppets

A stick puppet is a picture or object attached to a stick. It moves when the puppeteer moves the puppet up and down or from side to side, holding the stick.

Materials

paper, glue, scissors, crayons, popsicle sticks (or tongue depressors or cardboard strips)

Construction procedure

1. Characters and scenery can be drawn by children or pre-outlined. Depending on the age of the children, the characters and scenery can then be colored or both colored and cut out.
2. Older children may want to create their own figures.

Box Puppets

Materials

one small (individual size) box with both ends intact, one piece of white construction paper, 6″ × 9″, crayons or poster paints and brush, scissors, sharp knife, glue

Construction procedure

1. Cut box in half as in view 1, with one wide side uncut. Fold over as in view 2.
2. On construction paper, draw the face of a person or an animal. Color or paint features and cut out face.
3. Add yarn for hair, broomstraws for whiskers, and so on, if desired.
4. Cut face along line of mouth and glue to box as in view 4, so that lips come together as in view 5.

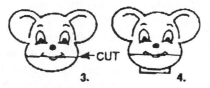

cern for protection of the various parts of the world has promoted global dialogues and joint projects focused on common goals. Many other endeavors, like the responses to natural disasters and political events, have also caused the global community to join together. Working together for the achievement of common goals promotes and builds global citizenship. Developing in individuals a broad sense of

---

::	**Let's Talk About . . . 7–3**

What Are the Characteristics of a Global Citizen?

Read the following comments made by two young adolescents and consider whether they depict a sense of themselves as global citizens.

"Earth is our home. And every patch of Earth is beautiful in its own way. That's exactly why I love this world. I love people, I try to understand them. I want to devote my life to it."

Vera (Age 13, Ukraine)

"I want the world to become a nice place to live in for animal and living things and people."

Satoshi (Age 13, Japan)

1. Would you say a global sense is reflected through Vera and Satoshi's comments? Why?

2. What characteristics would you say are expected from a citizen of the "global village"?

3. In your opinion, which characteristics are crucial for young children to develop during the early years?

4. Write down your comments and essential beliefs regarding effective global citizenship. Compare your views with friends and colleagues.

Source: Temple, 1993, pp. 13, 18.

---

social responsibility and the desire to contribute to the society at-large is critical to the survival of our society (Berman, 1997).

Developmentally appropriate practices (DAP), the cornerstone of early childhood education, support educational programs that prepare young children for membership in the global society. Helping the children to develop a sense of themselves as members of a world community through developmentally appropriate practices is a major goal of early childhood education (Bredekamp & Copple, 1997). Educators recognize that young children have an awareness of a large community outside their immediate environment. This is strongly reinforced through today's media and other current technologies. Although children's notions about a global society are vague, they exist at a very early age.

■■ Fostering Positive Values and
■■ Social Skills in Young Children

Every society has its own values. **Values** (see Chapter 3) are "decisions about the worth of some-

thing based on a standard we have set" (Sunal, 1990, p. 144). They are culturally bound and are learned through our contact and participation in a social group. They give a group its special identity. Passed on from generation to generation, values form a code of behavior that is followed by a group and its individual members. There are different types of values: aesthetic, educational, moral, religious, political, democratic, and others. Each different kind of value is utilized by individuals according to the circumstance.

The development of moral and democratic values is particularly important for success in a democratic society. Moral values indicate right and wrong and help people to make decisions and judgments (Savage & Armstrong, 1996). Research shows that people who do not have a clear understanding of moral values are more likely to exhibit inappropriate social behaviors (Committee for Children, 1992). Democratic values are centered in the recognition of the rights of each individual. They also describe socially acceptable behaviors. Moral and democratic values are essential for maintaining the lifestyle and the freedom we enjoy in the United States (see Figure 7–2).

FIGURE 7–2 Essential American Democratic and Social Values

freedom	respect for nature
patriotism	respect for others
justice	freedom of expression
loyalty	freedom to choose
friendship	freedom of worship
honesty	right to private ownership
compassion	right to have different
tolerance	ideas
equality and	right to participate
opportunity	right to lead a happy life
respect for life	

Fostering Values Development in the Early Childhood Classroom

When children come to the classroom, they bring with them values they have already acquired through their families and cultural groups. Appropriate practices establish the need to foster value development and clarify it further through classroom experiences. Direct teaching of values is not recommended. The goal is to create a classroom environment in which the values upheld by society are emphasized (Armento, 1981). Activities that provide

The classroom is instrumental in values development.

opportunities for children to interact socially present some of the most effective ways to clarify and develop the children's own values and to learn about the values held by others.

Values development is a long-term process. It progresses gradually, and it is dependent upon the individual's own developmental process. Three developmental elements influence the process of values development:

1. *the children's range of cognitive skills* (ability to process information from the environment);
2. *their social and emotional skills* (repertoire of behaviors used to respond to and cope with problems); and,
3. *the extent and quality of their personal experiences and interactions* (the range and kind of life experiences).

Awareness of these factors helps to establish consistent expectations about children's behaviors and responses. Planning activities aimed at enhancing the range of children's experiences contributes to the internalization or acquisition of values. In the case of young children, internalization occurs as they interact with others considered to be more socially skilled (Vygotsky, 1978). Active participation with others provides children with concrete examples of and experiences with behaviors and values. In this process of informal and formal social encounters, children gradually develop a sense about what is accepted and esteemed in society. One of the influential scenarios in which social encounters happen is in the classroom. Daily exchanges between teachers and children and between children and their peers provide opportunities to learn about behaviors and interactions with others. Through planned and unplanned activities in the classroom, children build social skills and acquire values every day. Concept Box 7–1 lists some of the many planned and unplanned instances in which social encounters occur in the classroom.

Through the process of social interaction, children gain what Piaget (1952) defined as development of socio-conventional knowledge (see Chapter 3) and what Vygotsky described as social and cul-

Concept Box 7–1   Opportunities for Formal and Informal Social Encounters in the Early Childhood Classroom

- Circle time or morning sharing time
- Group discussions
- Story-telling time
- Setting time to talk with individual children
- Working with children at the centers
- Free play
- Giving directions
- Talking to visitors
- Verbal and non-verbal responses to others (children, visitors, staff members, teachers)
- Answering calls (telephone, school messages)
- In the cafeteria
- Sharing opinions about events and incidents
- Behaviors during visits and field trips (see Chapter 6)
- Interacting outdoors

tural learning (see p. 57). In both theories, the role of interaction with others is highlighted as instrumental for appropriate social development. In values education interaction is the way adults and peers "scaffold" learning. Early childhood teachers not only provide examples and model behaviors but they also facilitate the learning process of specific behaviors as defined by society. Facilitation implies that time is provided for children to share their own interpretations of what they experience.

It is important to remember that a child's social interpretations are best demonstrated through sociodramatic play (see Chapter 3). Sociodramatic play engages children in make-believe situations of their own. As they create these play scripts, children reveal their interpretation of social interactions. Teachers should provide time and opportunities for play, because it is a developmentally appropriate way to foster social development. Careful observation of children interacting with each other while at play helps teachers to discover how children are progressing in their social development.

Because values are learned in action, experiences with other people provide the models of value-based behaviors that children then use to mold their own. Research reveals that children tend to be selective of those they use as **role models.** There are specific characteristics defining who will become a model (Berk, 1999):

1. Models are usually persons with qualities one admires and which one would like to possess.
2. Models have warm and responsive personalities.
3. They tend to exhibit consistent behaviors.
4. Models are seen as individuals who have power or authority.

Models are commonly found in the family, the neighborhood, and at school. Parents, family members, and teachers are powerful models for young children. Careful observations in early childhood classrooms reveal that the children model their own behaviors on those exhibited by their teachers. It is not unusual to find children responding and behaving in ways similar to their teachers'. Keen observers, children literally shape themselves based on what they witness other people do, especially those they consider important models. Because the teacher is seen as an authority figure, children will often copy the mannerisms, phrases, responses, and even food preferences of their teachers. Awareness of the powerful influence teachers exert on children and their behavior is essential. Early edu-

Teachers are relevant models for young children.

Concept Box 7–2   Good Resources to Foster Values Development

Web of Life (K–6)

Developed by the American Society for the Prevention of Cruelty to Animals (ASPCA), the program helps children to develop humane values. Caring and responsible attitudes toward animals are fostered through the many hands-on activities in the ASPCA resource kits. Available for a minimal fee, the Web of Life Resource Kits are designed for grades K–3 and 4–6.

The ASPCA also sponsors Animaland, a junior membership club for children ages 7–12. Both Animaland and *Yo quiero a los animales,* the Span-ish version for grades K–1 and 2–3, foster respect and responsibility toward animals. A teacher newsletter, *A is for Animal,* offers teaching suggestions, activities, and current events. For information, contact:

ASPCA
424 East 92nd Street
New York, NY 10128–6804

Information is also available through local Humane Societies or at ASPCA's Web site: http://www. aspca.org*

---

*Please note that Internet resources are of a time-sensitive nature and URL sites and addresses may often be modified or deleted.

---

cators need to use their influence to foster and instill socially and culturally appropriate values. It is important to remember that it is during the preschool years that teachers and others will most influence young children. Constant awareness of behaviors demonstrated by teachers in the classroom helps to project those behaviors that are deemed socially positive.

Modeling by teachers is very important because it translates values into actions and life experiences. Modeling also serves as a means for teachers to examine their own value systems in relation to the

---

■■ **Let's Talk About . . . 7–4**

Clarifying Our Own Values

Helping children to clarify their values requires each educator to have a clear understanding of his or her own value system. It requires the teacher to know the attitudes and opinions he or she has regarding such value-laden topics as racism, capital punishment, cheating, and related issues. We should also remember that many times our actions reflect different values from those we express verbally. On more than one occasion, children have surprised teachers by "reading" their non-verbal messages. Children are excellent at perceptual learning and can easily read your gestures and intonations. It is suggested that before you start a theme or read a story involving values, you take time to reflect on your own ideas and attitudes toward what is presented.

Remember that for young children, teachers are often the most powerful role models. Discuss the following with your colleagues:

1. Have you ever been "read" by a child? What did you do to correct the non-verbal message you did not intend to transmit?

2. What would you recommend doing to avoid sending conflicting messages?

3. How would you analyze your own attitudes and values with regard to a controversial topic? Pick one and use it as a demonstration.

value systems of the children they teach. This is especially important when dealing with culturally and religiously diverse groups in the classroom (see Chapter 9). For teachers, keeping a non-judgmental position regarding values is crucial. A non-judgmental position occurs when individuals avoid forming or expressing prior or unfounded opinions or statements about an event or person. Educators who adopt a non-judgmental perspective treat others with respect, even when they disagree with their views. They also give equal opportunities to others to present their ideas or positions. Teaching young children to do the same is essential for positive value development.

Approaches for Values Development

Two approaches to value development are particularly useful in the early childhood classroom. One approach stems from Kohlberg's moral development theory (cited in Santrock, 1998), which is based on moral developmental stages. To foster reflection and discussion of moral issues, Kohlberg proposes the presentation of *age-appropriate moral dilemmas* to children. An example of a moral dilemma appears in the vignette at the opening to this chapter. According to Kohlberg, as issues are discussed and analyzed, children improve their moral reasoning. Issues are selected from events happening in the classroom as well as from current events. More will be said about this theory when we discuss social morality in another section of this chapter.

Values clarification (Raths, Harmin & Simon, 1978) is another strategy that can be used for moral development of young children. It is based on the premise that one's values are chosen and then acted upon. According to Raths, Harmin, and Simon, values are "clarified" and defined through a seven-step process. The stages include: choosing freely, choosing freely among alternatives, choosing after thoughtful consideration of the consequences of each alternative, prizing and cherishing, affirming, acting upon choices, and repeating. This process leads children from the first step of selecting behaviors and beliefs to finally acting on them.

Exploration of values in the early childhood classroom requires attention to the developmental characteristics of children. Knowledge of where the child stands developmentally sheds light upon what he or she is capable of understanding and on the responses.

Consideration of the children's cultures is also essential. It is important to remember that values are relative to the individual's culture. Teachers will find it necessary to examine their own values and ideas, especially when these represent positions different from those of the children or of the community.

Good questioning techniques and effective clarification of responses are very important when fostering values. The way teachers use language is central to how children perceive and respond to ideas and values-based experiences. It is important to keep in mind that the way we use language communicates our feelings and helps to set the tone for the children responses. Be aware that through nonverbal gestures and body position, teachers also convey their feelings to children. Asking non-biased and open-ended questions is essential: Both will promote more honest and open discussions among the children.

Consider the following questions as examples of non-biased and open-ended questioning:

"What is your opinion about _____?"
"What else can you tell about _____?"
"I'd like to know more about your ideas. What can you tell me?"
"Can you tell me what happened?"
"Why would you like to do that?"
"Who can tell me more about this?"
"What would happen if _____? Let's find out together."
"How can we find out what would happen if _____?"

Allowing children to take time to think before they answer is highly recommended, particularly when discussing complex moral dilemmas. A sense of haste will inhibit the children's thought processes because of the pressure it will put on them. Clarifying responses in non-threatening ways that promote further thinking about an issue is especially valuable in teaching values. Also, teachers need to remember that

FIGURE 7–3 Using Literature to Foster Development of Values and Social Skills

Sample Monthly Literature-based Block Plan

Theme: Learning about Our Families   *Social Concepts:* family, cultural diversity   *Social Skills:* self-esteem, dealing with emotions, making friends   *Values:* friendship, respect, family love, dignity

This is my family (Meyer & Meyer, 1992)	*How my family lives in America* (Bradbury, 1992)	*Father and son* (Lauture, 1992)	*All kinds of families* (Simon, 1986)	*Tucking mommy in* (Loh, 1987)
Welcoming babies (Knight, 1992)	*The leaving morning* (Johnson, 1992)	*Sleep, sleep, sleep* (Van Laan, 1995)	*Mama, do you love me?* (Joose, 1998)	*Mama Provi and the pot of rice* (Casanova, 1994)
All the colors we are (Kissinger, 1994)	*Everybody has feelings* (Avery, 1992)	*Everybody bakes bread* (Dooley, 1996)	*Whoever you are* (Fox, 1997)	*How many days to America?* (Bunting, 1989)
The relatives came (Ryland, 1985)	*People say hello* (Barber, 1996)	*The patchwork quilt* (Flournoy, 1986)	*Bigmama's* (Crews, 1991)	*The chalk doll* (Pomerantz, 1989)
Frog and Toad are friends (Lobel, 1970)	*Home lovely* (Perkins, 1995)	*Jafta's father* (Lewin, 1982)	*I need a lunch box* (Cummings, 1988)	*Lizzie and Harold* (Winthrop, 1986)

their own body language and voice intonations can be dead give-aways of their attitudes and biases. Consider these guidelines when you are attempting to compose effective responses that will help clarify values:

■ Do not criticize or judge the child's reasons.
■ Direct the clarifying response at the individual child rather than the group.
■ Encourage the child to analyze the pieces of his or her response and consider the elements of the response.
■ Place the responsibility for the answer on the child.
■ Never frame your clarification with a predetermined answer in mind.
■ Avoid body language and voice intonations that may provide contradictory clues to the child.
■ Do not allow a clarifying response to turn into an extended discussion.

Children's literature and puppets are especially helpful when presenting moral dilemmas. They not only provide a source of issues but also include characters that children can easily relate to. For children, puppets become a voice other than the voice of the teacher that they can talk and respond to. A sample monthly block plan teachers can use to foster development of social skills and values by incorporating relevant themes from children's literature appears in Figure 7–3.

Effective use of puppets is part of many curricular programs. For example, the Second Step violence prevention curriculum (Committee for Children, 1992) uses the "Impulsive Puppy" puppet to portray impulsiveness. Several value-based children's books are also available with puppets. Examples are *Corduroy* (Freeman, 1986) and *Guess how much I love you* (McBratney, 1996). Puppets are also recommended for values clarification experiences. They provide a channel of expression for some children who are hesitant to share their views. A developmentally appropriate resource, puppets stimulate the imaginative and creative minds of preschoolers for whom puppet characters are real. Responding to puppets and creating fanciful situations allow children to exhibit ideas and personal views. For primary-age children, puppets foster cre-

---

Bringing Ideas into Practice 7–3   *Literature with Themes about Values*

Literature is one of the best sources for fostering social and democratic values and attitudes. Kilpatrick (1993) states that well-chosen stories are a powerful source for moral development. He also acknowledges that stories have traditionally been a way to pass on values and wisdom from one generation to the next. In the classroom, stories help children explore social issues in meaningful ways. Listed here are a few titles to help you get started in creating a list of your own. (Target values promoted in each title are indicated in parentheses.)

Bunting, E. (1990). *A day's work.* New York: Clarion. (work, perseverance)

Bunting, E. (1989). *How many days to America: A Thanksgiving story.* New York: Clarion. (freedom)

Cameron, A. (1988). *The most beautiful place in the world.* New York: Knopf. (patriotism)

Cowen-Fletcher, J. (1993). *Mamma zooms.* New York: Scholastic (respect for differences, love, family)

Fox, M. (1997). *Sophie.* San Diego, CA: Harcourt. (love, family love)

Fox, M. (1985). *Wilfrid Gordon McDonald Partridge* New York: Kane/Miller. (respect for elders)

Havill, J. (1986). *Jamaica's find.* New York: Houghton Mifflin. (honesty)

Hoffman, M. (1991). *Amazing Grace.* New York: Dial. (perseverance, self-confidence)

Nye, N. (1995). *Benito's dream bottle.* New York: Simon & Schuster. (helping others, kindness)

Pak, M.(1988). *Aekyung's dream.* Chicago, IL: Children's Press. (friendship, respect differences)

Patterson, K. (1990). *The tale of the mandarin ducks.* New York: Lodestar. (kindness, compassion)

Pomeranc, M. (1998). *The American Wei.* New York: Albert Whitman. (patriotism)

Williams, V. (1982). *A chair for my mother.* New York: Greenwillow. (family love, sacrifice)

Exploring ethics through children's literature by Elizabeth Saenger (1993) is a collection of children's stories aimed at promoting the discussion of value-laden issues. This guide is designed to help teachers of young children encourage their students to engage in examining ethics. Appropriate for grades 2 to 3, the guide includes suggestions for classroom activities. It is available from Critical Thinking Press, P.O. Box 448, Pacific Grove, CA 93950-0448.

---

ative writing. By using their own scripts and sometimes puppets of their own creation, children can share their personal experiences.

Values Exploration as Part of the Social Studies Content

Incorporating value clarification into the social studies content can be done in many different ways. Family, children's literature, classroom experiences, and current events all provide opportunities for children to examine values. Raths, Harmin, and Simon (1978) suggest the following curriculum techniques:

■ Use pictures without captions and allow children to engage in "what if" scenarios.

■ Present a problem and discuss the possible solutions with children.

■ Examine stories about TV characters and song lyrics and identify moral issues and values in them.

■ Use open-ended statements to complete the thoughts (i.e., I can count on my best friend because . . .).

It is important to allow children to analyze values and the decisions they make in values-related activities. One of the most effective ways to accomplish this is by presenting value conflicts found in children's literature and discussing them in large or small groups. One of the most important reasons for using literature for value clarification is getting the children to empathize with the characters and their predicaments. Other resources that will allow for value analysis are films, current events, family problems, photographs, and pictures. Allowing young children to feel and discuss the unpleasant, conflicting alternatives facing other individuals provides an appropriate setting for affective learning to take place (Derman-Sparks, 1989).

Here are some questions teachers can use to guide discussion with young children who have just read or heard a story that raises issues about conflicts in values:

1. Can you tell me what happens in this story?
2. What did (character) do?
3. Do you agree with what (character) did? Why?
4. How do you think (character) felt?
5. If you were (character) , what would you do? Can you tell me why?
6. Do you think that what (character) did was right?
7. Why was that wrong?
8. If you were (character) , what would you do?

There is no "best" way to promote values in young children. The important thing is that value education is incorporated into the social studies curriculum on a continuing basis. Values continue to be the framework individuals use to face social and personal decisions. Children of the twenty-first century will be faced with even more complex social, moral, and ethical dilemmas in the future. It is the responsibility of early childhood educators to provide young children with the best possible tools to resolve these conflicts in positive and effective ways.

The Importance of Social Skills

Successful citizens can be characterized as skillful social individuals. Appropriate social interactions are based on the individual's knowledge of social skills. Social skills are the abilities and behaviors individuals need to succeed in society. **Prosocial skills** help children to achieve positive interactions. Social skills are exhibited in most kinds of interactions in the classroom—working with peers, interacting with adults, and dealing with conflicts.

Social skills are learned both formally and informally. Informally, they are learned through interactions with people in various social environments such as the classroom, the home, and the community. Formal acquisition of social skills takes place during special lessons focused on specific skills like cooperation with peers, or as rules and instructions are given by the family.

Modeling plays a very significant role in young children's acquisition of social skills. Because children tend to imitate people they admire, how the role model relates to others influences, to a great extent, the types of behaviors the children will adopt. As avid observers, children grasp the behaviors and responses of others and add them to their repertoire of social skills. Role models include individuals in the family, teachers, personalities in the media, and fictional characters. Classroom teachers report that they often find children behaving in ways that reflect the interaction styles of both real and imaginary characters portrayed by the media. Research shows that when social skills are systematically taught, children improve their interpersonal interactions (Slaby, Roedell, Arezzo, & Hendrix, 1995).

The choice of specific social skills you should address with your young students is an important question. There are many types of social skills. They vary according to the circumstances prompting interactions. During the early years, social skill planning should include experiences that foster socially effective behaviors, establish positive relationships, teach individuals how to control their emotions during conflicts, and demonstrate prosocial behaviors (Maccoby, 1980; Bredekamp & Copple, 1997; Elias et al., 1997). Figure 7–4 identifies some of the specific skills to target in each of those areas.

Three points are important for successful learning of social skills:

1. *Developmentally appropriate expectations.* The need to keep expectations and experiences in accordance with the developmental characteristics of children establishes the basis for child-responsive experiences. Familiarity with the social milestones as well as with cultural characteristics

FIGURE 7–4 What Social Skills Should We Foster in the Classroom?

Basic social behaviors (necessary for effective social interactions):
- listening to others
- following directions
- waiting one's turn
- using nice talk
- using "manners" words ("thank you, please, excuse me")
- responding nicely to others
- asking questions
- showing respect to others

Establishing relationships with others (friendship):
- acknowledging others
- making eye contact
- "reading" how others feel
- listening
- smiling

- using manners (greeting others)
- showing consideration to others
- accepting differences
- participating with others
- helping others
- inviting others to play
- playing with others

Developing self-control (dealing with conflicts):
- listening before taking a stand
- using words to express emotions

Developing prosocial behaviors:
- helping others
- sharing
- showing empathy
- responding to others when in need
- defending others
- showing an initiative to help

Sources: Adapted from McGinnis, E., & Goldstein, A. (1990); Committee for Children (1992); Begun (1995); and Elias et al. (1997).

helps teachers to plan behaviors consistent with what the child is typically able to do. Development affects competence in social skills. As children mature, they increase their repertoire of skills and become more competent socially.

2. *Reinforcement.* Reinforcement of positive social skills is essential for expanding the child's behavioral repertoire. Consistent feedback helps children to identify and establish behaviors as a regular way of responding in a group.

3. *Teacher as a consistent role model.* Demonstrating behaviors in a consistent manner is essential. It reinforces their validity as acceptable behaviors. Teachers need to be constantly aware of the behaviors they model for children, as these behaviors will be used by children to establish their own patterns of behavior. Recognizing the family as a powerful role model of social skills is essential for teachers. Sharing with parents and families the behaviors targeted at school helps to create consistent models. However, there are cases where, despite the attempt to encourage certain

Concept Box 7–3   Sample Social Skills Curriculum

Second Step: A Violence Prevention Curriculum (Levels Pre-K/K and 1–3). Available from the Committee for Children, 172 20th Avenue, Seattle, WA 98122 (1–800–634–4449)

This curriculum is intended to build prosocial skills as a way of preventing socially aggressive behaviors. The program is literature-based, consisting of units that provide experiences for developing empathy, managing anger, and controlling impulses. Use of puppets and photographs stimulate presentation and discussion of child-appropriate situations. Participation of parents and families through home activities contributes to the development of target behaviors. Research has shown that *Second Step* improves the social skills of children when integrated into the curriculum (Hunt, 1998; Linde, 1997; Murray, 1998; and Renicks, 1998).

behaviors at home or in the immediate environment, the teacher's efforts will not succeed. This often occurs when dealing with children from other cultures, at-risk children, and children with special needs. These circumstances will present special challenges to teachers, the children, and their families.

■■ Developing Civic and
■■ Social Responsibilities

One of the most essential elements of citizenship is the ability to live successfully as a member of a social group. The early childhood years are the optimal time for building ideas and a concept about the child as a member of a society. As members of a social group, it is important to recognize that there are civic and social responsibilities as well as rights. **Civic and social responsibilities** describe the duties each member has to maintain and contribute to the well-being of the group. Good citizens are characterized by their sense of duty to collaborate with others in their society. Effective social participation of all members is a central characteristic of civic life in a democracy. Awareness of the duties and responsibilities of people is necessary for good citizenship. This is a quality that individuals develop early in life. In this section suggestions for appropriate curricular experiences aimed at fostering a sense of civic and social responsibility will be discussed.

Children as the Source
of the Civic Curriculum

Appropriate curricular practices establish the importance of building upon what is developmentally sound for children. Learning happens as the child interacts with many social groups: the family, the classroom, peers, friends, and the neighborhood. These groups also establish the context in which meaningful learning occurs.

Many times teachers have shared their concern about how to plan for so many areas and concepts (*"How can I plan for so many things?"*). Others have

expressed worry about the extent of curricular expectations posed on young children (*"Do they have to learn that, too? Oh, no; I have to follow those standards, too!"*). The answer to their concerns lies in having a clear understanding of what is implicit in the phrase "sound and developmentally appropriate." Essentially, it means becoming aware of when the child exhibits an interest in learning. Like windows, children do not always open up fully, but they do open to let ideas in.

A curriculum about the civic life of young children is both *formal* and *informal*. It is built from the topics that children indicate they are ready to learn about. Themes and activities evolve from the observations teachers make about the children's interactions. The incidents and behaviors children participate in and wonder about are the source of the social and civic education curriculum, both formal and informal. Formal activities are those teachers plan for. There are many ideas about civic life to be planned and integrated into the curriculum. However, because of the nature of this subject area, knowing how to use **"teachable moments"** is critical. These causal and unplanned instances, which describe the informal curriculum, are essential learning opportunities for young children. They are windows of opportunity when meaningful and child-initiated learning truly happens. Listening and knowing how to observe children will alert you not only to what is "teachable," but also to what they are ready and need to learn. Remember, curriculum is "what happens" (Jones & Nimmo, 1994, p. 12).

Using Appropriate Strategies:
Cooperative Learning

Let's put our heads together and dream the same dream!
—*Together* (Lyon, 1989)

Cooperative learning is a well-known strategy for developing positive social behaviors (Johnson, Johnson, & Holubec, 1988). It helps build skills for effective social interaction and collaboration. Cooperative learning experiences should be structured to mirror society's expectations and to encourage positive behavior outcomes for young children.

Cooperative learning helps children develop good interpersonal skills.

Coelho (1994) tells us that cooperative learning as a strategy contributes not only to the children's social growth, but also builds self-esteem and promotes the acceptance of others. It is a good framework for discovering the children's prior knowledge and for promoting higher level thinking skills. Cooperative learning experiences provide a meaningful setting for the development of children's prosocial skills and academic achievement.

Research has shown that benefits from cooperative learning encompass both the cognitive and social-emotional domains. In the early childhood years, use of cooperative learning activities contributes in the following ways:

Cognitive
1. Directly engages children in themes of interest to them as individuals and a group.
2. Provides hands-on experiences. Practice and trials are encouraged.
3. Encourages use of different sources to obtain information.
4. Favors use of children's diverse talents (multiple intelligences).
5. Provides opportunities to learn from and through peers.
6. Encourages discussion and sharing of ideas among children. Enhances and expands use of language to communicate ideas.

Social-Emotional
1. Fosters development of group interaction skills.
2. Provides opportunities to build friendships.
3. Fosters development of self-control.
4. Enhances sense of one's abilities (self-esteem).
5. Provides experiences to learn about respect for the ideas of others (tolerance).
6. Fosters participation and sense of belonging.
7. Builds sense of responsibility.

Teachers also need to structure and create meaningful and purposeful cooperative learning experiences that are well planned from the beginning to the end. Specific behaviors, instructional goals, and resources need to be identified, and children need to be prepared for the activities. When preparations are not made, children often grow restless, wander away from the group, and make comments like, "I don't know what you want me to do." When planning cooperative learning activities, it is important to:

1. *know the goals and the purpose:* The experience is built around a theme of common interest expressed by the children or an area of interest detected by the teacher. With the help of the teacher, children learn about the objectives to be met. Questions are encouraged, and modeling occurs to further clarify the goal of the activity (*What are we trying to accomplish? Why are we doing this?*)
2. *analyze the activity in terms of the tasks involved:* Define the tasks needed to achieve the goals. (*What do we need to do?*)
3. *assign the tasks:* Establish a specific role and responsibility for each group member. Group success is contingent upon each member's completion of his or her tasks. (*Who will do _____ ?*)
4. *provide support:* The teacher serves as a facilitator and provides support as needed. Children know the teacher is available for consultation and for help. While children are at work, the teacher observes the process, knowing when to offer ideas, or when to intervene to redirect the group process.
5. *share the accomplishments and the evaluation of accomplishments:* Children are encouraged to share what they have accomplished. Reflections

about the experience should also take place. This helps the group to assess its work and to make improvements in the activity. (The teacher should ask questions such as: *"How do you feel about what you did?" "Would you have done anything differently?" "What would you do the next time?" "Why?"*) (Johnson, Johnson, & Holubec, 1988)

Cooperative learning can be structured for small and large groups. Whatever format you select for your students, remember that the first thing is to establish the rules of acceptable behavior. Having the children participate in this process is essential, because it fosters a sense of ownership of the rules that are established. Ask the children's advice in identifying appropriate rules. Some rules may include the following:

■ Move into groups quietly.
■ Stay with the group.
■ Speak in low voices.
■ Let everyone participate.
■ Be polite to all members of the group.

Cooperative learning groups can consist of only two members, or they can be larger. In working with young children, groups of more than five may prove to be difficult. The content of the activity and the composition of the class are factors that determine the size of the groups. For example, discussing a poem can be done effectively with two or three children, while planning a trip to the zoo is suitable for a larger group. Teachers should also consider such characteristics of children as their interests, abilities, developmental readiness, personalities, and the special needs of children when selecting cooperative learning groups.

Adaptations for Children with Special Needs

Cooperative learning has been found to be an appropriate classroom strategy for children with special needs. It is important for teachers working in inclusive classrooms to be aware of the specific teaching strategies they can use to foster the appropriate development of key social behaviors. According to special educators Fad, Ross, and Boston

(1995), cooperative learning is one of the best strategies for developing social skills in children with special needs. They suggest a four-step approach:

1. *Target special social skills:* Begin by identifying a target skill for improvement. Select a target skill by using an observation instrument, choosing one of the skills most important for success in the mainstream environment, or asking the children to select the skills most relevant to them.

2. *Define the target skills clearly and behaviorally:* Establish a hierarchy of social skills in order to know what is to be learned first (see Figure 7–4). Using the hierarchy, select the target skills and set priorities according to the needs of the children. "Task-analyze" the skill to identify the specific behaviors children will exhibit. Convey the expectations to the children by using terms they understand. Making the skills concrete is crucial in working with children with special needs (and with young children in general). Use appropriate visuals and other aids to provide children with concrete clues.

3. *Design and implement the cooperative activities:* Specify both the academic and the social goals of the activity. Direct instruction and modeling of a targeted social skill are recommended for teaching children with learning or behavioral disabilities. Develop activities where everyone has a particular role to play. Discuss the criteria for success. Systematic, consistent, and frequent support and reinforcement must be built into the activities. Create groups: It is advisable to start with groups of two children, and when success has been demonstrated, move into groups of three members.

4. *Reflection and evaluation:* Use questioning to lead children to reflect on the activity. Have them comment about what they felt. Review the success criteria, and have children determine the effectiveness of the activity. Use process questions and statements such as: *How did the group function as a whole? How did each member help to make the group successful? What was your job? Show us your work—did you do your job? What should we do the next time?* (p. 33). Sentence starters ("My job was _____") and pictorial cues (happy/sad faces) can be used to process the experience. (Fad, Ross & Boston, 1995).

■■ Nurturing Civic Responsibility
■■ in Young Children

Lisa sat down with Corduroy on her lap and began to sew a button on his overalls.

"I like you the way you are" she said, "but you'll be more comfortable with your shoulder strap fastened."

"You must be a friend," said Corduroy; "I've always wanted to have a friend."

"Me too!" said Lisa, and gave him a big hug.

—*Corduroy* (Freeman, 1986)

Helping children to become aware of their behaviors and responsibilities toward others is a goal shared by both social studies and early childhood educators. Young children need to acquire the same sense of concern for others as is demonstrated by Lisa, who helped little Corduroy. Teachers' awareness of the children's social and cognitive development processes helps to establish appropriate classroom experiences and set expectations. It is important to remember that social knowledge is formed through our contacts with the environment. In young children, these contacts are limited by their repertoire of behaviors as well as by the children's cognitive knowledge.

The classroom is a social laboratory, the ground where children explore and inquire about the meaning of interactions with others. What they observe, say, and respond to, as well as how they interact with others, is used to build their own ideas about themselves and about social relationships. For many of them, it is a place where they learn for the first time what it is to be a member of a democratic, social group. Being aware of this and recognizing the different physical and social environments children come from will help teachers design effective developmentally appropriate activities.

Becoming A Part of Society:
Social Development of the Child

Becoming a part of a positive social environment is essential for the appropriate development of the individual. Knowing that each one "belongs" is what constitutes a cohesive society and what encourages its members to work for the group's betterment. For young children, becoming social members is one of the central tasks of the early years. You probably remember the little Velveteen Rabbit (Williams, 1985), who really wanted to become real. To be needed and cared for by the child gave him a reason to exist. Like the Velveteen Rabbit, children also seek to belong and be a part of a group.

[Velveteen Rabbit] "Does it happen all at once, like being wound out, or bit by bit?"

[Skin Horse] "It doesn't happen all at once. You become. It takes a long time."

—*The Velveteen Rabbit* (Williams, 1985)

As the Skin Horse said, it takes time to become a part of society. More important than the process of becoming is the outcome. Once you know that people care about you, you feel validated. The end of the

There are many ways to acknowledge positive skills and behaviors.

FIGURE 7–5 Developmental Levels of Social Perspective Taking (after Selman, 1980)*

Level 0: Egocentric Perspective (around ages 3–6): Children are generally unable to make clear distinctions between the ideas and feelings of one person and those of another. They may exhibit difficulties understanding that other people might hold a different point of view or have different feelings.

Level 1: Subjective and Social Informational Perspective (around ages 6–8): Children express an awareness of the different positions or ideas of other people in a particular situation.

A tendency to look at one perspective, rather than seeing the common elements between them, is still evident. However, children are able to see the views of a third person.

Level 2: Self-reflective perspective (around ages 8–10): Children are able to place themselves in the positions of others and understand how they feel or see their actions. Self-reflection about their own actions and ideas occurs. They believe others will understand and concur with the way they think and feel.

Source: Adapted from: J. Santrock. (1998). *Child development.* (8th ed.). Boston, MA: McGraw Hill; R. Berndt (1997). *Child development.* (2nd ed.). Madison, WI: Brown & Benchmark.

*Ages are approximate.

Velveteen Rabbit has a powerful message and an important implication for early childhood teachers: how strongly children feel about themselves as social individuals is the result of those who helped them "become" in the early part of their social development:

> "Why, he looks just like my old Bunny that was lost when I had scarlet fever!"
> But he never knew that it really was his own Bunny, come back to look at the child who had first helped him to be real.
>
> (Williams, 1985)

Children's concepts about social relationships develop over time. Their emerging social life must be considered by the teacher as part of curriculum planning. Awareness of the social characteristics in relation to child development guides teachers in their selection of activities and materials and establishes the basis for child-appropriate expectations. Two aspects are of particular importance: the children's perspective-taking ability and sense of morality.

Children's Sense of Perspective-Taking

Perspective-taking is the ability to place oneself in the place of others. It is what makes people capable of seeing the viewpoints, feelings, and emotions of others. More importantly, it is what prepares individuals to exhibit prosocial behaviors, an essential characteristic of democratic civic life. Perspective taking is an ability that evolves gradually. It develops as the child learns more about himself (Berndt, 1997). During the preschool years children tend to be egocentric—their thinking still tends to be centered on themselves. According to Robert Selman (cited by Berndt, 1997, and Santrock, 1998), children tend to judge and look at others using their own frame of reference, rather than taking into account that others may have different ideas or motivations (see Figure 7–5). Both Selman and Piaget (see Chapter 3) state that children's egocentricity impedes them from perceiving what others see, think, or believe. However, with increased social experience, children's ability to see the position of others as different from their own increases. This allows for greater understanding and tolerance in human interactions. Positive social interactions create opportunities to exhibit civic and socially acceptable behaviors. Planned and unplanned classroom experiences are among the many ways children expand their understanding about others.

Young Children's Ideas about Morality

Morality is socially and culturally bound. It is described as the society's way of measuring social behavior, learned through contacts and interactions formed by customs and traditions, rooted in religious and cultural principles. Defined in the context of development, "moral [behavior] concerns rules and conventions about what people should do in their interactions with others" (Santrock, 1998, p. 435). **Moral thinking** is directly tied to development and social maturity.

According to Piaget, as children mature, their ability to think morally becomes more sophisticated, and thus, more adult-like. Through his observations, Piaget found that peer interactions played a significant role in fostering moral thinking.

Two distinct patterns of moral thinking were observed by Piaget: *heteronomous* and *autonomous*. The first stage, heteronomous thinking, is exhibited by young children ages four through seven, and it is characterized by a tendency to believe there are consequences if one goes against what has been established as right. Right behaviors are believed to be a part of "the world," and children are bound to obey them. Because offenses of these behaviors carry punishments, young children who break a rule often look worried and will even hide what they did to prevent themselves from "being punished." Piaget also identified a transitional pattern typical of children ages seven through ten. By the time children have developed the second pattern of moral thinking—autonomous thinking—typically at around age 10 or older, they demonstrate an awareness of rules as having been created by people and also as the intentions guiding a person's actions. Piaget observed that autonomous thinkers developed an understanding of punishment as not always having to occur; rather, these children had found that it depended upon those witnessing the offenses.

Kohlberg (1969) also developed a theory about moral reasoning. Through the many interviews he conducted, Kohlberg concluded that there are three levels of moral thinking: *preconventional thinking, conventional,* and *postconventional* (see Figure 7–6). He points out that individuals move through each

level as they mature developmentally and socially. Level I, preconventional thinking, specifically describes moral reasoning of young children (under age nine). Like Piaget, Kohlberg placed emphasis on the influence of peer interactions as a condition to advanced moral reasoning (Santrock, 1998). Exchanges with peers grant children opportunities to perceive the position of others and internalize concepts about what is an appropriate behavior. Positive modeling though interactions with the family and other adults is another source used in the process of internalization. For Kohlberg, **internalization** is the key to moral reasoning. It is a way to establish developmental change in children. The way the child processes a situation and takes a stand serves as a measure of social and cognitive maturity. Appropriately designed classroom experiences and careful teacher monitoring are essential for building the children's social cognition and sense of morality.

Moral Development in a Diverse Society

In a socially diverse society like the United States, finding people who have different perspectives about what is right and wrong is not uncommon. Essential differences emerge when cultural ideas of individuals more closely bound to group religious conventions and practices come in contact with those of mainstream American culture (Damon, 1988). Traditionally, American mainstream has placed the emphasis on the individual sense of morality rather than on collective moral behavior. Teachers who work in culturally diverse communities often encounter clashes between moral ideas of the child's family, the morality of the mainstream American culture, and even their own moral code. This discord occurs when the child is encouraged to develop an autonomous stand at school while he or she is being taught at home to follow the moral code of the cultural group. The collective morality learned from the family and the neighborhood is the dominant one for the child. It establishes what is socially accepted and in the best interests of the group. In cases where teachers and students have to

FIGURE 7–6 A Summary of Kohlberg's Stages of Moral Reasoning

1. **Level I: Preconventional thought (under age 9):** Moral reasoning is based on external rewards and punishment. Social conventions and norms are considered by children as they make their judgments. Egocentric reasoning and selectively chosen perspectives (assuming the position of an individual with no enduring relationship to anyone else, as in the case of superheroes) are exhibited in their moral reasoning.

   ■ *Stage 1—Punishment and obedience (heteronomous thinking):* Children obey what family members and significant others (teachers, neighbors, etc.) tell them to obey.

   ■ *Stage 2—Individualism and self-interest:* Children consider more than one opinion. They are able to identify differences between opinions and obey the one they find convenient. Interest in getting rewards defines what is good and right to do.

2. **Level II: Conventional thought (ages ten through adolescence):** Internalization of social conventional rules is more evident. Children follow own ideas about what to do and use rules established by others.

   ■ *Stage 3—Interpersonal morality:* Children follow the rules of their group. The child sees caring, trust, and a sense of loyalty to others as important values. Importance of role models is evidenced during this period, for children tend to emulate the behaviors of those they admire.

   ■ *Stage 4—Social system morality:* Behaviors reflect an understanding of the social codes as well as the codes of the children's affiliations (religious).

3. **Level III: Postconventional thought (after age 25)**—the highest morality level.

   ■ *Stage 5—Individual rights and community rights:* Individuals have internalized an understanding about individual and society's moral values.

   ■ *Stage 6—Universal morality:* Individuals respond to the needs of their society even if it means placing themselves at risk.

Source: Adapted from Kohlberg, cited in Berns, R. (1994). *Topical child development.* Albany, NY: Delmar.

deal with such dilemmas, the following suggestions may prove helpful:

1. Learn about the sociomoral ideas of the cultural groups represented by the children in your classroom. Talking to colleagues and family members helps in understanding their culture and society.
2. Highlight what is common between both cultural groups. The fact there are universal moral values should be always stressed.
3. Encourage children to discuss and share their opinions about moral dilemmas and issues. Expressing one's opinion is an essential part of a positive civic and democratic life.
4. Turn the presence of diversity in your classroom into an opportunity to learn about the right to have a different view. This is an essential char-

acteristic and an intrinsic value of democracy. Tolerance of others' ideas is learned through examples. It is also fundamental to positive social interactions.

Fostering an awareness of other people's opinions and positions they take on issues is an important part of what we do in the classroom. As a mini-society, classrooms representing different viewpoints help children to experience how people handle similar situations in daily life.

Fostering a Sense of Social Responsibility

Social responsibility is an essential characteristic of an effective democratic society. Development of a sense of social responsibility is a process that

<table>
<tr><td>

Let's Talk About . . . 7–5

The Moral Codes of My Classroom

Most early childhood educators have dealt with the presence of other cultures in their classrooms. In today's society, anything less would seem unnatural. Diversity, however, presents some unique opportunities and challenges (see Chapter 9). Keep a journal for a week and record all the issues and situations that were related to diversity, and discuss with your colleagues the following:

1. How were the issues and experiences you recorded related to the moral code of the particular group?

2. What is the most interesting issue you dealt with?

3. How did you solve or respond to the issue?

4. What role did the children play in the response or the solution?

5. What are three things you learned from the issues you confronted?

6. What advice would you give others regarding your experience?

</td></tr>
</table>

FIGURE 7–7 Typical Behaviors of People Exhibiting Social Responsibility

Socially responsible individuals:

- have a positive image about themselves as individuals.
- are a part of a group.
- demonstrate prosocial attitudes (share and work collaboratively, help others, protect and defend others).
- participate actively in decisions concerning their groups.
- demonstrate an initiative to help whenever it is necessary.
- contribute to the well-being of their society.
- treat others with respect, fairness, tolerance, and equality.
- listen before reaching conclusions.
- resolve conflicts nonviolently.
- show pride about their culture and ethnicity as well as that of others.

evolves through life but begins in the early childhood years (Slaby, Roedell, Arezzo, & Hendrix, 1995; Berndt, 1997). People who have a sense of social responsibility exhibit a core of positive behaviors (de Melendez & Ostertag, 1996; Berman, 1997; Elias et al., 1997). These behaviors, learned during the early years, should be the focus of civic and social curricular experiences in the classroom (Figure 7–7).

Strategies to Build Social Responsibility

According to Berman (1997), there are four central strategies that can help children become socially responsible individuals (Figure 7–8). He believes they are the key to building "social consciousness" in children. Berman's strategies are based on three important elements: First, signifi-

cant others, adults, and the environment serve as models on which children base their own social ideas and behaviors. Second, families and teachers are instrumental in fostering positive social ideas. Third, it is important to take a stance against violence. Berman's strategies resemble other curriculum models for the prevention of violence (Committee for Children, 1992; Slaby, Roedell, Arezzo, & Hendrix, 1995).

Connecting Social Development with the NCSS Social Studies Standards

The central goal of the social studies curriculum is to contribute to the individual's development of effective social competence. Early childhood education offers many opportunities to foster social development in the classroom. This is an aspect that permeates the national social studies standards. However, it is addressed specifically through Strands I, IV, and X. Each of these strands, or themes, suggests ways to address social competence and integrate it into the curriculum:

FIGURE 7–8 A Summary of Berman's Strategies for the Development of Social Consciousness in Children

- **Develop a warm and caring classroom environment:** A sense of being secure characterizes the environment. Children know they have people who care about them, who listen to them, and who are concerned about their needs. Guidance is used to help children develop self-control and appropriate behaviors. Prosocial skills are developed as children engage in experiences and interactions with others. Children participate in the decision-making processes.
- **Model prosocial and ethical behaviors:** Adults (families, teachers, and adults) display prosocial and ethical behaviors. Opportunities to behave prosocially are encouraged.

- **Plan activities that foster perspective-taking:** Developmentally based activities are offered in order to promote consideration for the views and ideas of others. Preschoolers are guided to gain a sense of what happens to others through interactions with peers and adults, planned experiences, and group activities. Expressions of feelings and emotions are encouraged.
- **Encourage children to take action against injustice:** The awareness of social injustice and responsibility to take action is fostered through the program. Opportunities are offered for children to take action against unfair behaviors and actions. Non-violent strategies are implemented and modeled.

Source: Adapted from: Berman, S. (1997). *Children's social consciousness and the development of social responsibility.* Albany, NY: SUNY Press.

Strand I: Culture.

Recognition of our culture contributes to understanding who and what we are. Culture is the force that shapes people and through which we learn the beliefs, ideals, and values used to guide our lives. Development of a sense of pride about one's cultural roots is essential for proper, individual social development. It is also instrumental in effective social membership. "Culture helps us understand ourselves as both individuals and members of various groups" (NCSS, 1994, p. 21). As children learn to recognize their culture, they become aware of the existence of other cultural behaviors. In a multi-cultural society, social competence is directly related to the individual's ability to interact with a variety of cultural codes and behaviors. Learning about our cultural similarities and differences fosters appreciation of the many things that give people their unique character. Suggested topics to incorporate into the classroom curriculum are:

- Who I am, who we are.
- We are alike and different, too.
- I am proud of my cultural roots.

- Celebrating the cultures in our classroom.
- Things I like to do.
- Things we can do together.
- Friends everywhere.
- Showing respect for the ideas of others.
- My favorite folktales from other cultures.
- Singing songs that celebrate my culture/country.

Strand IV: Individual Development and Identity.

One's identity is the result of one's interactions with others in society. Through social exchanges in various contexts, people develop their own ways and behaviors, which come to define them as individuals. Acknowledgement of culture as a shaping force for individual identity is essential for positive individual and social development. Becoming aware of the influence of social groups such as the family, friends, neighborhood, and community contributes to an understanding of how individuals become who they are (NCSS, 1994). Changes in our social behavior over time is another important aspect for children to learn. Suggested topics to explore in the classroom include the following:

- Things I like to do.
- Things I used to do before; things I can do now.
- This is my family.
- My family is special.
- My favorite pet.
- My favorite hobby.
- These are my friends.
- Things I like to do with my friends.
- This is what we do at school.
- I know how to work with others.
- I help others.

Strand X: Civic Ideals and Practices.

At the heart of social life in a democracy is the development of a conscience about the values held by the society. An understanding about the rights and responsibilities people have in a democratic society is what establishes its success. According to the National Council for the Social Studies (NCSS), "An understanding of civic ideals and practices of citizenship is critical to full participation in society as is central to the purpose of the social studies" (NCSS, 1994, p. 30). Individual awareness of the important role each person plays in society is what contributes to the success and continuity of democracy. These are characteristics built early in life. Suggested topics to foster development of effective citizenship in the classroom include the following:

- I collaborate with my family.
- My family helps each other.
- I like to work in groups.
- Helping each other.
- Learning about special people who help others.
- I know my rights.
- We all have rights and responsibilities.
- We help in the classroom.
- We are all equal.
- We follow rules.
- I know the rules of my classroom.

- Helping my friends.
- Things I do to help my community.
- Community helpers.
- Important people who built our society.
- I am a good citizen.

Teaching Social and Civic Concepts in the Early Childhood Classroom

Like all learning in the early childhood years, the social and civic education curriculum stems from the child. By listening to the children's questions, dialogue, and comments and through observations, teachers can collect clues to use in planning relevant and appropriate learning experiences. We cannot emphasize this enough: *Social and civic curricula should stem from the interests and motivations of the child and should not be based upon a prescribed curriculum.*

Children, through their interactions with people, form social ideas and skills. The various family members, the peers in the classroom, the people in the community, and media personalities are the ones who influence the development of the child's social and civic concepts the most. In planning activities aimed at developing social concepts, teachers need to know the children's patterns of behavior in their interactions with others and the current situations the children face. This is of utmost relevance, because it will assist the teacher in planning a responsive and developmentally effective curriculum.

Figure 7–9 lists key social concepts to develop in young children. These are by no means the only ones. Working with children and closely observing them will alert teachers to other concepts and tasks to include in the curriculum.

Living in a Democratic Society: Political Concepts

A democratic environment provides the best setting for learning about the rights and responsibilities of citizenship. Such an environment also facilitates the understanding of the people's need for government. Children begin to acquire their under-

FIGURE 7–9 Key Themes for Building Social and Civic Skills

Social Skills:
- I am important.
- I can do many things.
- My family cares about me.
- I like to be with my family.
- I value my friends.
- Keeping my friends.
- I use my listening skills.
- I help others.
- I use the magic words ("please, thank you, excuse me").

- I use my happy face.
- I follow rules.
- I treat others with respect.
- I take care of my pets.
- I express my feelings with words.

Civic Themes:
- Respecting others.
- We are alike.
- Expressing our ideas.
- Making decisions.

- Together we can do many things.
- Helping our friends.
- Keeping our classroom/school clean.
- Feeling proud about our community.
- I know our community helpers.
- Following rules.
- Our family rules.
- Sharing and helping our group/community.

For discussion:
1. How many other topics would you include?
2. Which of these topics are most appropriate for preschoolers?

standing of basic political concepts like "government," "rules," and "power" very early in life. For example, infants acquire a sense of the source of authority when someone feeds them when they are hungry or picks them up when they are crying. A three-year-old knows the meaning of rules and recognizes that approval can result in a reward and that disobeying the "no" of a parent can bring on punishment. This kind of awareness on the part of the child is not only a phase of development, but also the beginning of an extensive lifelong process called **political socialization.**

Political socialization begins in childhood and focuses on building knowledge about the role of government and its relationship to the individual in a democracy (Savage & Armstrong, 1996). Political socialization—development of an understanding about power, rules, and the role of government as an authority—is grounded in politics, not in partisan politics, but rather in politics as a framework for implementing the rules of democracy. Politics is a broad field and describes the activities and behaviors that people exhibit in relation to the power structure and the governing processes (Ellis, 1995). Political activities with peers or adults take place in

all the settings where children interact: at home, in the classroom, and around the neighborhood (Parker & Kaltsounis, 1986). Activities such as expressing one's ideas about an issue, electing someone, choosing a position, deciding what game to play, resolving a conflict, following rules, and recognizing authority are just a few of the political activities children experience during the early years.

Children's progressive acquisition of the concept of politics has been documented through research. The results of one study indicate that a sense of politics is acquired even "before the child enters kindergarten" (Parker & Kaltsounis, 1986, p. 16). Concept Box 7–4 lists some of the major findings regarding young children's awareness of politics that have some important implications for teachers.

A democratic classroom is essential for the development of positive political concepts in young children. An atmosphere in which ideas, questions, participation, and involvement in decision making are welcome creates a positive environment for building democratic political concepts. Active participation and engagement of children in exploration of child-meaningful political themes help children to

Concept Box 7–4   Key Research Findings Regarding Children's Ideas about Politics

■ The concept of politics begins during the early years and continues to evolve through life experiences.

■ Basic attachments to political figures and identifications are part of the first political perspectives children acquire.

■ Children's earliest perceptions of political figures define them as positive, benevolent figures. They tend also to be very personal (the governor, the president, the mayor).

■ Emotions and feelings toward political concepts are built before there is a knowledge-based understanding about what these concepts represent.

■ An understanding of the political process tends to appear between the end of middle childhood and adolescence.

Source: W. Parker and T. Kaltsounis. Citizenship and law-related education (p. 18). In V. Attwood (Ed.). (1986). *Elementary school social studies: Research as guide to practice.*

FIGURE 7–10 How Much Do Young Children Understand about Politics?

Children exhibit their political sense in many ways:
. . . *through the positions they assume.*
. . . *by expressing their views.*
. . . *by inquiring about things that happened.*
. . . *when they participate in making decisions.*
. . . *when making choices.*
. . . *by acknowledging the existence of a governing source.*
. . . *by supporting the ideas of others.*
. . . *by participating in class and group activities.*
. . . *by showing preferences.*
. . . *by taking the initiative.*
. . . *by promoting change.*

build and exhibit their political identities (Figure 7–10).

An effective way to help children learn about politics and political processes is by engaging them in theme-based activities based on political topics. A well-planned classroom environment where such activities can take place is essential. Concept Box 7–5 has information that will help you create such experiences for your children.

Learning about Political Symbols

Society uses many different symbols that convey its identity and political orientation. *Patriotic symbols* like the flag, the national anthem, the Pledge of Allegiance, patriotic songs and slogans, and special colors are among the symbols that reflect the pride people feel for their country. *National symbols* include a variety of items that identify a country and define its culture. They include characters who are either historical (e.g., Dr. Martin Luther King; Toussaint L'Ouverture in Haiti) or legendary (Uncle Sam and Johnny Appleseed in the United States); songs (e.g., *America the Beautiful*); typical costumes; national landmarks (e.g., the Washington Monument); music; and, even food (e.g., "as American as apple pie").

Children get their first-hand knowledge about political symbols from interactions with the family, the neighborhood, and the school. They learn the symbols and recognize their uses in many informal ways. For example, children notice that the flag is displayed in many more places during the Fourth of July holiday. They know that the national anthem is sung at the opening of every baseball game. Through such experiences, children learn to associate meanings with symbols and begin to grasp their significance. By the time they come to school, most are familiar with the flag, the anthem, and the character most representative of their country.

Political symbols are too abstract for young children to understand. This fact establishes the need to design activities that are both concrete and mean-

---

Concept Box 7–5   Suggested Concepts about Politics

Experiences related to politics cover a wide range of areas familiar to the child. You may want to use this list as a starter for activities.

Concepts: rules, establishing rules, following rules, rights and responsibilities, tasks and roles, participation, choosing, making decisions, leaders, authority figures, law, law enforcers, government

Themes:

- All families have rules.
- Tasks I do at home.
- I follow rules at home.
- We know our classroom rules.
- There are rules for the playground.
- I know my rights.
- We all have responsibilities (at home, in the school).
- Establishing rules for a field trip (see p. 165).
- Learning about what the school principal does.
- Community leaders.
- Leaders from many places.

- Police officers are community helpers.
- Learning about our leaders.
- Recognizing rule-based symbols (traffic lights, international road signs, school bell, ambulance's siren).

Suggested Children's Books:

Fritz, J. (1987). *Shh! We're writing the constitution.*

Garza, C. L. (1990). *Family pictures/Cuadros de familia.*

Hopkinson, D. (1993). *Sweet Clara and the freedom quilt.**

Kurusa. (1998). *The street is ours [La calle es nuestra].*

Lindbergh, R. (1990). *Johnny Appleseed.*

Provenesen, A. (1990). *The buck stops here.*

Sis, P. (1991). *Follow the dream: The story of Christopher Columbus.*

Spier, P. (1987). *We the people: The Constitution of the United States of America.*

*Suitable for retelling or for older children.

---

ingful to young students. Ideas about the meanings of symbols such as the flag should be integrated into the social studies curriculum. For example, flags that are familiar to children, such as those representing sports teams, are a way of building symbolic knowledge. The flags can be displayed in the classroom and discussed. Symbols (logos, colors, mascots) used by the local and national sports teams are also considered good sources of knowledge about representations. Children can also create a classroom flag. Other activities that foster knowledge about national and patriotic symbols are:

- *Flags:* It is important to display the flag in the early childhood (preschool) classroom, even though children typically do not show an understanding of its symbolism until the elementary grades (Hess & Torney, 1996). Besides the national flag, state flags and different local flags should also be displayed. A center (*Flags of Our Global Friends*) displaying selected flags from other countries can portray the flag as common symbol of all people. Flags can be changed monthly, or according to celebrations. Displaying the flag of the country where a story takes place or where the author of the story was born is another way of learning about flags.

- *Music:* Exposing children to patriotic songs promotes their political socialization. Tapes and recordings of such songs as *America the Beautiful* and others representing American ideals can be included in the listening center. They can be enjoyed and discussed before or after reading a story with a related topic. Music and the anthems from other countries should be included in the listening center as well.

- *Illustrations of National Characters and Landmarks:* Pictures and photographs of national, historical, and legendary characters, as well as pictures of national landmarks, help to develop

---

Concept Box 7–6   Children's Comments about National and Patriotic Symbols

Comments about the flag:

"A flag is like a big piece of cloth that includes all of us" (Darren, age 6)

"These are my colors . . . ["Why are those your colors?"] . . . Because I see them in the flag and my teacher said so." (Gisela, age 5)

"I have many in my house. Daddy hangs them for the 4th of July." (Etienne, age 8)

"You see all those stars, I am one of them." (Reynaldo, age 5)

Comments about the anthem:

"I like it because we all stand up and sing, and then go YEA!!!!" [gesturing and cheering] (Anne, age 4)

"I can't sing it, but I know I have to stand up." (Ben, age 7)

"Daddy puts his hand here" [placing his open hand on his chest]. (Mike, age 4)

---

young children's ideas about political symbols. Photographs of the town and state landmarks should be displayed and included in the classroom materials. Postcards are a good and inexpensive source of landmark visuals. Easy to display, they can be used to create books about "special places." National landmarks of other countries should also be included. For example, one of the ways to illustrate the common use of political symbols and promote global awareness is to display pictures of the presidential houses in other countries along with a picture of the White House.

■ *Literature:* There are many stories and poems available that help children to build concepts about different political symbols. Here are a few suggestions:

Bates K. L. (1994). *O beautiful, for spacious skies* [patriotic music]

Blumberg, R. (1994). *Bloomers!* [political characters: Susan B. Anthony, Amelia Bloomer, and Elizabeth Stanton Cady]

Cohn, A. (1994). *From sea to shining sea.* [excellent collection of stories and songs about American historical and political events]

Johnson, J. (1994). *Lift every voice and sing.* [considered to be the African-American anthem]

Spier, P. (1973). *The Star-Spangled Banner.* [based on the U.S. national anthem]

Political symbols are a part of everyday life in American society. Emphasizing their importance and clarifying their meaning to young children will help build their understanding of the basic prin-

---

Concept Box 7–7   Celebrating Flag Day and Independence Day

Songs for Independence Day:

Wave a Little Flag
(to the tune of *"I'm a little teapot"*)

Wave a little flag
Red, white, and blue.
Our country belongs
To you and me.
So, all together we can say:
"Happy Independence Day!"

Independence Day
(to the tune of *"Mary had a little lamb"*)

Fireworks go snap, snap, snap!
Crack, crack, crack! Zap, zap, zap!
Fireworks make me clap, clap, clap!
On Independence Day!

ciples of democracy and strengthen their ability to grasp abstract concepts. Teaching and learning about political symbols is fun for teachers and children alike, as it provides opportunities to engage in multi-disciplinary multi-media activities. It is also an opportunity to explore cross-cultural and global similarities and differences among people and their societies.

Recommended Children's Books

Bunting, E. (1994). *Smoky night.* [Spanish (1999): *Noche de humo.*] San Diego, CA: Harcourt Brace.

Bunting, E. (1998) *The day the whale came.* San Diego, CA: Harcourt Brace.

Carlson, N. (1994). *How to lose all your friends.* New York: Viking.

Christiansen, C. (1997). *The willow tree.* New York: Fulcrum.

Cohen, M. (1967). *Will I have a friend?* New York: Simon & Schuster.

De Rolf, S. (1996). *The crayon box that talked.* New York: Random House.

Freeman, D. (1986). *Corduroy.* New York: Puffin.

Freeman, D. (1987). *Dandelion.* New York: Puffin.

Hallinan, P. K. (1997). *Let's care about sharing!* New York: Ideals Children's Books.

Hallinan, P. K. (1998). *That's what a friend is.* New York: Ideals Children's Books.

Henkes, C. (1988). *Chester's way.* New York: Greenwillow.

Joose, B. M. (1998). *Mama, do you love me?* San Francisco, CA: Chronicle Books.

Lewison, W. (1995). *The rooster who lost his crow.* New York: Dial.

McBratney, S. (1996). *Guess how much I love you.* Cambridge, MA: Candlewick Press.

Samuels, B. (1989). *Duncan and Dolores.* New York: Aladdin.

Torres, L. (1993). *Subway sparrow.* [Spanish (1997): *Gorrión del metro.*] New York: Farrar, Straus, & Giroux.

Williams, M. (1985). *The velveteen rabbit.* New York: Dragonfly.

Zolotow, C. (1990). *Mr. Rabbit and the lovely present.* New York: Harper Trophy.

ACTIVITIES

Keeping Track of What You Learn: Your Personal Activity Log

In this chapter we discussed citizenship and civic responsibility as social studies topics appropriate for young children. Here are some additional activities for your PAL.

A. Reflections

1. Create a values continuum for your classroom that identifies two polar positions such as "strongly agree" and "strongly disagree." Use it on a regular basis by having children place a face with their name it on the spot that expresses their opinion during value-related discussions and moral dilemmas. This is a good way for the children to visualize how they and others feel about an issue.

2. Write several open-ended sentences that focus on values, citizenship, and civic responsibility on strips of butcher paper and put them up around the classroom. They can be topics for discussion, and serve as activities any time the opportunity arises. Some examples include: "I can count on my best friend to . . ." "A good President is . . ." "My neighborhood is different because . . ."

3. Plan a classroom election (as a game). Have the children pick the officers to elect; define the issues; make slogans and other campaign materials; conduct the campaign; and elect the candidates. Have the class make a "big book" about the experiences.

B. Collections

1. Collect election memorabilia from your local party headquarters, and use it in activities with children. Ask family members to contribute to your collection.

2. Cut from magazines and newspapers pictures that represent values and civic responsibility. Use them for projects in the classroom.

3. Over a period of time, have children take pictures of each other that represent socially responsible behaviors. Make a class record using the pictures and appropriate captions.

C. Internet Resources*

■ **ASKERIC**

Web site:
http://www.eric.sys.edu/virtual/lessons

The ERIC database has lesson plans and activities about civics and character education.

■ **The Gateway Educational Materials**

Web site: http://www.thegateway.org

This is a searchable database, with materials, units, and lesson plans about civics, character education, values, and related topics.

■ **United Nations Cyber School Bus**

Web site: http://www.un.org/pubs/cyber

Many resources for observing the International Day of Peace (the third Tuesday of September) and a list of schools around the world that celebrate this day are provided at this site.

*Please note that Internet resources are of a time-sensitive nature and URL sites and addresses may often be modified or deleted.

References

Armento, B. (1981). A matter of values. In J. Allen. *Education in the 80's*. Washington, DC: National Education Association, pp. 113–118.

Begun, R. W. (Ed.). (1995). *Ready-to-use social skills lessons & activities for grades 1–3*. West Nyack, NY: The Center for Applied Research in Education.

Berk, L. (1999). *Infants, children and adolescents*. Upper Saddle River: Merrill.

Berman, S. (1997). The development of children's social consciousness. *ESR Forum, 14*(3), pp. 1–5.

Berman, S. (1997). *Children's social consciousness and the development of social responsibility*. Albany, NY: SUNY Press.

Berndt, T. (1997). *Child development* (2nd ed.). Madison, WI: Brown & Benchmark.

Berns, R. (1994). *Topical child development*. Albany, NY: Delmar.

Bredekamp, S., & Copple, C. (1997). *Developmentally appropriate practices in early childhood programs* (rev. ed.). Washington, DC: National Association for the Education of Young Children.

Center for Civic Education. (1994). *National standards for civics and government*. Calabasas, CA: Author.

Coelho, E. (1994). *Learning together in the multicultural classroom*. Portsmouth, NH: Heinemann.

Committee for Children. (1992). *Second step: A violence prevention curriculum (Grades Pre-K/K; 1–3)*. Seattle, WA: Author.

Damon, W. (1988). *The moral child*. New York: Free Press.

Derman-Sparks, L. (1989). *The anti-bias curriculum: Tools for empowering children*. Washington, DC: National Association for the Education of Young Children.

Ellis, A. (1995). *Teaching and learning elementary social studies* (5th ed.). Boston, MA: Allyn & Bacon.

Elias, M., Zins, J., Weissberg, R., Frey, K. Greenberg, M., Haynes, N., Kessler, R., Stone, M., & Shriver, T. (1997). *Promoting social and emotional learning: Guidelines for educators*. Alexandria, VA: Association for Supervision and Curriculum Development.

Fad, K., Ross, M., & Boston, J. (1995, Summer). We're better together: Using cooperative learning to teach social skills to young children. In K. Fad, M. Ross, & J. Boston (Eds.), *Teaching exceptional children* (pp. 28–34).

Hess, R., & Torney, J. (1996). *The development of political attitudes in children*. New York: Anchor Books.

Horse, H. (1997). *A friend for little bear*. London, UK: Walker Books.

Hunt, L. (1998). *Developing pro-social skills as a way to counteract violent behaviors in a group of kindergart-*

ners. Graduate Teacher Education Program Master's Practicum. Ft. Lauderdale, FL: Nova Southeastern University.

Johnson, D., Johnson, R., & Holubec, E. (1988). *Cooperation in the classroom* (Rev. ed.). Edina, MN: Interaction Book Company.

Jones, E., & Nimmo, J. (1994). *Emerging curriculum*. Washington, DC: National Association for the Education of Young Children.

Kilpatrick, W. (1993, Summer). The moral power of stories. *American Educator*, pp. 24–35.

Kneip, W. (1986, October). Defining global education by its content. *Social Education, 50*, 445–50.

Kohlberg, L. (1969). Stage and sequence: The cognitive developmental approach to socialization. In D. Goslin, (Ed.). *Handbook of socialization*. Chicago, IL: Rand McNally.

Linde, D. (1997). *Prosocial problem-solving techniques for conflict resolution in the kindergarten classroom*. Graduate Teacher Education Program Master's Practicum. Ft. Lauderdale, FL: Nova Southeastern University.

Maccoby, E. (1980). *Social development*. New York: Harcourt Brace Jovanovich.

Machado, J. (1999). *Early childhood experiences in language arts* (6th ed.). Albany, NY: Delmar.

Maxim, G. W. (1991). *Social studies and the elementary school child* (4th ed.). New York: Merrill.

Mayesky, M. (1998). *Creative activities for young children* (6th ed.). Albany, NY: Delmar.

McGinnis, E., & Goldstein, A. (1990). *Skillstreaming in early childhood: Teaching prosocial skills to the preschool and kindergarten child*. Champaign, IL: Research Press.

McGuffee, M. (1996). *The day the earth was silent*. Bloomington, IN: Inquiring Voices Press.

Murray, M. (1998). *Improving the behavior of second grade students through the Second Step discipline program*. Graduate Teacher Education Program Master's Practicum. Ft. Lauderdale, FL: Nova Southeastern University.

National Council for the Social Studies (1989). *Social studies for early childhood and elementary school children: Preparing for the 21st century*. Washington, DC: Author.

National Council for the Social Studies (1994). *Expectations for excellence: Curriculum standards for social studies*. Washington, DC: Author.

Parker, W., & Kaltsounis, T. (1986). Citizenship and law-related education. In V. Atwood. (Ed.). *Elementary school social studies: Research as guide to practice.* (Bulletin no. 79). Washington, DC: National Council for the Social Studies.

Piaget, J. (1952). *The origins of intelligence in children.* New York: International Universities Press.

Raths, L., Harmin, M., & Simon, S. (1978). *Values and teaching.* Columbus, OH: Merrill.

Robles de Melendez, W., & Ostertag, V. (1996, September). *Helping children to build a sense of community.* Paper presented at the Annual Conference of the Early Childhood Association of Florida, Orlando, FL.

Renicks, L. (1998). Sample social studies integrated activity packet. Course assignment. Ft. Lauderdale, FL: Nova Southeastern University, Graduate Teacher Education Program.

Santrock, T. (1998). *Child development* (8th ed.). Boston, MA: McGraw Hill.

Savage, T., & Armstrong, D. (1996). *Effective teaching in the elementary social studies* (3rd ed.). Englewood Cliffs, NJ: Prentice Hall.

Slaby, R., Roedell, W., Arezzo, D., & Hendrix, K. (1995). *Early violence prevention.* Washington, DC: National Association for the Education of Young Children.

Sunal, C. (1990). *Early childhood social studies.* Columbus, OH: Merrill.

Temple, L. (Ed.). (1993). *Dear world: How children around the world feel about the environment.* New York: Random House.

Vygotsky, L. (1978). *Mind in society.* Cambridge, MA: Harvard University Press.

CHAPTER 8

Integrating the Arts and Creative Expression into the Social Studies Curriculum

. . . no one can claim to be truly educated who lacks basic knowledge and skills in the arts.

. . . the arts have been an inseparable part of the human journey; indeed we depend on the arts to carry us toward the fullness of our humanity.

—NATIONAL STANDARDS FOR ARTS EDUCATION
(1994, Introduction, p. 5)

Chapter Questions

After reading this chapter, you should be able to answer the following questions:

- What constitutes the arts and creative expression for young children?
- How can we create developmentally appropriate arts experiences for young children?
- How can the arts and creative expression be integrated into the early childhood social studies curriculum?

Key Terms and Concepts

aesthetics	culture
art process	folk group
art product	folklife
the arts	folklore
creative expression	visual arts

Classroom Portrait: **A Visit to the Arts and Crafts Fair**

Children in Mr. Nelson's second grade classroom have been preparing themselves for a visit to the local crafts fair. Every year community artists and crafters celebrate the holiday season with the special pre-holiday fair. Musicians, painters, wood carvers, quilt makers, and this year, children, take part in the event. Every year Mr. Nelson looks forward to taking his class to the fair. This year he has decided to invite the children's families to participate. "It's a good way for all of us to learn about the many artists in our community," he told his colleagues. Preparing the children and the families to appreciate what they were about to experience was just as important to Mr. Nelson as the visit itself. One morning, just as Mr. Nelson was getting ready to begin the discussion about the fair and unveil the fair's new poster, Mrs. Rossi, a parent of one of the children, entered the classroom. Mr. Nelson immediately noticed that she was holding the pink paper on which he sent the note about the fair home to the families. The letter announced the activity as "an opportunity to learn about the arts."

"Well, Mr. Nelson, I see you are planning to go to the fair next week," said Mrs. Rossi in an irritated voice.

"That's right. Are you joining us?" he asked. At that moment a big "WOW!" resounded through the classroom as Mr. Nelson's student intern unfolded the colorful poster.

"Mrs. Rossi, you can see how excited the children are about the visit to the fair. I do hope you can come with us and help us enjoy it." Mr. Nelson flashed his best smile at Mrs. Rossi, who was frowning.

"No, I won't be coming with you," she replied. "In reality I came to talk to you about this idea of going to the fair."

As both of them stepped into the hallway, Mr. Nelson asked the parent to share her concern.

"You know," explained Mrs. Rossi, "it's not that I'm opposed to art, but don't you think that the children need that time to do more important school work? Taking time to go see some home-made pictures and holiday gifts is not as important as spending time teaching the children to read. I just think that you should not take children out of school when my Ben and his friends are having trouble reading. I understand that you think the arts are important, and we have some wonderful museums for that, but . . . the fair? What is so special about our arts and crafts fair?"

Mr. Nelson smiled as once again he heard the familiar question. "You gave me the answer, Mrs. Rossi. What makes it special is that it's 'ours'!"

■■ Defining the Arts
■■ and Creative Expression

In 1988 the U.S. Congress commissioned the National Endowment for the Arts (NEA) to assess the status of art education in American schools. The extensive study revealed that arts education was in jeopardy. Art, music, dance, painting, and other means of creative expression were viewed as frivolous and were not awarded the same respect and importance as reading, mathematics, science, and the other more traditional curriculum subjects. Ten years later, educators still cannot agree on the role of art in the curriculum. Education objectives in the arts and creative expression are difficult to define, or totally lacking in many school systems. Yet, art is what endures and embodies the essence of the human spirit. Art knows no national or cultural boundaries. The arts also nurture the human spirit and promote universal understanding. Creative expression leaves an indelible mark on the world and makes it a more beautiful place.

The arts are considered to be a universal language, common to all people. They convey many aspects of the human experience. They are the immortal records of historical events and personalities and representations of various groups' customs and emotions, often interpreted through innovative media. The arts are a chronicle of our development as a species.

The arts are defined as the "creative works [of people] and the process of producing them" (National Standards for Arts Education, 1994, Preface).

Let's Talk About . . . 8–1

What Is Your Perception of the Arts?

Many of us do not really understand what the arts are. We think of the arts only as the paintings we see in a museum or a ballet performance we watch at the theater. The arts tell stories of humankind. They link us to the past, mirror the present, and predict the future. The arts are an integral part of all human cultures and histories. Take time to think about the following:

1. How do you perceive the arts?
2. How would you describe your knowledge about the arts?
3. What is the value of art to you personally and to society in general?
4. What is the role of the arts in the early childhood curriculum?

FIGURE 8–1 The Arts

- **Music:** singing, performing, creating, and responding to sounds, pitch, and rhythm.
- **Dance:** body movements, responding to music, experiences and sounds; improvisation; movement exploration.
- **Visual arts:** creative expressions of one's experiences and perceptions through the use of a variety of media, tools, and processes.
- **Dramatic arts:** representations of one's experiences and perceptions by means of actions (improvisations, pantomimes), dialogues, costumes, and characterization.
- **Literature:** expressions of people's experiences, feelings, emotions, and imaginary concepts, depicted in different genres (poetry, fiction, narrative, traditional folktales, biographies).

Source: Consortium of National Arts Education Association. (1994). National standards for arts education. In *Dance, music, theatre, visual arts: What every young American should know and be able to do in the arts.* Reston, VA: Music Educators National Conference.

They show the full range of **creative expression** people use to convey their ideas and feelings through various media. The arts include dance, music, visual arts, and drama.

The arts are one of the best outlets young children use to express themselves. They are the essential language children use to communicate and explore the world. Literature, traditionally a part of the humanities, is included among the arts in the list in the National Standards for the Arts (Figure 8–1), because it is the oral and written connection that links the arts and gives additional meaning to the human expression.

The **visual arts** represent a category that has several branches of its own. The most familiar branch, the fine arts, brings to mind visions of Renoir's paintings and Michelangelo's sculptures. With the advent of modern times, however, the category of the visual arts has expanded to include several other branches that are not so widely known.

In examining the various categories of the arts, one can see that they are a part of key human endeavors. It is therefore essential to expose children to the arts in an approach that balances content and experience. Early childhood educators know that allowing children to express themselves through the various art media is an essential part of their devel-

Concept Box 8–1   The Visual Arts

Fine arts: drawing, painting, sculpture, printmaking
Communication and design arts: films, television, graphics
Environmental arts: architecture, landscape, urban, and interior design
Folk arts: pottery, weaving, jewelry design, wood carving, and others

Source: Consortium of National Arts Education Association. (1994). National standards for arts education. In *Dance, music, theatre, visual arts: What every young American should know and be able to do in the arts.* Reston, VA: Music Educators National Conference.

opment. However, it is equally valuable to help children to learn and appreciate art through its content.

Development of the Aesthetic Sense in Young Children

Human beings experience life through their senses. The senses help us create the images of our world and navigate through life. They are the essential learning tools of young children. Through the senses, children form their first perceptions of life and build their mental repertoire. Perceptions are not merely reflections of the senses. They are also guided by the emotional feelings that experiences arouse in the individual. For example, the emotions a child feels as he or she listens to a piece of music, or as he or she looks at a painting, define the child's own sense of what is meaningful.

How we perceive and judge art experiences has much to do with our individual sense of **aesthetics.** An aesthetic sense defines the individual's response to creative expression. Our sensory perceptions and the emotional reactions they evoke form the basis for the way each one of us perceives "beauty." Our own aesthetic sense determines which things and forms of expression we consider beautiful.

The aesthetic sense is an important human characteristic. It establishes the need as well as the criteria for what is attractive and appealing. There are many ways in which the aesthetic sense of individuals or groups is demonstrated, from their participation in the visual arts to the decoration of community areas. Aesthetics influence the ways culturally diverse individuals and groups express themselves. Every cultural group has a unique sense of beauty that is reflected in how its members dress, how they decorate their homes, and what they recognize as beautiful. Learning to show respect and to be tolerant of other's aesthetic ideas is an important social task of the early childhood education.

To develop an attachment to aesthetics, children also need daily experiences with objects and events that require them to use their senses. They also need time to share their perceptions and to express the feelings, thoughts, reactions, and creative ideas the experiences evoke in them. Teachers who pro-

Concept Box 8–2   Organizations with Information about the Arts and Art Education

Getty Center for Education in the Arts
401 Wilshire Blvd., Suite 950
Santa Monica, CA 90401
(310) 395–6657

American Council for the Arts
1 East 53rd Street
New York, NY 10022
(212) 223–2787

Music Educators National Conference
1806 Robert Fulton Drive
Reston, VA 22091
(703) 860–4000

vide opportunities for such experiences, and listen without judging, will contribute to the children's developing sense of aesthetics.

The Child's Need for the Arts

The ability to find personal meaning in different experiences is fundamental to the development of each child's emotional and social identity. Finding personal meaning also strengthens the child's ability to form attachments to the concrete (i.e., a school, hometown, or particular landscape) and the abstract things in life like the sense of happiness, safety, and love a personally meaningful artistic experience can evoke.

Developmentally, children are born with a unique capacity to express themselves artistically. The ability they have to use their senses to explore and learn about their social and physical environments is also indicative of the children's natural disposition toward the arts. In early childhood social studies, the arts represent a way to sharpen and refine "the [children's] capacity to use their senses and minds joyfully and confidently in experiencing their environment" (Herbeholz & Hanson, 1995, p. 2). For young children, the arts represent a way to express their perceptions, feelings, and emotions about social phenomena.

Bringing Ideas into Practice 8–1   *Discovering Artistic Preferences: Talents and Behaviors*

In order to discover the "artists" in your classroom, try to find out the answers to the following questions:

1. What seems to attract (catch) the child's attention?
2. What kind of actions and behaviors does the child seem to follow?
3. Is the child introducing any changes in his/her behavior?
4. Does the child seem to use the same materials to express different ideas?
5. Does the child show confidence when using or handling materials and objects to express his/her ideas and views?

6. What kind of gestures, body movements, and verbalizations does the child exhibit? Is the child aware of these behaviors?
7. What kind of expressive channels does the child seem to prefer?
8. What does the child say about his/her preferences?

The answers to these questions will provide you with a lot of information that will help you design your arts curriculum and select appropriate resources for your students.

Source: Adapted from G. Forman & D. Kuschner. (1998). *The child's construction of knowledge: Project for teaching children.* Washington: DC: National Association for the Education of Young Children, p. 141.

Observations of young children reveal how each child uses the arts to construct and reenact life experiences. As early as infancy, children tend to reveal their perceptions through their movements and facial expressions. In the classroom, the youngsters' earliest art works and expressions are examples of their emerging individual preferences. The colors, patterns, body movements, sounds, and rhythm the children prefer are indications of their developing aesthetic sense. Having the opportunity to use the arts to communicate his or her own ideas is indispensable to the appropriate cognitive, emotional, and social development of any child.

The arts foster creativity and a sense of aesthetics.

The Arts and Child Development

In addition to building a sense of aesthetics and nurturing the human spirit, the arts and creative expression foster human development by playing an important role in each of the developmental domains (Brittain, 1979). Some of the ways in which the arts benefit children's development are defined here.

■ *Cognitive domain:*
Through the arts, children find opportunities to explore their environment and build ideas about it. Individual visualizations of reality are best constructed through artistic representations. For the young child, the arts become a tool for building concepts about the social and natural phenomena

encountered in the environment. The arts offer children opportunities to convey in a representational way ideas that they would have difficulties expressing with words. Properly described as the creative processes, the arts are also a source of experimentation and decision making (see Figure 8–2).

Creative and artistic behaviors also foster the development of thinking skills. They reinforce the child's ability to use imagination when learning about the environment. The arts provide a channel for divergent thinking, an invaluable critical thinking skill. As teachers observe children's development, they will see opportunities to identify each individual's cognitive capacities and strengths. The existence of multiple intelligences, as theorized by Gardner (1983), has particularly helped to validate the artistic abilities of individuals. The arts advocate this diversity and encourage development of the "other cognitive ways" children may have.

■ *Social and emotional domain:*
When observing children engaged in artwork, one can see their feeling of personal success. Through the arts, children find ways to express and convey their feelings and emotions to others. Having opportunities to express themselves enhances the children's self-esteem. Through sing-

ing, drawing, or body movements, children find ways to communicate what they feel and perceive. The arts are also essential for fostering the development of basic social behaviors, such as working with individuals and groups, learning to show respect for the ideas and opinions of others, participating with others in achieving a common goal, sharing and taking turns, and gaining a sense of belonging.

The arts provide ways to learn about the social and emotional foundations of one's culture. Cultural art expressions are ways people share their social and cultural beliefs. For children, this is a way of learning their culture and their cultural group's social codes and behaviors. Giving children opportunities to express their inner thoughts through socially acceptable means offers them a way to connect with the society to which they belong. More importantly, it helps children to identify with their groups.

■ *Physical and motor domain:*
The arts engage the whole child. Art activities provide opportunities for the continued growth and development of motor and physical abilities. Art experiences develop body awareness and motor coordination. Recognition of one's own body movements and of one's body image is encouraged through music, dance, and dramatic representations. Visual and motor coordination is enhanced while the child engages in the exploration of different art media. Artistic work also fosters good auditory and visual discrimination skills.

FIGURE 8–2 Actions that Occur During the Creative Process

- ■ Using imagination to look at reality
- ■ Developing and playing with ideas
- ■ Accepting challenges
- ■ Exploring possible solutions and options
- ■ Evaluating and selecting possible solutions
- ■ Putting ideas into action
- ■ Examining and analyzing results
- ■ Creating a different way to do things

Source: S. Parnes. (1981). *The magic of your mind.* New York: Creative Education Foundation.

The Arts and Children with Special Needs

The arts provide learning opportunities for all children. Children with special needs can find in the arts a vehicle for personal fulfillment and success. Participation in art experiences serves as a developmental channel for them. Socially, the arts offer a way to participate in and belong to a group. Developmentally based curricular experiences will challenge and engage the children on the cognitive level. Consideration of each child's specific conditions and needs should guide the selection and plan-

FIGURE 8–3 Planning Art Activities for Children with Special Needs

For children with physical disabilities:
- select large objects for printing and collage experiences. Have pre-cut shapes and pictures available when doing collage experiences.
- have appropriate scissors available.
- use containers (for glue, paint, water) that are easy to handle. A piece of sandpaper or of corrugated paper around the container will provide a better grip.
- attach glue or paint containers to the table surface with a piece of tape or with Velcro.
- provide a lap tray, which will provide a firm and even surface when painting or gluing things. The tray also helps children to do the activity in any area of the classroom.
- allow markers to be used instead of crayons. They require less force to be applied while coloring or drawing.
- have helmets available for dance and movement experiences.

For children with visual disabilities:
- designate areas by using tape to set boundaries. Use carpet squares to create boundaries.
- use the buddy system and pair children during art experiences.

- select large objects to trace or cut.
- use big lettering to label containers.
- arrange paint containers in a pattern easy for children to recall.
- "texturize" paint by adding sand, rice, sawdust, and salt to help children identify the colors they want to use.
- use a variety of tactile silhouettes to label bottles.
- select fabric scraps with different textures.
- add scent to glue to facilitate its recognition.

For children with hearing impairments:
- face the child and give clear verbal directions.
- use signals and gestures to facilitate understanding.
- prepare charts with step-by step directions for activities.

For children with cognitive disabilities:
- provide simple directions; break down each process in steps.
- use visual cues.
- use gestures and signals when explaining experiences.
- provide a variety of multi-sensory materials.
- have charts available with step-by step direction.

Sources: Broughton, B. (1986). *An arts curriculum for young children—including those with special needs: Creative experiences.* Chapel Hill, NC: Chapel Hill Training Outreach Project. Deiner, P. L. (1983). *Resources for teaching young children with special needs.* New York: Harcourt Brace Jovanovich.

ning of materials and experiences. Good selection of materials will offer opportunities for children with physical and motor conditions to experience the arts (Figure 8–3).

Developmentally Appropriate Art Experiences: Emphasis on Process, Not Product

One of the major goals of art experiences is to foster creativity in young children. This takes place through the **art process**—the act of producing the art—and is demonstrated by the **art product** itself. The product reflects the process followed by the artist, a willingness to accept the challenge to do things in another fashion, and the ability for each individual to find a different way to express himself or herself. In this sense, the process is a valuable learning experience that is independent of the product itself. Emphasizing the process over the product is the way art should be viewed in the early grades. From this perspective, early childhood educators are able to create developmentally appropriate experiences for young children.

Concept Box 8–3   Professional References for the Arts with the Special Needs Child

Broughton, B. (1986). *An arts curriculum for young children—including those with special needs: Creative experiences.* Chapel Hill, NC: Chapel Hill Training-Outreach Project.

Cook, R., Tessier, A., & Klein, D. (1992). *Adapting early childhood curricula for children with special needs.* New York: Merrill. [general references and guidelines]

In designing art experiences for young children, it is again important to remember that each of us is unique. This statement also applies to the artistic abilities of children. While some individuals may ex-

cel in drawing and movement, they may not be able to carry a tune. A child who performs a part perfectly in a play may not be able to make a collage.

The aim of the arts in the early childhood classroom is not to produce perfect art, but to enhance children's ability to create. While the end product will not always be a masterpiece according to general art standards, the *process* is what gives value and importance to art experiences (Mayeski, 1995).

Providing an environment in which each child finds he or she is invited to participate and try things out is essential to providing appropriate art experiences. The true value of the arts lies in the process children decide to follow as they encounter materials and use their imagination (Edwards, 1997). To engage children in creating expressions that reflect their unique perceptions and ideas is the essence of art education in early childhood.

Bringing Ideas into Practice 8–2   *Creating an Environment that Fosters Creativity*

An inviting and appealing environment is essential for developing the creative and thinking abilities of children. Here are some suggestions for creating a stimulating classroom oriented toward the arts:

■ Design the classroom environment with bright and subtle color contrasts. Use paper borders, mobiles, banners, and carpets to create a variety of color patterns and contrasts.

■ Consider the ceiling as a part of the room that can stimulate creative ideas. Hang up mobiles and tape pictures, shapes, and silhouettes to the ceiling.

■ Include a balance of artwork. Decorate the room with artwork made by children and include printed artwork such as posters, pictures, and photographs.

■ Display artwork of the famous masters along with the children's art.

■ Display art pieces at the children's eye level.

■ Use music throughout the day. Select both classical and popular music.

■ Provide a variety of media. Clay, paper, finger paint, crayons, markers, brushes, paint, chalk, fabrics,

beads and sequins, and other media should be made available for children to use.

■ Have "unusual art materials," such as recyclable and natural materials (leaves, sticks, dried fruits, and seeds).

■ Designate an area for dance and movement exploration.

■ Include reference books about the arts (with pictures and text about dance performers, famous artists and their work, architecture, etc.).

■ Have an abundance of dress-up materials in the dramatic area. Encourage children to explain and share ideas through dramatic representation.

■ Visit museums and other places in the community.

■ Stimulate mental imagery. Provide guided imagery to foster the power of imagination.

■ Value individual creative efforts. Recognize the work of each child and encourage the children to share their creative ideas and visions.

The young artist. This five-year-old proudly stands by her artwork. The arts are a developmentally appropriate way to foster self-esteem. (Courtesy of Ivan Robles)

Freedom of expression is essential in process-oriented experiences. According to Edwards (1997, p. 27), the *product* becomes the personal creative expression, "or whatever results from the child's need to communicate thoughts or feelings." Developmentally appropriate practices remind us that art experiences are built from and by the child. The teacher and the materials provide a stimulus to create, but the real masterpiece is constructed in the child's mind and brought to life in ways the child finds appropriate.

■■ Integrating the Arts and
■■ Creative Expression into
the Social Studies Curriculum

An effective social studies education curriculum includes the experiences from the arts and creative expression. For young children, these experiences offer meaningful opportunities to better understand and relate to social concepts, historical events, and geographical abstractions. Any child-appropriate and appealing social studies curriculum for young children includes rich experiences in the arts and creative expression. The following three techniques will help you design such a curriculum.

1. *Theme-based curricular infusion:* An effective curricular infusion occurs when the theme and the scope of the content are clearly defined. Art and other creative experiences are selected purposefully to enhance understanding and enrich the concepts. Selection of experiences emerges from, or is suggested by, the content. For example, children can be engaged in learning a dance from Africa while exploring the theme, "All people celebrate"; discussions of the paintings of Norman Rockwell and Claude Monet can be added to the theme, "Family activities now and in the past." More opportunities to use artistic experiences to integrate multi-cultural themes are discussed in Chapter 9; historic themes are discussed in Chapter 5.

2. *A balanced menu of art experiences:* The curriculum should include experiences that are representative of all the arts. The experiences should represent as many different artistic areas of human expression as possible. Experiences in music, dance, art appreciation, movement, and the visual arts should all be studied and represented in the equally in the curriculum. Remember, art experiences facilitate the development of multiple intelligences of children. More importantly, they offer opportunities for all children to recognize their own strengths and abilities.

3. *Meaningful, challenging, and logical use of the arts:* Art and creative expression experiences should evolve logically from the various curriculum themes. An art experience should be used as an opportunity to clarify and enhance a concept, not viewed as a way to fill in the time with "busy work." Art experiences should be also used as ways to depict abstract ideas (e.g., a historical era or a cultural belief).

Concept Box 8–4 Basic Classroom Art Materials	
Easels (at least two)	String, yarn
Paints (tempera) of different colors, including brown and black	Cardboard tubes
	Paper of different shapes and colors
Butcher paper	Old newspapers
Brushes of different types	Containers for paint (i.e., plastic trays, disposable plates, empty margarine containers)
Crayons and color pencils, including chubby crayons for younger children or children with motor disabilities	
	Fabric scraps, notions, ribbons, raffia, buttons
Markers (fine and wide-tip)	Glue (non-toxic)
Aprons or old shirts	Musical instruments
Scissors, including scissors for left-handed children and scissors with easy grip	Ethnic musical instruments (i. e., maracas, güiro, Irish drum)
Flour (for papier mâché activities)	Recordings
Recyclable and found materials	Tape-player and record player
Clay	Dress-up kits (masks, costumes, hats, shoes, necklaces)
Rolling pins	

In order to integrate the arts effectively into the curriculum, teachers should ask themselves the following questions:

■ "What is the purpose of the activity?"
■ "How does it contribute to the selected theme or topic?"
■ "What will children gain from it?"

Connecting the Arts with the NCSS Social Studies Standards

Effective curricular planning requires consideration of the ten thematic social studies standards for the primary grades (NCSS, 1994). These ten standards (see Appendix I, p. 271) are aimed at establishing meaningful ways to develop socially competent individuals. If we consider the arts as the source of expression for the many voices children have within themselves, we will immediately find connections between the arts and the social studies standards. Specifically, the arts provide opportunities to integrate three of the ten curricular strands—*Culture* (I), *Individual Development and Identity* (IV), and *Global Connections* (IX)—into the curriculum.

Culture is present throughout any art activity. In fact, the arts are bound to cultural ideas. How we see and identify what is considered art is influenced by culture. In the classroom, integration of the arts offers a child-appropriate way to explore cultural diversity. Best practices tell us that when we involve children in singing, drama, or any visual arts activity, their interest is boosted. The interactive, dynamic, and personal nature of the arts also helps to engage children in exploring their culture and the cultures of others.

At the individual level, opportunities to share and validate one's culture are enhanced through the arts. In the classroom, reaffirmation of each child's ethnic pride is enhanced when, for example, children dance and sing music that is representative of their cultural groups. Encouraging children to present and express their ideas, using their own codes, also contributes to the reinforcement of their cultural selves. Appreciation of one's cultural heritage promotes self-esteem and contributes to the development of a sense of acceptance and belonging.

At the group level, art activities foster understanding of the community's cultural make-up. Observation and appreciation of the multi-faceted ways to create art, as defined by each culture, are other ways to promote a sense of tolerance and respect for the ideas of others (see Chapter 9). The arts are one of the best sources of information about other cultures. Consistent exposure to artistic representations allows children to learn about cultural similarities and differences. It also promotes the skills children need to interact effectively with people of cultures different from their own.

In the classroom, connecting culture to the arts can happen in a variety of ways. Here are a few of the many activities teachers can explore with children:

- Include, on a regular basis, art supplies representing a variety of materials used by different cultural groups.
- Integrate music from other cultures into the daily schedule. Target specific cultural groups as they relate to classroom topics.
- Learn and sing songs from different cultural groups.
- Learn the dances and rhythmic movements of cultural groups in the community.
- Create an area to exhibit cultural art pieces or replicas.
- Include prints from artistic reproductions.

Through the arts, the theme of *individual development and identity* (curricular strand IV) is continuously addressed. The arts are, by definition, a way to share individual ideas, values, and interpretations. In the classroom, planned experiences aimed at encouraging children to express themselves foster individual development. Art not only offers opportunities to discover and validate individual abilities, as well as perceptual skills, but it also provides channels for each child to build a sense of himself or herself. It also contributes to the individual's development of participatory and collaborative skills.

The social identities of families and communities are also manifested and learned through the arts. Among the many activities that support the arts and the theme of identity:

- planning for individual expression through the arts on a regular basis.

- providing access to a variety of materials and inviting children to select freely the ones they prefer to communicate their ideas.
- providing individual recognition for individual art works.
- encouraging children to suggest ways to express ideas through the arts (by writing songs, creating a dance, or designing symbols).
- creating opportunities for participation in dance and choral groups.
- planning collaborative activities such as mural making.
- taking field trips to explore examples of artistic representations in their communities.
- visiting local museums and art galleries.
- inviting community members to share their artistic skills with the class.

Through the arts, children find *global connections* (see strand IX)—meaningful ways to relate with people around the world. A universal language, the arts serve as bridges to the world's many cultures and their expressions. Teachers can use the arts to build and enhance the interrelationships that exist among people (see Chapter 9). Some of the ways teachers can foster the idea that "they" are "we" include:

- learning songs from other countries and singing the lyrics in other languages.
- learning dances from other parts of the world.
- examining and creating musical instruments used in other countries.
- learning and playing games from other countries.
- exploring and appreciating the works of artists from other places.
- using art materials that artists use in other countries.
- learning about folktales and fables from other countries and comparing them to American (i.e., U.S.) folktales.
- discussing artworks by children from other countries.
- discussing the themes used in global art works. Exploring similarities and differences between topics addressed by other artists and children.

National Standards for Arts Education

The arts were acknowledged by *Goals 2000* as an essential content area of study in the national education agenda. In 1994 the National Standards for Arts Education further defined the importance and the role of the arts in the school curriculum. The arts standards address four essential areas: dance, music, theatre, and the visual arts. They are also a very valuable educational resource for several reasons: First, the standards provide a valuable planning framework for art education at all levels. Second, they offer specific information regarding the basic concepts and processes in each of the key areas of the arts. Third, the standards help teachers to integrate the rich cultural diversity of the United States and of its global neighbors into the curriculum. These reasons attest to the importance of the National Standards for the Arts for the development and integration of arts experiences into the curriculum.

The art standards support the notion that the knowledge about the arts is built progressively throughout the school years. The scope of arts education in the early years is defined in the following five expectations. If the arts curriculum is appropriate and effective, children should be able to:

1. **communicate at a basic level in the four art disciplines.**
   In early childhood, this means that: Children express their ideas through drawings (*visual arts*), respond to music with corporal movement (*dance*), role-play stories (*theatre*), and sing together (*music*).
2. **communicate proficiently in at least one art form.**
   In early childhood, this means that: Children are encouraged to select the art form of their preference. Opportunities are offered for them to share their feelings and ideas through their preferred art form.
3. **develop and present basic analyses of works of art according to structural, historical, and cultural perspectives.**
   In early childhood, this means that: Children share comments about a song that they heard.

Children describe an outfit as being from "long ago." When observing the illustrations by an artist such as Sendak, they can compare the characters with those in books by Dr. Seuss.

4. **be acquainted with exemplary works of art from a variety of cultures and historical periods.**
   In early childhood, this means that: Individual children express their views about the paintings that they have seen during a visit to the local museum. During quiet time, children can recognize the music from *"The Nutcracker"* while it plays in the background. Children can relate wooden sculptures shown in a photograph to African culture.
5. **relate the knowledge and skills of the various types of art.**
   In early childhood, this means that: Children use corporal movements to respond to music while role-playing a story.

(National Standards for Arts Education, 1994, pp. 18–19)

For early childhood teachers, the art standards are a valuable source of ideas for developing experiences that foster young children's appreciation and

---

Concept Box 8–5   Good Teaching Resources about the Visual Arts

Helpful teaching resources include:

- Fitzpatrick, S., & Parrish, G. (1995). *Art tells a story about . . .* Cypress, CA: Creative Teaching Press. Three themes are included in this series: families, communities, make believe. This book includes posters of famous paintings by American painters, as well as artists from other countries.
- Gomez, A. (1992). *Crafts of many cultures: 30 authentic craft projects from around the world.* New York: Scholastic.
- Loumaye, J. (1994). *Art for children* series. New York: Chelsea House. This series includes, among others, da Vinci, Chagall, Degas, Matisse, Miró, and Picasso.

involvement in the arts. It is important to remember that the arts—sometimes called "the other 'R' " in education—are one of the best channels for nurturing and learning about human creativity.

Promoting the Arts through Active Learning Experiences

Including the arts as part of the social studies curriculum provides a source of interesting experiences for young children. It also offers a great variety of activities based on active engagement. Thematic teaching and use of different learning centers are among the best strategies for bringing the arts into the classroom.

■ *Thematic teaching*
A theme study offers an opportunity to venture into the many facets of social concepts and events from the present and from the past. Human experiences in any time period always include artistic expressions. As a theme is selected, it is important to brainstorm its possible connections to the arts. Use of a brainstorming matrix will help teachers identify what art experiences to include (see Figure 8–4). Rather than using the arts as a culminating experience, consider art experi-

ences as a part of the ongoing activities of the theme children are exploring.

■ *Learning Centers*
An art center is an essential element in any early childhood classroom. Usually consisting of an easel along with drawing and painting tools, this interest center can be enhanced to include materials and elements about all of the arts. A variety of materials stimulates children's thinking skills and promotes creativity and artistic expression. Suggested arts materials include:

☐ *Sculpture:* Include a variety of materials such as modeling clay, different types of dough, play dough, potters' clay, paper mâché mixture, soft and pliable materials (e.g., foam, sponges)

☐ *Painting and printmaking:* a variety of painting and printable surfaces (canvas, paper, butcher paper, paper plates; fabric, newspapers, cans, stones, etc.), brushes, sponges, stencils, "textured paint" (sand, glitter, rice, salt)

☐ *Folk arts:* materials found in nature, recyclable materials, fabric scraps, glue, scissors, sewing notions

☐ *Dance:* a variety of classical and popular and multi-cultural music, streamers, scarves, hair accessories, pictorial books about dance and dancers

---

FIGURE 8–4 Infusing the Arts into the Curriculum—A Planning Matrix

Theme: *Exploring the Rain Forest.* **Age group:** Pre-K and Kindergarten

Music	Visual Arts	Dance/Movement	Drama	Literature
■ Listening to selected music by Villalobos while looking at pictures about rain forests ■ Making a rain stick	■ Drawing an imaginary rain forest ■ Working in cooperative groups to prepare a model of a rain forest	■ Using body movements to respond to music	■ Role-playing: Using their voices to imitate their favorite animal from the rain forest	■ Reading: *Koala Lou* (M. Fox, 1988) ■ *Crocodile beat* (L. Jorgensen, 1989) ■ *The great kapok tree* (L. Cherry, 1989)

FIGURE 8–5 Art-Based Prop Boxes

History Prop Box
(see Chapter 5 for more ideas):
Hats, clothes, shoes from olden times
Selected paintings about activities in the past
Old photographs and illustrations
Sample artifacts (folk art pieces)
Masks
Costumes
Songs from times past
Illustrations about dance performance in the past

Geography Prop Box
(see Chapter 6 for more ideas):
Songs about different geographic places
Multi-cultural holiday music
Music typical of geographic regions (for example,
  jazz music for the South; salsa for the Caribbean)

Music reflecting the environment (for example,
  Rimsky-Korsakov's *"The Flight of the
  Bumblebee"*)
Instruments that reproduce geographic elements
  (animal sounds, city sounds)
Selected paintings from great artists that have
  geographic elements
Artifacts representing different cultural groups

Civic and Democratic Values Box
(see Chapter 7 for more ideas):
Songs with lyrics that embody civic and social skills
Paintings and photographs with civic and social
  themes
Costumes for dramatic play
Hats and masks to represent characters from
  stories

☐ *Music:* a variety of musical recordings, a tape-player with earphones for children's use, musical instruments, gourds, materials that can be used for percussion (e.g., wood, sticks, empty cans, etc.), photographs and illustrations of musical instruments and performers, informational books about performers from the past and the present

Concept Box 8–6   Music: Professional Music References for Teachers

Levene, D. (1993). *Music through children's literature: Theme variations.* Englewood, CO: Teacher Ideas Press.
McLean, M. (1988). *Make your own musical instruments.* Minneapolis, MN: Do It Yourself Books.
Wirth, M., Stassevich, V., Shotwell, R., & Stemlerr, R. (1983). *Musical games, fingerplays and rhythmic activities for early childhood.* West Nyack, NY: Parker Publishing Co.

☐ *Drama and theatre:* an area designated for dramatic representation, costumes, clothes and accessories, wigs, shoes, hats, masks, old bed sheets and flowing materials
■ *Art-Based Prop Boxes*
The use of prop boxes is another very effective strategy for providing arts experiences. A *prop box* is a container that holds a variety of manipulatives and accessories, all based on a common theme. Sample art prop boxes can be created around many different social studies themes (see Figure 8–5).

Including the Arts in the Curriculum

Integrating the arts into the social studies curriculum has many benefits. The arts are an effective way for young children to work with abstract concepts. Learning about the arts is also an appealing and versatile way for children to learn about life. To ensure meaningful integration of the arts into the curriculum, teachers will find it useful to begin the process by exploring the themes found in the classroom. As a theme is chosen and brainstorming be-

FIGURE 8–6 Exploring the Theme of the Farm through the Arts

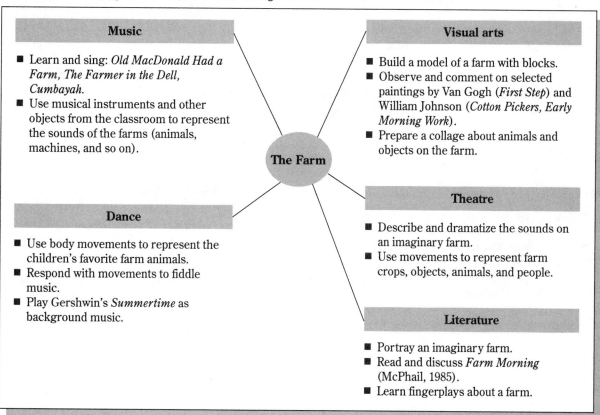

gins, include connections between the theme and the various arts. Think about the ways they can be explored in the classroom. Figure 8–6 provides an example of the art connections found in one social studies theme. Working with a colleague helps to find more connections with the arts. Consider including the arts and the music teachers in the planning process. Their expertise will provide valuable guidance.

Selecting Materials for Arts Experiences

Early childhood classrooms typically have art, music, and drama centers. The purpose of these centers is to promote the children's developmental skills and creativity through rich experiences. If

these goals are to be achieved, the centers must have an abundance of interesting and age-appropriate materials. It is important for teachers to know what to choose and how to choose it. *What to choose* is determined by the age level, developmental characteristics of the group, and special needs of individual children in the class. Knowledge about the themes to be explored helps establish the materials to be selected. Considering the cultural characteristics of the children in choosing the materials is also very important. *How to choose* is determined by each material's appropriateness for children and safety features. Safety and ease of manipulation are of primary importance in selecting tools and materials for the very young. Art tools, for instance, should be geared to the varying skill and ability lev-

Bringing Ideas into Practice 8–3   *Bringing Music and Singing into the Classroom*

Singing in the classroom has always been an activity that children enjoy. Singing has maintained many of our country's traditions and those of other countries of the world. You can help to make this important activity a part of your classroom by planning what music and songs to share with your students. Taking the following steps will be helpful.

■ Make a list of the songs *you* know and compare them with those the children know. This will give you an idea of which ones you can incorporate more easily into the curriculum.

■ Post a list titled "Songs We Know." Enjoy singing them with the children over and over again.

■ Select songs with the following characteristics: strong melody, a complex melody, simple lyrics, child-appropriate themes, repetitive phrases.

■ Include music and singing into daily activities. For example, use music as background during free play, while working on projects, during quiet time and snack time.

■ Sing during special parts of the day and to set the mood for activities. Sing a "morning song" to start the day, introduce a special song for working on projects, mark daily transitions with songs, sing before story-telling begins. Begin the afternoon and end the day with a group song.

■ Review the themes you are planning to explore with children. Look for songs and music that match the theme. Find music representative of American traditions as well as those from other cultures. Remember, music is one of the best bridges for building global connections.

■ Build your own "musical resource inventory." Create a computer database of music and songs related to the themes typically explored in the early childhood classroom. You can also use index cards or a binder to keep your inventory. Update your database periodically.

■ Use the musical resources in your school and in the community. Others will be happy to contribute their art and music to your classroom.

■ Learn songs and practice them. Make it a point to search for and learn new songs.

■ If you feel singing is not one of your special gifts, remember that your enthusiasm and persistence will make you a success. Children will follow you!

els of children. The following suggestions for appropriate selection of materials should be considered:

Visual Arts: Select materials that offer opportunities to explore and use a variety of media and tools. To spark creativity, include materials used at home, as well as recyclable materials. Materials typically used by different cultural groups should be also incorporated; for example, include natural, discarded, and found materials. Provide cans, lids, plastic trays, and containers of different sizes and shapes (these objects can be used for construction projects and for tracing). Have a variety of notions (lace, buttons, sequins, etc.) available to children. Include scissors with a variety of cutting shapes. Have different types of brushes available at the easel.

Music: Always designate an area as the music center. If space is limited, a plastic container labeled "Music Center" that can hold a variety of items should be placed in the drama center or in another prominent location. Have a variety of musical instruments available for children to use. Instruments typical of other cultures should also be incorporated. Recordings (tapes, records, and compact discs) should be made available for children to use individually and in groups. Be sure to include a variety of recorded music. Include posters and pictures of musical instruments and of performers. If available, photographs or pic-

Concept Box 8–7   Four Ways of Presenting Songs to Children

Presenting a song to your class will depend on the mood and the nature of the song itself (Mayeski, 1998). Four methods are highly recommended:

1. *Phrase-wire method:* The song is introduced with a brief story, question, or discussion. Introduce the song by singing one phrase, and ask children to repeat it. Follow with two phrases, and so on. This method is especially appropriate for learning songs having more than one stanza or paragraph.
2. *Whole-song method:* Use a variety of active approaches to make the song appealing to the group. For example, dancing, body movements, playing instruments, and dramatization

will spark the children's interest in the song. Remember to select ways that will involve all children, including those with special needs.

3. *Combination of phrase-wire and whole-song methods:* Teachers sing the whole song, and then ask children to act as a chorus, singing the easiest phrases.
4. *Using recordings:* Always listen to the recording first. Use the whole-song method. Have children listen to the song, inviting them to respond to it with movement and clapping or using musical instruments. Clarify phrases and ask children to repeat the easiest lines.

tures of well-known performers and musicians from America and other countries should be displayed.

Theatre: The drama center is the home of theatrical arts. Make sure to include costumes, hats, and other accessories. Masks and items representing other cultures should also be incorporated. A few yards of fabric or an old bed sheet always come in handy. Decorative items such as garlands and jewelry or holiday decorations will also spark the children's dramatic ideas. Puppets (hand puppets, finger puppets, stick puppets) are necessary items for dramatic activities.

Dance and Movement: Both dance and movement can be incorporated into any theme. Body movement and dance allow children to communicate in very unique ways. A multipurpose area (story-telling, large group meeting area) can be designated as the stage for dance and movement. Include a variety of dress-up items such as scarves, lightweight fabrics, hats, and other kinds of accessories. Ribbons, crepe paper, and handkerchiefs should also be available.

The Folk Arts

Folklife or folklore is an integral element of social life. As reflection of the group's heritage, **folklore** describes the beliefs, customs, behaviors, values, and practices common to people belonging to a particular cultural group. Bringing folklife into the classroom helps children to validate the activities and social behaviors of people in their own cultural and social groups (Sidener, 1997, p. 3). It also fosters the understanding of the ideas and beliefs of people from other cultures. Using folklife as a source of the curriculum reinforces developmentally and culturally appropriate practices. According to the National Standards for Folklife Education, "teaching students through their own experiences is good pedagogy" (Sidener, 1997, p. 13).

The folk arts, the expressions of members of a cultural group, are an exciting way to learn about people and about their unique lifestyles. Folk arts are also an interesting source of documentation about the past. The folk arts are a universal cultural element and a common way for communities to share their experiences. The folk arts encompass all of the arts: music, dance, visual arts, and theatre.

■■ Let's Talk About . . . 8–2

Foodways, as a Part of Folklife

Whenever food is mentioned, it always catches people's attention. Food is considered an important element of life and a concrete way to portray a culture. Foodways define not only the food items of a folk group, but also the processes, the events, the cultural context, as well as the beliefs attached to the preparation and consumption of traditional foods. Think about the "folk" or cultural group to which you belong, and develop a web to identify some of those foodways. Do the same with the children in your classroom.

My Foodways

- typical dishes
- my favorite breakfast dish
- food preparation
- typical ingredients
- contexts in which they are served
- food for special events (holidays, celebrations)

Folk arts are ways to preserve traditions.

They are a key source of information about what a cultural group considers "beautiful, useful, and representative of the group's beliefs" (Sidener, 1997, p. 48). A **folk group** is a group of people who meet together and share at least one common element,

---

Concept Box 8–8   Characteristics of Folk and Popular Culture Items

According to Sidener (1997, p. 32), here are some key characteristics you can use to distinguish items that are *folk art* from those that are *expressions of popular culture.*

Folk expressions are:

- produced by individuals for the use of their own folk group members.
- shared and taught in person-to-person settings.
- made by hand, using locally available resources.
- not uniform but have accepted variations.
- accessible to the group.
- unofficial representations.

(Can you think of any examples of folk art items?)

Popular expressions are:

- mass produced in mechanized ways.
- marketed via mass media.
- accessible to population.
- associated with commercial influences.
- recognizable by the majority.
- usually uniform.

(What popular items can you mention?)

Source: Adapted from Sidener, D. (1997). *National Standards for Folklife Education,* Immaculata, PA: Pennsylvania Folklife Education Committee, p. 32.

FIGURE 8–7 Folk Arts: Sample Objects

handicrafts	furniture
paintings	accessories (such as
dances	head ornaments,
music	jewelry)
songs	dresses
musical instruments	weavings
wood carvings	quilts
leather works	toys
metal works	children's garments
pottery	cooking utensils

How many others can you add?

processes entailed in the production, use, and transmission are a good basis for determining whether an item is either an authentic folk item or a popular object (see Concept Box 8–8).

Finding examples of folk arts to share in the classroom is not a very difficult task. Figure 8–7 lists some types of folk art to look for. In fact, to locate some of these items, we should begin by checking what we have in our homes. Family and community members are an excellent source. Not only do most families have a treasury of sample folk art pieces, but many times some family members are also good craft makers. They will be pleased to come to the classroom and share their experiences. Most communities have local craft makers who can be contacted. You can arrange for some these local artists to visit your school.

Global Connections: Using Children's Folklore

Children around the world share common traditions and practices like toys, games, songs, and rhymes. These traditions benefit individual children and also serve as valuable resources for the social studies curriculum. They offer developmentally

"such as ethnicity, language, age, family, occupation, gender, region, [or] religion" (Sidener, 1997, p. 48). Folk arts are a tangible way for children to learn about diversity and about the commonalities across cultural groups.

Sharing folk items in the classroom is an exciting and valuable experience. When selecting what to share, keep in mind that the items should reflect what is authentic to the group. Often times, popular cultural expressions mislabel folk art. According to the National Standards for Folklife Education, the

Games are also a way to pass on traditions.

Concept Box 8–9   Using Traditional Games from Around the World in the Classroom

Development of a multi-cultural curriculum is a process that requires time. We suggest phasing into multi-cultural teaching by changing one small portion of the curriculum. Planning a unit around a theme of interest to both children and teachers is an appropriate way to start. For example, games can provide an exciting way to learn about various cultures.

Building on the importance of play as a child-appropriate strategy, a first grade teacher created a thematic unit about traditional games. Her goal was to increase the children's knowledge of their own cultures and those of other groups around the world. By talking to families, community members, and colleagues, the teacher was able to gather a list of the games, musical games, and songs they all recalled from their childhood. With the help of the media specialist, who led her to related references and a search on the Internet that provided additional sources, the teacher was ready to begin her unit. The result was an appealing curriculum in which children were guided to explore their own diversity and to learn about others.

Theme: It's Playtime!

Standards: Social Studies: Culture (I), Individual development and identity (IV), People, places, and environments (III), Global Connections (IX)

Goal: To become familiar with traditional children's games from our families and neighborhoods and from other places

Activities:
1. Explore favorite games of our families
2. Play sample traditional games
3. Sing the songs of musical games
4. Identify traditional games from the following cultural groups:
   - African-American families: *hot butter beans; skelly; roly-poly; tin-can alley; hand soccer; four squares; hand-clapping games*
   - European-American families: *hide and seek; jump-rope; hopscotch; tops; hand-clapping games*
   - Hispanic families: *Arroz con leche*, Doña Ana, Ambos-a-dos; Candela*
5. Play the following group games from other cultures:
   - Ghana—*The clapping hand***
   - Zaire—*Catching stars****
   - Taiwan—*Clapstick blind man buff***
   - Haiti—*Manee Gogo***
   - Jamaica—*Sally Water***
   - Chile—Guessing game (*¿Quién es?*)**
6. Discuss the different rules for the games
7. Use a world map and globe to locate the different countries where games come from
8. Select our favorite games

Resources:
- colored chalk
- world globe
- world map
- tops
- recordings (Matilde Cintron, *Doce Juegos Folklóricos* [Twelve folkloric games]. Camera Mundi
- Reference materials:
  Benjamin, F. (1995). *Skip across the ocean.* New York: Orchard Books.
  *Delacre, L. (1992). *Arroz con leche.* New York: Scholastic
  Lankford, M. (1992). *Hopscotch around the world: Nineteen ways to play the game.* New York: Beech Tree.
  **Nelson, W., & Glass, B. (1992). *International playtime: Classroom games and dances from around the world.* Carthage, IL: Fearon Teacher Aids.
  ***Orlando, I. (1993). *The multicultural game book: More than 70 traditional games from 30 countries.* New York: Scholastic.
  Reck, D. (1977). *Music of the whole Earth.* New York: Scribner's.
  Walters, C. (1995). Multicultural music: Lyrics to familiar melodies and native songs. Minneapolis, MN: T. S. Dennison.

appropriate ways of learning about the oral traditions of the local community and other communities around the world. Folklorist Samuel Bronner (1988) states that children's folklore is also a way to learn about cultural changes. "The customs, games, and verses of childhood reminds us of society's cherished values and attitudes" (p. 28). He describes children's folklore as a valuable socialization tool. For example, children's games, songs, and rhymes are based on themes that reflect the group's social rituals and beliefs. A closer look at the ideas presented in the lyrics of a song or the rules of a game reveals how these elements change as children grow. Another important benefit of children's folklore is its ability to reflect the folk arts and foster global connections in a child-appropriate manner.

A closer look at the topics and themes explored in the curriculum will provide directions as to when and where to incorporate children's folklore. Several resources will provide teachers with ways to integrate folk arts along with other forms of creative expression into the curriculum.

Recommended Children's Books

Aukerman, R. (1994). *Move over, Picasso! A young painter's primer.* New Windsor, MD: Pat Depke Books.

Bjork, C. (1985). *Linnea in Monet's garden.* New York: R&S Books.

Bronner, S. (1988). *American children's folklore: A book of rhymes, games, jokes, stories, secret languages, beliefs and camp legends for parents, grandparents, teachers, counselors and all adults who were once children.* Little Rock, AR: August House.

Clayton, E. (1996). *Ella's trip to the museum.* New York: Crown.

Fitzpatrick, S., & Parrish, G. (1995). *Art tells a story about . . .* Cypress, CA: Creative Teaching Press.

Fox, M. (1988). *Koala Lou.* San Diego, CA: Harcourt Brace.

Fung, S. (1993). *Chinese children's games* (5th ed.). New York: A.R.T.S. Incorporated.

Gomez, A. (1992). *Crafts of many cultures: 30 authentic craft projects from around the world.* New York: Scholastic.

Grunfield, F. (1975). *Games of the world: How to make them, how to play them, how they came to be.* New York: Holt, Rinehart & Winston.

Jorgensen, L. (1989). *Crocodile beat.* New York: Aladdin Books.

Lamarche, H. (1986). *Miró for children.* Montreal, Canada: Montreal Museum of Fine Arts.

Lankford, M. (1992). *Hopscotch around the world: Nineteen ways to play the game.* New York: Beech Tree.

Loumaye, J. (1994). *Art for children* series. New York: Chelsea House.

McPhail, D. (1985). *Farm morning.* New York: Atheneum.

Montañez, M. (1994). *Juegos de mi isla [Games from my island]* (3rd ed.). New York: A.R.T.S. Incorporated.

Nelson, W., & Glass, H. (1992). *International playtime: Classroom games and dances from around the world.* Carthage, IL: Fearon Teacher Aids.

Pienkowski, J. (1996). *Une chambre à louer* [published in English as *Boticelli's bed and breakfast*]. France: Seuil Jeunesse.

Sherry, L. (1989). *The great kapok tree: A tale of the Amazon rain forest.* San Diego, CA: Harcourt Brace.

Stanley, D., & Nolan, D. (1994). *The gentleman and the kitchen maid.* New York: Dial Books.

Winter, J. (1991). *Diego.* New York: Knopf.

ACTIVITIES

Keeping Track of What You Learn: Your Personal Activity Log

This chapter dealt with the inclusion of the arts and creative expression in the early childhood curriculum. You may want to record these additional ideas in your PAL for future planning.

A. Reflections

1. Create an annual calendar of the arts with your children. Make sure that all the artistic areas are represented. Every month, feature a famous artist from our country and from other countries around the world. Have children discuss and replicate their works, make collections and displays and decorate the classroom.

2. Develop a plan to organize an art fair for your grade level. Present your ideas to your colleagues and set the plan in motion. Include students, parents, community guests, and resource people in the event.

3. Write your own philosophy of art education. Use it as a road map for teaching the arts to young children.

4. View several videos of famous museums, art collections, and works of famous artists. Write new information and ideas in an art journal. Review your art journal periodically and incorporate your ideas into the curriculum.

5. Research the information on how to make a mural. Once you know the steps, engage the class in the process by selecting a theme and producing a mural.

B. Collections

1. Organize a resource collection of materials and props for each of the art areas: art activities, construction activities, creative dramatics, and music and dance. Use posters, pictures from calendars, brochures from exhibits and performances, children's books, artifacts, clothing and costumes, music, and folk art and organize them in themes. These collections can be used as resources for thematic units or as materials for the different classroom art centers.

2. Collect art objects and photographs of artistic performances for display in the classroom "art gallery." This permanent section of the classroom can be used to display the children's artistic achievements throughout the year.

C. Internet Resources*

Resources about the arts are plentiful. The ones listed here are only a few of those that are available through the Internet.

■ The Smithsonian Institution

Web site: http://www.si.edu

This is an ideal Web site. The Smithsonian Institution encompasses several museums that cover the arts and the humanities as well as science. Of particular interest are:

■ The Center for Folklife Programs and Cultural Studies

Web site: http://www.si.edu/folklife

Provides information about cultural activities and about recordings by noted musicians and performers of the United States and other countries. An ideal resource for indigenous music at affordable prices.

■ The National Portrait Gallery

Web site: http://www.npg.si.edu:80/index

A collection of the best examples of the art of portraiture, representing many famous people as well as the less famous subjects of the best portrait artists. Many of the best examples from this collection are digitized and can be viewed on-line. A treat for children!

ACTIVITIES (continued)

■ The National Museum of American Art

Web site: http://www.nmaa-ryder.si.edu

An excellent collection of the finest American art works. Its educational department sponsors programs to integrate the arts through technology. A member of the "The Electronic Museum in the Classroom," this museum makes art images and lesson plans available though Internet.

■ National Endowment for the Humanities

Web site: http://www.neh.gov

This is the home page for the organization that promotes the preservation of the humanities in the United States. It offers links to all the state councils for the humanities and includes a list with digital pictures of the current museum exhibitions.

*Please note that Internet resources are of a time-sensitive nature and URL sites and addresses may often be modified or deleted.

References

American Alliance for Theatre & Education, National Art Education Association, Music Educators National Conference, & National Dance Association. (1994). *National Standards for Art Education.* Washington, DC: Authors.

Brittain, W. L. (1979). *Creativity and the young child.* New York: Macmillan.

Bronner, S. (1988). *American children's folklore: A book of rhymes, games, jokes, stories, secret languages, beliefs and camp legends for parents, grandparents, teachers, counselors and all adults who were once children.* Little Rock, AR: August House.

Broughton, B. (1986). *An arts curriculum for young children—including those with special needs: Creative Experiences.* Chapel Hill, NC: Chapel Hill Training-Outreach Project.

Caballero, J. (1990). *Children around the world.* Atlanta, GA: Humanics.

Consortium of National Arts Education Association. (1994). National standards for arts education. In *Dance, music, theatre, visual arts: What every young American should know and be able to do in the arts.* Reston, VA: Music Educators Conference.

Cook, R., Tessier, A., & Klein, D. (1992). *Adapting early childhood curricula for children with special needs.* New York: Merrill.

Deiner, P. L. (1983). *Resources for teaching young children with special needs.* New York: Harcourt Brace Jovanovich.

Edwards, L. C. (1997). *The creative arts: A process approach for teachers and children* (2nd ed.). Upper Saddle River, NJ: Merrill.

Fitzpatrick, S., & Parrish, G. (1995). *Art tells a story about . . .* Cypress, CA: Creative Teaching Press.

Forman, G., & Kuschner, D. (1998). *The child's construction of knowledge: Project for teaching children.* Washington, DC: National Association for the Education of Young Children.

Gardner, H. (1983). *Frames of mind: The theory of multiple intelligences.* New York: Basic Books.

Herberholz, B., & Hanson, L. (1995). *Early childhood art* (5th ed.). Madison, WI: Brown & Benchmark.

Levene, D. (1993). *Music through children's literature: Theme variations.* Englewood, CO: Teacher Ideas Press.

Mayeski, M. (1998). *Creative activities for young children* (6th ed.). Albany, NY: Delmar.

McLean, M. (1988). *Make your own musical instruments.* Minneapolis, MN: Do It Yourself Books.

Orlando, L. (1993). *The multicultural game book: More than 70 traditional games from 30 countries.* New York: Scholastic.

Parnes, S. (1981). *The magic of your mind.* New York: Creative Education Foundation.

Robles de Melendez, W., & Ostertag, V. (1997). *Teaching young children in multicultural classrooms: Issues, concepts, and strategies.* Albany, NY: Delmar.

Sidener, D. (1997). (Ed.). *National standards for folklife education: Integrating language arts, social studies, arts, and science through students' traditions and culture.* Immaculata, PA: Pennsylvania Folklife Education Committee.

Wirth, M., Stassevich, V., Shotwell, R., & Stemlerr, R. (1983). *Musical games, fingerplays and rhythmic activities for early childhood.* West Nyack, NY: Parker Publishing Co.

CHAPTER 9

Growing Up in a Multi-cultural Society

America is not like a blanket—one piece of unbroken cloth, the same color, the same texture, the same size. America is more like a quilt— many pieces, many colors, many sizes, all woven together by a common thread.

—JESSE JACKSON (1998)

Chapter Questions

After reading this chapter, you should be able to answer the following questions:

■ What are the characteristics of a multi-cultural society?
■ What is multi-cultural education?
■ What skills should children develop to live in a multi-cultural society?
■ What are the characteristics of multi-cultural activities?

Key Terms and Concepts

anti-bias
bias
culture
diversity
equality
equity

global education
multi-cultural education
multi-cultural literature
nationality
race/ethnicity
stereotype

Classroom Portrait: **Discovering the Colors of People**

A first grade class was working on a project, "Friends Across the Border," when the teacher discovered that most of the children thought that the people in countries neighboring the United States were "not white." This incited a protest from some fair-skinned Hispanics who refused to be described as "not white," arguing that their skin was as light as that of others in the class. Everything reached a climax when several members of the class agreed: "They can't be white because they speak Spanish." The teacher understood that the children were using not only race, but also language, to define others. She decided to do something immediately to correct the misconceptions.

The teacher proceeded to divide the class into teams of five. Then, using different shades of clay that resembled various skin colors, she asked the children to match the clay to the skin tones of their five best friends.

The results were recorded on a graph. Upon completing the survey, the teacher entered all the names of colors the children had chosen during the discussion.

The descriptions of skin tones ranged from peachy, rose, and dark peach to tan, burnt brown, and "kind of creamy vanilla." Then the groups began to share their findings. At the end, the column that read "white" was empty, and the entries for the skin colors of their friends appeared in all of the other categories.

"What do we see in this graph?" the teacher asked the class. "Where do we have most of the names? Where do we have the least names, or no names?" she asked the children.

Without hesitation, the children's answers began to show the truth. Most colors were entered in categories, with a variety of fancy names other than white. "No one is really 'white,'" said a child of very fair skin, who described his own skin color as "golden vanilla."

"Why do they say that people are white or black? They lied to us," said one girl.

The teacher, by using self-discovery, helped the children to clarify their ways of looking at others and ensured continuous harmony in the class.

▦ Our Multi-cultural Society

The United States is a showcase of world cultures. Built by immigrants in search of freedom and liberty, the United States mirrors different cultures around the world. The many different people living in our country have created the largest example of a multi-cultural society on Earth. This diversity is also reflected in the student populations of our schools.

Growing up in a multi-cultural society is an exciting social experience. It presents a multiplicity of challenges to young children who are learning to be both national and global citizens and who are trying to act in accordance with the many social codes they find in the communities where they live.

Multi-cultural education has been acknowledged as a group of effective instructional strategies for helping individuals meet the demands of a dynamic and diverse society. In this section, the need to incorporate a multi-cultural perspective in the social studies curriculum will be explored.

Immigration—the Foundation of Multi-culturalism

Every day, people from places near and far arrive in the United States, hoping for a better future for themselves and their families. The impact of immigration is reflected in the racial and ethnic makeup of our country. Today, the demographic composition of the United States has been transformed from what used to be a mostly biracial society "into a multiracial and polyethnic society" (Rong, p. 395).

Virtually all of us have roots that we can trace to somewhere else in the world. The reasons our ancestors or we had for coming to the United States may differ, but the truth is, unless our ancestors

Classrooms reflect the diversity of our society.

From *The American Wei*, 1998, by Marion Hess Pomeranc. Reproduced with permission from Albert Whitman & Company.

Bringing Ideas into Practice 9–1
Learning about Immigration in the Early Childhood Classroom

The experience of immigration has different significance for people who are immigrants and those who interact with them. Immigration is a major element of American society, so it is important to help young children learn about its significance. Exploring the many reasons and circumstances that cause people to leave their homelands helps children to become sensitive to the process of immigration. As immigration is explored in the classroom, children are also led to appreciate their own roots and to value the presence of new immigrants in our communities.

Early childhood educators favor the use of selected children's literature as an appropriate strategy for studying the complex topic of immigration (McBee, Bone, Mossop, & Owens, 1998; Singer & Harbour-Ridley, 1998). The following titles will help you explore this topic in your classroom. Remember to add your own resources to this list. A list of publishers of children's books about global and multi-cultural topics appears in Appendix III (p. 282).

Immigration:

Bunting, E. (1988). *How many days to America: A Thanksgiving story.* New York: Clarion.

Cohen, B. (1983). *Molly's pilgrim.* New York: Lothrop, Lee & Shepard.

Dorros, A. (1995). *Isla.* New York: Dutton.

Leighton, M. (1994). *An Ellis Island Christmas.* New York: Puffin.

Levine, E. (1989). *I hate English.* New York: Scholastic.

Polacco, P. (1988). *The keeping quilt.* New York: Simon & Schuster.

Pomeranc, M. H. (1998). *The American Wei.* Morton Grove, IL: Whitman.

Say, A. (1993). *Grandfather's journey.* Boston, MA: Houghton Mifflin.

Uchida, Y. (1993). *The bracelet.* New York: Philomel.

FIGURE 9–1 A View of the World

"When I came to catch my flight, I never thought that I would have such a remarkable experience. The hour and a half that I had to spend because of a flight delay showed me the real face of America. Everything started when I decided to have a second cup of coffee. I went to the coffee bar in one of the concourses, where they serve the best "cortadito" (espresso with milk) and "pastelitos" (guava and cheese pastries). A smiling Cuban lady served me the aromatic coffee. While sipping it, I saw an airport employee greeting a friend just returning from his hometown in Nicaragua. At the same time, several Haitians chatted while also sipping coffee. Two Colombians joined the group in front of the coffee stand. I noticed two Indian ladies, who wore the prettiest saris, chatting about their children. I finally made the line to board my flight, where I heard a father call his child in very distinct Arabic. As we flew out, a thought came to my mind: my country is not just a country; it's a world in itself, a world that I see in my classroom."

Source: Rosales 1992 (p. 9).

The photographs on the immigrant wall at Ellis Island remind us that we are all immigrants.

were Native Americans, our families all immigrated (Figure 9–1). Becoming aware of our common immigrant status helps young children understand why people still leave their countries and come to the United States today. Learning about immigration also helps children appreciate our country as a model of democratic life in action. American educators have a responsibility for nurturing in children the democratic values that have brought immigrants from all over the world to the United States.

■■ Let's Talk About . . . 9–1

Discovering Our Immigrant Nature: Where Did Your Family Come From?

One way to learn to appreciate the immigrant nature of our society is by exploring the roots of our own families. We encourage you to discover your origins—the country where your relatives and ancestors originally lived. Begin by talking to your family members and close relatives about your ancestors. Take time to search through family photographs and artifacts. We suspect that you will find many exciting details about your ancestors and about yourself. We hope that as a result of your search, you will realize that immigration is a characteristic we share as Americans.

Celebrating Our Multi-cultural Character

The many diverse groups that have come to the United States have given it its multi-cultural identity. The variety of ideas and traditions immigrants have brought to American communities has made our country an exciting cultural mosaic. When we consider the many different characteristics found in every town and state, we realize the magnitude of the social impact diverse cultures have had on our society. Through technology, music, food patterns, and ways of dress, newcomers continue to enrich and transform the United States.

Life in a multi-cultural and diverse society is constantly changing and evolving. In describing the significance of multi-culturalism, Maureen Cech (1991, p. 6) remarks:

FIGURE 9–2 Main Cultural Groups in the United States

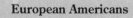

European Americans		Non-European Americans

European Americans

Formed by all those born or descending from Europeans. For example:

- English
- Scottish
- Irish
- Spaniards
- French
- Portuguese
- Italians
- Greeks
- Scandinavians
- Eastern Europeans

American ethnic groups

Native Americans

These two groups include all the indigenous groups in the continental U.S. and Alaska. Native Americans represent all the groups belonging to the Indian Nations.

Non-European Americans

Includes all those ethnic groups with origins other than European. For example:

- Hispanics
- African-Americans
- Pacific Islanders
- Asian-Americans
- Caribbean Islanders
- Middle Easterners
- Indo-Americans

We all belong to the United States!

Source: Based on U.S. Bureau of the Census data.

Bringing Ideas into Practice 9–2
Becoming Aware of the Multi-cultural Nature of Our Society

Many of us do not realize how multi-cultural our country has become. Neighborhoods and communities all over the country are becoming more culturally diverse each day. The schools across this nation mirror this phenomenon. For us as educators, and as early childhood educators in particular, it is crucial to recognize the existence of the various cultures in our classrooms. To see how aware and knowledgeable you are about the many cultures in your community and in your classroom, we suggest doing a brief "cultural inventory." A sample "Community Cultural Inventory" is included in Appendix IV (p. 284). Five key areas are inventoried: language, people/ethnic groups, religion/beliefs, holidays, and food.

After you have completed the cultural inventory of your community, first, consider your findings and share them with your colleagues. Second, incorporate your findings into the curriculum. If you find your community is an example of diversity, make sure that your teaching and your curriculum reflect it. Even if you find your community is not very diverse culturally, you still should be sure to incorporate experiences about diversity into the curriculum. As educators, we are responsible for preparing children to live in a culturally diverse society. This responsibility is carried out only when the curriculum provides opportunities for children to learn about the many cultures that form American society.

Multiculturalism is a sharing of cultures. It empowers individuals, who then share that strength among groups. It expands cultural consciousness.

America will continue to transform itself well into the twenty-first century as a result of the growing influx of people that arrive on our shores daily. Figure 9–2 shows the major ethnic groups found in American society.

The Need for Multi-cultural Education

Culture (see p. 236) is a major force that shapes the lives of individuals and groups. People from the same cultural group follow a similar social code and principles, which they use to interpret reality. In a society where many cultures interact, deciphering the cultural behaviors of others is a never-ending challenge. For example, the "American way" reflects the distinctive cultural patterns of our mainstream culture. In communities throughout our country, both the immigrants and the Americans are confronted with each other's ways on a daily basis. Blending the "American way" with the diverse ways of other groups can be a complex, never-ending process. For some individuals, interacting with people who have diverse cultural patterns is not always a smooth experience. Sadly, lack of acceptance of different cultural patterns has sometimes reinforced religious and racial prejudices or **stereotypes** that, in turn, undermine the basic principles of our democratic society. In order to prevent this from happening, it is important for all of us to acquire the social skills that are needed for successful interaction in an increasingly diverse society.

Diversity and Education for All

Equality and diversity are two essential traits of our democratic society. These two characteristics are also related, in that the U.S. Constitution guarantees equal treatment under the law to all, who are racially, sexually, religiously, and culturally diverse. **Diversity** is a concept that encompasses the many unique ways in which people are different. Figure

FIGURE 9–3 Elements of Diversity

- **Nationality:** refers to the country of origin where one was born or from where one's parents came.
- **Race/Ethnicity:** defines the cultural traditions of a group that serve to shape one's identity.
- **Religion:** defines the belief systems affiliations one holds.
- **Social class:** describes the social group to which one belongs. It is defined by income, education, occupation, lifestyles, and values typically held by a group.
- **Language:** describes the language of one's origin.
- **Gender:** describes the socially acceptable roles and expectations assigned to males and females.
- **Exceptionality:** describes the individual with various physical and emotional disabilities, or with special abilities, like the gifted and talented individuals.
- **Age:** establishes the socially acceptable roles and expectations assigned to people based on their age group. The roles and expectations differ according to one's cultural group.

9–3 describes the many forms of diversity found in society. Because of the variety of human characteristics in both the American and global societies, diversity is a key social issue. Respect for diversity is central to fulfilling the aspirations of a peaceful and equitable society.

We begin to develop social competence—the behaviors and skills necessary for effective interaction amidst social diversity—early in life (Kendall, 1983; Derman-Sparks & The A. B. C. Task Force, 1989). As children have a variety of experiences in different settings—at home, in the neighborhood, in the classroom, in the community, through the media—they develop a sense of equality and social diversity. Appropriate classroom experiences are among the best vehicles for creating positive attitudes about the differences in people. The classroom is also an

Ellis Island's Word Tree shows how our language reflects our diversity.

invaluable setting for learning about the things that makes us equal despite our differences. Multi-cultural education accomplishes this through well-planned experiences. This methodology prepares children to live and interact successfully in a diverse society like ours.

What is Multi-cultural Education?

Multi-cultural education is an essential educational strategy. It evolved out of the search for equal rights and opportunities for all children. Today, it is acknowledged as a curricular priority across age

Exceptionalities represent another component of diversity.

levels. The purpose of multi-cultural education is to develop a sense of pride in one's roots and cultural background and to empower all children to live productively in a socially and culturally diverse society. James Banks, a noted multi-culturalist, defines multi-cultural education as both an approach and an educational philosophy based on the ideal of social equality (Banks & Banks, 1993). Nieto (1992, p. 307) states that multi-cultural education is a process of comprehensive and basic education for all students (see Concept Box 9–1). In her opinion, it openly "challenges racism and other forms of discrimination" and reaffirms the cultural diversity that characterizes American society.

A curriculum with a multi-cultural focus helps children to build concepts about the similarities and the uniqueness of people. Fostering knowledge about one's own culture and about people who are culturally diverse establishes the foundation for social equality and equity and supports the goal of multi-cultural education. In early childhood, multi-cultural education provides opportunities for children to develop positive interactions based on fairness with individuals and groups different from themselves. This is essential for preventing the development of prejudices and biases. Research has shown that prejudiced and biased behaviors are learned through interactions in the environment (Derman-Sparks & The A. B. C. Task Force, 1989). Failure to provide experiences and to guide children early in life to learn about the similarities people have, notwithstanding their differences, places social harmony at risk (Robles de Melendez & Ostertag, 1997). Because of the diversity of cultural groups in American society, the need for multi-cultural education is even more compelling.

Multi-cultural Education and Global Education

Both multi-cultural and global education have as a common goal—the development of an individual who will be culturally knowledgeable and sensitive to the cultures of others. Becoming knowledgeable about cultures and recognizing their impact on peo-

Concept Box 9–1 What Is Multi-cultural Education?

According to educator, Sonia Nieto, **multi-cultural education is . . .**

. . . *antiracist education:* It creates an awareness of discriminatory practices and behaviors. It empowers children to take action against discrimination and promotes a sense for fairness and equity.

. . . *basic education:* It provides essential knowledge and skills for interacting effectively in a multi-cultural and global society.

. . . *important for all students:* It is an essential curriculum component for all children, regardless of their cultural characteristics. A curriculum lacking multi-cultural experiences would "mis-educate" children.

. . . *pervasive:* It permeates the entire curriculum. The subject standards movement acknowledges this characteristic. No curriculum would be deemed appropriate and effective if it did not incorporate a multi-cultural focus.

. . . *education for social justice:* It promotes the development of social fairness and equity. Classroom experiences built with a multi-cultural focus lead children to examine social situations and empower them to take action against unfair events.

. . . *a process:* It creates a social laboratory where attitudes and values are experienced and clarified. Multi-cultural education is essentially a dynamic and continuous experience in which children are encouraged to get a taste of social reality. Classroom activities empower children to explore and learn about interactions in a positive, multi-cultural environment.

. . . *critical pedagogy:* It examines knowledge and considers ideas and events from a variety of perspectives. Children are encouraged to examine events critically and to analyze them in search for fairness and equity. These practices, in turn, develop social fairness and **equity. Anti-bias** education is an example of critical pedagogy appropriate for young children (Derman-Sparks & The A. B. C. Task Force, 1989).

Source: Adapted from Nieto, S. (1992). *Affirming diversity: The sociopolitical context of multicultural education.* New York: Longman, pp. 208–219.

■■ **Let's Talk About . . . 9–2**

Do We Need Multi-cultural Education?

Multi-cultural education has long been advocated as an educational strategy. In fact, the roots of this movement date back to the 1930s. In Cech's opinion (1991, p. 6), "It is no longer an option in education, it is an integrated part of any well-developed program." Cech's ideas reflect the position of many multi-cultural educators and of the national educational organizations like the National Council for the Social Studies (NCSS) and the National Association for the Education of Young Children (NAEYC). However, in spite of this, some people still do not acknowledge the need for a multi-cultural approach. Still others believe it is only needed in communities and schools that serve many children from minority groups.

1. What do you think about the need for multi-cultural education?

2. How important is it compared to the traditional subjects taught in school?

3. Why is there resistance toward it?

Concept Box 9–2   Characteristics of Global and Multi-cultural Education

■ **Multi-cultural education:** provides children with awareness and knowledge about their own cultures, about those of people in their own neighborhoods and in their country. For example, multi-cultural curricular activities are developed to examine family activities, celebrations at home, and cultural activities in their communities (e.g., New Year's traditions observed by different cultural groups in the community).

■ **Global education:** promotes awareness of cultures of people around the world. For example, children explore the similarities and differences of customs and traditions of people in towns and villages from other parts of the world (e.g., birthday celebrations in India, China, and Guatemala).

---

ple's lives are considered essential survival skills in today's social context. This supports the need for students to have curricular experiences that are both multi-cultural and global in scope. The common link between multi-cultural and global education is the aim to promote knowledge about different cultures and social competence to interact with the members of these cultures. The difference between multi-culturalism and globalism is in their *perspective:* The former focuses on the immediate cultural environment and the latter targets the international cultural milieu. Concept Box 9–2 defines the characteristics of both multi-cultural and global education.

Developmentally and Culturally Appropriate Practices: DCAP

An appropriate early childhood education program is grounded in the characteristics of the children it serves. The concept of developmentally appropriate practices—DAP (Bredekamp & Copple, 1997)—discussed extensively in Chapters 2 and 3,

establishes the basis for responsive experiences. Early educators know that DAP acknowledges consideration of developmental characteristics as one of the essential elements of planning. In response to the social traits and needs of American society, "DAP" has become "DCAP"—that is, *developmentally and culturally appropriate practices.* The newly added "C" recognizes *culture* as a major element that provides the framework for people's lives. This is highly significant, because it stresses the importance of including cultural perspectives in the curriculum. The position statement published by the NAEYC, *Responding to Culturally and Linguistically Different Children* (1996) supported consideration of the many cultural elements in the lives of children. NAEYC's statement acknowledged the need to plan curricula with a cultural perspective. This mandate reiterates the need for multi-cultural education. Implications for social studies experiences are clear: Appropriate social studies curriculum needs to consider what is typically age-appropriate, along with the cultural characteristics of children.

■■ Connecting Multi-cultural ■■ Education with the NCSS Social Studies Standards

Multi-cultural education relates to two *themes,* or *curricular strands,* in the social studies standards: Strand I—*Culture,* and Strand IX—*Global Connections.* Both strands address multi-cultural education in the following ways:

Culture. The study of culture prepares students to answer questions such as: What are the common characteristics of different cultures? How do belief systems, such as religion or political ideals, influence other parts of the culture? How does the culture change to accommodate different ideas and beliefs? What does language tell us about the culture? In schools, this theme typically appears in units and course dealing with geography, history, sociology, and anthropology, as well as multicultural topics across the curriculum.

(NCSS, 1994, p. x).

FIGURE 9–4 Performance Expectations (for the Primary Grades) for Standards in Culture and Global Connections

I. Culture

   a. Explore and describe similarities and differences in the ways groups, societies and cultures address similar human needs and concerns.

   b. Give examples of how experiences may be interpreted differently by people from diverse cultural perspectives and frames of reference.

   c. Describe ways in which language, stories, folktales, music, and artistic creations serve as expression of culture and influence behavior of people living in a particular culture.

   d. Compare ways in which people from different cultures think about and deal with their physical environment and social conditions.

   e. Give examples and describe the importance of cultural unity and diversity within and across groups.

IX. Global Connections

   a. Explore ways that language, arts, music, belief systems, and other cultural elements may facilitate global understanding or lead to misunderstanding.

   b. Investigate concerns, issues, standards, and conflicts related to the universal human rights, such as the treatment of children, religious groups, and effects of war.

Source: National Council for the Social Studies. (1994). *Expectations for Excellence: Curriculum Standards for Social Studies.* pp. 33, 44. Washington, DC: Author.

Global Connections. The realities of global interdependence require understanding the increasingly important and diverse global connections among world societies and the frequent tension between national interests and global priorities. Students will need to be able to address such international issues as health care, the environment, human rights, economic competition, and interdependence, age-old ethnic enmities, and political and military alliances. The theme typically appears in units or courses dealing with geography, culture, and economics but may also draw upon the natural and physical sciences and the humanities.

(NCSS, 1994, p. xii).

Both standards seem very complex and almost impossible to simplify for young children. However, NCSS (1994) offers some excellent examples of what the expectations are for the early grades. Figure 9–4 shows specifically what the standards mean.

Multi-cultural education permeates other social studies standards as well. Early childhood teachers are encouraged to browse through them for additional ideas when planning the curriculum (see the Social Studies Standards in Appendix I). Additionally, district and state guidelines must be considered in curriculum planning. It is especially important for new teachers to be aware of these and ensure that they are observed. Local guidelines generally have priority over personal convictions and beliefs, as well as federal mandates. Early childhood educators, therefore, have a complex task of incorporating curriculum guidelines from many different sources when selecting what to teach to young children in their classrooms.

Suggestions for Planning Social Studies with a Multi-cultural Focus

We know that creating a curriculum based on the ideas of diversity is a difficult task that will not be accomplished overnight. We also recognize that the progress for some of you may be slow if you are required to follow a state or a district curriculum. In spite of these constraints, we ask you to recognize that in order to implement an optimum program, you must focus on what is most valuable for children.

As you begin to bring in social studies themes on multi-culturalism, there are key points to remember that will facilitate the transition from what you do now to teaching from a multi-cultural perspective (Robles de Melendez & Ostertag, 1997). These points are equally helpful in following any pre-scribed curriculum.

Planning social studies with a multi-cultural perspective:

■ Begin by reviewing the content of your current curriculum to determine what was successful and what felt comfortable.

■ Go through your lesson plan book and identify the topics developed in class.

■ Find in your curriculum *where* you could add or expand the children's views by including an-other perspective. Determine *what* other perspec-tive you can add. Begin with only one additional perspective; then, as you gain confidence, add others.

■ Adopt a flexible thematic teaching approach that will facilitate the integration of topics and views. This will also help guide children into examining things they like or have demonstrated an interest in. Use of an "emergent curriculum" fosters flexi-bility (Jones & Nimmo, 1994).

■ When including a second perspective, think about the ways in which it relates to the chil-dren's own cultural experiences. Remind yourself to always center your selections first on what is connected to the lives of your students.

■ Include as many concrete experiences as possi-ble. Children need things to see, touch, and ma-nipulate if they are to construct new knowledge. In dealing with views and perceptions about oth-ers, present common daily-life situations in which children can see the meaningfulness and the im-pact of their behavior.

■ Make sure the experiences will offer accurate portrayals of individuals and groups and not pre-sent stereotypes. Avoid what is exotic, and in-clude what defines the current realities of a cul-ture (Derman-Sparks, 1992). For example, when presenting folklore and traditional dress or cus-toms, clarify that they describe or represent what happens during a holiday or a festivity, but are not necessarily a part of everyday life.

■ Present perspectives in time frames that define the *here/now* first, and then move into the *then/now*. Bring in ideas about a place (*here/there*) that have elements children can relate to, like common cli-mate, topography, and so on.

■ If you are uncertain about the details of a particu-lar culture, postpone presenting it until you have learned about it. Remember that children see you as an authority. They will accept what you say as the truth.

Selecting Multi-cultural Learning Materials

One of the ways young children learn about dif-ferent cultures is through appropriately selected curriculum materials. For young children, instruc-tional materials serve as tools to experience, create, and process ideas. Instructional materials are neces-sary resources that help children acquire and shape knowledge. According to Forman and Kuschner (1983), instructional materials are an important re-source for provoking cognitive construction in the child. Because of this, teachers need to become aware of what happens when children use the entire classroom environment as a learning resource.

Appropriate selection of materials begins with teachers answering the question, *"Are these re-sources developmentally appropriate?"* A summary of Forman and Kuschner's recommendations (1983) for the selection of developmentally appropriate classroom materials is presented in Concept Box 9–3. Their suggestions offer teachers ways to choose resources following the Piagetian construc-tivist cognitive position (see Chapter 3). These guidelines are also pertinent because multi-cultural education for young children follows the principles of child development.

Culturally Appropriate Materials: Avoiding Biases and Stereotypes

Good multi-cultural classroom materials need to be free of biases, stereotypes, and misrepresenta-

---

Concept Box 9–3   Selecting Quality Developmental Instructional Materials

Teachers should exercise caution when choosing materials for young children. Here are some helpful tips for selecting items for the early childhood multi-cultural classroom.

1. Do not rely on the titles of commercial materials. Sometimes they are deceiving! Take time to carefully read the instructions and examine the materials.

2. Choose materials with various ranges of difficulty that present challenges. Avoid materials that only serve one purpose or one skill level. They will be interesting for children when seen for the first time, but they will not hold their interest for long.

3. Select materials that will make the child think. Try to stay away from resources that are too simple or easy for a child to figure out.

4. Choose materials that can be transformed. It is preferable to have items that can be used in different ways.

5. Have materials that allow children freedom to work with them. For instance, avoid items that do little to encourage the child to try several possible answers.

Source: Adapted from Forman, G., & Kuschner, D. (1983). *The child's construction of knowledge: Piaget for teaching children.* Washington, DC: National Association for the Education of Young Children, pp. 189–191.

---

tions regarding diverse cultures. **Bias** is "any attitude, belief, or feeling that results in, and helps to justify unfair treatment of an individual because of his or her identity" (Derman-Sparks & The A.B.C. Task Force, 1989, p. 3). Teachers need to be especially careful when selecting multi-cultural materials, because of the tendency to seek what is "beyond the usual" (Thompson, 1993, p. 29.) Morris (1983)

Bringing Ideas into Practice 9–3
Guidelines for the Selection of Culturally Appropriate Resources

In Matsumoto-Grah's (1992) opinion (cited in Byrnes & Kiger, p. 105), there are seven areas to consider when selecting materials that include all aspects of diversity. In her view, appropriate diversity materials should:

1. present the contributions of groups other than European-Americans. Materials [should] also reflect a cross-cultural perspective of what women have contributed.

2. portray people, including women, across socioeconomic classes and religions. Find an absence of stereotypes. (For instance, European Americans [often] are portrayed as the upper class, and minorities as poor.)

3. depict religious issues appropriately "when religion is integral to the context of the subject."

4. give a socially balanced view about "famous people," that is, include the outstanding people from both the privileged and the working classes.

5. reflect the cultures and ethnicities of the classroom children and of their community.

6. exhibit and include the native languages present in the class. (For example, if the class has children who speak Spanish and French-Creole, materials in those languages should be available.)

7. [be] at the developmental level of the children and offer challenges with opportunities to experience success.

Source: Matsumoto-Grah, K. (1992). Checklist for diversity. In D. A. Byrnes & G. Kiger (Eds.). *Common bonds: Anti-bias teaching in a diverse society* (2nd ed.). Wheaton, MD: Association for Childhood Education International: p. 105.

warns that teachers cannot simply rely on what a resource seems to have, but rather they need to verify the nature of didactic materials by asking, "Do these materials present an accurate, bias- and stereotype-free picture of diversity?" A **stereotype** is "an oversimplified generalization about a particular group's race, or sex, which usually carries [a] derogatory implication" (Derman-Sparks & The A.B.C. Task Force, 1989, p. 3).

Early educators Kendall (1983) and Derman-Sparks and The A.B.C. Task Force (1989) emphasized attention to classroom resources. They recommend that teachers take time to examine what is brought into the classroom to ensure it is totally bias-free. In their opinion, during children's formative years, it is of utmost importance to make the classroom a place where the children will experience and encounter human and social differences as something typical of all people. The emphasis should be placed first on targeting unbiased representations in materials. Attention to *what* is presented and *how* cultural groups are presented through resources is essential (see Figure 9–5).

Using Art to Enhance Awareness of Multi-culturalism

In early childhood education the art center is a very important place in the classroom. Art provides children with opportunities to explore ways to use the materials to represent what they perceive through their senses. Art is a powerful source of learning that can also be used to facilitate learning about diversity.

The colors of the paints are the first art objects that should be changed. Adding more browns, tans, and black induces the child to notice other color tones. Creative ways of developing these tones include using chocolate, which can be diluted to create various shades of brown. Having children work with such color tones is an appropriate way to facilitate understanding about the role of melanin as the agent responsible for the different skin tones of people.

The colors white and black have been associated with the symbolism of good and evil in the western society. Unfortunately, this concept has been extended into the racial context that children encounter very early in life. Classroom activities can be designed to disperse and correct these unfounded views. Teachers can set aside specific days when the only art items to be used are those of less frequently used colors, like blacks and browns. This is a way of helping children overcome any socially based fear of these colors. A preschool or a kindergarten class can also take a field trip around their neighborhood to see all the things that are the various shades of brown or black. We can already anticipate a long list of items! The realization that these colors are a part of our daily life can start the children thinking that there is nothing mysterious or negative about them.

FIGURE 9–5 Selecting Culturally Appropriate Materials

What should be presented?
- a variety of gender roles, racial, and cultural backgrounds.
- a variety of occupations.
- a variety of ages.
- a variety of abilities (include special-needs individuals from different backgrounds).
- a variety in time (past and present) and place (local, national, international).

How should it be presented?
- in an assortment of social contexts.
- in settings presenting contrasting lifestyles and configurations.
- in a variety of languages (those of the children must be acknowledged first, and then others, as chosen by the teacher).
- in an assortment of representations or symbols to depict a given event or fact.
- different social and racial groups should be represented.
- in an accurate portrayal of racial characteristics. (Pictures should not use the Caucasian facial traits to depict different races/ethnic groups.)

According to Allport (1954), one of the most damaging myths is that people are divided by the color of their skins. Art experiences contribute to dispelling such myths. In the art section, tempera paints, crayons, and markers can be selected to include more colors reflecting the range of human skin tones. Today, there are many effective multi-cultural art materials, such as the "multi-cultural crayons" and "multi-cultural construction paper" that contain many varieties of skin shades. Another very useful item is the multi-cultural modeling clay. Regular clay can be also be shaded by teachers to produce various skin shades by using powdered tempera and even cocoa powder (Thompson, 1993). Whether teacher-made or commercially produced, multi-cultural art supplies and materials should be available in the classroom at all times.

Felt in shades of brown and black is another important material to include in the art center. Draw-

---

Concept Box 9–4   Making Your Own Multi-cultural Clay

You can easily make your own multi-cultural clay for your students. Simply follow the recipe we have included here. Remember that you can save the clay in plastic bags or in a tightly closed container.

You will need the following ingredients:
4 cups cornstarch
1 cup salt
1½ cup water
powdered tempera (brown or red) or cocoa
2½ cups water

Mix all the ingredients. The amount of tempera or cocoa to add will depend on the skin colors you want to make. Place on medium heat for 5 minutes, until the dough thickens. Remove from heat. Cover the pot with a wet paper towel. When cool, knead for about 5 minutes, working on a surface covered with wax paper. Make objects. Allow objects to dry before painting.

Concept Box 9–5   The Arts and Multi-cultural Education

■ Through the arts, children express their ideas and find a variety of ways to learn.

■ The arts offer a channel to communicate ideas and emotions beyond the barriers of language (see Chapter 8). Children and adults who are linguistically different find in the arts a medium where they can share their views and ideas.

■ The arts offer an enjoyable source for learning and individual success.

■ Through the arts, children experience how to work collaboratively, to share ideas and materials, and to experience group success.

■ For educators, the arts are a source of discovery and awareness of the gifts and abilities of children. They also provide valuable examples for authentic assessment.

Source: Goldberg, M. (1997). *Arts and learning: An integrated approach to teaching and learning in multicultural and multilingual settings.* New York: Longman, pp. 14–15.

---

ing and craft paper should also be changed and varied (Thompson, 1993). Traditionally, only white paper has been used in the classroom. However, when children are drawing pictures or making figures of themselves, family, and friends, they should find paper in shades that more accurately reflect their reality. It is important to remember that the shades of tan and natural are more appropriate than plain white paper. Packing paper, which comes in a natural shade, is an inexpensive source that resembles most skin tones more closely. Brown grocery bags are also useful. Manila folders and a roll of manila paper are additional sources of art materials.

Crafts are one of the universal elements that define people across cultures (Gomez, 1992). Crafts have the power to captivate the interest and the imagination through artistic expression. Crafts are an excellent source of learning experiences about ourselves and about other people. Because art and crafts represent how individuals have learned to create art with whatever is present in their environments, they become a source for valuing and appreciating people's resourcefulness and creativity.

Arts and crafts activities contribute to the holistic development of the child by providing opportunities for "actively solving problems, thinking critically, becoming visually literate, making aesthetic decisions, weighing and measuring, expressing themselves, using their imaginations, communicating with peers, and developing motor skills" (Gomez, 1992, p. 7). Children need to have access to the materials used in handicrafts in order to explore and experiment. Part of the classroom art area should include selected art forms and handicrafts from the children's own cultural groups, as well as from other groups about which they will learn. A sample of the materials listed below can enhance the child's perspective of other people. We have indicated the cultural groups that more frequently use these art and craft materials. You may add some others.

- *Caribbean, African, Native American groups:*
  dry gourds, dry coconut shells, beans, seeds, leaves
- *Latin American, Native American groups:*
  feathers, clay, colored beads, strings, leather scraps
- *Asian, European, Latin American groups:*
  yarn, scraps of fabric, sequins, glitter, watercolors, clay
- *Latin American, African, Asian groups:*
  straw, sticks, twigs, raffia
- *Caribbean, Asian groups:*
  sea shells, dry fish scales, coral rocks, driftwood, seeds

Using Children's Literature to Integrate Multi-cultural Themes

Literature is one of the most powerful sources of ideas, personal values, and wisdom. Donna Norton (1995) says that literature plays an important role in helping people learn and appreciate their own cultural heritage. She further maintains that literature is of critical relevance in a multi-cultural society like ours:

> Carefully selected literature can illustrate the contributions and values of the many cultures. It is especially critical to foster an appreciation of the heritage of the minorities in American society. A positive self-concept is not possible unless we respect others as well as ourselves; literature *can contribute considerably* toward our understanding and thus our respect.
>
> (Norton, 1995, p. 4, emphasis added)

Some of the impressions, fantasies, and words many of us still cherish are from the stories, rhymes, and poems we heard or read when we were children. Our favorite books made us dream of new places and people, both real and "make-believe." The benefits of literature go beyond the pleasure

---

■■   Let's Talk About . . . 9–3

Teachers Are Always Resourceful!

We've often been told often by teachers that finding appropriate art materials is not an easy task. However, visiting and observing teachers in classrooms across the nation, we have been amazed at the creativity and resourcefulness of early childhood educators in locating good materials. As you read the following anecdote, consider how this teacher's idea helped to turn a throwaway into valuable art material for her class.

The first grade teacher ran out of art paper one day. She found some brown boxes that had been discarded and had an idea. She cut the boxes into pieces of various sizes; she placed them on the art table, and waited for the reactions. When children asked what they were, she said they were "special art canvases for pictures they could easily hang after they finished them." The result was a lot of "artistic canvases" the children displayed around the classroom. The experience was so successful that the teacher decided to make corrugated cardboard a permanent part of the art supplies.

and enchantment it gives us. Literature is a complementary developmental element for the young child. Joan Glazer (cited by Norton, 1995) has listed four ways that literature promotes good emotional development. According to Glazer, there are four ways in which a good selection of books in the classroom benefits children:

1. Books help children see that other people also share emotions and feelings, just as they do.
2. They facilitate the exploration of feelings and emotions from a variety of perspectives.
3. They show different ways to deal with emotions and feelings.
4. They demonstrate that, at times, what we might feel might be in conflict with our own emotions.
(Norton, 1995, p. 25).

Literature is one of the common denominators of all cultures. We can learn about the ideas, beliefs, values, and struggles of any country around the world through literature. Because of its powerful ability for cultural transmission, literature is an ideal resource for multi-cultural education. In the opinion of Tway (cited by Norton, 1995, p. 224), "In a country of multicultural heritage, children require books that reflect and illuminate that varied heritage."

The emphasis on whole language teaching has opened the door to more quality literature for children. With it, a profusion of **multi-cultural literature** has also emerged, because of the recognition given to the absence and misrepresentation of cultural groups. Today, most classrooms have a good supply of multi-cultural books depicting ethnic groups and other elements of cultural diversity. Discovering what kinds of books are in the classroom is important because of the power literature has for young children. Neugebauer (1992) recommends assessing the classroom library corner to determine:

1. how the books portray the characters;
2. the type of situations they present;
3. the value, accuracy, and appropriateness of the illustrations;
4. the nature of the messages conveyed in the stories;

Bringing Ideas into Practice 9–4
Sources of Good Multi-cultural Literature

Selecting multi-cultural books is an exciting experience. Many book publishers include titles covering all aspects of diversity. For example, Scholastic Books (see p. 283) has an extensive series of multi-cultural titles. Among them are the *Big Multicultural Tales*, which include stories from Russia ("Little Masha and Misha the Bear"), Haiti ("Horse and Toad"), and Kenya ("The Crocodile and the Ostrich"), and a story about the Pueblo Indians ("Coyote and the Butterflies"), among others. There are several book publishers and distributors that also specialize in the distribution of ethnic literature. Among those, you may want to check the following: Savanna Books, Holiday House, BridgeWater Books, Just Us Books, Children's Book Press, Children's Press, and Jacaranda. A visit to the children's section of your local library will probably reveal an exciting number of titles to share with your class.

---

5. the credibility of the author and illustrator to tell the story and portray the characters;
6. whether the stories depict the ethnic groups and the diversity of the class and of the community.
(Neugebauer, 1992)

Using Journals, Magazines, and Newspapers in the Early Childhood Classroom

Journals, newspapers, and magazines are another type of contemporary literature that can be used to enhance the children's learning process. They are also excellent sources of pictures children can view while learning about their world and the worlds of others who inhabit our society. Periodicals and newspapers in different languages should be included in the classroom literature areas. They provide unique opportunities for the children to explore the linguistic symbols of other languages.

Analyses of the various sections, such as the advertising section, found in foreign newspapers can turn into interesting activities for the children. Teachers can obtain foreign papers and journals from local bookstores, at airport newspaper stands, and in some cases, from local ethnic stores. Other sources are donations made by the children's parents, or by staff members who buy ethnic publications. Teachers are advised to examine the donated literature materials carefully to verify the appropriateness and the quality of the content.

There are many journals and magazines that can be added to the book center. For example, the *National Geographic* and *World* (both from the National Geographic Society), *Faces: The Magazine about People* (Cobblestone Publishing), and the *Smithsonian* (from the Smithsonian Institution) are good additions to the classroom literature corner. They can be found in most public and school libraries.

Newspapers are an inexpensive source of rich cultural materials. They offer glimpses into the realities of other individuals and groups. A newspaper also reports on current views, attitudes, conflicts, and values of different ethnicities. Newspapers can help children discern a variety of human characteristics through their portrayals in pictures and text of people living in our communities and around the world.

Using Postcards as a Teaching Resource

Postcards are another inexpensive source of good pictures. When traveling, most people are tempted to bring home cards that end up not being used. These postcards can become an excellent resource in the classroom. Robles de Melendez and Ostertag (1997) recommend that early educators use what they call the "teacher's eye" in selecting postcards while traveling. The good "teacher's eye" alerts us to images children enjoy and savor.

Postcards can easily be used to make picture books that will expand the literacy resources. When using postcards from around the world, a map or a world globe should always be close by to help the children learn more about diversity. The notion of "here and there" portrayed by maps and globes (see Chapter 6) encourages children to compare and contrast people and their cultures for the purpose of finding out what makes us so alike!

Bucher and Fravel, Jr. (1991) report that using postcards is an effective way to teach about communities and about local history. Their postcards were organized into thematic areas (architecture and historical scenes; major industry scenes, agriculture, transportation; environment and tourist sites) that provided a wealth of perspectives for children. Teachers can also organize their postcards by major themes, and either file them by those topics, or make picture books with them. Figure 9–6 presents a list of possible themes commonly found in postcards.

Enhancing the Literature Area

Story-telling is an optimal literature resource. Grandparents, senior citizens, and other volunteers can be invaluable sources of information and anecdotes of other people's ways. Teachers can have the

---

Bringing Ideas into Practice 9–5
Using Newspapers to Build a Multi-cultural Picture File

There are always many inexpensive and creative ways to enhance learning. A second grade teacher who wanted to build awareness of physical diversity developed a project about people solely from newspapers. Instead of discarding newspapers, the children's families donated them to the classroom. Every week, the teacher and the students enjoyed searching through the papers to find pictures of people. During the entire year, the students saved the pictures they thought best portrayed different people. The pictures provided opportunities to clarify and expand ideas about the variety of physical characteristics of individuals and groups. Over 800 pictures pasted on tag board became a permanent picture file that captivated the children's imagination throughout the year.

FIGURE 9–6 Sample Themes from Postcards

dresses for special occasions	places to visit
things to eat	people's hats
animals from different weather zones	musical instruments
	celebrations/festivals
	houses and buildings
flowers and trees	games
children's faces	colors and decorations

A variety of "persona dolls" can make multi-cultural issues and world events "come alive" in the classroom.

elderly visit the classroom as guest "tellers," and record their stories to create an additional "story bank" for the children's enjoyment. Story-telling is also a way to save the wisdom of the past for future generations and to develop an appreciation for the elderly, a diversity group frequently overlooked.

Using Persona Dolls

All of us have enjoyed the stories told by puppets at one time or another in our lives, largely because we believed they were real. That is precisely why the persona doll is another child-appropriate resource. Developed by Kay Taus, a *persona doll* is a vehicle for telling stories about the lives of children and their families. According to Taus (cited in Derman-Sparks, 1989, p. 16), persona dolls also bring into the classroom the lives of people who have "differences that do not exist within one classroom." Each doll acquires a "persona" from a character it represents in a story. The doll, who periodically "visits" the classroom, is accompanied by a script. Intended to serve as a teacher resource, persona dolls should be kept in the teacher's area. However, the dolls should be made available to children whenever they ask for them.

Stories with persona dolls are created from three main sources:

1. issues emerging from the children's lives and experiences.
2. current world and community events.
3. information considered relevant by the teacher—the children should learn significant historical events

(Derman-Sparks & The A.B.C. Task Force, 1989, p. 18.)

Bringing Ideas into Practice 9–6
Preserving the Stories of Our Grandparents

Patricia Raymond (1992), a kindergarten teacher from Ocala, Florida, developed an oral history project with the elders in her community. It was her goal "to build a bridge of memories past and present by joining kindergarten students with grandparents" (p. 224-L). With the support of a mini-grant from ACEI, she began taping the stories of grandparents to enhance her classroom listening center. Raymond (1992, pp. 224-L to 224-P) describes the benefits as follows:

Our classroom listening center became a time machine as students listened to older members of the community read familiar stories on tape and record re-enacted situations and instances from their lives. The readers readily shared personal glimpses of their childhood that delighted the children. . . . Even on tape the warm, soothing voices of older friends bring smiles to children's faces.

Recommended Children's Books

Bernier-Grand, C. (1994). *Juan Bobo: Four folktales from Puerto Rico.* New York: Harper Trophy. (on Hispanics)

Brill, M. (1998). *Tooth tales from around the world.* Watertown, MA: Charlesbridge. (on diversity)

Brusca, M. (1991). *On the pampas.* New York: Holt. (on South Americans, Hispanics)

Bunting, E. (1998). *How many days to America: A Thanksgiving story.* New York: Clarion. (Americana)

Cohen, B. (1983). *Molly's pilgrim.* New York: Lothrop, Lee & Shepard. (Americana)

Cooper, E. (1997). *Country fair.* New York: Greenwillow. (on American mainstream culture)

Cowen-Fletcher, J. (1994). *It takes a village.* New York: Scholastic. (on African-Americans)

Delacre, L. (1990). *Las navidades: Popular Christmas songs from Latin America.* New York: Scholastic. (on Hispanics)

DeRolf, S. (1996). *The crayon box that talked.* New York: Random House. (on diversity)

Dorros, A. (1991). *Abuela.* New York: Puffin. (on Hispanics)

Dorros, A. (1991). *Tonight is carnaval.* New York: Puffin. (on Hispanics)

Dorros, A. (1995). *Isla.* New York: Puffin. (on Hispanics)

Dwight, L. (1992). *We can do it!* New York: Checkerboard Press. (on exceptionalities)

Fazio, B. (1996). *Grandfather's story.* Seattle, WA: Sasquatch Books. (on Asian-Americans)

Fox, M. (1989). *Wilfrid Gordon McDonald Partridge.* New York: Kane/Miller. (on intergenerational)

Fox, M. (1997). *Whoever you are.* San Diego, CA: Harcourt Brace. (on diversity)

Himmelman, K. (1996). *Hooray! It's Passover!* New York: HarperCollins. (on Jewish-Americans)

Kocher, A. (1994). *Ravi's Diwali surprise.* Cleveland, OH: Modern Curriculum Press. (on Indo-Americans)

Leighton, M. (1994). *An Ellis Island Christmas.* New York: Puffin. (on immigration)

Levine, E. (1989). *I hate English.* New York: Scholastic.

Longfellow, H. W. (1855/1983). *Hiawatha.* New York: Puffin. (on Native Americans)

Mitchell, R. (1997). *The talking cloth.* New York: Orchard Books. (on African-Americans)

Moxley, S. (1995). *Skip across the ocean: Nursery rhymes from around the world.* New York: Orchard Books. (on diversity)

Pico, F. (1994). *The red comb.* New York: BridgeWater. (on Puerto Ricans, Hispanics)

Polacco, P. (1988). *The keeping quilt.* New York: Simon & Schuster. (on Jewish-Americans)

Pomeranc, M. H. (1998). *The American wei.* Morton Grove, IL: Albert-Whitman & Company. (on diversity, immigration)

Riehicky, J. (1993). *Cinco de Mayo.* Chicago, IL: Children's Press. (on Hispanics)

Rosa-Casanova, S. (1997). *Mama Provi and the pot of rice.* New York: Atheneum. (on diversity)

Rosen, M. (1997). *Elijah's angel: A story for Chanukah and Christmas.* San Diego, CA: Harcourt Brace.

Say, A. (1999). *Tea with milk.* Boston, MA: Houghton Mifflin. (on Asian-Americans)

Soto, G. (1997). *Snapshots from a wedding.* New York: Putnam. (on Mexican-Americans, Hispanics)

Stutson, C. (1996). *Prairie primer.* New York: Dutton. (on Americana)

Suyenaga, R. (1994). *Obon.* Cleveland, OH: Modern Curriculum Press. (on Japanese-Americans)

Swamp, Chief Jake. (1995). *Giving thanks: A Native American good morning message.* New York: Lee and Low. (on Native Americans)

Swartz, L. (1992). *A first Passover.* Cleveland, OH: Modern Curriculum Press. (on Jewish-Americans)

Uchida, Y. (1993). *The bracelet.* New York: Philomel. (on Asian-Americans)

Vezza, D. (1997). *Passport on a plate: A round-the-world cookbook for children.* New York: Simon & Schuster. (on diversity)

Zalben, J. (1988). *Leo and Blossom's Sukkah.* New York: Holt. (on Jewish-Americans)

Zalben, J. (1990). *Beni's first Chanukkah.* New York: Holt. (on Jewish-Americans)

Zalben, J. (1991). *Goldie's Purim.* New York: Holt. (on Jewish-Americans)

ACTIVITIES

Keeping Track of What You Learn: Your Personal Activity Log

This chapter dealt with multi-culturalism and diversity in the early childhood curriculum. You may find these additional ideas helpful for future planning.

A. Reflections

1. Define the concept of culture in your own words. Write a description of how your culture influences the way you are.
2. Consider the ideas presented throughout this chapter on the need for multi-cultural education. Select those you consider to be most relevant, and give a reason for your selection.
3. Based on the ideas explored thoughout this chapter, develop your own definition of *multi-cultural education.*
4. In your opinion, what topics should be addressed in a multi-cultural and global social studies curriculum for young children?

B. Collections

1. Find out how you or your family came to the United States. Collect any stories or photographs that describe the arrival.
2. Create a visual sampler about the cultural groups present in the community where your school is located.
3. Create a collage of the cultural groups present in your classroom.

4. Observe children in your classroom and in the neighborhood, and make a list of the things they do and say that reveal their culture.

C. Internet Resources*

There are many resources about multi-cultural education available on the Internet. Here are two we consider relevant:

■ **The American Immigration Home Page**

Web site: http://www.bergen.org/AAST/ Projects/Immigration/index.html

This Web site was originally developed as a class project. Today it is an excellent source for information about topics related to immigration.

■ **The Multicultural Pavilion**

Web site: http://curry.edschool.virginia. edu/go/multicultural

This Web page has helpful educational information about educational resources. It includes links to many interesting sources. The links to resources about children's literature are very valuable.

*Please note that Internet resources are of a time-sensitive nature and URL sites and addresses may often be modified or deleted.

References

Allport, G. (1954). *The nature of prejudice.* Garden City, NJ: Doubleday.

Banks, J., & Banks, C. (Eds.). (1993). *Multicultural education: Issues and perspectives* (2nd ed.). Needham Heights, MA: Allyn & Bacon.

Bredekamp, S., & Copple, C. (1997). *Developmentally appropriate practices in programs serving young children* (rev. ed.). Washington, DC: National Association for the Education of Young Children.

Bucher, K., & Fravel Jr., M. (1991, January–February). Local history comes alive with postcards. *Social Education, 3*(3), pp. 18–20.

Cech, M. (1991). *Globalchild: Multicultural resources for young children.* Menlo Park, CA: Addison Wesley.

Derman-Sparks, L. (1992). *Reaching potential through antibias, multicultural curriculum.* In S. Bredekamp & T. Rosegrant (Eds.). *Reaching potential: Appropriate curriculum for young children.* (Vol. 1.) (pp. 114–128). Washington, DC: National Association for the Education of Young Children.

Derman-Sparks, L., & The A.B.C. Task Force (1989). *The anti-bias curriculum: Tools for empowering children.* Washington, DC: National Association for the Education of Young Children.

Dickinson, G., & Leming, A. (1990). *Understanding families: Diversity, continuity and change.* Boston, MA: Allyn & Bacon.

Forman, G., & Kuschner, D. (1983). *The child's construction of knowledge: Piaget for teaching children.* Washington, DC: National Association for the Education of Young Children.

Glazer, J. (1981). In D. Norton (1995). *Through the eyes of a child: An introduction to children's literature* (4th ed.). Englewood Cliffs, NJ: Merrill.

Goldberg, M. (1997). *Arts and learning: An integrated approach to teaching and learning in the multicultural and multilingual settings.* New York: Longman.

Gomez, A. (1992). *Crafts of many cultures: Thirty authentic crafts projects from around the world.* New York: Scholastic.

Kendall, F. (1983). *Diversity in the classroom: A multicultural approach to the education of young children.* New York: Teachers College Press.

Jones, E., & Nimmo, J. (1994). *Emergent curriculum.* Washington, DC: National Association for the Education of Young Children.

Matsumoto-Grah, K. (1992). Checklist for diversity. In D. A. Byrnes & G. Kiger (Eds.). *Common bonds: Antibias teaching in a diverse society* (2nd ed.). Wheaton,

MD: Association for Childhood Education International: p. 105.

McBee, R., Bone, K., Mossop, G., & Owens, C. (1998). Teaching immigration in elementary classrooms. *Social Education, 62*(7), pp. 417–419.

Morris, J. (1983). *Classroom methods and materials.* In O. Sarocho & B. Spodek (Eds.). *Understanding the multicultural experiences in early childhood education* (pp. 77–90). Washington, DC: National Association for the Education of Young Children.

Morrison, G. (1995). *Early childhood education today* (6th ed.). Englewood Cliffs, NJ: Merrill.

National Association of the Education of Young Children. (1996). *Responding to culturally and linguistically different children.* Washington, DC: Author.

National Council for the Social Studies. (1994). *Curriculum standards for social studies: Expectations of excellence.* Washington, DC: Author.

Neugebauer, B. (1992). *Alike and different: Exploring our humanity with children* (rev. ed.). Washington, DC: National Association for the Education of Young Children.

Nieto, S. (1992). *Affirming diversity: The sociopolitical context of multicultural education.* New York: Longman, pp. 208–219.

Norton, D. (1995). *Through the eyes of a child: An introduction to children's literature.* Englewood Cliffs, NJ: Merrill.

Pomeranc, M. H. (1998). *The American wei.* Morton Grove, IL: Albert Whitman & Company.

Raymond, P. (1992). Oral history: A bridge to children's literature experience. [1991 Mini-grant winner] *Childhood Education, 68*(4), (Summer), pp. 224-L–224-P.

Robles de Melendez, W., & Ostertag, V. (1997). *Teaching young children in multicultural classrooms: Issues, concepts, and strategies.* Albany, NY: Delmar.

Rong, L. X. (1998). The new immigration: Challenges facing social studies professionals. *Social Education, 62*(7), pp. 393–399.

Rosales, L. (1992). *Listen to the heart: Impressions and memories of a teacher.* Unpublished manuscript.

Singer, J., & Harbour-Ridley, T. (1998). Young children learn about immigrants to the United States. *Social Education, 621*(7), pp. 415–416.

Thompson, B. (1993). *Words can hurt you: Beginning a program of anti-bias education.* Menlo Park, CA: Addison Wesley.

Tway, E. (1989). Dimensions of multicultural literature for children. In D. Norton (1995). *Through the eyes of a child: An introduction to children's literature* (4th ed.). Englewood Cliffs, NJ: Merrill.

CHAPTER 10

Economics, the Environment, and Social Issues: Preparing Children to Make Informed Choices

Bring me back the aroma and the swords
that fall from the sky,
the solitary peace of pasture and rock,
the damp of the river-margins,
the smell of the larch tree . . .

—PABLO NERUDA, "OH, EARTH WAIT FOR ME" (1962)

Chapter Questions

After reading this chapter you should be able to answer the following questions:

- How do young children experience economics in their lives?
- What is environmental education?
- Why is environmental education important for young children?
- How do we make young children aware of social issues?

Key Terms and Concepts

consumption

distribution

economics

exchange

production

scarcity

supply and demand

Classroom Portrait: **Images of Today**

Yesterday, the group of four-year-olds visited the zoo. It was a happy experience. They sang and solved animal riddles on the bus. As the bus moved through the streets, children saw the contrasts between well-kept buildings and run-down places. There were some people pushing carts and other people huddled under the overpass. One child noticed that many people were lined up to get food that was being served. But the excitement of going to the zoo had overshadowed all this and had captured their attention all that day.

The next morning the class was sharing what they saw at the zoo. Ms. Garcia was writing down all the things they had seen during their visit. When Eric's turn came, his answer surprised her. He said, "There were people sleeping under the bridge. Were they cold?" At first, the teacher did not know what to say. Then another child added: "... and they were not clean!" Eric replied to that comment from his class-

mate stating that perhaps the people living under the bridge "don't have a mommy." Other children shared their impressions about the people "out in the streets." When a child asked why they were not sleeping in their house, Ms. Garcia had to respond.

By now it was clear that her class had, indeed, noticed one of today's social realities: homelessness. She hesitated for a second, but then quickly put aside the discussion about the zoo. "It's time," she thought, "to talk about what happens in our community." In fact, this teacher of four-year-olds was pleased to find how her class had become aware of this issue. She felt it was her responsibility to help them find out for themselves why the people they saw were living on the streets. She asked a question to lead her group into exploring the meaning of homelessness: "Have you ever thought what would happen if you did not have a house?" asked Ms. Garcia. She knew that many interesting conversations would follow.

■■ Bringing the "Outside World" into
■■ the Early Childhood Classroom

Today, society faces a multiplicity of challenges. Many of these challenges are pressing issues that directly and indirectly affect our lives. In part, they include aspects of economics, the environment, current events, and special issues such as homelessness.

As you read in the Classroom Portrait at the beginning of this chapter, children are exposed to life's difficult challenges on a daily basis. Providing appropriate classroom experiences to explore and clarify these issues as they arise is an educational responsibility. It is also necessary to build knowledge and sensitivity about the society to which children belong. Learning that the problems and issues of their communities are theirs, too, establishes the bases for creating socially responsible citizens. It also fosters socially acceptable attitudes and desirable moral characteristics in a diverse society. A responsive social studies curriculum includes opportunities for chil-

dren to learn about these issues. This chapter presents suggestions to incorporate experiences about other social issues in a child-appropriate manner.

Finding Connections Between Current Issues and the NCSS Social Studies Standards

There are many connections with the social studies standards related to the areas of economics, environmental issues, current events, and social issues. Essentially, standards VII (*Production, Distribution and Consumption*), VIII (*Science, Technology, and Society*), and IX (*Global Connections*) are addressed through these areas.

Standard VII relates to the development of a concept of economics. It establishes the need to incorporate in the curriculum "experiences that provide for the study of how people organize the production, distribution, and consumption of good and services" (NCSS, 1994, p. 27). As such, it establishes the importance of planning activities to build concepts about the use and origin of personal and group resources. In the early childhood classroom, this standard establishes guidelines to help the child learn how to make appropriate economic decisions. Understanding the difference between wants and needs is the central goal to build a beginning sense about economics. There are many classroom opportunities to foster this kind of knowledge. Furthermore, research supports the fact that children are able to make good economic decisions if teachers consistently provide age-appropriate experiences in the classroom (Laney & Schug, 1998). Some of the ways to integrate and connect standard VII in the classroom are:

■ plan, on a regular basis, experiences about economics.
■ use real-life experiences such as planning a snack, a classroom party, a field trip, and others. Select experiences pertinent to the child's environment.
■ after economic-related activities, always provide time for discussion to foster understanding about the consequences of economic decisions.
■ create learning centers with a focus on economics. Include props to foster dramatic play.
■ read stories with themes related to economics. Use role-playing to clarify concepts.

Standards VIII and X are reflected through the areas related to the environment, current events, and social issues. Today, social and environmental issues are of concern to people around the world. As the world uses technology to communicate more effectively, we share the concerns of other global citizens, as well as the effects of situations happening in places remote from our country.

In the classroom, as teachers address these areas, they should incorporate experiences to help children learn about how issues affecting others also touch us. Development of a sense of shared social and global responsibility is at the heart of the goals set by standards VIII and X.

A complex and long-range goal, the sense of responsibility toward others begins in the early childhood years. Classroom activities that can help young children develop an awareness of this responsibility include:

■ daily discussions of "what happens in the world."
■ reading and discussing stories about social issues.
■ writing letters to express support for civic and global causes (environmental issues, peace, hunger).
■ projects to benefit others or the community.
■ learning about what individuals are doing to help people in our country and in other places.
■ exploring the use of technology in the family and in the community.
■ using technology to learn about others in other places.

Learning about Economics

All of us make daily decisions about the goods and services we need and want. We also face decisions how to satisfy unlimited wants with limited resources. These choices are grounded in economics. Basic principles of economics are based on the theory of **supply and demand** as it relates to scarcity. Because of scarcity of goods, services, resources, etc., humans have developed ways to produce more with less, through innovation and specialization. From this evolved an interdependence or reliance on people and societies on one another to satisfy each other's needs. The result of these efforts produced market systems through which buyers and sellers produce and exchange goods and services (Saunders & Gilliard, 1996).

Economics is the field that examines the production and distribution of goods and services (Saunders & Gilliard, 1996). Knowledge about economics is essential in making effective and positive personal choices about issues that have short- and long-term effects on our lives. An economically literate individual uses good critical thinking skills to guide decisions (NCSS, 1989). Knowing how to make good decisions about one's personal resources and becoming cognizant of which goods and services to obtain is one of the key characteristics of good citizens.

As the National Council on Economic Education (1996) has noted, "the aims of economic education are targeted at fostering lifelong knowledge and skills." Individuals who develop a good grasp of economics become:

- productive members of the work force
- responsible citizens
- knowledgeable consumers
- prudent savers and investors
- effective participants in a global economy
- competent decision makers.

(National Council on Economic Education, 1996, p. 3)

Because economics plays such an important part in American society, it is important for each of us to understand the basic economic concepts of scarcity, production, distribution, exchange, and consumption. Teaching these in an early childhood classroom is possible if teachers use concrete and child-appropriate ways to present them within the experiential framework of the children.

Developing children's understanding of work and the contributions workers make to society is also developed through economics. By learning about the different jobs people do, children build a sense of the importance of work. An understanding of the dignity of all types of honest work is also fostered through the study of economics.

Economics—the field that studies the use, production, distribution, and acquisition of goods and services—is a crucial discipline that needs to be emphasized even more in the school curriculum as we expand globalism and enter the new era in the twenty-first century. Future generations will be faced with even greater economic challenges as the Earth's resources decline and the environment erodes. Preparing students to respond to them with deeper understanding of the issues facing the global economy is in the best interests of human kind.

Voluntary Standards for Economics Education

Teaching of economics in the early grades has always promoted many debates among educators.

Some hold that the basic concepts of economics are much too complex for young children and are better left for later grades. Others believe that educating very young children helps them to become better consumers, producers, and voters. The lack of cohesiveness in the education community on the issue of economics education has resulted in a set of recommended standards, the Voluntary National Content Standards for Economics (Meszaros & Engstrom, 1998). They do not represent federal and state mandates but they do provide valuable guidelines to curriculum writers, teachers, and school districts regarding appropriate content in the area of economics.

The first voluntary standard targets the students in kindergarten through second grade and states:

Students will understand that:
Productive resources are limited. Therefore, people cannot have all of the goods and services they want; as a result, they must choose some things and give up others.

Students will be able to use this knowledge to:
Identify what they gain and what they give up when they make choices.

The first standard comprises 15 benchmarks that indicate what students in kindergarten through second grade should know and be able to do:

1. People make choices because they cannot have everything they want. (Grades K–1)
2. Economic wants are desires that can be satisfied by consuming a good, service, or leisure activity. (Grades K–1)
3. Goods are objects that can satisfy people. (Grades K–1)
4. Services are actions that can satisfy peoples' wants. (Grades K–1)
5. People's choices about what goods and services to buy and consume determine how resources are used. (Grades 1–3)
6. Whenever a choice is made, something is given up. (Grades 1–2)
7. The opportunity cost of a choice is the value of the best alternative. (Grades 1–2)
8. People whose wants are satisfied by using goods and services are called consumers. (Grade 1)

9. Productive resources are the natural resources, human resources, and capital goods available to make goods and services. (Grade 2)

10. Natural resources, such as land, are "gifts of nature"; they are present without human intervention. (Grade 2)

11. Human resources are the quantity and quality of human efforts directed toward producing goods and services. (Grade 2)

12. Capital goods are goods produced and used to make other goods and services.

13. Human capital refers to the quality of labor resources, which can be improved through investments in education, training, and health. (Grade 2)

14. Entrepreneurs are people who organize other productive resources to make goods and services. (Grades 2)

15. People who make goods and provide services are called producers. (Grade 2)
    (Meszaros & Engstrom, 1998, pp. 8–10)

The sixteenth standard addresses the economic concepts for grades three and four. That standard includes the following two benchmarks:

Students will know that:

1. Governments provide certain kinds of goods and services in market economy. (Grade 3)

2. Governments pay for the goods and services they use or provide by taxing or borrowing from people. (Grades 3–4)
   (Meszaros & Engstrom, 1998, p.10)

Early childhood teachers are invited to incorporate the benchmarks into the economics education for their young students. They are a rich resource for many developmentally appropriate activities the children will enjoy. Upon review, it is also evident that many of the benchmarks are present in the daily behaviors and experiences of young children. It goes to prove that economics has always been a part of the early childhood classroom.

Essential Economic Concepts

The five key economic concepts—scarcity, production, distribution, exchange, and consumption—are developed through the study of economics.

Teaching young children about these concepts engages them in exploring the following content:

■ **Scarcity:** learning how to deal with the limited resources available to supply the demand, learning about needs and wants.

■ **Production:** exploring what the community/country produces, the different jobs people have, learning about goods and services.

■ **Distribution:** investigating how products reach the market, how goods and services are made available to people, learning about the different sources where goods can be found.

■ **Exchange:** exploring how people acquire products in the community, how trading among communities and countries makes goods available.

■ **Consumption:** deciding between wants and needs, making appropriate use of the available resources.

All five categories involve the ability to make decisions, another important skill associated with economics. Young children begin to learn how to make positive and effective decisions from birth. Including decision-making based on economic issues adds to their repertoire of skills that will make them more effective adults.

Another essential ingredient of economics is *money.* Money is, in fact, a highly abstract concept. Young children acquire a sense of money and the

Appropriate activities promote the awareness of economic concepts.

What are Children's Ideas about Money?

According to cognitive research, children have difficulty understanding money because their sense of conservation and ability to deal with operations is still evolving. Take the opportunity to observe or think about experiences in which children are engaged in trading or exchanging money.

1. What comments do children make about money?

2. What are some assumptions children make about money?

3. What common misconceptions do they have regarding money?

role it plays in the lives of people over time. Their understanding of money as a concept is not fully achieved until they master the key cognitive conservation tasks (see p. 50). Teachers need to provide meaningful activities to foster gradual development about the concept of money. Learning about what money represents also involves children in decision-making. Exercises that show how much they can buy, what they need, and what they are able to have are examples of situations engaging children in learning about the use of money and in making decisions. It is important, in this context, to help children develop a responsible attitude towards money as early in life as possible.

At first glance, the key economic concepts appear too abstract and too complex for young children to understand. Our intent is to show you that many activities based on economic concepts can be made meaningful and appropriate for children with effective planning and some imagination.

Developing Thematic Activities Based on Economics

The classroom offers many opportunities for children to build their knowledge of economics. For example, some basic themes grounded in economics that are appropriate for children to explore include the following:

- Goods and services (production and distribution)
- Where things come from (scarcity and production)
- Saving to get what we need and want (exchange and consumption)
- Jobs (production, distribution, exchange, and consumerism)
- Places where we get what we need (distribution, exchange, and consumerism)

Experiences with an economics theme begin to acquaint the child with economic activities in his or her own life. Early childhood educators need to remember that these thematic activities will be more effective if learning centers are added. Centers and prop boxes can be created to facilitate explorations of the concepts of production, services, and occupations. Both centers and prop boxes are also excellent sources of hands-on experiences for children.

"Things I would like to have" can become an interesting thematic experience. Geared to building ideas about needs and wants, this theme emphasizes items that appeal to children. Reading stories, such as *A Friend for Little Bear* (Horse, 1997), will initiate a good discussion about those things that are really important and really needed as opposed to those that are merely wanted. Children can search through magazines to make a collage about items they need and want. Group and individual discussions about their collages will provide opportunities for children to find out why and when an item is *necessary* and when it is just *desired*. Good questioning will lead children to reflect on the items chosen in their collages. A visit to the grocery store or to a shopping mall will also help to establish the difference between needs and wants. Discussion about the things we can find at these two places will provide opportunities to classify items that we actually *need* and those that we simply *want*.

Learning about economics from the context of the family offers meaningful experiences for young children. Consider, for instance, the concept of ser-

---

Concept Box 10-1   Sample Prop Boxes with Economics Themes

Concept: Production

■ *The bakery:*
 Props—baking molds, flour, mixing bowls, rolling pin, measuring cups, bread trays, cookie molds, apron, empty boxes of cookies, empty bread wrappers, brown paper bags

■ *The pizza place:*
 Props—flour, rolling pin, pizza boxes, cans of pizza sauce (empty), containers of grated cheese (empty), plastic pizza shapes, paper plates, plastic pizza cutter, paper and markers to write down prices, order forms

■ *The print shop/bookbinding shop:*
 Props—brown or white butcher paper, markers, inkpads (washable ink), stamps (with a variety of designs), glue, construction paper, scissors, lace or ribbon (for tying pages together)

Concept: Services and Occupations

■ *The travel office:*
 Props—airline and train ticket covers, travel brochures, maps, old keyboard

■ *The post office:*
 Props—used stamps and play stamps, envelopes, paper, empty boxes, tape, used letter mailers, stamp pad and date stamp, map, mail carrier bag, mail carrier hat

■ *The grocery store:*
 Props—plastic fruits and vegetables, sample groceries (empty boxes), grocery basket, cash register, calculator, brown paper bags (avoid the use of plastic bags for safety reasons), apron or grocer smock

■ *The repair shop:*
 Props—plastic tools (screwdriver, hammer, etc.), cleaning rags, items to repair (such as an old radio, toy cars, etc.), mechanic or repair person uniform

■ *The bank:*
 Props: old checkbook covers, pieces of paper to be used as checks, stamp and date stamp, calculator, play money (bills and coins)

---

vice as it relates to the tasks and chores the family performs. Needs and wants explored from the perspective of the family help children to understand society's most important social unit. Figure 10–1 describes possible economics themes to explore within the setting of the family.

Many good literature resources can also be used to foster understanding at a child-appropriate level. For example, *The Forgotten Toys* (Stevenson, 1995), is a story about a toy bear and a doll that find themselves thrown into the garbage after the holidays. To the surprise of the toys, they are discarded simply because the children who owned them received new toys. This story is an excellent opportunity for children to explore the concept of needs and wants. It will enable children to reflect upon the concept of *scarcity*—a very difficult idea, but central to the study of economics. *Bread is for Eating* (Gershator & Gershator, 1995) is another story that presents economic concepts such as production and distribu-

tion. Through its colorful illustrations and use of Spanish phrases throughout the text, the story teaches children about the process of making bread. Appreciation for the significance of bread as a symbol of food and of the work of many is emphasized in the story. The lyrics of the song included at the end of the story assist children in developing awareness of the importance of bread as a staple food for people.

Saving money and goods is another important theme to explore. This can easily be connected to the experiences used in *needs and wants*. For example, a classroom bank center can provide opportunities to role-play transactions. Children can save money "earned" while working at learning centers, such as a restaurant or a travel agency center. The importance of savings can also become a group experience. Primary-age children could open a "class savings account." Money can be saved for field trips or for other special events. A class ice cream party

FIGURE 10–1 Exploring Economics through the Context of the Family

Key Concept: Consumption
Needs and wants: Learning about things we need and things we would like to have:
- Things we all need (shelter, food, affection, and protection).
- Our house: We all need a home!
  Houses here and there.
  My favorite foods; favorite foods my family cooks.
  A visit to the grocery store.
  My family cares about me.
  We all take care of each other.
  I'm safe at home.
  People in the community who help to keep me safe (integrates the concept of occupations).

Key Concept: Production
Occupations: Exploring the roles of family members (parents; children; extended family); learning about jobs:
  Chores I do at home.
  We take care of our home. Chores my family does at home.
  I am proud of my parents' jobs.
  Learning about what my parents do at work.
  Family members work in the community.
  It's important to work.
  I'm proud I can work.

became the savings goal of a group of kindergartners we know. In another case, a group of third graders saved money that later was used to buy a television set for a senior citizen center.

Children can be "paid" for cleaning up, or other chores. This play money can later be used to purchase a limited number of items from a school "store" that has been set up for that purpose. Pencils, toys, children's costume jewelry, or play groceries could be available in the store. Students could role-play a 20-minute marketing activity on a weekly basis. Children should then be led in a discussion of the purchases they made, whether they fell into the category of a need or a want, and whether or not they wished to re-sell the items to another class member for profit or at a loss.

Exploring where and how goods are produced is another theme to develop with young children. This

---

Bringing Ideas into Practice 10–1   *Analysis of* Bread is for Eating

Carefully selected literature provides appropriate ways to explore abstract concepts such as those found in the field of economics. Taking time to analyze the concepts embedded in a story allows teachers to maximize the use of a selection. An analysis like the one presented here will reveal opportunities to bring challenging issues and concepts to a level children can understand. It will also prove that there are many ways and reasons for sharing a story.

- *Production:*
  Farming: "Think of the farmer who tills the soil, hoping the rains will come on time."*

Jobs: "Think of the worker, who loads the grain and takes it to town." "Think of the miller . . .", ". . . the cook", ". . . the baker . . ."
- *Distribution:* "Think of the storekeeper . . ."
- *Consumption and scarcity:* "Think of the people around the world dreaming of bread"; ". . . the families working all day to put bread on the table."
- *Integration of subject areas:* science; math; language arts; music.

Sources: Gershator, D., & Gershator, P. (1995). *Bread is for eating.* New York: Holt.

*pages are unnumbered

Bringing Ideas into Practice 10–2
Opportunity Cost

Laney and Schug (1998) suggest teaching children about a theoretical concept of economics, which they call *"opportunity cost."* They explain that the cost of some things cannot always be seen in dollars and cents, but rather in terms of other things that choices might cost, such as time. Teachers can ask students questions such as the ones that follow:

- Sleeping late on Saturday morning.
- Being late to school.
- Buying a fast food meal.
- Owning a puppy.
- Not wearing your eyeglasses to school.
- Fighting on the playground.
- Staying up late to watch television.
- Reading a book.
- Going to a movie.

Source: Laney, J. D. & Schug, M. C. (1998). Teach kids economics and they will learn. *Social Studies and the Young Learner 11*, 13–17.

---

is a theme that easily lends itself to learning about jobs and employment, another key economic concept. Selection of topics to explore should be based on those available in the community. A field trip to the town would help launch the theme. Exploring the variety of jobs should lead children to appreciate all kinds of occupations, from the humblest to the highest-paying ones. Emphasizing appreciation for the diverse jobs parents and family members hold is essential. Teachers need to ensure that opportunities exist for children to learn that work is a dignifying experience.

The sample activities in this chapter are intended to make the teaching of economics more approachable to the early childhood educators. We hope that they will give you ideas for additional experiences that you can provide for your young students. It is important to remember that whatever you introduce in the classroom must be developmentally appropriate and within the experiential frame of reference of the children you teach. Teachers also need to convey ideas in the most concrete and child-appropriate way. Age- and child-appropriate activities are developed when teachers have sound knowledge about the environment in which children live and about their prior experiences. An example of this is the very special guest a teacher had for her three-year-old class members (see photo). The group, in a suburb in South Florida, was learning about animals from the farm. Aware that one child had a pet pot-bellied pig, the teacher did not hesitate to invite "Salami" to visit the classroom.

Bringing Ideas into Practice 10–3   *Creating A Restaurant Center*

Learning centers are an ideal instructional strategy for young children. A *restaurant center* is among the many centers with an economic theme that can be included in the classroom. A pre-first grade teacher, Kathleen Richards, created such a center, which provided her students with many opportunities to engage in all five basic economics concepts. With the help of her class, the restaurant was opened using a table and two chairs for "the customers." A simple menu designed by the children included items like pizza, eggs, juices, and sandwiches. Prices were determined by the children during one of their meetings. "Employees" took turns working in the restaurant. Plastic manipulatives representing food items (pizza, hot dogs, and eggs) and laminated cutouts of meals (found by the children in magazines) were used to serve the customers. The restaurant was so successful that is was necessary for a "bank" to be added. Money transactions performed by "bank tellers" included credit card charges, cashing of checks, and savings deposits. A year later, children and visiting adults (including one of the authors) were still enjoying the service at the restaurant. This successful experience led Ms. Richards to keep the classroom restaurant as a permanent learning center.

"Salami" visits three-year-olds outside their classroom.

The entire preschool turned out to meet the visitor. For those who had never seen a real pig, it was an unforgettable experience.

Successful planning will only be possible if the developmental and cognitive needs of children are kept in mind. As activities relate to the world of the children, understanding about the meaning of economics will be fostered.

■■ Becoming Environmentally
■■ Responsible Citizens

Humanity's disregard for the surroundings and the rapid rate of unrestricted technological growth has produced an unprecedented global environmental emergency (Maxim, 1991, p. 433). The uncontrolled air, sewage, and chemical pollution; hazardous nuclear disposal; the destruction of the rain forests; and use of toxic pesticides are among the many man-made disasters that threaten the existence of our planet.

Most of the environmental problems have been caused by the progress of mankind. It is the price the human race has paid for a more comfortable, technologically advanced existence. Unfortunately, progress cannot continue on a planet devoid of essential resources like clean air, potable water, and essential food. This realization has brought the envi-

ronmental crisis to the forefront of the global agenda.

Helping to improve and preserve the environment is a priority of the entire human race. As communities grow and industries expand, the demands for resources are continuously increasing. With many of the Earth's natural resources destroyed or improperly used, the need for all citizens to join in improving their protection is fundamental. One of the ways to accomplish that is through environmental education, beginning at an early age. The purpose of environmental education is to help citizens become conscious of the shared responsibility they have for proper usage and preservation of resources. This is an important cause that must be nurtured early in life.

Environmental Awareness and Global Education

Environmental education is often associated with globalism, because environmental issues and concerns transcend local and national borders (Maxim, 1991, p. 433). Today, as the world becomes one big neighborhood, we understand the responsibility of all people to protect the Earth's environment. Becoming effective citizens in a global society means acquiring a sense of responsibility, not only for the local and the national environment, but also for the global environment. It is crucial for the citizens of our planet to undertake the responsibility for the preservation of resources of all. According to Kniep (1986), awareness of the global environmental responsibility is important because it makes people sensitive to their actions and decisions related to the environment.

> Of all human species that make up life on the planet, human beings, because of our capacity to manage and exploit, maintain and destroy, have become the most critical actors in the ecological system. Global education [must] . . . help students to feel part of the living world, to respect it and their unique place in it, and *to undertake actions only after consideration of their actions on the whole ecological system.*
>
> (Kniep, p. 440, emphasis added)

Many critical concerns about the environment have resulted in a major push to include environmental education in the K through 12 curriculum. The NCSS has moved to make environmental education part of the social studies curriculum and has stated that the approach must be interdisciplinary, meaning that all areas of the curriculum must be combined to teach the students environmental awareness (Maxim, 1991, p. 433).

Key Concepts about Environmental Awareness

Environmental education is aimed at: 1) developing an awareness about the importance of our environment; 2) fostering an understanding about the effects of human actions upon the environment; and, 3) promoting attitudes and actions to preserve the environment.

Recognizing that young children are eager to explore their world, some teachers may wish to focus their efforts on making the children aware of the elements that place the environment in danger. Others may wish to foster a sense of duty for protection of the natural resources. Development of classroom experiences based on the latter approach can be centered on the following key concepts:

- keeping our environment clean
- protecting the homes of animals in our community
- recycling
- saving our trees and plants
- protecting Earth's resources

Concept Box 10–2   Suggested References for Teachers

- Miles, B. (1991). *Save the earth: An action handbook for kids.* New York: Knopf.
- Temple, L. (1993). *Dear World: How children around the world feel about the environment.* New York: Random House.

Becoming aware of the needs of the environment requires individuals to develop proactive attitudes. Environmentally aware children will help to preserve the cleanliness of their surroundings and appreciate the natural resources in their community.

Good environmental attitudes also depend upon effective skills of observation, classification, analysis, and evaluation. Appropriate environmental skills and attitudes are fostered through classroom experiences that build these skills.

■■ Guidelines for ■■ Environmental Education

The North American Association for Environmental Education (NAAEE) developed a set of curriculum guidelines in order to promote environmental knowledge. The guidelines for excellence for grades K through four are intended to foster environmental awareness in young children. According to NAAEE, the purpose of the guidelines is:

> . . . to develop a world population that is aware of, and concerned about, the environment and its associated problems, and which has the knowledge, skills, attitudes, motivations, and commitment to work individually and collectively toward solutions of current problems and the prevention of new ones.
>
> (NAAEE, 1997, p. 4).

The guidelines for excellence (1997) present four essential themes that focus on the development of both personal skills and knowledge about the environment. The four themes appear in Figure 10–2. They provide a wide variety of appropriate directions for classroom activities.

Developing Experiences with the Environment

Although there are many good literary resources to help children develop knowledge about the environment (see p. 268), environmental knowledge is best developed through field projects based on concepts familiar to children. The school, the

FIGURE 10–2 Four Key Themes of Environmental Education (Grades K–4)

■ *Theme #1—Knowledge of environmental processes and systems:* An important building block in the foundation of environmental literacy is an understanding of the processes and systems that comprise the environment. Environmental literacy depends on an understanding of the Earth as a physical system, the living environment (including diversity, interdependence of organisms, flow of matter and energy through living systems), and humans and their societies. The guidelines under this theme begin with overarching ideas that are common to the search for knowledge about the natural and human systems.

■ *Theme #2—Inquiry skills:* Developing environmental literacy depends on learners' willingness and ability to ask questions about the work around them, to speculate and hypothesize, to seek information, and to develop answers to their questions. Environmental literacy requires a familiarity with some basic modes of inquiry, a mastery of fundamental skills for gathering and organizing information, and an ability to interpret and synthesize information and develop explanations. Learners rely on these abilities to understand the environment and to investigate environmental problems and issues using a variety of techniques.

■ *Theme #3—Skills for decision making on an action:* Environmentally literate people are able to draw conclusions, develop solutions, make decisions, and participate in resolving issues. (Learners are able to develop generalizations based on the information they have collected, processed, and analyzed.) They are able to consider the implications of alternative courses of action and arrive at their own conclusions about what, if anything, should be done. Ultimately, environmental literacy requires an understanding of the ideals, principles, and practices of citizenship in our democratic republic, as well as competence in skills necessary for citizen action.

■ *Theme #4—Personal responsibility:* Environmentally literate citizens are motivated and empowered to act on their own conclusions about what should be done to ensure environmental quality. As learners develop and apply concept-based learning and skills for inquiry, analysis, and action, they cultivate an understanding that what they do as individuals and in groups can make a difference.

community, our homes, and the classroom are all places where meaningful environmental experiences occur. Additional topics like air, water, food, animals, land, and the planets also lend themselves to experiences that address environmental concerns. These same topics also offer opportunities to link ecological issues within the context of a global neighborhood. Early childhood educators should consider incorporating the following themes and activities in their curricula:

Learning about recycling: Placing recycling containers in the classroom. Identifying and classifying items for recycling (glass, paper, metal, and plastic).

■ *Recognizing the recycling symbol:* Displaying it in the classroom. Using a magnifying glass to examine containers to see if they have the symbol.

■ *Cleaning campaign:* "Leaving things cleaner than you found them" can be used as a motto for the class. Engaging children in maintaining a clean classroom should be a year-round experience. A "clean environment" group with a rotating membership can be created throughout the year.

Conservation of resources: Development of attitudes that promote the conservation of resources includes effective use of home and classroom materials such as water and paper. Themes such as the rain forests will foster appreciation for the resources they provide to people. Exploring the resources used to produce paper will help children understand the

Bringing Ideas into Practice 10–4
Service Projects

- Clean up a vacant lot.
- Plant flowers or vegetables.
- Protect animal habitats (vacant lots, trees [bird nests], ponds [frogs, etc]).
- Pull weeds around the school and home.
- Adopt and maintain a section of the school lawn/yard.
- Join a wildlife organization such as "Save the Manatee," as a group.
- Set out food and water for birds during migration periods.
- Care for neighbor's pet while they are on vacation.
- Take a stand against animal abuse (write a letter to local paper or Humane Society).
- Celebrate Arbor Day (plant a tree).

Source: Lewis, B. A. (1995). *The kids' guide to service projects.* Minneapolis: Free Spirit Publishing.

■■ Let's Talk About . . . 10–2
Saving Our Global Environment

Global citizenship establishes the need to work together to preserve our vanishing environment. As you read the following quote from Chief Seattle (1855), consider how it defines our responsibility to protect the Earth:

> Humankind has not woven the web of life. We are but one thread within it. Whatever we do to the web, we do to ourselves. All things are bound together. All things connect. Whatever befalls the earth befalls also the children of the earth.

1. How did Chief Seattle perceive our responsibility towards the environment?

2. How would you convey this message to children?

3. What message would you send to the citizens of out global society?

need to avoid paper waste. A weekly chart depicting ways to conserve paper, energy, and water at home will engage children and their families in environmental conservation experiences.

Protecting animal habitats: Identifying animals that live in the community. Field visits to locate their habitats. Developing a campaign to preserve animal habitats. Investigating endangered animals. Learning about the endangered animals in the community. Discussing beneficial insects. Planting flowers to attract beneficial species (e.g., ladybugs, butterflies—creating a "butterfly garden").

Field trips: Taking children to examine the neighborhood will develop an awareness of ecological problems. Action plans can be devised to correct problems. Visits to recycling plants will provide information regarding what happens to discarded items.

Environmental vocabulary: Learning key terms such as *pollution, litter, pollutants, habitat, recyclable,* and others will help children to convey ideas and suggestions related to the environment.

Fostering Positive Environmental Attitudes

Action-oriented activities are indispensable for the development of positive attitudes and a sense of responsibility toward the environment. Using current issues about the environment is an effective way to engage children in such activities. For example, keeping a bulletin board with clippings from the local newspaper and from magazines about ecological issues provides opportunities for discussion and action-oriented projects. Having a camera handy for children to capture examples of ideal and damaged environments is another way to foster environmental responsibility. This approach worked well with a group of urban third graders, who used disposable

Bringing Ideas into Practice 10–5   *Project Earth Day*

At the Native Village of Eyak in Cordova, Alaska, Earth Day became a very special event. It was an opportunity to foster awareness about environmental issues. Under the leadership of Kate Williams, the environmental program coordinator, preschool and elementary children participated in the groceries project. According to Williams, developing awareness about the importance of recycling was a need of the community. Recycling in this community—reachable only by boat or airplane—poses a real challenge. As Williams started the project, she soon found that obtaining paper gro-

Children's messages decorate recycled grocery bags.

cery bags was not an easy task. The local grocers used only plastic bags. With the help of the organizer of the project, Mark Ahlness, she contacted Colleen Shine from the American Forest and Paper Association. Six hundred paper bags, along with educational materials, were sent at no cost to the village.

Having distributed the bags at the preschool and elementary school, Williams thought about the best way to promote environmental awareness further. Knowing the Post Office was the major recycler in town, she then contacted the local postmaster, who agreed to display a few "favorite" bags from each grade for a month. The display helped to increase awareness about recycling; moreover, it thrilled the children.

For Williams, the project proved to be a very rewarding experience. The manager of one local grocery store even commented that use of paper bags was the right thing to do and that he would consider offering them as an option. Williams plans to continue the project. In her opinion, "the simple act of offering people a choice: 'paper or plastic', can make a difference—especially when those paper bags are decorated by children concerned for the future of their environment."

We thank Kate Williams for sharing her successful experience at the Native Village of Eyak.

cameras to capture some local cases of environmental "ouches" while they were on classroom field trips.

Promoting public awareness is another strategy children will enjoy. An example of this is the Earth Day Groceries Project. This global campaign engages children from the United States and from several countries around the world in activities to promote environmental awareness. The project, initiated by Mark Ahlness, a third grade teacher from Seattle, Washington, uses the Internet to engage thousands of children in classrooms throughout the country and in several places around the world. The

goal is to make people aware of the importance of recycling to protect our environment. To participate, children need to contact their local grocers to get paper grocery bags. At school, children decorate bags with messages encouraging people to protect and care for the environment. Decorated bags are returned to the grocery stores to observe Earth Day, April 22 (see photos in box above). These decorated bags are used to bag groceries on Earth Day, sending messages to households throughout the community. A description of one of the grocery bag projects appears in "Bringing Ideas into Practice 10–5."

Using Children's Literature to Promote Environmental Awareness

There are many good literary resources to help children develop knowledge about the environment. Some of the titles available are listed here, with the main concept they emphasize indicated in parentheses.

Albert, R. (1996). *Alejandro's gift*. New York: Chronicle Books.

Berenstain, S., & Berenstain, J. (1996). *The Berenstain bear scouts and the coughing catfish*. New York: Scholastic.

Cannon, J. (1997). *Verdi*. San Diego, CA: Harcourt Brace Jovanovich. (environmental awareness)

Grindley, S. (1996). *Peter's place*. (contamination)

Johnson, P. (1995). *Farmer's market*. New York: Orchard.

Kurusa. (1996). *La calle es libre*. [The street is free]. Caracas, Venezuela: Ediciones Ekare. (environmental awareness)

Livingston, M. L. (1986). *Earth songs*. (environmental awareness)

Ryan-DiSalvo, D. (1994). *City green*. New York: Morrow.

Schimmel, S. (1997). *Children of the Earth . . . Remember*. ME: NorthWord Press.

Tamar, E. (1996). *The garden of happiness*. San Diego: Harcourt Brace. (cleaning the environment)

■■ Teaching about Special ■■ Social Issues

Daily, the media reveals the variety of social issues and current events affecting society. As consumers of the media, young children are being exposed to these realities. Although many of these issues are beyond the children's level of understanding, they arouse curiosity, as well as an array of emotions. Educators of young children cannot afford to ignore these realities. Since children are affected by these social issues, the principle of developmentally and culturally appropriate practices underlines the importance of the curriculum to be valid and pertinent. It also establishes the need to discuss these issues in the classroom as questions arise or issues surface. Suggestions about when and how to incorporate these special issues are discussed in this section.

Current Events

Current events are an important part of the social studies curriculum. They are also a part of children's lives. Sound curricular practices indicate the importance of including these events in the classroom. There are reasons that support the inclusion of current social events: Essentially, children benefit when the curriculum fosters the development of a sense about what happens in the community and in other places. Awareness of what happens provides a sense about reality. It also strengthens individual identification with society.

A well-informed citizen is characterized by having knowledge about the events taking place in his or her society. In early childhood classrooms, discussion of current, important events should routinely be part of the classroom activities. In fact, the daily sharing of news during circle or planning time is an example of time dedicated to getting an update on those things that are considered important to children. When an important event happens, the television news replays it so often that children know about it, and they often want to ask questions about it. Although it may not be pleasant to speak of death or divorce, these are facts of life that frequently have an impact on the lives of children.

Many teachers find it difficult to engage children in discussion about current events in the community and beyond. Some still believe it is too early for children to learn about some of life's realities. Others contend that young children are unable to process and understand these experiences. While it is true that some topics may be too difficult to be understood by a young child, it is important to consider the risk of not discussing them in the classroom. Avoiding such topics has results similar to what happens when educators believe children are unaware of color and ethnic differences.

Misconceptions and even biased interpretations may emerge from situations children see or learn about from the news, from their friends, and from adult's comments. *What* to discuss and *when* is a decision teachers need to make about these issues. In some cases, the events will be of interest to young children and, thus, it would be a sound decision to share them in the classroom. This would be the case with momentous occasions related to scientific or social or political events, such as the launching of a space shuttle, the discovery of new dinosaur fossils, the dedication of an important building, or the local elections.

Any other issues in which children express an interest should also be considered. Listening attentively to what children comment on with peers, after reading a story or during sharing time, will provide indications of issues requiring clarification. It is a developmentally appropriate practice to offer children opportunities to examine and discuss issues in which they show an interest or about which misguided comments have been made. These "teachable opportunities" are windows for learning that should not be disregarded.

Safety Issues

Children often express their fears concerning their personal safety. Early childhood curricula usually include several issues that can be used to ensure that children believe they are being cared for by their parents and by the school. Several organiza-

---

> **Concept Box 10–4   Current Events and Topics of Interest to Young Children**
>
> ■ Heroic feats
> ■ Events happening in nature (i.e., local weather, news about animals and plants, natural disasters)
> ■ Scientific discoveries and happenings (i.e., launch of a space vehicle, discovery of fossils and ancient cities)
> ■ Sport events (i.e., games, news about sport teams, players)
> ■ News about constructions in the community
> ■ News about the arts (i.e., information about a children's musical, an exhibit)
> ■ News related to their own neighborhood and community

---

tions can and will provide information, materials, and demonstrations that will *reassure* children, as well as educate them.

Crime Watch, a community-oriented crime deterrent project, will provide a demonstration in the schools using puppets to teach safety lessons. These free shows are provided at childcare centers, preschools, and elementary schools, or any other place where there are young children, such as apartment complexes, churches, synagogues, and so on. The puppet shows included are "Stranger Danger," "Traffic Safety," "Stop, Drop, and Roll" (fire safety), and "Shoplifting," to name a few. A police officer from the community usually speaks to the children before and after each show to reinforce the lessons. Almost every community, urban and rural, has this valuable resource available. Using imitations of these puppet shows, children can stage their own shows for each other.

Another valuable resource for safety information and education is the local fire department. Firemen will provide demonstrations and materials that will be of interest to children.

Pedagogically, preparing oneself to discuss topics and issues is an essential educational practice.

> **Concept Box 10–3   Web Site about Safety**
>
> There are Web sites that address the topic of fire safety that appeal directly to children. One such site is sponsored by Bic, the writing pen manufacturers. A Dalmatian puppy named Hero teaches children to "Play safe! Be safe!" He spreads the word about smoke alarms and how they can help to save lives in the case of fire. The address for this very interesting Web site is: http://kplane@netcom.com

---

■■ Let's Talk About . . . 10-3

Staying Well Informed about Current Events

Helping children to be aware of things happening in society requires educators to be knowledgeable about current events. There are several ways to keep oneself well informed. Reading newspapers and informational periodicals, watching the news, and talking to people are some of the ways to know "what's taking place." Take time to think about how often you use any informational source to know about what is happening in your community and in the world. To help you learn how current you are about daily events, we invite you to answer the five questions listed here.

1. Do you receive or buy the local newspaper?
2. Do you read the newspaper? How often?
3. Do you buy and read news magazines (i.e., *Time, Newsweek, The Washington Post*)
4. Do you watch or listen to the news report on a daily basis?
5. Do you take time to discuss about events and news with others?

Teachers should take time to inform themselves about any topic, issue, or concept presented to children. There are several ways to prepare oneself: Conversations with other colleagues can help to clarify the relevance of an issue and to learn about ways to approach these issues with children. Talking to others in the community and to family members offers additional perspectives on an issue. Reading the local newspapers and watching the news can help you to get important details, especially those children might have heard or seen. Some current events and issues are easier to talk about. Others are not, especially when they entail critical social issues. However, when one is aware of what is happening, deciding how to approach and share simple and difficult events will be easier.

Sources of Information about Current Events

Events and issues of current interest are reflected through the media. Use of newspapers, magazines, and other sources of printed media should become a regular classroom activity. Fostering in children a sense of the informational purpose of media is also important. Learning about the purpose and types of media, as well as how to use printed media, helps to build skills in communication and the use of information.

A bulletin board is a simple and effective strategy for keeping children informed about events of interest. The bulletin board should be located in a conspicuous place. This will ensure that children will have a chance to view and discuss what is posted. Pictures and clippings from newspapers and magazines about issues and special events should be included. These should be changed periodically to keep the class abreast of what is happening.

Some teachers prefer to designate a time and a day in the schedule to focus on current events. With preschool children, however, events should be brought in as they arise and as the children show an interest. At the primary level, selecting a specific day to review the most important events is a suggested strategy. Individual children can share the news they consider important and give reasons for their selection. Cooperative groups can also be formed to review newspapers and to select the items they believe to be relevant.

Current Social Issues: Homelessness, AIDS, Violence

The daily news reflects the many challenging issues that society faces. These are special issues and problems, requiring answers that are still being sought. Issues such as the incident of homelessness, the efforts to prevent AIDS, the presence of violence and crime in communities across the country, and the fight against drug and alcohol abuse are among the most pressing problems in our society. Young children are not exempt from their impact.

In many classrooms, children express their reactions to these issues. Through their comments and during their play activities, teachers get a sense of how these issues touch the children's lives. In a recent visit to a local early childhood school, the authors were told that many of the children need to take a nap when they get to school because they have been kept awake all night "by fights or bullets." Such conditions are more common than many of us realize, especially in urban areas.

The need to prepare children effectively to deal with society establishes why these special issues require early childhood educators to consider appropriate ways to incorporate them into the curriculum. Keeping oneself aware of how these special issues impact children's lives and their community will provide direction as to *when* and *to what extent* they need to be clarified in the classroom. Listening to what children comment upon will lead teachers to decide when it is important to discuss these special issues.

On the other hand, some special issues are more overt to children. Discussion about homeless families and about violence provides ideal opportunities to continue building socially valid attitudes and behaviors.

Homelessness, a characteristic of today's economic diversity, is an issue that requires attention. Time should be given for children to express their views and ideas and to clarify what it means to be "homeless." During the same time period when space travel is routine and technological wonders are commonplace, homelessness among children has risen to staggering proportions. According to Mary Ann Gleason, director of National Council on Homelessness, a seven-year-old boy named Jacob is so disturbed by the fact that there are children who have no home that he buys two sets of school supplies, one for himself and one so that a homeless child can experience opening a new box of crayons. Information about this project is available on the Internet (http://nch.ari. net/jacob.html).

Violence is another topic must be discussed in the classroom. The daily news makes violent behaviors a constant presence in our lives. Many school children live in homes where violent behavior is a

---

Bringing Ideas into Practice 10–6
Discussions about Violence

During "circle time," ask the children to talk freely about violent events, incidents, or objects that are familiar to them. A few topics should be designated "off-limits," because of their extremely violent nature and inappropriate treatment in the media. Ask the children to sit very still and think of a response to a violent issue. After a wait period (silently count to 50), allow any child to speak on the topic, expressing his or her fears, problems, and proposed solutions. Summarize the children's responses on the board.

---

fact of life. Discussing violence in the classroom provides opportunities to help children develop peaceful ways to address conflicts.

"Violence touches the life of every child in the country, some more than others" (NAEYC Position Statement, 1999, p. 2). Early childhood educators play an important role in the healthy development of children's emotional lives. Modeling positive conflict-resolution strategies may prevent later violent behaviors. "Although high-quality early childhood programs are not an inoculation against the destructive effects of violence, positive early childhood experiences and warm, nurturing relationships with teachers are known to be critical contributors to children's ability to cope with stress and trauma" (NAEYC Position Paper, 1999, p. 1). This statement concludes that early childhood educators ". . . must address issues of violence in children's lives through partnerships with parents and other professionals; early childhood programs and curriculum; and professional preparation, development and support" (p. 6).

Using Literature about Special Issues

Literature provides a child-appropriate venue to discuss special social issues. A visit to the local library will help to identify many other valuable lit-

---

Concept Box 10–5   Violence in the United States

- An estimated 2.7 million children were reported to child protection agencies in 1991 as victims of neglect, physical abuse, sexual abuse, or emotional maltreatment; nationwide the number of children reported abused or neglected has tripled since 1980 (Children's Defense Fund, 1992).

- Gun-related violence takes the life an American child at least every three hours and the lives of at least 25 children—the equivalent of a whole classroom—every three days. In 1990 alone, guns were used to kill 222 children under the age of 10 and 6,795 young people under the age of 25. Another 30 children are injured every day by guns (Edelman, 1993). Every day, 100,000 children carry guns to school.

- In one Chicago public housing project all of the children had witnessed a shooting by the age of five (Dodd, 1993). A child growing up in Chicago is 15 times as likely to be murdered as

a child growing up in Northern Ireland (Garbarino, 1992).

- By the age of 18 the average child will have seen 26,000 killings on television (Tuchscherer, 1988). *TV Guide* reports that a violent incident is shown on television, on the average, every six minutes (Edelman, 1993). The number of violent acts depicted on television has tripled since deregulation of the industry.

- In a national survey, 91 percent of the responding teachers reported increased violence among children in their classrooms as a result of cross-media marketing of violent cartoons, toys, videos, and other licensed products (Carlsson-Paige & Levin, 1991).

- In a recent survey of New Orleans fifth graders, more than half reported they had been victims of some type of violence; 70 percent had witnessed weapons being used (Zero to Three, 1992).

Source: http://www.naeyc.org National Association for the Education of Young Children. (1999). *Violence in the lives of children*. Washington, DC: Author.

---

erary resources. Titles such as *Fly away home* (Bunting, 1991), a story about a father and child who live in an airport, brings the issue of homelessness to a level appropriate for children to understand. Awareness of issues related to homelessness such as economic pressures and social class are explored by such titles as *The black snowman* (Mendez, 1989), *Bajo la luna de limón* [*Under the lemon moon*] (Fine, 1999), *Gettin' through Thursday* (Cooper, 1998), and *A chair for my mother* (Williams, 1982). The issue of violence is addressed in a child-appropriate manner by titles such as *The quarreling book* (Zolotow, 1975), *The hating book* (Zolotow,

1963), *Smoky night* (Bunting, 1999), and *Being bullied* (Petty & Firmin, 1991). These titles help children explore and learn about the topic of conflict.

Peace is also another special issue related to the issue of violence and a topic to be discussed in the classroom. *Sadako and the thousand paper cranes* (Coerr, 1993) provides opportunities for children to discuss what it means to live in a world at peace. Shea's *The whispering cloth: A refugee's story* (1995) helps children to learn about the life of those forced to leave their homelands.

Other suggested titles for children on economics and other current issues are listed on p. 266.

Recommended Children's Books

See also suggested titles about the environment on pp. 259 and 263.

Anderson, J. (1995). *The forgotten toys*. London, UK: Scholastic.

Bunting, E. (1991). *Fly away home*. New York: Harper & Row.

Bunting, E. (1999). *Smoky night*. New York: Harper & Row.

Brown, M. (1990). *Arthur's pet business*. New York: Little Brown.

Coerr, E. (1993). *Sadako and the thousand paper cranes.** New York: Putnam.

Cooper, M. (1998). *Gettin' through Thursday*. New York: Lee & Low.

Cosgrove, S. (1978). *The muffin muncher*. Los Angeles: Price Stern Sloan.

Day, A. (1989). *Carl goes shopping*. [boardbook] New York: Farrar, Strauss & Giroux.

de Paola, T. (1973). *Charlie needs a cloak*. New York: Simon & Schuster.

Dorros, A. (1992). *This is my house*. New York: Puffin.

Fine, E. (1999). *Bajo la luna de limón*. [*Under the lemon moon.*] New York: Lee & Low.

Fox, M. (1988). *Koala Lou*. San Diego, CA: Harcourt Brace.

Gershator, D., & Gershator, P. (1995). *Bread is for eating*. New York: Holt.

Grifalconi, A. (1986). *The village of round and square houses.** New York: Little Brown.

Grossman, P. (1994). *Saturday market.** New York: Lee & Lothrop.

Hall, D. (1997). *The milkman's boy*. New York: Walker & Co.

Hoberman, M. A. (1982). *A house is a house for me*. New York: Viking.

Horse, H. (1997). *A friend for little bear*. London, UK: Walker Books.

Hutchins, P. (1986). *The doorbell rang*. New York: Mulberry Books.

Joffe, L. (1985). *If you give a mouse a cookie*. New York: Harper Collins.

Johnson, B. (1997). *Farmer's market*. New York: Orchard.

Lewis, B. A. (1995). *The kid's guide to service projects*. Minneapolis: Free Spirit Publishing.

Life, K. (1996). *Finding a job for Daddy*. Morton Grove, IL: Whitman.

Lisa-Nikola, W. (1997). *Till year's good end: A calendar of medieval labors*. New York: Atheneum.

Loomis, C. (1993). *At the mall*. New York: Scholastic.

McCully, E. (1993). *The bobbin girl*. New York: Dial.

McDonald, M. (1996). *My house has stars.** New York: Orchard.

McPhail, D. (1990). *Pig Pig gets a job*. New York: Dutton.

Mendez, P. (1989). *The black snowman*. New York: Scholastic.

Merrill, J. (1972). *The toothpaste millionaire*. New York: Houghton Mifflin.

Miranda, A. (1997). *To market, to market*. San Diego, CA: Harcourt Brace.

Mitchell, M. K. (1993). *Uncle Jed's barbershop.** New York: Simon & Schuster.

Morris, A. (1992). *Loving.** New York: Lothrop.

Morris, A. (1995). *Houses and homes*. New York: Mulberry.

Petty, K., & Firmin, C. (1991). *Being bullied*. New York: Aladdin.

Rey, M., & Shalleck, A. (1988). *Curious George and the pizza*. New York: Houghton Mifflin.

Robinson, B. L. (1997). *A street called home*. San Diego, CA: Harcourt Brace.

Shea, P. D. (1995). *The whispering cloth: A refugee's story*. Honesdale, PA: Boyds Mills.

Viorst, J. (1978). *Alexander who used to be rich last Sunday*. New York: Aladdin.

Williams, V. (1982). *A chair for my mother*. New York: Greenwillow.

Williams, V. B. (1983). *Something special for me*. New York: Greenwillow.

Zolotow, C. (1963). *The hating book*. New York: Harper & Row.

Zolotow, C. (1975). *The quarreling book*. New York: Harper & Row.

*Fosters global connections.

ACTIVITIES

Keeping Track of What You Learn: Your Personal Activity Log

A. Reflections

1. Describe your position in reference to teaching children about the special social issues mentioned in this chapter. Take into consideration the implications of the philosophy about developmentally and culturally appropriate practices.

2. What issues would you say are appropriate to discuss with young children?

3. Besides the issues mentioned in this chapter, what others do you consider important to explore in the classroom? Why?

4. Consider the position of parents and families in your community and describe what their reactions would be to the discussion of special social issues. What strategies would you use to help them understand why these topics need to be addressed in the classroom?

5. Some people believe learning about economics is not relevant for young children. What arguments would you use to emphasize its importance?

B. Collections

1. Develop a concept web about the special social issues faced by the community/ communities where children live. Identify those issues you consider more relevant.

2. Prepare a bank of literary resources about special social issues. Remember to include music and poetry.

3. Create a reference file about economic activities in the community. Identify those sites most suitable for field trips.

4. Water conservation and recycling are among the most pressing environmental issues. Search the Internet to find information and classroom resources on water conservation and recycling.

5. Find the two most important environmental issues in the community where you live. Develop a thematic unit targeted at fostering awareness about these issues.

C. Internet Resources*

There are many resources available on Internet about economics, the environment, and other special social studies topics. Here are a few of those we consider informative.

■ **Earth Day Groceries Project**

> Web site: http://www.halcyon.com/ arborhts/earthday.hml

This is the Web site about the paper bag groceries project. You will find information about how to get involved with this activity. It also includes reports from the schools that have participated. A world map describes the geographical locations where the project has been developed.

■ **Project WET**

Web site: http://www.montana.edu:80/wwwwet/

This site offers information about water conservation. Projects developed throughout the country are described. Information about classroom resources is also offered.

■ **United Nations Agencies**

Of interest to all teachers is the information provided by the agencies from the United Nations. Through their Web sites, valuable data and ideas can be gathered. Some of those agencies considered relevant to early education are listed here.

United Nations Children's Fund (UNICEF)

> Web site: http://www.unicef.org

Information about activities and programs for children worldwide is found here. Activities for the classroom as well as lists of resources are offered.

ACTIVITIES (continued)

United Nations Environment Program (UNEP)

Web site: http://www.unep.org

This Web site provides reference information about global projects and issues related to the protection of the environment.

■ **Department of Public Information: UN CyberSchoolBus**

Web site: http://un.org/pubs/cyberschoolbus

An informative and interactive Web site, it offers resources and current information about global events.

*Please note that Internet resources are of a time-sensitive nature and URL sites and addresses may often be modified or deleted.

References

Carlsson-Paige, N., & Levin, D. E. (1991). The subversion of healthy development and play. *Day Care and Early Education, 19*(2), 14–20.

Children's Defense Fund (CDF). (1992). *The state of America's children, 1992.* Washington, DC: Author.

Dodd, C. (1993). Testimony prepared for the Joint Senate-House Hearing on Keeping Every Child Safe: Curbing the Epidemic of Violence. 103rd Congress, 1st session, March 10, 1992.

Edelman, M. W. (1993). Testimony prepared for the Joint Senate-House Hearing on Keeping Every Child Safe: Curbing the Epidemic of Violence. 103rd Congress, 1st session, March 10, 1992.

Garbarino, J. (1992, November). *Helping children cope with the effects of community violence.* Paper presented at the Annual Conference of the National Association for the Education of Young Children, New Orleans, LA.

Kniep, W. (October 1986). Defining global education by its content. *Social Education, 50,* 445–450.

Laney, J. D., & Schug, M. C. (1998). Teach kids economics and they will learn. *Social Studies & the Young Learner, 11,* 13–17.

Maxim, G. M. (1991). *Social studies and the elementary school child* (4th ed.). New York: Merrill.

Meszaros, B., & Engstrom, L. (1998, Nov./Dec.). Voluntary National Content Standards in Economics: 20 enduring concepts and benchmarks for beleaguered teachers. *Social Studies and the Young Learner, 11*(2), pp. 8–10.

North American Association for Environmental Education. (1994). *Environmental education guidelines for excellence: What school-age learners should know and be able to do.* Oregon, IL: Author.

National Council for the Social Studies (1989). *Social studies for early childhood and elementary school children: Preparing for the 21st century.* Washington, DC: Author.

National Association for the Education of Young Children. (1999). *Violence in children's lives.* Position paper. Washington, DC: Author.

Saunders, P., & Gilliard, J. (1996). *A framework for teaching basic economic concepts.* New York: National Council on Economic Education.

Tuchscherer, P. (1988). *TV interactive toys: The new high tech threat to children.* Bend, OR: Pinnaroo Publishing.

Weiner, T. (1991, March 13). Senate unit calls U.S. most violent country on earth. *The Boston Globe,* p. 3.

Zero to Three. (1992). *Can they hope to feel safe again? Impact of community violence on infants, toddlers, their parents and practitioners.* Arlington, VA: National Center for Clinical Infant Programs.

Appendices

APPENDIX I

Social Studies Standards—The Primary Grades

Curricular Strand	*Performance Expectations*	*Child-Appropriate Themes*
I. Culture: Examines culture and cultural diversity in the contexts of our country and of our global community	a. Explore and describe similarities among people in the way they address similar human needs and concerns.	■ Play, toys, and games in different communities and cultures
	b. Give examples of how experiences may be interpreted differently by people from diverse cultural perspectives and frames of reference.	■ School activities in different cultures
	c. Describe ways in which language, stories, folktales, music, and artistic creations serve as expressions of culture and influence behavior of people living in a particular culture.	■ Favorite story characters in different communities and cultures
	d. Compare ways people from different cultures think about and deal with their physical environment and social conditions.	■ How alike and different people are
	e. Give examples and describe the importance of cultural unity and diversity within and across groups.	■ Eating patterns in different cultures
		■ Ways people dress across cultures
		■ Holidays people celebrate
		■ Ornaments, decorations people use across cultures

Curricular Strand	*Performance Expectations*	*Child-Appropriate Themes*
II. Time, continuity, and change	a. Demonstrate an understanding that different people may describe the same event or situation in diverse ways, citing reasons for the differences in views. b. Demonstrate an ability to use correctly the vocabulary associated with time such as past, present, future, and long ago; read and construct simple timelines; identify examples of change; and recognize examples of cause and effect. c. Compare and contrast different stories or accounts about past events, people, places or situations, and identify how they contribute to our understanding of the past. d. Identify and use various sources for reconstructing the past, such as documents, letters, diaries, maps, textbooks, photos, and others. e. Demonstrate an understanding that people in different times and places view the worlds differently. f. Use knowledge of facts and concepts drawn from history, along with elements of historical inquiry, to inform decision-making about and action-taking on public issues.	■ Toys that our parents and grandfathers used and played with ■ Home utensils from long ago ■ Things I wore and did when I was a baby ■ Looking at school and school activities from long ago ■ Communities from long ago
III. People, places, and environments	a. Construct and use mental maps of locales, regions, and the world that demonstrate understanding of relative location, direction, size, and shape. b. Interpret, use, and distinguish various representations of the earth such as maps, globes, and photographs. c. Use appropriate resources, data sources, and geographic tools such as atlases, databases, grid systems, charts, graphs, and maps to generate, manipulate, and interpret information. d. Estimate distances and calculate scale. e. Locate and distinguish among varying landforms and geographic features, such as mountains, plateaus, islands, and oceans.	■ Places where my friends live ■ The neighborhood where I live ■ My friends' neighborhood ■ Planning a trip to my favorite place ■ Houses in other places ■ Plants and animals in our community ■ Animals from other places ■ Where is the sea? ■ Going to the beach ■ Helping to protect our environment

Curricular Strand	Performance Expectations	Child-Appropriate Themes
	f. Describe and speculate about physical system changes, such as seasons, climate and weather, and the water cycle.	
	g. Describe how people create places that reflect ideas, personality, culture, and wants and needs as they design homes, playgrounds, classrooms, and the like.	
	h. Examine the interaction of human beings and their environment, the use of land, building of cities, and ecosystem changes in selected locales and regions.	
	i. Explore ways that the Earth's physical features have changed over time in the local region and beyond and how these changes may be connected to one another.	
	j. Observe and speculate about social and economic effects of environmental changes and crises resulting from phenomena such as floods, storms, and drought.	
	k. Consider existing uses and propose and evaluate alternative uses of resources in home, school, community, the region, and beyond.	
IV. Individual development and identity	a. Describe personal changes over time, such as those related to physical development and personal interests. b. Describe personal connections to place—especially place as associated with immediate surroundings. c. Describe the unique features of one's nuclear and extended families. d. Show how learning and physical development affect behavior. e. Identify and describe ways family, groups, and community influence the individual's daily life and personal choices. f. Explore factors that contribute to one's personal identity such as interests, capabilities, and perceptions.	■ This is me ■ Things I like to do ■ Our favorite games ■ My family ■ Families here and there ■ This is where our families came from ■ Things my friends and I can do

Curricular Strand	*Performance Expectations*	*Child-Appropriate Themes*
	g. Analyze a particular event to identify reasons individuals might respond to it in different ways. h. Work independently and cooperatively to accomplish goals.	
V. Individuals, groups, and institutions	a. Identify roles as learned behavior patterns in group situations such as students, family member, peer play group, or club member. b. Give examples of and explain group and institutional influences such as religious beliefs and government policies and laws. c. Identify examples of institutions and describe the interactions of people with institutions. d. Identify and describe examples of tensions between and among individuals, groups, or institutions, and how belonging to more than one group can cause internal conflicts. e. Identify examples of tension between an individual's beliefs and government policies and laws. f. Give examples of the role of institutions in furthering both continuity and change. g. Show how groups and institutions work to meet individual needs and promote the common good; identify examples of where they fail to do so.	■ Animal families ■ Community helpers ■ Celebrations in our neighborhood ■ Special family celebrations ■ School helpers ■ Our classroom
VI. Power, authority, and governance	a. Examine the rights and responsibilities of the individual in relation to his or her social group, such as family, peer group, and school class. b. Explain the purpose of government. c. Give examples of how government does or does not provide for needs and wants of people, establish order and security, and manage conflict.	■ We all have responsibilities ■ Helping in the classroom ■ We help at home ■ I respect others ■ We follow the classroom rules ■ We establish rules for our classroom

Curricular Strand	*Performance Expectations*	*Child-Appropriate Themes*
	d. Recognize how groups and organizations encourage unity and deal with diversity to maintain order and security.	■ Sharing and helping others ■ Learning about the local government
	e. Distinguish among local, state, and national government and identify representative leaders at these levels such as mayor, governor, and president.	
	f. Identify and describe factors that contribute to cooperation and cause disputes within and among groups and nations.	
	g. Explore the role of technology in communications, transportation, information processing, weapons development, or other areas as it contributes to or helps resolve conflicts.	
	h. Recognize and give examples of the tensions between the wants and needs of individuals and groups, and concepts such as fairness, equity, and justice.	
VII. Production, distribution, and consumption	a. Give examples that show how scarcity and choice govern our economic decisions.	■ Things that come from the farm ■ At the grocery store ■ Going to the store ■ Things we need to live ■ Jobs I do ■ I can do many things! ■ Places where people work in our community ■ Jobs people do ■ Things I like to have ■ Food comes from different places ■ Re-using and recycling in our school
	b. Distinguish between needs and wants.	
	c. Identify examples of private and public goods and services.	
	d. Give examples of the various institutions that make up economic systems such as families, workers, banks, labor unions, government agencies, small businesses, and large corporations.	
	e. Describe how we depend upon workers with specialized jobs and the ways in which they contribute to the production and exchange of goods and services.	
	f. Describe the influence of incentives, values, traditions, and habits on economic decisions.	
	g. Explain and demonstrate the role of money in everyday life.	
	h. Describe the relationship of price to supply and demand.	

Curricular Strand	*Performance Expectations*	*Child-Appropriate Themes*
	i. Use economic concepts such as supply, demand, and price to help explain events in the community and nation. j. Apply knowledge of economic concepts in developing a response to a current local economic issue, such as how to reduce the flow of trash into a rapidly filling landfill.	
VIII. Science, technology, and society	a. Identify and describe examples in which science and technology have changed the lives of people, such as in homemaking, childcare, work, transportation, and communication. b. Identify and describe examples in which science and technology have led to changes in the physical environment, such as the building of dams and levees, offshore oil drilling, medicine from rain forests, and loss of rain forests due to extraction of resources or alternative uses. c. Describe instances in which changes in values, beliefs, and attitudes have resulted from new scientific and technological knowledge, such as conservation of resources and awareness of chemicals harmful to life and the environment. d. Identify examples of laws and policies that govern scientific and technological applications, such as the Endangered Species Act and environmental protection policies. e. Suggest ways to monitor science and technology in order to protect the physical environment, individual rights, and the common good.	■ Helping to save our environment ■ Means of transportation in our community ■ I communicate with friends in other places ■ Important inventors and their inventions ■ Inventions we use at school ■ Helping to save the animals ■ I know how to recycle
XI. Global connections	a. Explore ways that language, art, music, belief systems, and other cultural elements may facilitate global understanding or lead to misunderstanding.	■ We all come from somewhere in the world ■ Food from other places ■ Dance and songs from other places

Curricular Strand	Performance Expectations	Child-Appropriate Themes
	b. Give examples of conflict, cooperation, and interdependence among individuals, groups, and nations. c. Examine the effects of changing technologies on the global community. d. Explore causes, consequences, and possible solutions to persistent, contemporary, and emerging global issues, such as pollution and endangered species. e. Examine the relationships and tensions between personal wants and needs and various global concerns, such as use of imported oil, land use, and environmental protection. f. Investigate concerns, issues, standards, and conflicts related to universal human rights, such as the treatment of children, religious groups, and effects of war.	■ We have friends everywhere ■ The rain forests ■ We all have the same needs ■ Helping people in other places ■ Celebrations around the world ■ Folktales from other places
X. Civic ideals and practice	a. Examine the origins and continuing influence of key ideals of the democratic republican form of government, such as individual human dignity, liberty, justice, equality, and the rule of law. b. Identify and interpret sources and examples of the rights and responsibilities of citizens. c. Locate, access, analyze, organize, and apply information about selected public issues—recognizing and explaining multiple points of view. d. Practice forms of civic discussion and participation consistent with the ideals of citizens in a democratic republic. e. Explain and analyze various forms of citizen action that influence public policy decisions. f. Identify and explain the roles of formal and informal political actors in influencing and shaping public policy and decision making.	■ Important rules in the classroom ■ This is our country ■ Important people in our community ■ Helping to keep our community clean ■ Sharing things in the classroom ■ Ways we can help people

Curricular Strand	*Performance Expectations*	*Child-Appropriate Themes*
	g. Analyze the influence of diverse forms of public opinion on the development of public policy and decision making.	
	h. Analyze the effectiveness of selected public policies and citizen behaviors in realizing the stated ideals of a democratic republican form of government.	
	i. Explain the relationship between policy statements and action plans used to address issues of public concern.	
	j. Examine strategies designed to strengthen the "common good," which consider a range of options for citizen action.	

Source: Adapted from *Expectations for Excellence: Curriculum Standards for Social Studies.* © 1994 National Council for the Social Studies, 3501 Newark Street, NW, Washington, DC 20016. Used with permission.

APPENDIX II

Lesson Plan Formats

Sample Lesson Plan Format #1

Age Level/Grade _____ Date: _____

Theme: _____

Special Events:

_____

_____

_____

_____

Learning Outcomes:

Group Activities:

Learning Centers/Activities

	Materials	Adaptations	Assessment
■ Social studies			
■ Housekeeping			
■ Literacy			
■ Math/Science			
■ The arts			
■ Cooking Experiences			
■ Playground/ Outdoors			

Sample Lesson Plan Format #2

Group _____ Date: from _____ to _____

Theme: _____

Goals:

_____

Social Studies Strand:

_____

Activities:

_____

Adaptations:

_____

Materials:

_____

Evaluation:

_____

Comments/Observations:

_____

Sample Lesson Plan Format #3

Planning Matrix for Literature-based Early Childhood Social Studies

Theme: *Diversity Is All Around Us*   Story:

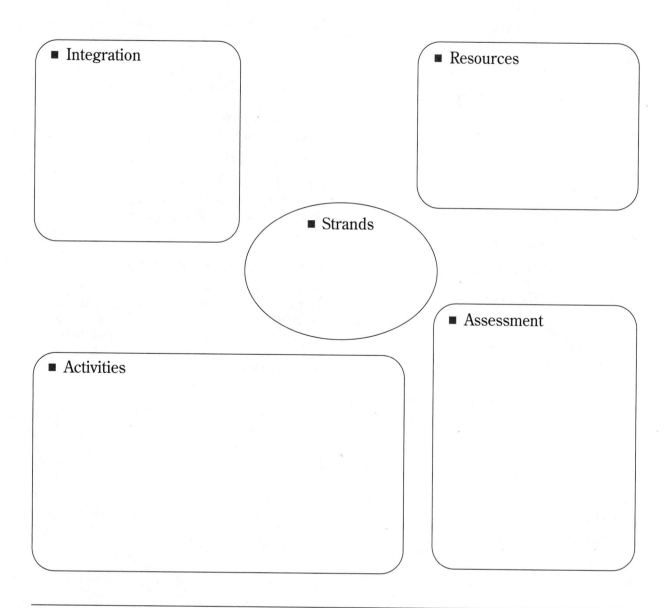

■ Integration

■ Resources

■ Strands

■ Assessment

■ Activities

APPENDIX III

Sources for Appropriate Social Studies Materials

■ General Materials for the Early Childhood Classroom

Lakeshore Learning Materials
2695 E. Dominguez Street
P.O. Box 6261
Carson, CA 90749
(800) 421-5354

Web site: http://www.lakeshorelearning.com

A good source for block play materials and resources for learning centers.

Constructive Playthings
13201 Arrington Road
Grandview, MO 64030
(800) 448-4115

E-mail: ustoy@ustoyco.com

A good source for materials for learning centers. They carry a wide variety of materials and manipulatives to support play behaviors.

Creative Teacher
2027 Central Avenue
Kearney, NE 68845
(800) 537-9060

They carry a good selection of materials to support play.

Kaplan
Lewisville-Clemmons Road
P.O. Box 609
Lewisville, NC 27023
(800) 334-2014

Web site: http://www.kaplanco.com

A source of learning materials to support all the curricular areas.

National Geographic Society
1145 17th St., NW
Washington, DC 20036

Excellent source for materials about geography, environmental science, and global studies.

Social Studies School Service
10200 Jefferson Boulevard, Room 1611
P.O. Box 802
Culver City, CA 90232
(800) 421-4246

Web site: http://www.socialstudies.com

An excellent source for materials covering all the social studies areas. They carry a good selection of posters, videotapes, recordings, and reference materials for teachers.

■ Selected Sources for Children's Books

The following are a selection of publishers or distributors of children's books about global and multi-cultural topics. See also the lists of titles in Chapter 9, Growing Up in a Multi-cultural Society.

Africa World Press
P.O. Box 236
Santa Barbara, CA 93102

Albert Whitman & Co.
6340 Oakton Street
Morton Grove, IL 60053

Carolrhoda Books, Inc.
Division of the Learner Publishing Company
241 First Avenue N
Minneapolis, MN 55401

Celebration Press
One Jacob Way
Reading, MA 01867
(800) 333-3328

Good source for books about social studies topics.
They carry a good selection of bilingual books for
children.

Children's Book Press
6400 Hollis Street
Emeryville, CA 94604

Children's Book Press
246 First Street, Suite 101
San Francisco, CA 94105

Children's Press
90 Sherman Turnpike
Dansbury, CT 06816

Holiday House
425 Madison Avenue
New York, NY 10017

Houghton Mifflin Co.
222 Berkeley Street
Boston, MA 02116

Jewish Publication Society
60 East 42nd Street
Suite 1339
New York, NY 10165

Lee & Low Books
95 Madison Avenue
New York, NY 10016

Puffin Books
375 Hudson Street
New York, NY 10014

Scholastic Books Inc.
P.O. Box 7502
Jefferson City, MO
(800) 724-6527

Web site: http://www.scholastic.com

The Wright Group
19201 120th Avenue NE
Bothell, WA 98011
(800) 523-2371

Web site: http://www.wrightgroup.com

Good source for big books.

APPENDIX IV

Sample Community Cultural Inventory

LANGUAGE

1. In this community, besides English, people speak the following languages:

2. I speak the following languages:

3. At school, children and their families use the following languages:

4. In this community, there are signs written in other languages:

   YES _____   NO _____

5. Newspapers are available in other languages.

   YES _____   NO _____

6. Programs in other languages are commonly broadcasted on the radio and on television.

   YES _____   NO _____

PEOPLE/ETHNIC GROUPS

1. There are people with a variety of physical ethnic characteristics.

   YES _____   (Can you identify them?)

   NO _____

2. At school, there are children and staff representative of different ethnic groups.

   YES _____   (Can you identify them?)

   NO _____

3. Ethnically, I consider myself to be _____

   _____

4. In this community, people use garments representative of different ethnic groups.

   YES _____   NO _____

RELIGION/BELIEFS

1. There are different religious denominations in the community.

   YES _____   NO _____

2. The following religious buildings are present in the community:

   _____ church

   _____ synagogue

   _____ temple

   _____ mosque

HOLIDAYS

1. The official holidays observed by this community are:

2. Other celebrations observed by people in this community are:

3. At school, children and their families and school staff observe the following holidays/celebrations:

FOOD

1. At the grocery store, there is a section with "ethnic food."

   YES _____   NO _____

2. There are "ethnic food" stores in the community.

   YES _____   (Identify)

   NO _____

3. Ethnic restaurants are available in the community.

   YES _____   (Identify)

   NO _____

4. I cook/eat ethnic food.

   YES _____   NO _____

5. At school, the lunch menu includes food representative of the community's ethnic groups.

   YES _____   NO _____

APPENDIX V

Using the Holidays and Special Events
to Deliver a Multi-cultural Social Studies Curriculum*

Adler, D.A. (1981). *A picture book of Jewish holidays.* New York: Holiday House.

Allsburg, C.V. (1985). *The polar express.* Boston, MA: Houghton Mifflin.

Angelou, M. (1994). *My painted house, my friendly chicken and me.* London: The Bodley Head.

Balian, L. (1983). *Leprechauns never lie.* Nashville, TN: Abingdon Press.

Barry, R. (1992). *Mr. Willowby's Christmas tree.* New York: McGraw Hill.

Barth, E. (1977). *Shamrocks, harps, and shillelaghs: The story of St. Patrick's Day symbols.* New York: Clarion Books.

Brown, M. (1983). *Arthur's Thanksgiving.* Boston, MA: Little, Brown.

———— (1980). *Arthur's Valentine.* Boston, MA: Little, Brown.

Brown, M. (1985). *Hand rhymes.* New York: E.P. Dutton.

Buchanan, K. (1992). *This house is made of mud.* Northland Publishing.

Bunting, E. (1988). *How many days to America?* New York: Clarion Books.

Burden-Patmon, D. (1992). *Imani's gift at Kwanza.* New York: Simon & Schuster.

Burnett, B. (1983). *Holidays.* NY: Franklin Watts.

Burgie, I. (1992). *Caribbean carnival.* New York: Tambourine Books.

Burden-Patmon, D. (1992). *Imani's gift at Kwanza.* Cleveland, OH: Modern Curriculum Press.

Corwin, J.H. (1987). *Jewish holiday fun.* New York: Simon & Schuster.

Delacre, L. (1990). *Las Navidades: Popular songs from Latin-America.* New York: Scholastic.

de Groat, D. (1996). *Roses are pink, your feet really stink.* New York: Mulberry Books.

de Paola, T. (1980). *The family Christmas tree book.* New York: Holiday House.

de Paola, T. (1994). *The legend of the Poinsettia.* New York: G.P. Putnam's Sons.

de Paola, T. (1976). *Things to make and do for Valentine's Day.* New York: Franklin Watts.

de Paola, T. (1980). *The legend of Old Befana.* New York: Harcourt Brace.

De Regniers, B.S., Moore, E., White, M.M., & Carr, J. (1988). *Sing a song of popcorn.* New York: Scholastic, Inc.

Devlin, H. and W. (1971). *Cranberry Thanksgiving.* New York: Four Winds Press.

Ets, M.H., & Labastida, A. (1959). *Nine days to Christmas.* New York: Viking.

Everix, N. (1991). *Ethnic celebrations around the world.* Carthage, IL: Good Apple.

Flournoy, V. (1985). *The patchwork quilt.* New York: Dial Books for Young Readers.

Fradin, D.B. (1990). *Halloween.* Hillside, NJ: Enslow Publishers.

Franco, B. (1995). *Vietnam: A literature-based multicultural unit.* Monterey, CA: Evan-Moor.

Freeman, D.R., & Macmillan, D.M. (1992). *Kwanza.* Hillside, New Jersey: Enslow Publishers.

Friedrich, P. & Friedrich, O. (1957). *The Easter bunny that overslept.* New York: Lothrop, Lee, & Shepard.

Gayle, S. (1994). *Kwanza: An African American holiday.* Watermill Press.

Gantos, J. (1990). *Happy birthday rotten Ralph.* Boston, MA: Houghton Mifflin.

Gavin, J. (1997). *Our favorite stories from around the world.* New York: DK Publishing.

Gellman, E. (1985). *It's Chanukah!* Rockville, MD: Kar-Ben Copies.

Ghazi, S.A. (1960). *Ramadan.* New York: Holiday House.

Goffstein, (1980). *Laughing Latkes.* New York: Farrar Straus Giroux.

Goss, L. and C. (1995). *It's Kwanza time.* New York: G.P. Putnam's Sons.

Gore, W.W. (1993). *Mother's day.* Hillside, NJ: Best Holiday Books.

Grayson, M.F. (1962). *Let's do finger plays.* Washington: Robert B. Luce.

Greene, C. (1982). *Holidays around the world.* Chicago, IL: Children Press.

Greenfield, E. (1988). *Grandpa's face.* New York: Philomel Books.

Guback, G. (1994). *Luka's quilt.* New York: Greenwillow.

Hadithi, M. (1984). *Greedy Zebra.* Hodder & Stoughton.

Haines, J.E. (1992). *Leading young children to music.* New York: Macmillan.

Hart, J. (1992). *Singing bees.* New York: Lothrop, Lee & Shepard.

Hodges, S. (1995). *Multicultural snacks.* Everett, Washington: Warren Publishing House.

Horse, H. (1996). *A friend for little bear.* London: Walker Brothers.

Hoyt-Goldsmith, D. (1993). *Celebrating Kwanza.* New York: Holiday House.

Hoyt-Goldsmith, D. (1995). *Mardi Gras: A Cajun country celebrations.* New York: Holiday House.

Hirsh, M. (1982). *Potato pancakes all around: A Hanukah tale.* Philadelphia, PA: The Jewish Publication Society of America.

Hume, B., & Sevier, A. (1991). *Starting with me: Topic ideas for teaching of history, geography, and religious education to infants.* England: Belair Publishing Company.

Jasmine, J. (1994). *Multicultural holidays: Share our celebrations.* Huntington Beach, CA: Teacher Created Materials.

Keats, E.J. (1968). *The little drummer boy.* London: The Macmillan Company.

Keens-Douglas, R. (1992). *The nutmeg princess.* Buffalo, NY: Firefly Books U.S.

Kimmel, E. (1985). *Hershel and the Hanukkah Goblins.* NY: Holiday House.

Kimmelman, L. (1992). *Hanukkah lights, Hanukkah nights.* New York: HarperCollins.

Kindersley, B. & A. (1995). *Children just like me: A unique celebration of children around the world.* Britain: A DK Publishing Book.

Kozodoy, R. (1981). *The book of Jewish holidays.* West Orange, NJ: Behrman House, Inc.

Krull, K. (1994). *Maria Molina and the days of the dead.* New York: Macmillan.

Lacapa, M. (1990). *The flute player: An Apache folktale.* Northland Publishing.

Lasky, K. (1994). *Days of the dead.* New York: Hyperion Books for Children.

Lasker, J. (1974). *He's my brother.* Chicago, IL: Albert Whitman & Company.

Lewin, H. (1983). *Jafta's father.* Minneapolis, MN: Carolrhoda Books.

Lewin, H. *Jafta's mother.* Minneapolis, MN: Carolrhoda Books.

Lewin, H. *Jafta and the wedding.* Minneapolis, MN: Carolrhoda Books.

Liestman, V. (1991). *Columbus Day.* Minneapolis, MN: Carolrhoda Books.

Livingston, M.C. (1985). *Celebrations.* New York: Holiday House.

Mc Elmeel, S.L. (1992). *Bookpeople: A multicultural album.* Englewood, CO: Teacher Ideas Press.

Macmillan, D. (1994). *Tet: Vietnamese New Year.* Hillside, NJ: Enslow Publishers.

Manushkin, F. (1990). *Latkes and Applesauce.* New York: Scholastic.

Manushkin, F. (1995). *The matza that Papa brought home.* New York: Scholastic.

McGuffee, M. (1996). *The day the earth was silent.* Bloomington, IN: Inquiring Voices Press.

Mendez, P. (1989). *The black snowman.* New York: Scholastic.

Millord, S. (1992). *Hands around the world.* Charlotte, VT: Williamson Publishing.

Moore, C.C. (1985). *The night before Christmas.* New York: Scholastic.

Nerlove, M. (1990). *Thanksgiving.* Morton Grove, IL: Albert Whitman & Company.

Osborn, S.T. & Tangvald, C. (1993). *Children around the world celebrate Christmas.* Cincinnati, OH: Standard Publishing.

Orozco, J.L. (1994). *De Colores and other Latin-American folksongs for children.* New York: Dutton Children's Books.

Page, N. (1995). *Sing and shine on! The teacher's guide to multicultural song leading.* Portsmouth, NH: Heinemann.

Pearl, L. (1983). *Pinatas and paper flower.* New York: Clarion Books.

Penn, M. (1994). *The miracle of the potato Latkes.* New York: Holiday House.

Presilla, M. (1992). *Feliz Nachebuena, Feliz Navidad. Christmas feasts of the Hispanic Caribbean.* New York: Holt.

Polacco, P. (1988). *The keeping quilt.* New York: Simon & Schuster.

Random House. (1993). *The Random Book of easy to read stories.* New York: Author.

Riordan, J. (1975). *Little Masha and Misha the bear.* New York: Scholastic.

Rose, M. (1994). *Day of delight. A Jewish Sabbath in Ethiopia.* New York: Dial Books.

Rosen, M. (1991). *Summer festivals.* New York: The Bookwright Press.

Rosen, M. *Spring festivals.* New York: The Bookwright Press.

Rosen, M. *Winter festivals.* New York: The Bookwright Press.

Rozakis, L. (1993). *Celebrate! Holidays around the world.* Santa Barbara, CA: The Learning Works.

Rutman, S.G. (1992). *Let's celebrate!* Mahwah, NJ: Troll Associates.

Say, A. (1991). *Tree of cranes.* Boston, MA: Houghton Mifflin.

Seuss, Dr. (1957). *How the Grinch stole Christmas.* New York: Random House.

Sherman, E.B. (1984). *The odd potato: A Chanukah story.* Rockville, MD: Kar-Ben Copies.

Silverthorne, E. (1992). *Fiesta, Mexico's great celebrations.* Brookfield, CT: The Millwood Press.

Spinelli, E. (1982). *Thanksgiving at the Tappletons'.* Reading, MA: Addison-Wesley.

Stevenson, J. (1996). *The forgotten toys.* London: Scholastic.

Tejada, I. (1993). *Brown bag ideas from many cultures.* Worcester, MA: Davis Publishers.

Terzian, A.M. (1993). *The kids art book.* Charlotte, VT: Williamson Publishing.

Tran, K.L. (1992). *Tet: The New Year.* Cleveland, OH: Modern Curriculum Press.

Van Allsburg, C. (1985). *The Polar Express.* Boston, MA: Houghton Mifflin.

Walker, B.K. (1993). *The most beautiful thing in the world.* New York: Scholastic.

Walters, C. (1995). *Multicultural music. Lyrics to familiar melodies and native songs.* Minneapolis, MN: T.S. Denison & Company.

Wan, E. (1990). *Lion dancer.* New York: Scholastic.

Washington, D. (1996). *The story of Kwanza.* New York: Harper Collins.

Watson, P. & M. (1994). *The market lady and the mango tree.* New York: Tambourine Books.

Ziefert, H. (1990). *Getting ready for a new baby.* Singapore: Harper Row, Publishers.

---

*Source: Developed by Audrey Henry and Wilma de Melendez

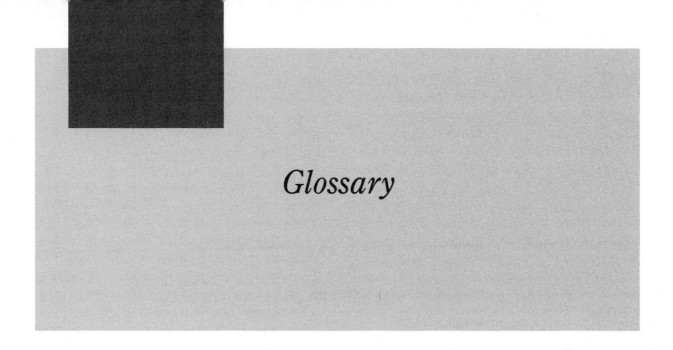

Glossary

aesthetics: A sense of beauty, which enables an individual to perceive, appreciate, and respond to beauty in nature and to artistic works created by humans. Each individual's sense of beauty is influenced by his or her culture and experiences.

affective objectives: A domain of learning consisting of behaviors focusing on emotional categories such as receiving, responding, valuing, organization, and characterization.

Americans with Disabilities Act: A legislative mandate affirming the nation's commitment to people with disabilities, particularly to children who are at risk or who have been diagnosed as having disabilities. The law requires that "appropriate education [be provided] to all children and youth with disabilities who require it."

anti-bias: A non-judgmental attitude toward others, based on acceptance of the individual differences between people in a diverse society. Anti-bias education fosters development of this outlook.

artifacts: Objects that are representative of different cultural elements.

the arts: Creative expressions that reflect life experiences. They include music, theater, dance and the visual arts.

art process: The activities and ways of thinking in which children engage for the purpose of creating an art product. A child-appropriate art process includes granting freedom to the child to select art materials, to use his or her imagination, and to invent procedures to create art products.

art product: An object produced by a child that represents his or her personal creative expression.

attitudes: Points of view that are often influenced by social and cultural experiences.

behavioral objectives: Specific, observable, and measurable behaviors to be attained through various learning methodologies.

bias: "Any attitude, belief, or feeling that results in, and helps to justify unfair treatment of an individual because of his or her identity" (Derman-Sparks & The A.B.C. Task Force, 1989, p. 3).

change: Alterations of animate and inanimate objects, people, events, attitudes, and other phenomena that are often affected by the passing of time.

children with special needs: Children who are experiencing a developmental delay in cognitive, physical, language-speech, social, or self-help development.

chronological thinking: Development of a clear sense of historical time that allows one to distinguish between the past, the present, and the future. Chronological thinking helps people to identify the time period in which events take place (NCHS, 1994).

chronology: The sequential organization of time.

citizenship: The political identity of an individual; a role that entails rights and responsibilities toward society.

civic responsibility: The sense of duty people have to contribute to their society. In American society this sense of responsibility establishes the use of democratic values in all aspects of social life, as well as the importance of effective social participation and respect for rights of individuals.

cognitive mapping: The child's ability to construct mental images of a place or location. Children combine their direct experiences with things and objects in their environment with information gathered through the media, literature, and other sources to build their knowledge about a specific area or place.

community: A place where one belongs; a group one is a part of as a result of social, emotional, and cultural ties. A community also represents a support network for an individual.

concept maps: Pictorial images of ideas and the interrelationships between them; concrete representations of mental concepts, often generated by brainstorming. See also **webs.**

concepts: Ways of organizing what is known.

consumption: Using resources; when consumers acquire goods or use services, they make distinctions between wants and needs and attempt to make appropriate use of the resources available.

cooperative learning: An instructional methodology in which learners work together to accomplish specific learning outcomes.

creative expression: Individual ways of expressing feelings, ideas, and experiences through the various artistic media. Artistic expressions can take a variety of forms, including music, painting, sculpture, dance, and others.

cultural diversity: A condition of society in which people of different cultures, races, exceptionalities, gender, age forums, and religions coexist. It is a characteristic of any society.

culture: The way of life of a social group, including all of its material and non-material products that are transmitted from one generation to the next (Dickinson & Leming, 1990, p. 16). Culture provides the framework people use to guide their lives.

curriculum: A framework for organizing instruction, both formal and informal.

curriculum strands: Specific themes identified in the national standards for social studies. The themes include: culture; time, continuity, and change; people, places, and environments; individuals, authority, and governance; power, authority, and governance; production and consumption; science, technology, and society; global connections; and civic ideals and practice.

developmentally appropriate practices (DAP): According to the NAEYC, DAP is a "framework, a philosophy, or an approach to working with young children that requires that the adult pays attention to at least two important pieces of information—*what we know* about how children develop and learn and *what we learn* about the individual needs and interests of each child in the group" (Bredekamp & Rosegrant, 1992, p. 4).

developmentally and culturally appropriate practices (DCAP): Educational practices (recommended by the National Association for the Education of Young Children (NAEYC)) that keep the curriculum responsive to the social and cultural realities of young children. In addition to incorporating knowledge about general principles of child development and recognizing the individual characteristics and needs of children, these practices are based on knowledge about the impact of culture and of the various environments experienced by children in their development. (Bredekamp & Copple, 1997, p. 9)

developmental milestones: Skills and behaviors that represent major accomplishments during the process of development. They include key achievements in all the developmental domains—cognitive, social, motor, physical, and language. Although most children exhibit these behaviors within a certain range of age levels, some individuals do not follow a typical pattern of development.

developmental planning: An approach to planning that considers the specific needs of the children taught, identifies new knowledge goals and intended outcomes, and selects the processes through which children will build the targeted ideas.

distribution: The ways products reach the market and goods and services from different sources are made available to consumers.

diversity: A condition of society reflecting the variety of cultural, social, linguistic, religious, racial, and ethnic characteristics found among its members.

dramatic activities: Activities designed to help children express their ideas and interpretations about a theme or an experience. Through pretend play, children are encouraged to share their own ideas without a written script or memorized dialogue.

economics: The field that studies the use, production, distribution, and acquisition of goods and services.

equality: A belief that everyone is the same.

equity: Fair, impartial treatment of individuals; the offering of the same opportunities to everyone.

ethnic identity: The sense of belonging to a cultural group.

exchange: The ways people acquire products in the community, including the ways that trade among communities and countries makes goods available.

family membership: Recognition of family members and awareness of belonging to a family.

folk group: A group of people who meet together and share at least one common element, "such as ethnicity, language, age, family, occupation, gender, region, [or] religion" (Sidener, 1997, p. 48).

folklife: "The skills, knowledge, beliefs, and practices learned through observation and imitation of one's folk group" (Sidener, 1997, p. 48).

folklore: Reflects "the familiar and creative ways . . . people . . . relate to one another [which contribute to] social cohesiveness" (Bronner, 1988, p. 29).

geographic literacy: The ability to understand and apply the characteristics and relationships of the environment to daily life.

geographic processes: The many ways in which the geography of our planet is transformed through natural forces or by people.

geography: "The study of people, places, and environments and the relationships among them" (National Geographic Society, 1994, p. 1).

global approach: An approach to teaching social studies that gives children "(t)he opportunity to discover and examine the many common points people here and there share. A global approach guides children to see themselves, their culture, and their lives as interconnected and dependent upon others in any part of the world." (Ellis, 1995, p.295).

global education: An approach that provides children with experiences that transcend social and political boundaries. It expands perspectives beyond national boundaries.

global identity: An awareness of being a part of the world.

goals: General statements of purpose that describe the targeted behaviors and achievements to be accomplished through various methods and experiences.

historical fiction: A literary genre in which historical facts and real and imaginary characters are blended to create stories about how life was in the past. This type of literature is a powerful way to help children gain a sense of events and people across time.

historical thinking: The ability "that enables children to differentiate [between] the past, present, and future time; raise questions; seek and evaluate evidence; compare and analyze historical stories, illustrations, and records from the past; [and] interpret the historical record, and construct historical narratives of their own" (NCHS, 1994, p. 2).

historical understanding: "What students should know about the history of their families, their communities, states, nation, and the world" (NCHS, 1994, p. 2).

history: The study of the past, including significant social, cultural, and natural events that have affected humanity.

history education: A study of the past intended to help children develop a sense of understanding about events, actions, and decisions made by individuals and groups in the past. History education also fosters an understanding and an appreciation of the existing conditions in life, one's roots and culture, as well as the origins of others.

humanities: The study of the fine arts, literature, and architecture.

inclusion: Educating children with special needs along with their non-disabled peers.

individual identity: Pride in oneself, in one's abilities and innate potential, and in the cultural background to which one belongs.

individuality: Recognition of self as a person.

integrated curriculum: A multi-faceted approach to teaching social studies, with an emphasis on the interrelationships between themes and subject areas.

internalization: The process of absorbing society's values and views of appropriate and inappropriate behavior, which helps children develop the ability to self-regulate their own behavior. Although young children are still developing their capacity to determine what is right and wrong, this ability begins to form early in life. It is influenced by parents and other family members, as well as by peers and adults the children interact with in their enviroment. The ideas children are exposed to through the media also have a powerful impact on this process.

learning centers: "A child-centered, exploratory way to get children involved in self-directed, autonomous behavior" (Ellis, 1995, p. 100).

lesson planning: Choosing activities and strategies to be used during a short-term period or throughout a specific day.

local, state, and national membership: Identifying with the community, neighborhood, town, state, and country where the individual lives.

macro-environmental cognition: Knowledge and the ability to perceive the overall physical characteristics found in the environment.

map: A symbolic representation of a geographical area.

moral thinking: The ability to reason about options in a situation according to codes of ethics (socially accepted moral codes). Moral thinking establishes the basis for taking action to defend an idea or to assume a position on an issue.

multi-cultural education: A philosophy and an educational strategy, based on the recognition of the concepts of equity and equality, that is aimed at empowering children.

multi-cultural literature: The collection of literature depicting ethnic groups and other elements of cultural diversity.

multiple intelligences: A theory developed by Howard Gardner that recognizes the existence of a variety of abilities or intelligences, such as kinesthetic, spatial, visual, musical, mathematical, interpersonal, intrapersonal, and naturalistic intelligences.

national identity: Recognition of one's nationality and role as a citizen of a country.

nationality: Refers to the country of origin where one was born or from where one's parents came.

older preschoolers: Children ages four to five. Compare **young preschoolers.**

operations: A Piagetian term referring to the child's ability to solve problems through logical thought processes. It is a process that evolves with growth.

oral history: The transmission of reports about events and the passing of traditions directly from person to person, in oral rather than written form.

peer group membership: Belonging to a group of biological and social equals.

performance objectives: Statements specifying the proficiency levels that learners should demonstrate as a result of instructional experiences.

perspective: Development of an awareness of the environment beyond the self.

perspective-taking: The ability "to be in the shoes of another person." Adopting someone else's perspective enables an individual to perceive the emotions and feelings of another individual. A moral perspective is developed over time and depends upon the opportunities for social interaction a person has.

play: Activities that are enjoyable, self-chosen, and spontaneous. Play can include both open-ended and process-oriented activities that engage children. See also **pretend play.**

political socialization: Development of a sense about the role and nature of authority, power, and rules, and about the existence of government.

position and orientation: Define the relationships between objects in an area and the points of reference describing their locations. **Position** answers the question "where." **Orientation** establishes the specific location of an object, using the cardinal points (north, south, east, west) as descriptors.

pretend play: Behaviors used to represent ideas and experiences. Toys, objects, gestures, movements, words, and actions are used by the child to convey views and concepts during pretend play.

primary-age children: Children ages six through eight.

production: The processes the community/country uses to produce goods and services.

project approach: "An in-depth study of a particular topic that one or more children undertake" (Katz and Chard, 1989, p. 2).

prosocial skills: Actions that promote positive and effective interactions with individuals and groups. These skills also enable the individual to take action on behalf of others.

psychosocial development: Development involving emotions, personality characteristics, and relationships with other people.

race/ethnicity: A group of individuals who share certain physical and biological characteristics, as defined by anthropologists. Compare **ethnic identity.**

recent past: Includes things that have taken place in a span of time as short as a class period.

role model: An individual who possesses characteristics and qualities that other individuals wish to emulate.

scale: A way to represent tht physical dimensions of and distances within an area that ensures accurate size-space relationships.

scarcity: Limited resources available to supply the demand for goods and services. Dealing with scarcity requires individuals and societies to make distinctions between needs and wants.

social and emotional development: The process through which children develop a sense of their own identity and learn about the social codes that govern the ways they interact with others.

social cognition: Knowledge and understanding of people and the dynamics of human interaction.

social competence: The ability to engage in successful social interactions with others and with the group to which one belongs.

social responsibility: An individual's sense of the rights and civic duties each person has in relation to other individuals in society. It includes the development of prosocial behaviors and skills that enable individuals to interact successfully in a diverse society. Essentially, fostering a sense of social responsibility helps children develop skills that will enable them to become good citizens.

social sciences: A curricular area that consists of disciplines such as history, geography, civics, economics, sociology, humanities, and anthropology.

social skills: Abilities and behaviors that are necessary for interacting and living in a social group.

social studies: Literally, "the study of things social;" an integrated discipline based on the social sciences, the humanities, mathematics, and the natural sciences.

socialization: The process by which children acquire knowledge about the acceptable behavior patterns of the group. Social behavior is learned through the members of society and is culturally defined.

space: The area where human and natural activities take place. The space is transformed by the actions of people and the changes caused by natural phenomena.

standards: Definitions of acceptable performance levels; in this book, a term referring to the national standards in the field of social sciences.

stereotype: "An oversimplified generalization about a particular group's race, or sex, which usually carries [a] derogatory implication" (Derman-Sparks & The A.B.C. Task Force, 1989, p. 3).

supply and demand: An economic principle of capitalism that refers to consumer-driven production and distribution of goods.

symbolic functioning: ". . . [T]he child's ability to understand, create, and use symbols to represent something that is not present" (Zigler & Stevenson, 1993, p. 315).

symbols: Represent the elements and objects in the area depicted on a map.

teachable moments: Brief and spontaneously occurring opportunities to lead children to meaningful learning. These are the moments when the child exhibits an interest or a curiosity about a topic or an idea. A teachable moment can be triggered through an encounter with something unusual or by a question, a classroom experience, or an outside event.

teaching strategy: A long-range view of ways to deliver content in an engaging and child-appropriate manner.

teaching technique: Day-to-day teaching activities.

thematic teaching: Teaching developed around a child-appropriate theme, which can be selected by the teacher, the children, or both. Thematic teaching integrates different types of subject matter and involves the study of one or more themes over a period of time.

time: A unit of measurement defining the duration and sequence of events in an experience. Time is an abstract and conventional concept. It is central to the study of history.

triple identity: A trifold perspective on identity; see **individual, national,** and **global identity.**

unit planning: Topical planning that extends over a longer period of time than daily lesson planning. A unit plan may be designed for a week or as long as a month.

values: Moral principles and ideas that individuals acquire through the family, religion, culture, and society.

visual arts: Painting, sculpture, filmmaking, and crafts.

visual literacy: Knowledge about the visible actions, objects, and symbols, natural and man-made, encountered in the environment (Fransecky & Ferguson, 1973).

webbing: The brainstorming process through which "tentative activity plans" are developed (Jones and Nimmo, 1995, p. 11). Webbing can also be used as a visual representation of other concepts.

webs: Maps of related ideas, often generated by brainstorming. See also **concept maps.**

young preschoolers: Children ages three to four. Compare **older preschoolers.**

Index

Page numbers in *italics* indicate figures; page numbers followed by C indicate concept boxes